Processes of Constitutional Decisionmaking

2017 Supplement

2017 Supplement

Processes of Constitutional Decisionmaking

Cases and Materials

Sixth Edition

Prepared by Jack M. Balkin

Paul Brest
Professor of Law, Emeritus and Former Dean
Stanford Law School
and President, The William and Flora Hewlett Foundation

Sanford Levinson
W. St. John Garwood & W. St. John Garwood, Jr.
Centennial Chair in Law
University of Texas Law School

Jack M. Balkin
Knight Professor of Constitutional Law
and the First Amendment
Yale Law School

Akhil Reed Amar
Sterling Professor of Law and Political Science
Yale Law School

Reva B. Siegel
Nicholas deB. Katzenbach Professor of Law
Yale Law School

 Wolters Kluwer

Published by Wolters Kluwer in New York.

Wolters Kluwer Legal & Regulatory U.S. serves customers worldwide with CCH, Aspen Publishers, and Kluwer Law International products. (www.WKLegaledu.com)

To contact Customer Service, e-mail customer.service@wolterskluwer.com, call 1-800-234-1660, fax 1-800-901-9075, or mail correspondence to:

Wolters Kluwer
Attn: Order Department
PO Box 990
Frederick, MD 21705

Printed in the United States of America.

1 2 3 4 5 6 7 8 9 0

ISBN 978-1-4548-8248-0

Certified Chain of Custody
Promoting Sustainable Forestry
www.sfiprogram.org
SFI-01028

About Wolters Kluwer Legal & Regulatory U.S.

Wolters Kluwer Legal & Regulatory U.S. delivers expert content and solutions in the areas of law, corporate compliance, health compliance, reimbursement, and legal education. Its practical solutions help customers successfully navigate the demands of a changing environment to drive their daily activities, enhance decision quality and inspire confident outcomes.

Serving customers worldwide, its legal and regulatory portfolio includes products under the Aspen Publishers, CCH Incorporated, Kluwer Law International, ftwilliam.com, and MediRegs names. They are regarded as exceptional and trusted resources for general legal and practice-specific knowledge, compliance and risk management, dynamic workflow solutions, and expert commentary.

Contents

**Chapter 9.   Liberty, Equality, and Fundamental
Rights: The Constitution, the Family, and the Body**   **173**

Processes of Constitutional Decisionmaking

2017 Supplement

Chapter 4

From Reconstruction to the New Deal: 1866-1934

Insert the following after note 7 on p. 457:

8. *Puerto Rico's status as a separate sovereign.* In Commonwealth of Puerto Rico v. Sanchez Valle, 2016 WL 3189527, The Supreme Court held that Puerto Rico was not a separate sovereign for purposes of the Double Jeopardy Clause of the Fifth Amendment. Under the dual-sovereignty doctrine, the Double Jeopardy Clause does not bar successive prosecutions if they are brought by separate sovereigns. The test of separate sovereignty hinges on a single criterion: the "ultimate source" of the power undergirding the respective prosecutions. United States v. Wheeler, 435 U.S. 313, 320 (1978). If two entities derive their power to punish from independent sources, then they may bring successive prosecutions. Conversely, if those entities draw their power from the same ultimate source, then they may not.

Justice Kagan, writing for six Justices, held that although the Commonwealth of Puerto Rico had its own constitution and passed its own criminal laws, its authority to do so rested on Public Law 600, a 1950 statute passed by Congress. Congress also approved Puerto Rico's draft constitution "subject to several important conditions accepted by the convention." Hence, the Court concluded, Puerto Rico was not a separate sovereign.

Justice Ginsburg, joined by Justice Thomas, concurred, but argued that the Court should reexamine the dual sovereignty doctrine, which allows for multiple prosecutions for the same offence. Justice Thomas concurred in the judgment, but argued that Indian tribes should not count as separate sovereigns, either.

Justice Breyer, joined by Justice Sotomayor, dissented, explaining that the Court's argument about the ultimate source of authority does not adequately distinguish the Philippines, which did not have the authority to make its own laws until Congress declared it independent. Nor does it distinguish most of the states, which began as federal territories. Congress must permit territories to organize and apply for statehood, and then it decides whether to admit states. Nor does the argument explain Congress's relationship to the Indian tribes: Congress maintains "plenary authority to limit, modify or eliminate the [tribes'] powers of local self-government," Santa Clara Pueblo v. Martinez, 436 U.S. 49, 56 (1978), and thus the tribes remain sovereign for purposes of the Double Jeopardy Clause only until Congress chooses to withdraw that power.

Breyer traced the history of American relations with Puerto Rico, and concluded that the "history of statutes, language, organic acts, traditions, statements, and other actions, taken by all three branches of the Federal Government and by Puerto Rico, convinces me that the United States has entered into a compact one of the terms of which is that the 'source' of Puerto Rico's criminal law ceased to be the U.S. Congress and became Puerto Rico itself, its people, and its constitution. The evidence of that grant of authority is far stronger than the evidence of congressional silence that led this Court to conclude that Indian tribes maintained a similar sovereign authority. Indeed, it is difficult to see how we can conclude that the tribes do possess this authority but Puerto Rico does not. Regardless, . . . I would hold for Double Jeopardy Clause purposes that the criminal law of Puerto Rico and the criminal law of the Federal Government do not find their legitimacy-conferring origin in the same 'source.'"

Chapter 6

Federalism, Separation of Powers, and National Security in the Modern Era

Insert on p. 724 before *NFIB v. Sebelius*:

TAYLOR v. UNITED STATES, 136 S.Ct. 2074 (2016). Petitioner Taylor was convicted under the Hobbs Act, which makes it a crime for a person to affect commerce, or to attempt to do so, by robbery. 18 U.S.C. §1951(a). The Act defines "commerce" broadly as interstate commerce "and all other commerce over which the United States has jurisdiction." §1951(b)(3). Taylor was part of a gang that broke into two homes in an unsuccessful search for marijuana. Taylor appealed his conviction on the ground that the government had to prove that the marijuana was part of interstate commerce; he contended that the marijuana was locally-grown.

Justice Alito, writing for six Justices (the case was decided after Justice Scalia's death), upheld Taylor's conviction. He argued that in order to satisfy the Act's element of affecting (or attempting to affect) commerce, the government simply needed to prove that Taylor attempted to rob marijuana dealers of their drugs and drug money. His opinion reaffirmed the reasoning of *Raich* and *Morrison*: "While [the] category [of activities that substantially affect interstate commerce in the aggregate] is broad, 'thus far in our Nation's history our cases have upheld Commerce Clause regulation of intrastate activity only where that activity is economic in nature.'" *Morrison*. "[T]he activity at issue, the sale of marijuana, is unquestionably an economic activity. It is, to be sure, a form of business that is illegal under federal law and the laws of most States. But there can be no question that marijuana trafficking is a moneymaking endeavor—and a potentially lucrative one at that."

Justice Alito explained that in *Raich* "[t]he Court reaffirmed 'Congress' power to regulate purely local activities that are part of an economic "class of activities" that have a substantial effect on interstate commerce.' The production, possession, and distribution of controlled substances constitute a 'class of activities' that in the aggregate substantially affect interstate commerce, and therefore, the Court held, Congress possesses the authority to regulate (and to criminalize) the production, possession, and distribution of controlled substances even when those activities occur entirely within the boundaries of a single State. Any other outcome, we warned, would leave a gaping enforcement hole in Congress's regulatory scheme." Because "the market for marijuana, including its intrastate aspects, is 'commerce over which the United States has jurisdiction,' . . . a robber who affects or attempts to affect even the intrastate sale of marijuana grown within the State affects or attempts to affect commerce over which the United States has jurisdiction." Justice Alito concluded: "Our holding today is limited to cases in which the defendant targets drug dealers for the purpose of stealing drugs or drug proceeds. We do not resolve what the Government must prove to establish Hobbs Act robbery where some other type of business or victim is targeted."

Justice Thomas dissented. "Although our modern precedents (such as *Wickard*) embrace the substantial-effects approach, applying that approach to the Hobbs Act is tantamount to abandoning any limits on Congress' commerce power—even the slight limits recognized by our expansive modern precedents. . . . [I]f the Hobbs Act is construed to punish a robbery that by itself affects only intrastate activity, then the Act defies the constitutional design." Justice Thomas argued that "[t]he Government may not obtain a conviction by proving only that the defendant's robbery affected intrastate commerce or other intrastate activity" because this is not necessary and proper to regulate interstate commerce. "To be 'necessary,' Congress' prohibition of robbery must be 'plainly adapted' to regulating interstate commerce." *McCulloch.* It "must have an 'obvious, simple, and direct relation' with the regulation of interstate commerce. . . . And for Congress' robbery prohibition to be 'proper,' it cannot be 'prohibited' by the Constitution or inconsistent with its 'letter and spirit.'" *McCulloch.*

Justice Thomas would apply the Hobbs Act only to robberies that actually affected interstate commerce, such as "those that affect the channels of interstate commerce or instrumentalities of interstate commerce. A robbery that forces an interstate freeway to shut down thus may form the basis for a valid Hobbs Act conviction. So too might a robbery of a truckdriver who is in the course of transporting commercial goods across state lines. But if the Government cannot prove that a robbery in a State affected interstate commerce, then the robbery is not punishable under the Hobbs Act. Sweeping in robberies that do not affect interstate commerce comes too close to conferring on Congress a general police power over the Nation."

Insert the following before subsection 4 on p. 776:

KING v. BURWELL, 135 S.Ct. 2480 (2015): Three years after *NFIB v. Sebelius*, litigation once again challenged the Affordable Care Act and its individual mandate; this time, however, it was through a debate about statutory interpretation.

Subsidies for health insurance through federal tax credits are a key feature of the Affordable Care Act. These tax credits allow individuals to purchase health insurance that they could not otherwise afford.

The Affordable Care Act gives each State the opportunity to establish its own online exchange for people to buy health insurance. It also provides, however, that the Federal Government will establish "such Exchange" if the State does not. 42 U.S.C. §§18031, 18041. The Act also provides that tax credits "shall be allowed" for any "applicable taxpayer," 26 U.S.C. §36B(a), but only if the taxpayer has enrolled in an insurance plan through "an Exchange established by the State under [42 U.S.C. §18031]," §§36B(b)-(c). An IRS regulation interprets that language as making tax credits available on "an Exchange," 26 CFR §1.36B–2, "regardless of whether the Exchange is established and operated by a State . . . or by HHS," 45 CFR §155.20.

Petitioners were four residents of Virginia who did not want to either purchase health insurance or pay the applicable tax for failing to insure. Virginia decided not to create a state health care exchange for buying health insurance and therefore employed a federal exchange.

Petitioners argued that the federal exchange used by Virginia residents does not qualify as "an Exchange established by the State under [42 U.S.C. §18031]" because the United States is not a "State." Therefore, they argued that it would be illegal for them to receive federal tax credits, and as a result health insurance would be too costly for them. Therefore they — and everyone else in their position in the 34 states then using a federal exchange — would be exempted from the requirements of the individual mandate.

In a 6-3 decision, written by Chief Justice Roberts, the Supreme Court rejected the petitioners' interpretation of the statute. "[W]hen read in context, 'with a view to [its] place in the overall statutory scheme,' the meaning of the phrase 'established by the State' is not so clear." It could refer only to exchanges actually created by a State. Nevertheless, the Court explained, other parts of the statute point to a different reading: "Section 18041 provides that [if the State fails to create an Exchange] the Secretary 'shall . . . establish and operate *such Exchange* within the State.' §18041(c)(1). By using the phrase 'such Exchange,' Section 18041 instructs the Secretary to establish and operate the *same* Exchange that the State was directed to establish under Section 18031." Moreover, "State Exchanges and Federal Exchanges are equivalent — they must meet the same requirements, perform the same functions, and serve the same purposes. Although State and Federal Exchanges are established by different sovereigns, Sections 18031 and 18041 do not suggest that they differ in any meaningful way."

Because, when read in context, the statute was susceptible of two meanings, the Court asked which reading was most consistent with the broader structure of the Affordable Care Act. " 'A provision that may seem ambiguous in isolation is often clarified by the remainder of the statutory scheme . . . because only one of the permissible meanings produces a substantive effect that is compatible with the rest of the law.' " "Here," the Court explained, "the statutory scheme compels us to reject petitioners' interpretation because it would destabilize the individual insurance market in any State with a Federal Exchange, and likely create the very 'death spirals' that Congress designed the Act to avoid. See New York State Dept. of Social Servs. v. Dublino, 413 U.S. 405 (1973) ("We cannot interpret federal statutes to negate their own stated purposes.")."

"The combination of no tax credits and an ineffective coverage requirement could well push a State's individual insurance market into a death spiral. One study predicts that premiums would increase by 47 percent and enrollment would decrease by 70 percent. Another study predicts that premiums would increase by 35 percent and enrollment would decrease by 69 percent. And those effects would not be limited to individuals who purchase insurance on the Exchanges. Because the Act requires insurers to treat the entire individual market as a single risk pool, premiums outside the Exchange would rise along with those inside the Exchange."

The Court therefore concluded that "[i]t is implausible that Congress meant the Act to operate in this manner. See National Federation of Independent Business v. Sebelius, 567 U.S. ____, ____, 132 S.Ct. 2566, 2674 (2012) (SCALIA, KENNEDY, THOMAS, and ALITO, JJ., dissenting) ("Without the federal subsidies . . . the exchanges would not operate as Congress intended and may not operate at all."). Congress made the guaranteed issue and community rating requirements applicable in every State in the Nation. But those requirements only work when combined with the coverage requirement and the tax credits. So it stands to reason that Congress meant for those provisions to apply in every State as well."

"A fair reading of legislation demands a fair understanding of the legislative plan," Chief Justice Roberts concluded. "Congress passed the Affordable Care Act to improve health insurance markets, not to destroy them. If at all possible, we must interpret the Act in a way that is consistent with the former, and avoids the latter."

Justice Scalia, joined by Justices Thomas and Alito, dissented: "The Court's decision reflects the philosophy that judges should endure whatever interpretive distortions it takes in order to correct a supposed flaw in the statutory machinery. That philosophy ignores the American people's decision to give *Congress* "[a]ll legislative Powers" enumerated in the Constitution. Art. I, §1. They made Congress, not this Court, responsible for both making laws and mending them. . . . This Court . . . concludes that [limiting tax credits to state exchanges] would prevent the rest of the Act from working as well as hoped. So it rewrites the law to make tax credits available everywhere. We should start calling this law SCOTUScare."

"Perhaps the Patient Protection and Affordable Care Act will attain the enduring status of the Social Security Act or the Taft–Hartley Act; perhaps not. But this Court's two decisions on the Act will surely be remembered through the years. The somersaults of statutory interpretation they have performed ("penalty" means tax, "further [Medicaid] payments to the State" means only incremental Medicaid payments to the State, "established by the State" means not established by the State) will be cited by litigants endlessly, to the confusion of honest jurisprudence. And the cases will publish forever the discouraging truth that the Supreme Court of the United States favors some laws over others, and is prepared to do whatever it takes to uphold and assist its favorites."

Discussion

1. King v. Burwell *as a continuation of the constitutional struggle over Obamacare*. Between 2009 and 2012, the United States engaged in a grand constitutional debate about the Affordable Care Act. Should Congress expand the social contract to include universal health insurance? Or was this an unjustified imposition on personal liberty and on state authority that was beyond Congress's powers? In *NFIB v. Sebelius*, the Court held that most of the Affordable Care Act was constitutional. It affirmed the change in the American social contract but with a few important qualifications. Americans would have (close to) universal health insurance. At the same time, individuals could opt out of health insurance by paying a tax, and states could decide whether to opt into health insurance for their poorest citizens. So altered, the Court legitimated this major change in American governance. See Jack M. Balkin, The Court Affirms Our Social Contract, The Atlantic, June 29, 2012, at http://www.theatlantic.com/national/archive/2012/06/the-court-affirms-our-social-contract/259186/

Mark Graber, however, has pointed out that the biggest constitutional issues are settled not when courts issue opinions but when one side gives up the fight. Mark A. Graber, "Settling the West: The Annexation of Texas, The Louisiana Purchase, and Bush v. Gore," in Sanford Levinson and Bartholomew Sparrow, The Louisiana Purchase and American Expansion, 1803-1898 83-110 (2005).

The decision in *NFIB v. Sibelius* hardly reconciled Republicans and conservatives to the Affordable Care Act. The House of Representatives attempted to repeal all or parts of the Act over 50 times, even though most of these attempts were largely symbolic. Republican politicians and conservative media repeatedly denounced the Act and predicted its imminent demise. Opposition to the Affordable Care Act, on both policy and constitutional grounds, remained the more or less official position of the Republican Party.

Meanwhile, lawyers and legal scholars opposed to the Act scoured the text of the law for new ways to attack it. One argument was based on the Origination Clause of Article I, section 7: "All Bills for raising Revenue shall originate in the House of Representatives; but the Senate may propose or concur with Amendments as on other Bills." Assuming as *Sebelius* held, that the individual mandate was a tax, it was unconstitutional under Article I, section 7, because the ACA did not originate in the House of Representatives. Instead—as sometimes happens when both houses work on a measure—the Senate took an unrelated House revenue bill and substituted the text of the Senate version of the ACA as an amendment. The Senate version of the ACA was ultimately enacted into law. This argument has not yet gotten very much traction. See Sissel v. United States Department of Health and Human Services, 760 F. 3d 1 (D.C. Cir. 2014)(rejecting the argument).

2. *Throwing sand in the gears of Obamacare*. The most promising line of attack was the challenge to federal tax credits that led to *King v. Burwell*. The goal was to cripple the Affordable Care Act in order to force a political reconsideration of its terms. By eliminating the tax credits for federally run exchanges,

many people could no longer afford health insurance. Because people could not afford health insurance, the individual mandate would not apply to them. And if millions of people were no longer insured, the Act's community ratings and guaranteed issue requirements would drive up health insurance costs, making health insurance unaffordable to even more people. By eliminating the tax credits, the challengers hoped simultaneously to destroy the effectiveness of the much despised individual mandate—the source of the original constitutional challenge in *Sebelius*—and to force Congress and the President to reconsider the entire Affordable Care Act.

The Affordable Care Act was passed when Democrats controlled the presidency and both houses of Congress. If the statutory challenge in *King v. Burwell* succeeded, the status quo would be untenable and Congress would have to act. Inertia would no longer be a possibility. But now the reconsideration would occur when Republicans controlled both Houses of Congress.

If the challenge succeeded, Republicans hoped to pressure President Obama into accepting significant changes in the law, like repeals of the employer and individual mandates. Perhaps more likely, Obama would have vetoed any changes and tried to blame the Republicans. In that case, the Republicans might wait for a Republican to win in 2016, leading to full repeal in 2017.

Either way, by throwing a monkey wrench into the law, the challengers hoped to force Congress and the President to alter or repeal the ACA, and achieve health care legislation more consistent with their political and constitutional principles.

Are legal campaigns deliberately designed to prevent major laws from operating legitimate? Supporters of the Affordable Care Act were outraged that the challengers sought to rob millions of Americans of affordable health insurance and potentially melt down the insurance markets. Nevertheless, there is a long history of such attempts, with different political valences. Consider, for example, the long running campaign by opponents of the death penalty to put up as many road blocks as possible to executions in the United States. Although supporters of the death penalty resent these strategies, opponents believe they are necessary to convince the public that the death penalty should be abolished. Are such tactics permissible if one believes that the law one is challenging is extremely unjust and hopes to change to public's mind?

3. *The Affordable Care Act as a framework statute*. The resolution of the statutory question in *King v. Burwell* is also implicitly a reaffirmation of the constitutional resolution reached in *Sebelius*. Guarantees of health care are increasingly embedded in the American social contract. Although legal challenges may continue, the Court seems to have sent a fairly clear message: The Affordable Care Act is part of the way we do things now in the United States, and it will continue to be until Congress repeals it.

In dissent, Justice Scalia objected that the Court was treating the ACA as its special favorite, and that by reading the Act to defend it from challenges it was responsible for keeping it in place. Hence, Scalia, remarked, it should be called "SCOTUScare." He acknowledged that the Act might be "enduring" like

Social Security or the Taft Hartley Act. But this should not affect how courts interpreted it.

By contrast, the majority treated the ACA as an important institutional arrangement like Social Security. It rejected the arguments of the challengers in *King* because it believed that the challengers' interpretation would seriously undermine the functioning of the act and was counter to its underlying purposes. The Court explained that its job was to interpret the Affordable Care Act according to Congress's purpose "to improve health insurance markets, not to destroy them."

4. *Framework statutes and American constitutional development.* Although Scalia thought he was criticizing the Court, he was actually describing how courts respond to big state-building exercises in American constitutional development, of which the Affordable Care Act is only the latest example. The American state has evolved through the creation of new institutions and programs, which reshape people's expectations about what government can do, must do, and should not do.

One need only compare Madison's veto of a federal bill for internal improvements in the 1810s with today's massive federal investments in highways, dams, and bridges. Or compare Grover Cleveland's veto of a disaster relief bill to alleviate the problems of drought-stricken Texas farmers in the 1880s with the federal government's multiple programs for disaster relief today. Statutes like Social Security, Medicare, and Medicaid, and programs like food stamps and unemployment insurance have constructed a social insurance system—sometimes called the social safety net—that did not exist in the 19th century but that most Americans today would be unwilling to do without. Add to this the modern expectation that Congress and the Federal Reserve will do their best to keep the economy humming—and to respond to recessions and depressions. Finally, note how modern American politics has created elaborate statutory systems for protecting civil rights, working conditions, and the environment. The American social contract has changed markedly over time through these and other state-building exercises. From *McCulloch v. Maryland*—which legitimated the creation of a national bank—to the present, many of the most important controversies in American constitutional history concern these exercises of state-building, either directly or indirectly. The fight over Obamacare is yet another example.

In general, courts legitimate big changes in the social contract by considering constitutional challenges to them. A good example is the constitutional struggle over the New Deal. At first, the Court, staffed by holdovers from the previous regime, rejected Roosevelt's proposed innovations to the social contract, symbolized by the National Recovery Act, struck down in the *Schechter Poultry* case. Roosevelt and the Democrats responded with different statutes—sometimes called the Second New Deal—including the Social Security Act and the Wagner Act. Eventually, the Supreme Court came around and ratified these changes to the social contract, and these framework statutes became important parts of our political and constitutional system.

Similarly, during the Civil Rights Revolution, the Warren Court upheld the Civil Rights Act and the Voting Rights Act against constitutional challenges, thus legitimating these major changes to American governance.

Framework statutes like Social Security and Medicare have a special status in the American system of government, and courts understand this implicitly. That is what made the Court's decision in *Shelby County v. Holder* so remarkable — it gutted a key part of a framework statute from the Civil Rights Revolution — the Voting Rights Act.

5. *The end of the struggle, or just the beginning?* Does the result in *King v. Burwell* mean that legal challenges to the ACA will die down? It is still too soon to tell. The law still hovers around 50 percent approval ratings and one of the nation's two major political parties is still publicly committed to its repeal. It is possible — as Democrats hope — that the ACA is here to stay, and that Republicans will simply get used to it, as they got used to other social insurance programs like Social Security and Medicare. Republicans no longer try to repeal these programs or have them declared unconstitutional; instead they attempt to alter them (usually in ways that Democrats don't like) while accepting their basic legitimacy.

Donald Trump's victory in the 2016 election gave Republicans control of both Congress and the Presidency. As this supplement went to press, Congressional Republicans are debating how to repeal and replace the Affordable Care Act. Although they have promised repeatedly to dismantle the ACA root and branch, the lack of 60 votes in the Senate means that Republicans can change the law only in certain ways, for example, by cutting back on the Medicaid expansion or making the ACA's insurance subsidies less generous.

The real test of whether an innovation is durable is whether it survives multiple changes of Administrations, including Administrations of both parties. The fate of the New Deal was not completely certain for many years after what — in hindsight — is now called the 1937 settlement. By 1952, however, when Dwight Eisenhower became the first Republican President elected since 1932, it became clear that the party had moved on and would no longer try to roll back the New Deal. Indeed, one of Eisenhower's great accomplishments was an enormous public works project that would have made New Dealers proud — the National Highway System.

One interesting feature of *King v Burwell* is that the Court held that access to tax subsidies on Federal exchanges was a requirement of the statute itself; it was not simply a reasonable interpretation by the IRS to which the Court would defer. Under the doctrine of Chevron U.S.A., Inc. v. National Resources Defense Council, 467 U.S. 837 (1984), federal courts defer to reasonable interpretations of statutes by administrative agencies when courts conclude that Congress has implicitly delegated the responsibility to fill in statutory gaps to the agency. Administrative agencies remain free to change their interpretations over time if they follow proper procedures. In *Burwell*, the Court held that "[t]t is especially unlikely that Congress would have delegated [a] decision [about subsidies] to the IRS, which has no expertise in crafting health insurance policy of this sort." Therefore it would not apply *Chevron* deference to the IRS's interpretation.

The Court's holding means that when Republicans once again control the White House, they will not be able to turn off the subsidies by having the IRS issue a new administrative regulation, thus provoking a political reconsideration of the Affordable Care Act. Instead, opponents will have to change the law through congressional statute. This feature of the Court's decision tends to increase the chances that the ACA will endure.

Add the following on p. 887 before note 9:

Note: The New Nationalism

Standard debates about federalism, as exemplified by cases like *Garcia*, *Printz*, and *Lopez*, revolve around the scope of state regulatory immunity and the limits of federal regulatory power. But the actual development of governance since the New Deal has changed federal-state relations in ways that do not map onto these debates particularly well.

The standard model assumes that centralization of power best serves national interests, while decentralization and devolution benefit the states and local interests. As national governance has become more complicated, however, it has also become clear that decentralization and devolution of power may also serve national interests. Conversely, states and local governments may actually increase their influence and power by structuring national policy debates and participating in national regulatory programs.

The "New Nationalism" refers to the body of scholarship that describes these phenomena.[1] This work focuses on the ways that decentralization shapes the national political process, and the ways that state power shapes the implementation of federal programs.

1. *How decentralization drives the national political process.* Many if not most policy and constitutional questions—including health care, immigration, voting rights, same-sex marriage, drug policy, education, and privacy—start in debates in state and local governments.[2] Different decisionmakers will reach different answers and compromises. Multiple jurisdictions for politics allow more sites in which politics can occur, which, in turn, shapes national debates.[3] In this way, the development of rights depends on federal structure; federal structure, in

---

1. See, e.g., Heather K. Gerken, Federalism as the New Nationalism: An Overview, 123 Yale L.J. 1889 (2013).

2. Heather K. Gerken, Windsor's Mad Genius: The Interlocking Gears of Rights and Structure, 95 B.U. L. Rev. 587 (2015); Heather K. Gerken, The Loyal Opposition, 123 Yale L.J. 1958 (2014).

3. See, e.g., Cristina M. Rodriguez, Federalism and National Consensus 4 (Oct. 2014) (unpublished manuscript); Jessica Bulman-Pozen, Partisan Federalism, 127 Harv. L. Rev. 1077 (2014); Jessica Bulman-Pozen, From Sovereignty and Process to Administration and Politics: The Afterlife of American Federalism, 123 Yale L.J. 1920 (2014).

turn, generates friction and controversy that engenders the political development of rights.[4]

Moreover, federalism continually produces oppositional politics that counteracts federal initiatives. American party politics operates counter-cyclically: when one party dominates national politics, the other party often gains in state and local governments who want to serve as a counter-weight to Washington, D.C. Finally, Heather Gerken argues that multiple jurisdictions allow groups to "dissent by deciding."[5] Political minorities at the national level are never shut out of politics as long as they can exert influence or possess majority control in state or local governments.

2. *The role of state power in the implementation of national programs.* As the federal government has grown, it has relied increasingly on state and local governments to implement its programs, ranging from social insurance programs (Medicaid, Obamacare) to educational policy (No Child Left Behind, Common Core) to criminal law enforcement (enforcement of marijuana and other drug laws).[6] Conversely, states have signed up to implement these programs, because the alternative is not to have a say in regulation at all.[7]

One irony of modern constitutional law is that as the formal power of the federal government increased following the New Deal and the Civil Rights Revolution, the practical power of the states in enforcing federal programs also increased in tandem. After setting up new programs, the federal government often relies on state and local governments to implement them, or it engages in continuous interaction with analogous state programs in order to coordinate efforts. Taken together, these practices create what is sometimes called "cooperative federalism."

In cooperative federalism, states and local governments willingly participate in federal initiatives. Yet because of the federal structure of politics, state and local governments are not simply loyal operatives of the federal government. Quite the contrary: they have independent bases of political power, and their own set of constituents to which they must answer. Their constituencies may differ in important ways from national constituencies. Hence when they work with the federal government, they always serve two masters, not one.

3. *Uncooperative federalism.* Heather Gerken and Jessica Bullman-Pozen point out that this dual loyalty may lead to the phenomenon of "uncooperative

---

4. Heather K. Gerken, Windsor's Mad Genius: The Interlocking Gears of Rights and Structure, supra.

5. Heather K. Gerken, Dissenting by Deciding, 57 Stan. L. Rev. 1745 (2005).

6. See, e.g., Abbe R. Gluck, Intrastatutory Federalism and Statutory Interpretation: State Implementation of Federal Law in Health Reform and Beyond, 121 Yale L.J. 534 (2011).

7. Abbe R. Gluck, Nationalism as the New Federalism (and Federalism as the New Nationalism): A Complementary Account (and Some Challenges) to the Nationalist School, 59 St. Louis U. L.J. 1045 (2015).

federalism."[8] States and local governments can resist, modify, or even partially nullify federal programs they do not like, because these federal programs cannot function without state and local implementation and cooperation. In this way, states and local governments can defend the values of local majorities in the construction and implementation of federal policies.

Even when state and local officials cooperate rather than obstruct federal programs, they exercise what Gerken calls "the power of the servant."[9] The federal government needs states and local governments as agents to implement its programs, but it cannot completely monitor or control what these agents do. Moreover, because these agents enjoy independent sources of political power, the federal government often negotiates and compromises with state and local officials as much as it gives orders to them.

4. *How state power affects the separation of powers.* Depending on the nature of the program, both Congress and the Executive may benefit from state and local governments' ability to shape implementation. For example, members of Congress may object to the way that the Executive is implementing Congressional statutes through administrative regulation. State and local actors can check executive aggrandizement and support Congress by pushing back at regulations, shaping how programs are implemented, and promoting compromises with federal officials.[10]

Conversely, states and local governments can empower the President. Congressional statutes often give the President the power to waive or modify certain features of programs—such as federal welfare laws, the Affordable Care Act, Medicaid, or No Child Left Behind—by making deals with the states about how they will implement them.[11] The result is that the President can reform or modify programs by striking deals with state and local regulators in ways he or she could never have achieved if the President attempted to pass the reforms through a polarized and dysfunctional Congress.[12] In fact, the use of waivers in federal programs is one of the most important methods of presidential lawmaking in a politically polarized system. At the same time, the President can justify the waivers on the grounds that this respects federalism and the value of using the states as laboratories for policy experimentation.

As a result, state and local officials are players in the national separation of powers. They can tilt toward one branch or the other depending on their constituents' needs, and they can shift their alliances as new issues arise.

---

8. Jessica Bulman-Pozen & Heather K. Gerken, Uncooperative Federalism, 118 Yale L.J. 1256 (2009).

9. Heather K. Gerken, Of Sovereigns and Servants, 115 Yale L.J. 2633 (2006).

10. Jessica Bulman-Pozen, Federalism as a Safeguard of the Separation of Powers, 112 Colum. L. Rev. 459 (2012).

11. See generally David J. Barron & Todd D. Rakoff, In Defense of Big Waiver, 113 Colum. L. Rev. 265 (2013); Sam Bagenstos, Federalism by Waiver After the Health Care Case, in The Health Care Case: The Supreme Court's Decision and its Implications 227 (Nathan Persily et al. eds., 2013).

12. Jessica Bulman-Pozen, Executive Federalism, 102 Va. L. Rev. 953 (2016).

5. *Criminal law enforcement.* The federal government can work with states in other ways. For example, although the federal government has extensive criminal laws on the books, it simply lacks the resources to enforce all of them. Therefore it has developed policies of cooperation with state law enforcement agencies. This approach has facilitated the decriminalization of marijuana use in some states.

The federal government has stated that its interest in prosecution is limited to what it regards as serious matters — like preventing the distribution of marijuana to minors; the diversion of revenues to cartels or criminal enterprises; and the use of violence in the cultivation and distribution of marijuana.[13] Conversely, it has stated that it is not interested in prosecuting minor possession offenses, leaving them to state and local officials under state law. It has also declined to assert that state laws are preempted by federal law. This relationship between state and federal law enforcement, in turn, has allowed states to effectively decriminalize marijuana possession and use within their borders.[14] And the federal government gets something out of the deal. It allows federal officials to experiment with different policies of decriminalization in different jurisdictions, which, given the likely political and legal response, it could never have been able to implement on its own.[15]

6. *The political safeguards of federalism, revisited.* Stepping back and looking at our current system of governance, we get the following picture: The federal government, through its New Deal powers of taxing, spending, and commerce, can regulate virtually any area of social life. Yet states, far from being crowded out by the expansion of federal power, have been ushered in as essential participants. Even so, the role of the states has changed considerably from the assumptions of the founding. States no longer have clear spaces of unencumbered regulatory power. Instead, their power comes from the fact that the federal government, no matter how great its powers may be in theory, cannot actually enforce its power everywhere. As a result, the federal government leaves a great deal of regulation to the states. And even where the federal government does regulate, states exercise considerable influence over how federal law actually operates (or does not operate) through implementation, negotiation, and resistance.

This picture requires us to rethink the debate over the political safeguards of federalism discussed in cases like *Garcia.*[16] The debate has usually been organized around whether states are adequately protected because they are

---

13. See, e.g., Memorandum from James M. Cole, Deputy Att'y Gen., to U.S. Attorneys, Guidance Regarding Marijuana Enforcement 2 (Aug. 29, 2013), http://www.justice.gov /iso/opa/resources/ 3052013829132756857467.pdf.

14. Robert A. Mikos, On the Limits of Supremacy: Medical Marijuana and the States' Overlooked Power to Legalize Federal Crime, 62 Van. L. Rev. 1421 (2009).

15. See Cristina M. Rodriguez, Negotiating Conflict Through Federalism: Institutional and Popular Perspectives, 123 Yale L.J. 2094 (2014).

16. Heather K. Gerken, Federalism and Nationalism: Time for a Détente?, 59 Wash. U. L. Rev. 997 (2015).

represented in the political process, for example, in the Senate. If states are adequately protected, judicial enforcement of federalism guarantees is unnecessary, but if states are not adequately protected, courts should step in. Defenders of national power have contended that states are generally adequately protected by the national political process; while defenders of state power have usually objected that these protections are illusory because of the way that national politics and national political parties have developed.

Cooperative federalism and related phenomena suggest a different account of how the national political process protects the interests of states, and, indirectly, the particular constituencies that states represent. States are protected politically because federal officials need to work with them and negotiate with them.[17] As a result, states can strike deals that secure their constituents different implementations of federal policies. Through their bargaining power and influence, different states can achieve a diversity of policy outcomes. This, in turn, serves many of the traditional goals of federalism, including experimentation, mutual learning, competition, and choice. Indeed, not only are states protected in this way, but so too are sub-state units like cities and counties, who are crucial partners in many different kinds of federal programs in areas ranging from health and educational policy to criminal enforcement, social services and immigration.

7. *Sovereigns and stakeholders.* This revised account of the political safeguards of federalism asserts that states and local governments are protected not as *sovereigns* (for after all, cities and counties are not sovereigns) but as *stakeholders* whose participation is crucial for the practical success of federal programs. We might even call this the *stakeholder model of federalism.* Instead of viewing the states as independent sovereigns in a federal system, we should think of states as indispensable stakeholders in the direction and implementation of federal policy.

8. *Institutional realism.* The new nationalist model argues that federalism debates should focus on the political world we are actually living in, rather than on an idealized world of federal-state relations that no longer exists. As the cases in this casebook suggest, throughout most of the nation's history, the historical debate over federalism has been waged in terms of whether it is a good idea for courts to guarantee states distinct spheres of regulatory control or enforce limitations on federal power to protect state autonomy. The goal of protecting state power, in turn, is to support individual liberty and act as a check on federal encroachment. (See the discussion in *Gregory v. Ashcroft* in the casebook at pp. 841-843, and note 6, at p. 850.).

The basic terms of dispute have become increasingly irrelevant following the New Deal. Even the Rehnquist and Roberts Court's federalism doctrines have altered the New Deal settlement only at the margins. There is very little that the federal government cannot do through its combination of powers if it possesses the political will to act. For example, in *Sebelius*, the federal government

---

17. ERIN RYAN, FEDERALISM AND THE TUG OF WAR WITHIN (2012).

was able to pass the individual mandate through the taxing power; and Chief Justice Roberts acknowledged that by structuring the Affordable Care Act differently, the Government could also have required the states to adopt the Medicaid expansion.

9. *Protecting states as stakeholders.* What are the doctrinal consequences of the new nationalism? Does it change how courts should decide federalism cases?

The model of cooperative federalism suggests that the best way to protect states may not be to carve out spheres of regulatory immunity or limited federal power. Rather, it is to accept the broad scope of federal power but give states bargaining leverage. States protect the interests of their citizens — their political base — through their influence and participation in federal governance. They exercise political power through their ability to implement (or not implement) federal programs and to structure the terms in which federal power will be exercised.

If, for example, you regard marijuana legalization as a victory for individual liberty, the victory has not come from judicial limits on the federal commerce power. (The Supreme Court upheld federal power to regulate marijuana in *Raich* and again this Term in *Taylor*.) Rather, the achievement is due to the fact that the federal government relies on the states for the enforcement of drug laws. This gives states bargaining leverage to push the federal government to experiment with different ways of organizing drug enforcement.

However, states can only exercise this role of protecting their citizens if they have (1) "skin in the game" — that is, a stake in federal governance — and (2) some form of bargaining leverage. It follows that the most important federalism doctrines might be those that give states both a stake *and* leverage in federal governance. If states increasingly protect their citizens and exercise their power as stakeholders, the courts assist them best when they protect their role as stakeholders.

How might this be accomplished? First, courts can adopt rules that require — or at least give incentives — for the federal government to bargain with states in regulatory initiatives rather than simply commanding states' obedience. Doing so puts friction into the system of federal power in order to encourage the federal government to negotiate and work with states. This might provide an additional justification for the anti-commandeering principle recognized in *Printz*[18] or the Court's construction of the spending power in *NFIB v. Sebelius*.[19] How would one write the majority opinions in these cases from a new nationalist perspective?

Note, however, that the consequence of this approach in *Sebelius* is that the federal government has to get the states to agree to expand Medicaid. It may not succeed. Some states will refuse for political and ideological reasons, with

---

18. Roderick M. Hills, Jr., The Political Economy of Cooperative Federalism: Why State Autonomy Makes Sense and "Dual Sovereignty" Doesn't, 96 MICH. L. REV. 813 (1998).

19. Heather K. Gerken, Federalism and Nationalism: Time for a Détente?, supra.

the result that many poor people, especially in red states, will not get Medicaid for many years, if at all. If you oppose the Medicaid expansion, that presents no problems. It is a genuine problem, however, if you support the federal government's expansion of medical care for the poor. Are the advantages of this model of federalism worth the costs?

On the other hand, are court-enforced limits on federal power actually necessary to give the states leverage in implementing federal programs? Suppose that *NFIB v. Sebelius* went the other way and the federal government was allowed to impose its Medicaid expansion on all of the states. Wouldn't recalcitrant states still have "the power of the servant," because they would implement the Medicaid expansion in their own way?

The difference between the two scenarios is that in the first scenario, poor people don't get Medicaid at all in some red states, while in the second, poor people in these states get Medicaid in the way that state opponents of Obamacare prefer. Which result in *NFIB v. Sebelius* is more consistent with the premises of the new nationalism? If both results are consistent, what advice does the model give to judges?

A second way for courts to implement the new nationalist model is to use clear statement rules rather than imposing simple limits on federal power. Clear statement rules do not prevent the federal government from acting; rather they require clear statements from Congress before federal power can be exercised in certain ways. Two examples are *Gregory v. Ashcroft* (Casebook p. 841) and *Bond v. United States* (Casebook p. 776). Clear statement rules require additional political capital to achieve certain goals. Therefore, they may indirectly enhance the role of states as stakeholders in federal policy.

If one adopted the new nationalist approach, would any of the cases you have read so far come out differently? Or is the primary value of this approach to give a different set of perspectives on how and when to empower states in their political relationships with the federal government?

Insert before Section III on p. 906:

ARIZONA STATE LEGISLATURE v. ARIZONA INDEPENDENT REDISTRICTING COMMISSION
135 S.Ct. 2652 (2015)

[In 2000, Arizona voters adopted Proposition 106, an initiative aimed at the problem of gerrymandering. Proposition 106 amended Arizona's Constitution, removing redistricting authority from the Arizona Legislature and vesting it in an independent commission, the Arizona Independent Redistricting Commission (AIRC). After the 2010 census, as after the 2000 census, the AIRC adopted redistricting maps for congressional as well as state legislative districts. The Arizona

Legislature challenged the map the Commission adopted in 2012 for congressional districts, arguing that the AIRC and its map violated the "Elections Clause" of the U.S. Constitution, Art. I, §4, cl. 1, which provides that "The Times, Places and Manner of holding Elections for Senators and Representatives, shall be prescribed in each State by the Legislature thereof; but the Congress may at any time by Law make or alter such Regulations." The Arizona Legislature contended that "Legislature" means the State's representative assembly; therefore, the Elections Clause prevents the public from using an initiative to create an independent commission for redistricting purposes.

In *Vieth v. Jubelirer,* 541 U.S. 267 (2004) (plurality opinion), the Court rejected the claim that voters could challenge partisan gerrymanders in the federal courts. A plurality of the Court held that the question was nonjusticiable. Justice Kennedy, the deciding vote in the case, did not believe that the plaintiffs had identified a workable standard, but left open the possibility that a suitable standard might be identified in later litigation.]

Justice GINSBURG delivered the opinion of the Court.

. . . .

I

A

Direct lawmaking by the people was "virtually unknown when the Constitution of 1787 was drafted." There were obvious precursors or analogues to the direct lawmaking operative today in several States, notably, New England's town hall meetings and the submission of early state constitutions to the people for ratification. But it was not until the turn of the 20th century, as part of the Progressive agenda of the era, that direct lawmaking by the electorate gained a foothold, largely in Western States.

The two main "agencies of direct legislation" are the initiative and the referendum. The initiative operates entirely outside the States' representative assemblies; it allows "voters [to] petition to propose statutes or constitutional amendments to be adopted or rejected by the voters at the polls." While the initiative allows the electorate to adopt positive legislation, the referendum serves as a negative check. It allows "voters [to] petition to refer a legislative action to the voters [for approval or disapproval] at the polls." "The initiative [thus] corrects sins of omission" by representative bodies, while the "referendum corrects sins of commission."

In 1898, South Dakota took the pathmarking step of affirming in its Constitution the people's power "directly [to] control the making of all ordinary laws" by initiative and referendum. In 1902, Oregon became the first State to adopt the initiative as a means, not only to enact ordinary laws, but also to amend the State's Constitution. By 1920, the people in 19 States had reserved for themselves the power to initiate ordinary lawmaking, and, in 13 States, the power to initiate amendments to the State's Constitution. Those numbers increased to 21 and 18, respectively, by the close of the 20th century.

The people's sovereign right to incorporate themselves into a State's lawmaking apparatus, by reserving for themselves the power to adopt laws and to veto measures passed by elected representatives, is one this Court has ranked a nonjusticiable political matter. *Pacific States Telephone & Telegraph Co. v. Oregon,* 223 U.S. 118 (1912) (rejecting challenge to referendum mounted under Article IV, §4's undertaking by the United States to "guarantee to every State in th[e] Union a Republican Form of Government"). But see *New York v. United States,* 505 U.S. 144 (1992) ("[P]erhaps not all claims under the Guarantee Clause present nonjusticiable political questions."). [relocated footnote — eds.]

B

For the delegates to Arizona's constitutional convention, direct lawmaking was a "principal issu[e]." By a margin of more than three to one, the people of Arizona ratified the State's Constitution, which included, among lawmaking means, initiative and referendum provisions. In the runup to Arizona's admission to the Union in 1912, those provisions generated no controversy.

In particular, the Arizona Constitution "establishes the electorate [of Arizona] as a coordinate source of legislation" on equal footing with the representative legislative body. The initiative, housed under the article of the Arizona Constitution concerning the "Legislative Department" and the section defining the State's "legislative authority," reserves for the people "the power to propose laws and amendments to the constitution." Art. IV, pt. 1, §1. The Arizona Constitution further states that "[a]ny law which may be enacted by the Legislature under this Constitution may be enacted by the people under the Initiative." Art. XXII, §14. Accordingly, "[g]eneral references to the power of the 'legislature' " in the Arizona Constitution "include the people's right (specified in Article IV, part 1) to bypass their elected representatives and make laws directly through the initiative."

C

Proposition 106, vesting redistricting authority in the AIRC, was adopted by citizen initiative in 2000 against a "background of recurring redistricting turmoil" in Arizona. Redistricting plans adopted by the Arizona Legislature sparked controversy in every redistricting cycle since the 1970's, and several of those plans were rejected by a federal court or refused preclearance by the Department of Justice under the Voting Rights Act of 1965.

Aimed at "ending the practice of gerrymandering and improving voter and candidate participation in elections," Proposition 106 amended the Arizona Constitution to remove congressional redistricting authority from the state legislature, lodging that authority, instead, in a new entity, the AIRC. Ariz. Const., Art. IV, pt. 2, §1, ¶¶ 3–23. The AIRC convenes after each census, establishes final district boundaries, and certifies the new districts to the Arizona Secretary of State. The legislature may submit nonbinding recommendations to the AIRC, and is required to make necessary appropriations for its operation. The highest ranking officer and minority leader of each chamber of the legislature each select one member of the AIRC from a list compiled by Arizona's Commission on Appellate Court Appointments. The four appointed members of the AIRC then choose, from the same list, the fifth member, who chairs the Commission. A Commission's tenure is confined to one redistricting cycle; each member's time in office "expire[s] upon the appointment of the first member of the next redistricting commission."

Holders of, or candidates for, public office may not serve on the AIRC, except candidates for or members of a school board. No more than two members of the Commission may be members of the same political party, and the presiding fifth member cannot be registered with any party already represented on the Commission. Subject to the concurrence of two-thirds of the Arizona Senate, AIRC members may be removed by the Arizona Governor for gross misconduct, substantial neglect of duty, or inability to discharge the duties of office.

In the current climate of heightened partisanship, the AIRC has encountered interference with its operations. In particular, its dependence on the Arizona Legislature for funding, and the removal provision have proved problematic. In 2011, when the AIRC proposed boundaries the majority party did not like, the Governor of Arizona attempted to remove the Commission's independent chair. Her attempt was stopped by the Arizona Supreme Court. [relocated footnote—eds.]

Several other States, as a means to curtail partisan gerrymandering, have also provided for the participation of commissions in redistricting. Some States, in common with Arizona, have given nonpartisan or bipartisan commissions binding authority over redistricting. The California Redistricting Commission, established by popular initiative, develops redistricting plans which become effective if approved by public referendum. Still other States have given commissions an auxiliary role, advising the legislatures on redistricting, or serving as a "backup" in the event the State's representative body fails to complete redistricting. Studies report that nonpartisan and bipartisan commissions generally draw their maps in a timely fashion and create districts both more competitive and more likely to survive legal challenge.

. . . .

II

We turn first to the threshold question: Does the Arizona Legislature have standing to bring this suit? . . . [T]he Arizona Legislature "must show, first and foremost," injury in the form of " 'invasion of a legally protected interest' that is 'concrete and particularized' and 'actual or imminent.' " *Arizonans for Official English v. Arizona,* 520 U.S. 43 (1997) (quoting *Lujan v. Defenders of Wildlife,*

504 U.S. 555 (1992)). The Legislature's injury also must be "fairly traceable to the challenged action" and "redressable by a favorable ruling." *Clapper v. Amnesty Int'l USA,* 568 U.S. ____, (2013). . . . [T]he Legislature's passage of a competing [redistricting] plan and submission of that plan to the Secretary of State . . . would directly and immediately conflict with the regime Arizona's Constitution establishes. . . . To establish standing, the Legislature need not violate the Arizona Constitution and show that the Secretary of State would similarly disregard the State's fundamental instrument of government.

[In] *Raines v. Byrd,* 521 U.S. 811 (1997), . . . this Court held that six *individual Members* of Congress lacked standing to challenge the Line Item Veto Act. The Act, which gave the President authority to cancel certain spending and tax benefit measures after signing them into law, allegedly diluted the efficacy of the Congressmembers' votes. The "institutional injury" at issue, we reasoned, scarcely zeroed in on any individual Member. "[W]idely dispersed," the alleged injury "necessarily [impacted] all Members of Congress and both Houses . . . equally." None of the plaintiffs, therefore, could tenably claim a "personal stake" in the suit. . . . [T]he Court "attach[ed] some importance to the fact that [the *Raines* plaintiffs had] not been authorized to represent their respective Houses of Congress." "[I]ndeed," the Court observed, "both houses actively oppose[d] their suit." Having failed to prevail in their own Houses, the suitors could not repair to the Judiciary to complain. The Arizona Legislature, in contrast, is an institutional plaintiff asserting an institutional injury, and it commenced this action after authorizing votes in both of its chambers, That "different . . . circumstanc[e]," was not *sub judice* in *Raines.*

Closer to the mark is this Court's decision in *Coleman v. Miller,* 307 U.S. 433 (1939). There, plaintiffs were 20 (of 40) Kansas State Senators, whose votes "would have been sufficient to defeat [a] resolution ratifying [a] proposed [federal] constitutional amendment" [giving Congress the power to ban child labor.] *Id.,* at 446. We held they had standing to challenge, as impermissible under Article V of the Federal Constitution, the State Lieutenant Governor's tie-breaking vote for the amendment. *Coleman,* as we later explained in *Raines,* stood "for the proposition that legislators whose votes would have been sufficient to defeat (or enact) a specific legislative Act have standing to sue if that legislative action goes into effect (or does not go into effect), on the ground that their votes have been completely nullified." Our conclusion that the Arizona Legislature has standing fits that bill. Proposition 106, together with the Arizona Constitution's ban on efforts to undermine the purposes of an initiative, would "completely nullif[y]" any vote by the Legislature, now or "in the future," purporting to adopt a redistricting plan. *Raines.*

The case before us does not touch or concern the question whether Congress has standing to bring a suit against the President. There is no federal analogue to Arizona's initiative power, and a suit between Congress and the President would raise separation-of-powers concerns absent here. The Court's standing analysis, we have noted, has been "especially rigorous when reaching the merits of the dispute would force [the Court] to decide whether an action taken by one of the other two branches of the Federal Government was unconstitutional." *Raines.* [relocated footnote — eds.]

III

[W]e summarize this Court's precedent relating to appropriate state decision-makers for redistricting purposes.

A

[*Ohio ex rel.*] *Davis v. Hildebrant,* [241 U.S. 565 (1916),] involved an amendment to the Constitution of Ohio vesting in the people the right, exercisable by referendum, to approve or disapprove by popular vote any law enacted by the State's legislature. A 1915 Act redistricting the State for the purpose of congressional elections had been submitted to a popular vote, resulting in disapproval of the legislature's measure. State election officials asked the State's Supreme Court to declare the referendum void. That court rejected the request, holding that the referendum authorized by Ohio's Constitution, "was a part of the legislative power of the State," and "nothing in [federal statutory law] or in [the Elections Clause] operated to the contrary." This Court affirmed the Ohio Supreme Court's judgment. In upholding the state court's decision, we recognized that the referendum was "part of the legislative power" in Ohio, legitimately exercised by the people to disapprove the legislation creating congressional districts. For redistricting purposes, *Hildebrant* thus established, "the Legislature" did not mean the representative body alone. Rather, the word encompassed a veto power lodged in the people. See *id.,* at 569 (Elections Clause does not bar "treating the referendum as part of the legislative power for the purpose of apportionment, where so ordained by the state constitutions and laws").

Hawke v. Smith [(*No. 1*), 253 U.S. 221 (1920),] involved the Eighteenth Amendment to the Federal Constitution. Ohio's Legislature had ratified the Amendment, and a referendum on that ratification was at issue. Reversing the Ohio Supreme Court's decision upholding the referendum, we held that "ratification by a State of a constitutional amendment is not an act of legislation within the proper sense of the word." Instead, Article V governing ratification had lodged in "the legislatures of three-fourths of the several States" sole authority to assent to a proposed amendment. The Court contrasted the ratifying function, exercisable exclusively by a State's legislature, with "the ordinary business of legislation." *Davis v. Hildebrant,* the Court explained, involved the enactment of legislation, *i.e.,* a redistricting plan, and properly held that "the referendum [was] part of the legislative authority of the State for [that] purpose."

Smiley v. Holm [285 U.S. 355 (1932),] raised the question whether legislation purporting to redistrict Minnesota for congressional elections was subject to the Governor's veto. The Minnesota Supreme Court had held that the Elections Clause placed redistricting authority exclusively in the hands of the State's legislature, leaving no role for the Governor. We reversed that determination and held, for the purpose at hand, Minnesota's legislative authority includes not just the two houses of the legislature; it includes, in addition, a make-or-break role for the Governor. In holding that the Governor's veto counted, we distinguished instances in which the Constitution calls upon state legislatures to exercise a function other than lawmaking. State legislatures, we pointed out, performed an "electoral" function "in the choice of United States Senators under Article I, section 3, prior to the adoption of the Seventeenth Amendment," a "ratifying" function for "proposed amendments to the Constitution under Article V," as explained in *Hawke v. Smith,* and a "consenting" function "in relation to the acquisition of lands by the United States under Article I, section 8, paragraph 17."

In contrast to those other functions, we observed, redistricting "involves law-making in its essential features and most important aspect." Lawmaking, we further noted, ordinarily "must be in accordance with the method which the State has prescribed for legislative enactments." In Minnesota, the State's Constitution had made the Governor "part of the legislative process." And the Elections Clause, we explained, respected the State's choice to include the Governor in that process, although the Governor could play no part when the Constitution assigned to "the Legislature" a ratifying, electoral, or consenting function. Nothing in the Elections Clause, we said, "attempt[ed] to endow the legislature of the State with power to enact laws in any manner other than that in which the constitution of the State ha[d] provided that laws shall be enacted."

The Chief Justice, in dissent, features, indeed trumpets repeatedly, the pre-Seventeenth Amendment regime in which Senators were "chosen [in each State] by the Legislature thereof." Art. I, §3. If we are right, he asks, why did popular election proponents resort to the amending process instead of simply interpreting "the Legislature" to mean "the people"? *Smiley,* as just indicated, answers that question. Article I, §3, gave state legislatures "a function different from that of lawgiver;" it made each of them "an electoral body" charged to perform that function to the exclusion of other participants. So too, of the ratifying function. As we explained in *Hawke,* "the power to legislate in the enactment of the laws of a State is derived from the people of the State." Ratification, however, "has its source in the Federal Constitution" and is not "an act of legislation within the proper sense of the word."

Constantly resisted by The Chief Justice, but well understood in opinions that speak for the Court: "[T]he meaning of the word 'legislature,' used several times in the Federal Constitution, differs according to the connection in which it is employed, depend[ent] upon the character of the function which that body in each instance is called upon to exercise." *Atlantic Cleaners & Dyers, Inc. v. United States,* 286 U.S. 427 (1932) (citing *Smiley*). Thus "the Legislature" comprises the referendum and the Governor's veto in the context of regulating congressional elections. *Hildebrant*; *Smiley*. In the context of ratifying constitutional amendments, in contrast, "the Legislature" has a different identity, one that excludes the referendum and the Governor's veto. *Hawke.*

The list of constitutional provisions in which the word "legislature" appears
. . . is illustrative of the variety of functions state legislatures can be called
upon to exercise. For example, Art. I, §2, cl. 1, superseded by the Seventeenth
Amendment, assigned an "electoral" function. See *Smiley*. Article I, §3, cl.
2, assigns an "appointive" function. Article I, §8, cl. 17, assigns a "consenting" function, see *Smiley*, as does Art. IV, §3, cl. 1. "[R]atifying" functions are
assigned in Art. V, Amdt. 18, §3, Amdt. 20, §6, and Amdt. 22, §2. See *Hawke*.
But [the Elections Clause of] Art. I, §4, cl. 1, unquestionably calls for the exercise of lawmaking authority. That authority can be carried out by a representative
body, but if a State so chooses, legislative authority can also be lodged in the
people themselves. [relocated footnote—eds.]

In sum, our precedent teaches that redistricting is a legislative function, to be
performed in accordance with the State's prescriptions for lawmaking, which
may include the referendum and the Governor's veto. The exercise of the initiative, we acknowledge, was not at issue in our prior decisions. But as developed
below, we see no constitutional barrier to a State's empowerment of its people
by embracing that form of lawmaking.

B

[Justice Ginsburg holds that Arizona's redistricting commission is consistent with the 1911 Reapportionment Act, 2 U.S.C. §2a(c), which provides that:
"Until a State is redistricted in the manner provided by the law thereof after any
apportionment, the Representatives to which such State is entitled under such
apportionment shall be elected in the following manner: [setting out five federally prescribed redistricting procedures].

From 1862 through 1901, the decennial congressional apportionment Acts
provided that a State would be required to follow federally prescribed procedures for redistricting unless "the legislature" of the State drew district lines.
In drafting the 1911 Act, Congress focused on the fact that several States had
supplemented the representative legislature mode of lawmaking with a direct
lawmaking role for the people, through the processes of initiative (positive legislation by the electorate) and referendum (approval or disapproval of legislation
by the electorate). To accommodate that development, the 1911 Act eliminated
the statutory reference to redistricting by the state "legislature" and instead
directed that, if a State's apportionment of Representatives increased, the State
should use the Act's default procedures for redistricting "until such State shall
be redistricted *in the manner provided by the laws thereof.*" (emphasis added).

[A]s this Court observed in *Hildebrant,* "the legislative history of th[e] [1911
Act] leaves no room for doubt . . . [that] [t]he change was made to safeguard to
"each State full authority to employ in the creation of congressional districts its
own laws and regulations." The 1911 Act, in short, left the question of redistricting "to the laws and methods of the States. If they include initiative, it is
included." [Congress used virtually identical language when it enacted §2a(c) in
1941. [relocated footnote—eds.]] . . . The 1941 provision, like the 1911 Act, thus

accorded full respect to the redistricting procedures adopted by the States. So long as a State has "redistricted in the manner provided by the law thereof"—as Arizona did by utilizing the independent commission procedure called for by its Constitution—the resulting redistricting plan becomes the presumptively governing map. . . . [Although] four of the five default redistricting procedures [have become obsolete because of] [t]he one-person, one-vote principle announced in *Wesberry v. Sanders,* 376 U.S. 1 (1964), . . . [this] does not bear on the question whether a State has been "redistricted in the manner provided by [state] law." . . .

C

[W]e hold that the Elections Clause permits the people of Arizona to provide for redistricting by independent commission. . . . The history and purpose of the Clause weigh heavily against [a contrary result], as does the animating principle of our Constitution that the people themselves are the originating source of all the powers of government.

[D]ictionaries, even those in circulation during the founding era, capaciously define the word "legislature." Samuel Johnson defined "legislature" simply as "[t]he power that makes laws." 2 A Dictionary of the English Language (1st ed. 1755); *ibid.* (6th ed. 1785); *ibid.* (10th ed. 1792); *ibid.* (12th ed. 1802). Thomas Sheridan's dictionary defined "legislature" exactly as Dr. Johnson did: "The power that makes laws." 2 A Complete Dictionary of the English Language (4th ed. 1797). Noah Webster defined the term precisely that way as well. Compendious Dictionary of the English Language 174 (1806). And Nathan Bailey similarly defined "legislature" as "the Authority of making Laws, or Power which makes them." An Universal Etymological English Dictionary (20th ed. 1763). . . .

Illustrative of an embracive comprehension of the word "legislature," Charles Pinckney explained at South Carolina's ratifying convention that America is "[a] republic, where the people at large, either collectively or by representation, form the legislature." 4 Debates on the Federal Constitution 328 (J. Elliot 2d ed. 1863). Participants in the debates over the Elections Clause used the word "legislature" interchangeably with "state" and "state government." [relocated footnote—eds.]

As to the "power that makes laws" in Arizona, initiatives adopted by the voters legislate for the State just as measures passed by the representative body do. See Ariz. Const., Art. IV, pt. 1, §1 ("The legislative authority of the state shall be vested in the legislature, consisting of a senate and a house of representatives, but the people reserve the power to propose laws and amendments to the constitution and to enact or reject such laws and amendments at the polls, independently of the legislature."). See also *Eastlake v. Forest City Enterprises, Inc.,* 426 U.S. 668 (1976) ("In establishing legislative bodies, the people can reserve to themselves power to deal directly with matters which might otherwise be assigned to the legislature."). As well in Arizona, the people may delegate their legislative authority over redistricting to an independent commission just as the representative body may choose to do.

1

The dominant purpose of the Elections Clause, the historical record bears out, was to empower Congress to override state election rules, not to restrict the way States enact legislation. As this Court explained in *Arizona v. Inter Tribal Council of Ariz., Inc.,* 570 U.S. 1 (2013), the Clause "was the Framers' insurance against the possibility that a State would refuse to provide for the election of representatives to the Federal Congress." (citing The Federalist No. 59 (A.Hamilton)).

The Clause was also intended to act as a safeguard against manipulation of electoral rules by politicians and factions in the States to entrench themselves or place their interests over those of the electorate. As Madison urged, without the Elections Clause, "[w]henever the State Legislatures had a favorite measure to carry, they would take care so to mould their regulations as to favor the candidates they wished to succeed." 2 Records of the Federal Convention 241 (M. Farrand rev.1966). Madison spoke in response to a motion by South Carolina's delegates to strike out the federal power. Those delegates so moved because South Carolina's coastal elite had malapportioned their legislature, and wanted to retain the ability to do so. The problem Madison identified has hardly lessened over time. Conflict of interest is inherent when "legislators dra[w] district lines that they ultimately have to run in."

Arguments in support of congressional control under the Elections Clause were reiterated in the public debate over ratification. . . . Timothy Pickering of Massachusetts . . . urged that the Clause was necessary because "the State governments *may* abuse their power, and regulate . . . elections in such manner as would be highly inconvenient to the people." He described the Clause as a way to "ensure to the *people* their rights of election."

While attention focused on potential abuses by state-level politicians, and the consequent need for congressional oversight, the legislative processes by which the States could exercise their initiating role in regulating congressional elections occasioned no debate. That is hardly surprising. Recall that when the Constitution was composed in Philadelphia and later ratified, the people's legislative prerogatives—the initiative and the referendum—were not yet in our democracy's arsenal. The Elections Clause, however, is not reasonably read to disarm States from adopting modes of legislation that place the lead rein in the people's hands.

The Chief Justice, in dissent, cites *U.S. Term Limits, Inc. v. Thornton,* 514 U.S. 779 (1995) . . . There, we held that state-imposed term limits on candidates for the House and Senate violated the Clauses of the Constitution setting forth qualifications for membership in Congress, Art. I, §2, cl. 2, and Art. I, §3, cl. 3. We did so for a reason entirely harmonious with today's decision. Adding state-imposed limits to the qualifications set forth in the Constitution, the Court wrote, would be "contrary to the 'fundamental principle of our representative democracy,' . . . that 'the people should choose whom they please to govern them.' " (quoting *Powell v. McCormack,* 395 U.S. 486 (1969)). [relocated footnote — eds.]

2

The Arizona Legislature maintains that, by specifying "the Legislature thereof," the Elections Clause renders the State's representative body the sole "component of state government authorized to prescribe . . . regulations . . . for congressional redistricting." . . . But it is characteristic of our federal system that States retain autonomy to establish their own governmental processes. See *Alden v. Maine,* 527 U.S. 706 (1999) ("A State is entitled to order the processes of its own governance."); The Federalist No. 43 (J. Madison) ("Whenever the States may choose to substitute other republican forms, they have a right to do so."). "Through the structure of its government, and the character of those who exercise government authority, a State defines itself as a sovereign." *Gregory v. Ashcroft,* 501 U.S. 452 (1991). . . .

This Court has "long recognized the role of the States as laboratories for devising solutions to difficult legal problems." . . . Deference to state lawmaking "allows local policies 'more sensitive to the diverse needs of a heterogeneous society,' permits 'innovation and experimentation,' enables greater citizen 'involvement in democratic processes,' and makes government 'more responsive by putting the States in competition for a mobile citizenry.' "

We resist reading the Elections Clause to single out federal elections as the one area in which States may not use citizen initiatives as an alternative legislative process. Nothing in that Clause instructs, nor has this Court ever held, that a state legislature may prescribe regulations on the time, place, and manner of holding federal elections in defiance of provisions of the State's constitution. . . . .

We add, furthermore, that the Arizona Legislature does not question, nor could it, employment of the initiative to control state and local elections. In considering whether Article I, §4, really says "No" to similar control of federal elections, we have looked to, and borrow from, Alexander Hamilton's counsel: "[I]t would have been hardly advisable . . . to establish, as a fundamental point, what would deprive several States of the convenience of having the elections for their own governments and for the national government" held at the same times and places, and in the same manner. The Federalist No. 61. The Elections Clause is not sensibly read to subject States to that deprivation.

3

The Framers may not have imagined the modern initiative process in which the people of a State exercise legislative power coextensive with the authority of an institutional legislature. But the invention of the initiative was in full harmony with the Constitution's conception of the people as the font of governmental power. As Madison put it: "The genius of republican liberty seems to demand . . .

not only that all power should be derived from the people, but that those intrusted with it should be kept in dependence on the people." [The Federalist] No. 37.

The people's ultimate sovereignty had been expressed by John Locke in 1690, a near century before the Constitution's formation:

"[T]he Legislative being only a Fiduciary Power to act for certain ends, there remains still in the People a Supream Power to remove or alter the Legislative, when they find the Legislative act contrary to the trust reposed in them. For all Power given with trust for the attaining an end, being limited by that end, whenever that end is manifestly neglected, or opposed, the trust must necessarily be forfeited, and the Power devolve into the hands of those that gave it, who may place it anew where they shall think best for their safety and security." Two Treatises of Government §149, p. 385 (P. Laslett ed.1964).

Our Declaration of Independence, drew from Locke in stating: "Governments are instituted among Men, deriving their just powers from the consent of the governed." And our fundamental instrument of government derives its authority from "We the People." U.S. Const., Preamble. As this Court stated, quoting Hamilton: "[T]he true principle of a republic is, that the people should choose whom they please to govern them." *Powell v. McCormack,* 395 U.S. 486 (1969) (quoting 2 Debates on the Federal Constitution 257 (J. Elliot ed. 1876)). In this light, it would be perverse to interpret the term "Legislature" in the Elections Clause so as to exclude lawmaking by the people, particularly where such lawmaking is intended to check legislators' ability to choose the district lines they run in, thereby advancing the prospect that Members of Congress will in fact be "chosen . . . by the People of the several States," Art. I, §2. . . .

4

Banning lawmaking by initiative to direct a State's method of apportioning congressional districts would do more than stymie attempts to curb partisan gerrymandering, by which the majority in the legislature draws district lines to their party's advantage. It would also cast doubt on numerous other election laws adopted by the initiative method of legislating.

The people, in several States, functioning as the lawmaking body for the purpose at hand, have used the initiative to install a host of regulations governing the "Times, Places and Manner" of holding federal elections. Art. I, §4. For example, the people of California provided for permanent voter registration, specifying that "no amendment by the Legislature shall provide for a general biennial or other periodic reregistration of voters." The people of Ohio banned ballots providing for straight-ticket voting along party lines. The people of Oregon shortened the deadline for voter registration to 20 days prior to an election. None of those measures permit the state legislatures to override the people's prescriptions. The Arizona Legislature's theory—that the lead role in regulating federal elections cannot be wrested from "the Legislature," and vested in commissions initiated by the people—would endanger all of them.

The list of endangered state elections laws, were we to sustain the position of the Arizona Legislature, would not stop with popular initiatives. Almost all state constitutions were adopted by conventions and ratified by voters at the ballot box, without involvement or approval by "the Legislature." Core aspects of the electoral process regulated by state constitutions include voting by "ballot" or "secret ballot," voter registration, absentee voting, vote counting, and victory thresholds. Again, the States' legislatures had no hand in making these laws and may not alter or amend them.

The importance of direct democracy as a means to control election regulations extends beyond the particular statutes and constitutional provisions installed by the people rather than the States' legislatures. The very prospect of lawmaking by the people may influence the legislature when it considers (or fails to consider) election-related measures. Turning the coin, the legislature's responsiveness to the people its members represent is hardly heightened when the representative body can be confident that what it does will not be overturned or modified by the voters themselves.

* * *

Invoking the Elections Clause, the Arizona Legislature instituted this lawsuit to disempower the State's voters from serving as the legislative power for redistricting purposes. But the Clause surely was not adopted to diminish a State's authority to determine its own lawmaking processes. Article I, §4, stems from a different view. Both parts of the Elections Clause are in line with the fundamental premise that all political power flows from the people. *McCulloch v. Maryland.* So comprehended, the Clause doubly empowers the people. They may control the State's lawmaking processes in the first instance, as Arizona voters have done, and they may seek Congress' correction of regulations prescribed by state legislatures.

The people of Arizona turned to the initiative to curb the practice of gerrymandering and, thereby, to ensure that Members of Congress would have "an habitual recollection of their dependence on the people." The Federalist No. 57 (J. Madison). In so acting, Arizona voters sought to restore "the core principle of republican government," namely, "that the voters should choose their representatives, not the other way around." Berman, Managing Gerrymandering, 83 Texas L.Rev. 781 (2005). The Elections Clause does not hinder that endeavor.
 . . . .

Chief Justice ROBERTS, with whom Justice SCALIA, Justice THOMAS, and Justice ALITO join, dissenting.

Just over a century ago, Arizona became the second State in the Union to ratify the Seventeenth Amendment. That Amendment transferred power to choose United States Senators from "the Legislature" of each State, Art. I, §3, to "the people thereof." The Amendment resulted from an arduous, decades-long campaign in which reformers across the country worked hard to garner approval from Congress and three-quarters of the States.

What chumps! Didn't they realize that all they had to do was interpret the constitutional term "the Legislature" to mean "the people"? The Court today performs just such a magic trick with the Elections Clause. Art. I, §4. That Clause vests congressional redistricting authority in "the Legislature" of each State. An Arizona ballot initiative transferred that authority from "the Legislature" to an "Independent Redistricting Commission." The majority approves this deliberate constitutional evasion by doing what the proponents of the Seventeenth Amendment dared not: revising "the Legislature" to mean "the people."

The Court's position has no basis in the text, structure, or history of the Constitution, and it contradicts precedents from both Congress and this Court. The Constitution contains seventeen provisions referring to the "Legislature" of a State, many of which cannot possibly be read to mean "the people." Indeed, several provisions expressly distinguish "the Legislature" from "the People." See Art. I, §2; Amdt. 17. This Court has accordingly defined "the Legislature" in the Elections Clause as *the representative body* which ma[kes] the laws of the people." *Smiley v. Holm,* 285 U.S. 355 (1932) (quoting *Hawke v. Smith (No. 1),* 253 U.S. 221 (1920); emphasis added).

The majority largely ignores this evidence, relying instead on disconnected observations about direct democracy, a contorted interpretation of an irrelevant statute, and naked appeals to public policy. Nowhere does the majority explain how a constitutional provision that vests redistricting authority in "the Legislature" permits a State to wholly exclude "the Legislature" from redistricting. Arizona's Commission might be a noble endeavor — although it does not seem so "independent" in practice — but the "fact that a given law or procedure is efficient, convenient, and useful . . . will not save it if it is contrary to the Constitution." *INS v. Chadha,* 462 U.S. 919 (1983). No matter how concerned we may be about partisanship in redistricting, this Court has no power to gerrymander the Constitution. I respectfully dissent.

I

[T]he Elections Clause both imposes a duty on States and assigns that duty to a particular state actor: In the absence of a valid congressional directive to the contrary, States must draw district lines for their federal representatives. And that duty "shall" be carried out "in each State by the Legislature thereof."

[T]he majority concedes that the unelected Commission is not "the Legislature" of Arizona. The Court contends instead that the people of Arizona as a whole constitute "the Legislature" for purposes of the Elections Clause, and that they may delegate the congressional districting authority conferred by that Clause to the Commission. The majority provides no support for the delegation part of its theory, and I am not sure whether the majority's analysis is correct on that issue. But even giving the Court the benefit of the doubt in that regard, the Commission is still unconstitutional. Both the Constitution and our cases make clear that "the Legislature" in the Elections Clause is the representative body which makes the laws of the people.

A

The majority devotes much of its analysis to establishing that the people of Arizona may exercise lawmaking power under their State Constitution. Nobody doubts that. This case is governed, however, by the Federal Constitution. The States do not, in the majority's words, "retain autonomy to establish their own governmental processes," if those "processes" violate the United States Constitution. In a conflict between the Arizona Constitution and the Elections Clause, the State Constitution must give way. Art. VI, cl. 2. The majority opinion therefore largely misses the point.

The relevant question in this case is how to define "the Legislature" under the Elections Clause. . . . The Court seems to conclude, based largely on its understanding of the "history and purpose" of the Elections Clause, that "the Legislature" encompasses any entity in a State that exercises legislative power. That circular definition lacks any basis in the text of the Constitution or any other relevant legal source.

The majority's textual analysis consists, in its entirety, of one paragraph citing founding era dictionaries. The majority points to various dictionaries that follow Samuel Johnson's definition of "legislature" as the "power that makes laws." The notion that this definition corresponds to the entire population of a State is strained to begin with, and largely discredited by the majority's own admission that "[d]irect lawmaking by the people was virtually unknown when the Constitution of 1787 was drafted." . . . Any ambiguity about the meaning of "the Legislature" is removed by other founding era sources. "[E]very state constitution from the Founding Era that used the term legislature defined it as a distinct multimember entity comprised of representatives." The Federalist Papers are replete with references to "legislatures" that can only be understood as referring to representative institutions. *E.g.,* The Federalist No. 27 (A.Hamilton) (describing "the State legislatures" as "select bodies of men"); No. 60 (contrasting "the State legislatures" with "the people"). Noah Webster's heralded American Dictionary of the English Language defines "legislature" as "[t]he body of men in a state or kingdom, invested with power to make and repeal laws." 2 An American Dictionary of the English Language (1828). It continues, "The legislatures of most of the states in America . . . consist of two houses or branches."

I could go on, but the Court has said this before. As we put it nearly a century ago, "Legislature" was "not a term of uncertain meaning when incorporated into the Constitution." *Hawke.* "What it meant when adopted it still means for the purpose of interpretation." "A Legislature" is "the representative body which ma[kes] the laws of the people;" see *Smiley* (relying on this definition).

B

The unambiguous meaning of "the Legislature" in the Elections Clause as a representative body is confirmed by other provisions of the Constitution that use the same term in the same way. When seeking to discern the meaning of a word in the Constitution, there is no better dictionary than the rest of the Constitution itself. Our precedents new and old have employed this structural method of inter- pretation to read the Constitution in the manner it was drafted and ratified—as a unified, coherent whole. See, *e.g., NLRB v. Noel Canning,* (SCALIA, J., concur- ring in judgment); *McCulloch v. Maryland; Martin v. Hunter's Lessee;* Amar, Intratextualism, 112 Harv. L.Rev. 747 (1999).

The Constitution includes seventeen provisions referring to a State's "Legislature." Every one of those references is consistent with the understand- ing of a legislature as a representative body. More importantly, many of them are only consistent with an institutional legislature—and flatly incompatible with the majority's reading of "the Legislature" to refer to the people as a whole.

Start with the Constitution's first use of the term: "The House of Representatives shall be composed of Members chosen every second Year by the People of the several States, and the Electors in each State shall have the Qualifications req- uisite for Electors of the most numerous Branch of the State Legislature." Art. I, §2, cl. 1. This reference to a "Branch of the State Legislature" can only be referring to an institutional body, and the explicit juxtaposition of "the State Legislature" with "the People of the several States" forecloses the majority's proposed reading.

The next Section of Article I describes how to fill vacancies in the United States Senate: "if Vacancies happen by Resignation, or otherwise, during the Recess of the Legislature of any State, the Executive thereof may make tempo- rary Appointments until the next Meeting of the Legislature, which shall then fill such Vacancies." §3, cl. 2. The references to "the Recess of the Legislature of any State" and "the next Meeting of the Legislature" are only consistent with an institutional legislature, and make no sense under the majority's reading. The people as a whole (schoolchildren and a few unnamed others excepted) do not take a "Recess."

The list goes on. Article IV provides that the "United States shall guarantee to every State in this Union a Republican Form of Government, and shall pro- tect each of them against Invasion; and on Application of the Legislature, or of the Executive (when the Legislature cannot be convened), against domestic Violence." §4. It is perhaps conceivable that all the people of a State could be "convened"—although this would seem difficult during an "Invasion" or out- break of "domestic Violence"—but the only natural reading of the Clause is that "the Executive" may submit a federal application when "the Legislature" as a representative body cannot be convened.

Article VI provides that the "Senators and Representatives before mentioned, and the Members of the several State Legislatures, and all executive and judicial Officers, both of the United States and of the several States, shall be bound by Oath or Affirmation, to support this Constitution." Cl. 3. Unless the majority is prepared to make all the people of every State swear an "Oath or Affirmation, to support this Constitution," this provision can only refer to the "several State Legislatures" in their institutional capacity.

Each of these provisions offers strong structural indications about what "the Legislature" must mean. But the most powerful evidence of all comes from the Seventeenth Amendment. Under the original Constitution, Senators were "chosen by the Legislature" of each State, Art. I, §3, cl. 1, while Members of the House of Representatives were chosen "by the People," Art. I, §2, cl. 1. That distinction was critical to the Framers. As James Madison explained, the Senate would "derive its powers from the States," while the House would "derive its powers from the people of America." The Federalist No. 39. George Mason believed that the power of state legislatures to select Senators would "be a reasonable guard" against "the Danger . . . that the national, will swallow up the State Legislatures." 1 Records of the Federal Convention of 1787, p. 160 (M. Farrand ed.1911). Not everyone agreed. James Wilson proposed allowing the people to elect Senators directly. His proposal was rejected ten to one.

Before long, reformers took up Wilson's mantle and launched a protracted campaign to amend the Constitution. That effort began in 1826, when Representative Henry Storrs of New York proposed — but then set aside — a constitutional amendment transferring the power to elect Senators from the state legislatures to the people. Over the next three-quarters of a century, no fewer than 188 joint resolutions proposing similar reforms were introduced in both Houses of Congress.

At no point in this process did anyone suggest that a constitutional amendment was unnecessary because "Legislature" could simply be interpreted to mean "people." See *Hawke* ("It was never suggested, so far as we are aware, that the purpose of making the office of Senator elective by the people could be accomplished by a referendum vote. The necessity of the amendment to accomplish the purpose of popular election is shown in the adoption of the amendment."). In fact, as the decades rolled by without an amendment, 28 of the 45 States settled for the next best thing by holding a popular vote on candidates for Senate, then pressuring state legislators into choosing the winner. All agreed that cutting the state legislature out of senatorial selection entirely would require nothing less than to "Strike out" the original words in the Constitution and "insert, 'elected by the people'" in its place. Cong. Globe, 31st Cong., 1st Sess., 88 (1849) (proposal of Sen. Jeremiah Clemens).

Yet that is precisely what the majority does to the Elections Clause today — amending the text not through the process provided by Article V, but by judicial decision. The majority's revision renders the Seventeenth Amendment an 86–year waste of time, and singles out the Elections Clause as the only one of the Constitution's seventeen provisions referring to "the Legislature" that departs from the ordinary meaning of the term.

[T]he majority observes that "the Legislature" of a State may perform different functions under different provisions of the Constitution. Under Article I, §3, for example, "the Legislature" performed an "electoral" function by choosing Senators. The "Legislature" plays a "consenting" function under Article I, §8, and Article IV, §3; a "ratifying" function under Article V; and a "lawmaking" function under the Elections Clause. All true. The majority, however, leaps from the premise that "the Legislature" performs different *functions* under different provisions to the conclusion that "the Legislature" assumes different *identities* under different provisions.

As a matter of ordinary language and common sense, however, a difference in function does not imply a difference in meaning. A car, for example, generally serves a transportation function. But it can also fulfill a storage function. At a tailgate party or a drive-in movie, it may play an entertainment function. In the absence of vacancies at the roadside motel, it could provide a lodging function. To a neighbor with a dead battery, it offers an electricity generation function. And yet, a person describing a "car" engaged in any of these varied functions would undoubtedly be referring to the same thing.

The Constitution itself confirms this point. Articles I and II assign many different functions to the Senate: a lawmaking function, an impeachment trial function, a treaty ratification function, an appointee confirmation function, an officer selection function, a qualification judging function, and a recordkeeping function. Art. I, §1; §3, cls. 5, 6; §5, cls. 1, 3; §7, cl. 2; Art. II, §2, cl. 2. Yet the identity of the Senate remains the same as it discharges these various functions.

Similarly, the House of Representatives performs different functions, including lawmaking, impeachment, and resolving Presidential elections in which no candidate wins a majority in the Electoral College. Art. I, §1; §2, cl. 5; §7, cl. 2; Amdt. 12. The President is assigned not only executive functions, Art. II, but also legislative functions, such as approving or vetoing bills, convening both Houses of Congress, and recommending measures for their consideration, Art. I, §7, cl. 2; Art. II, §3. Courts not only exercise a judicial function, Art. III, §1, but may also perform an appointment function, Art. II, §2, cl. 2. And so on. Neither the majority nor the Commission points to a single instance in which the identity of these actors changes as they exercise different functions.

The majority attempts to draw support from precedent, but our cases only further undermine its position. In *Hawke,* this Court considered the meaning of "the Legislatur[e]" in Article V, which outlines the process for ratifying constitutional amendments. The Court concluded that "Legislature" meant "the representative body which ma[kes] the laws of the people." The Court then explained that "[t]he term is often used in the Constitution *with this evident meaning*." *Ibid.* (emphasis added). The Court proceeded to list other constitutional provisions that assign different functions to the "Legislature," just as the majority does today.

Unlike the majority today, however, the Court in *Hawke* never hinted that the meaning of "Legislature" varied across those different provisions because they assigned different functions. To the contrary, the Court drew inferences from the Seventeenth Amendment and its predecessor, Article I, §3 — in which "the Legislature" played an *electoral* function — to define the "Legislature" in Article V, which assigned it a *ratification* function. The Court concluded that "Legislature" refers to a representative body, whatever its function. As the Court put it, "There can be no question that the framers of the Constitution clearly understood and carefully used the terms in which that instrument referred to the action of the legislatures of the States. When they intended that direct action by the people should be had they were no less accurate in the use of apt phraseology to carry out such purpose." *Ibid.* (citing Art. I, §2).

Smiley, the leading precedent on the meaning of "the Legislature" in the Elections Clause, reaffirmed the definition announced in *Hawke.* In *Smiley,* the petitioner argued — as the Commission does here — that "the Legislature" referred not just to "the two houses of the legislature" but to "the entire legislative power of the state . . . however exercised." The Court did not respond by holding, as the majority today suggests, that " 'the Legislature' comprises the referendum and the Governor's veto in the context of regulating congressional elections," or that " 'the Legislature' has a different identity" in the Elections Clause than it does in Article V. Instead, the Court in *Smiley* said this:

"Much that is urged in argument with regard to the meaning of the term 'Legislature' is beside the point. As this Court said in *Hawke* . . . the term was not one 'of uncertain meaning when incorporated into the Constitution. What it meant when adopted it still means for purposes of interpretation. A Legislature was then the representative body which made the laws of the people.' " (quoting *Hawke*).

Remarkably, the majority refuses to even acknowledge the definition of "the Legislature" adopted in both *Smiley* and *Hawke,* and instead embraces the interpretation that this Court unanimously rejected more than 80 years ago.

C

The history of the Elections Clause further supports the conclusion that "the Legislature" is a representative body. The first known draft of the Clause to appear at the Constitutional Convention provided that "Each state shall prescribe the time and manner of holding elections." 1 Debates on the Federal Constitution 146 (J. Elliot ed. 1836). After revision by the Committee of Detail, the Clause included the important limitation at issue here: "The times and places, and the manner, of holding the elections of the members of each house, shall be prescribed *by the legislature of each state* ; but their provisions concerning them may, at any time, be altered *by the legislature of the United States.*" *Id.,* at 225 (emphasis added). The insertion of "the legislature" indicates that the Framers thought carefully about which entity within the State was to perform congressional districting. And the parallel between "the legislature of each state" and "the legislature of the United States" further suggests that they meant "the legislature" as a representative body.

As the majority explains, the debate over the ratification of the Elections Clause centered on its second part, which empowers Congress to "make or alter" regulations prescribed by "the Legislature" of a State. Importantly for our purposes, however, both sides in this debate "recognized the distinction between the state legislature and the people themselves."

The Anti–Federalists, for example, supported vesting election regulation power solely in state legislatures because state "legislatures were more numerous *bodies,* usually *elected annually,* and thus more likely to be in sympathy with the interests *of the people*." Alexander Hamilton and others responded by raising the specter of state legislatures — which he described as "local administrations" — deciding to "annihilate" the Federal Government by "neglecting to provide for the choice of persons to administer its affairs." The Federalist No. 59. As the majority acknowledges, the distinction between "the Legislature" and the people "occasioned no debate." That is because everybody understood what "the Legislature" meant.

The majority contends that its counterintuitive reading of "the Legislature" is necessary to advance the "animating principle" of popular sovereignty. But the ratification of the Constitution was the ultimate act of popular sovereignty, and the people who ratified the Elections Clause did so knowing that it assigned authority to "the Legislature" as a representative body. The Elections Clause was not, as the majority suggests, an all-purpose "safeguard against manipulation of electoral rules by politicians." Like most provisions of the Constitution, the Elections Clause reflected a compromise — a pragmatic recognition that the grand project of forging a Union required everyone to accept some things they did not like. See The Federalist No. 59, at 364 (describing the power allocated to state legislatures as "an evil which could not have been avoided"). This Court has no power to upset such a compromise simply because we now think that it should have been struck differently. As we explained almost a century ago, "[t]he framers of the Constitution might have adopted a different method," but it "is not the function of courts . . . to alter the method which the Constitution has fixed." *Hawke*.

D

In addition to text, structure, and history, several precedents interpreting the Elections Clause further reinforce that "the Legislature" refers to a representative body.

McPherson v. Blacker, 146 U.S. 1 (1892) . . . . involved a constitutional provision with considerable similarity to the Elections Clause, the Presidential Electors Clause of Article II: "Each State shall appoint, in such Manner *as the Legislature thereof* may direct, a Number of Electors . . . ." §1, cl. 2 (emphasis added). The question was whether the state legislature, as a body of representatives, could divide authority to appoint electors across each of the State's congressional districts. The Court upheld the law and emphasized that the plain text of the Presidential Electors Clause vests the power to determine the manner of appointment in "the Legislature" of the State. That power, the Court explained, "*can neither be taken away nor abdicated.*" 146 U.S., at 35 (emphasis added; internal quotation marks omitted).

Against that backdrop, the Court decided two cases regarding the meaning of "the Legislature" in the Elections Clause. In *Ohio ex rel. Davis v. Hildebrant,* 241 U.S. 565 (1916), the Ohio Legislature passed a congressional redistricting law. Under the Ohio Constitution, voters held a referendum on the law and rejected it. A supporter of the law sued on behalf of the State, contending that the referendum "was not and could not be a part of the legislative authority of the State and therefore could have no influence on . . . the law creating congressional districts" under the Elections Clause.

This Court rejected the challenger's constitutional argument as a nonjusticiable claim that the referendum "causes a State . . . to be not republican" in violation of the Guarantee Clause of the Constitution. The Court also rejected an argument that Ohio's use of the referendum violated a federal statute, and held that Congress had the power to pass that statute under the Elections Clause. *Hildebrant* in no way suggested that the state legislature could be displaced from the redistricting process, and *Hildebrant* certainly did not hold — as the majority today contends — that "the word ['Legislature' in the Elections Clause] encompassed a veto power lodged in the people." *Hildebrant* simply approved a State's decision to employ a referendum *in addition to* redistricting by the Legislature. The result of the decision was to send *the Ohio Legislature* back to the drawing board to do the redistricting.

In *Smiley,* the Minnesota Legislature passed a law adopting new congressional districts, and the Governor exercised his veto power under the State Constitution. As noted above, the Minnesota secretary of state defended the veto on the ground that "the Legislature" in the Elections Clause referred not just to "the two houses of the legislature" but to "the entire legislative power of the state . . . however exercised." This Court rejected that argument, reiterating that the term "Legislature" meant "the representative body which made the laws of the people." The Court nevertheless went on to hold that the Elections Clause did not prevent a State from applying the usual rules of its legislative process — including a gubernatorial veto — to election regulations prescribed by the legislature. As in *Hildebrant,* the legislature was not displaced, nor was it redefined; it just had to start on a new redistricting plan.

The majority initially describes *Hildebrant* and *Smiley* as holding that "redistricting is a legislative function, to be performed in accordance with the State's prescriptions for lawmaking, which may include the referendum and the Governor's veto." That description is true, so far as it goes. But it hardly supports the result the majority reaches here. There is a critical difference between allowing a State to *supplement* the legislature's role in the legislative process and permitting the State to *supplant* the legislature altogether. Nothing in *Hildebrant, Smiley,* or any other precedent supports the majority's conclusion that imposing some constraints on the legislature justifies deposing it entirely.

* * *

The constitutional text, structure, history, and precedent establish a straightforward rule: Under the Elections Clause, "the Legislature" is a representative body that, when it prescribes election regulations, may be required to do so within the ordinary lawmaking process, but may not be cut out of that process. Put simply, the state legislature need not be exclusive in congressional districting, but neither may it be excluded.

The majority's contrary understanding requires it to accept a definition of "the Legislature" that contradicts the term's plain meaning, creates discord with the Seventeenth Amendment and the Constitution's many other uses of the term, makes nonsense of the drafting and ratification of the Elections Clause, and breaks with the relevant precedents. In short, the effect of the majority's decision is to erase the words "by the Legislature thereof" from the Elections Clause. That is a judicial error of the most basic order. "It cannot be presumed that any clause in the constitution is intended to be without effect; and therefore such a construction is inadmissible." *Marbury v. Madison.*

II

The Court also issues an alternative holding that a federal statute, 2 U.S.C. §2a(c), permits Arizona to vest redistricting authority in the Commission. The majority does not contend that this statutory holding resolves the constitutional question presented, so its reading of Section 2a(c) is largely beside the point . . .

III

[T]here is no real doubt about what "the Legislature" means. The Framers of the Constitution were "practical men, dealing with the facts of political life as they understood them, putting into form the government they were creating, and prescribing in language clear and intelligible the powers that government was to take." *South Carolina v. United States,* 199 U.S. 437 (1905). We ought to give effect to the words they used.

The majority today shows greater concern about redistricting practices than about the meaning of the Constitution. I recognize the difficulties that arise from trying to fashion judicial relief for partisan gerrymandering. See *Vieth v. Jubelirer,* 541 U.S. 267 (2004). But our inability to find a manageable standard in that area is no excuse to abandon a standard of meaningful interpretation in this area. This Court has stressed repeatedly that a law's virtues as a policy innovation cannot redeem its inconsistency with the Constitution. "Failure of political will does not justify unconstitutional remedies."

Indeed, the Court has enforced the text of the Constitution to invalidate state laws with policy objectives reminiscent of this one. Two of our precedents held that States could not use their constitutions to impose term limits on their federal representatives in violation of the United States Constitution. *Cook* [*v. Gralike*], 531 U.S. 510 [(2001)]; *U.S. Term Limits, Inc. v. Thornton,* 514 U.S. 779 (1995). The people of the States that enacted these reforms surely viewed them as measures that would "place the lead rein in the people's hands." Yet the Court refused to accept "that the Framers spent significant time and energy in debating and crafting Clauses that could be easily evaded." *Term Limits.* The majority approves just such an evasion of the Constitution today.

The Court also overstates the effects of enforcing the plain meaning of the Constitution in this case. There is no dispute that Arizona may continue to use its Commission to draw lines for state legislative elections. The representatives chosen in those elections will then be responsible for congressional redistricting as members of the state legislature, so the work of the Commission will continue to influence Arizona's federal representation.

Moreover, reading the Elections Clause to require the involvement of the legislature will not affect most other redistricting commissions. As the majority notes, many States have commissions that play an "auxiliary role" in congressional redistricting. But in these States, unlike in Arizona, the legislature retains primary authority over congressional redistricting.

The majority also points to a scattered array of election-related laws and constitutional provisions enacted via popular lawmaking that it claims would be "endangered" by interpreting the Elections Clause to mean what it says. Reviewing the constitutionality of these farflung provisions is well outside the scope of this case. Suffice it to say that none of them purports to do what the Arizona Constitution does here: set up an unelected, unaccountable institution that permanently and totally displaces the legislature from the redistricting process.

. . . .

The people of Arizona have concerns about the process of congressional redistricting in their State. For better or worse, the Elections Clause of the Constitution does not allow them to address those concerns by displacing their legislature. But it does allow them to seek relief from Congress, which can make or alter the regulations prescribed by the legislature. And the Constitution gives them another means of change. They can follow the lead of the reformers who won passage of the Seventeenth Amendment. Indeed, several constitutional amendments over the past century have involved modifications of the electoral process. Amdts. 19, 22, 24, 26. Unfortunately, today's decision will only discourage this democratic method of change. Why go through the hassle of writing a new provision into the Constitution when it is so much easier to write an old one out?

I respectfully dissent.

Justice SCALIA, with whom Justice THOMAS joins, dissenting.

I do not believe that the question the Court answers is properly before us. Disputes between governmental branches or departments regarding the allocation of political power do not in my view constitute "cases" or "controversies" committed to our resolution by Art. III, §2, of the Constitution. . . . I would dismiss this case for want of jurisdiction. . . .

Normally, having arrived at that conclusion, I would express no opinion on the merits unless my vote was necessary to enable the Court to produce a judgment. In the present case, however, the majority's resolution of the merits question ("legislature" means "the people") is so outrageously wrong, so utterly devoid of textual or historic support, so flatly in contradiction of prior Supreme Court cases, so obviously the willful product of hostility to districting by state legislatures, that I cannot avoid adding my vote to the devastating dissent of the Chief Justice.

Justice THOMAS, with whom Justice SCALIA joins, dissenting.

Reading today's opinion, one would think the Court is a great defender of direct democracy in the States. As it reads "the Legislature" out of the Times, Places and Manner Clause, U.S. Const., Art. I, §4, the majority offers a paean to the ballot initiative. It speaks in glowing terms of the "characteristic of our federal system that States retain autonomy to establish their own governmental processes." And it urges "[d]eference to state lawmaking" so that States may perform their vital function as " 'laboratories' "of democracy.

These sentiments are difficult to accept. The conduct of the Court in so many other cases reveals a different attitude toward the States in general and ballot initiatives in particular. Just last week, in the antithesis of deference to state lawmaking through direct democracy, the Court cast aside state laws across the country — many of which were enacted through ballot initiative — that reflected the traditional definition of marriage. See *Obergefell v. Hodges.*

. . . .

How quickly the tune has changed. And how striking that it changed here. The ballot initiative in this case, unlike those that the Court has previously treated so dismissively, was unusually democracy-reducing. It did not ask the people to approve a particular redistricting plan through direct democracy, but instead to take districting away from the people's representatives and give it to an unelected committee, thereby reducing democratic control over the process in the future. The Court's characterization of this as direct democracy at its best is rather like praising a plebiscite in a "banana republic" that installs a strongman as President for Life. And wrapping the analysis in a cloak of federalism does little to conceal the flaws in the Court's reasoning.

I would dispense with the faux federalism and would instead treat the States in an evenhanded manner. That means applying the Constitution as written. Although the straightforward text of Article I, §4, prohibits redistricting by an unelected, independent commission, Article III limits our power to deciding cases or controversies. Because I agree with Justice SCALIA that the Arizona Legislature lacks Article III standing to assert an institutional injury against another entity of state government, I would dismiss its suit. I respectfully dissent.

Discussion

1. What is a Legislature? The constitutional question in *Arizona Independent Redistricting Commission (AIRC)* is whether the State of Arizona can transfer the power to redistrict to an independent commission, which was created by a constitutional amendment passed through the initiative process. The Arizona Legislature objected to having this power taken away from it. It argued that this violated the Elections Clause of Art. I, §4, cl. 1, which provides that "The Times, Places and Manner of holding Elections for Senators and Representatives, shall be prescribed in each State by the Legislature thereof; but the Congress may at any time by Law make or alter such Regulations." The Court ruled 5-4, in an opinion by Justice Ginsburg, that the Elections Clause allowed Arizona to use an independent commission for creating and revising Congressional districts. (No one on the Court denied that Arizona could use an independent commission to create state legislative districts).

AIRC raises a recurrent problem in constitutional interpretation. How do we interpret words in the text for situations that the framers and ratifiers didn't expect or didn't even imagine would occur? The most obvious examples involve new technologies. Thus, in Kyllo v. United States, 533 U.S. 27 (2001), the Court held that using a thermal imaging device constituted a "search," even though government agents never breached the wall of the defendant's house. In Pensacola Tel. Co. v. Western Union Tel. Co., 96 U.S. 1 (1877), the court held that Congress could regulate telegraph communication as part of its powers to regulate foreign and interstate "commerce." In each case the Court looked to what it regarded as the purposes behind the text to apply it to unforeseen situations.

AIRC concerns a political innovation rather than a technological innovation — the development of the initiative and referendum in the late 19th and early 20th centuries to wrest some law-making power away from legislatures or to check legislative misbehavior. These innovations responded to the perceived corruption of representative democracy during the Gilded Age. Because legislatures were corrupt or easily bought off by powerful interests, reformers sought to return important questions to the public.

The framers did not expect that states would implement direct democracy. Many of them knew about similar institutions in ancient democracies, and they distrusted direct rule by the public. They were, however, worried about the problem of representatives entrenching themselves so that they could not be dislodged, even when they no longer commanded majority support. This is reflected not only in the Elections Clause, but also in Article IV section 4's guarantee of republican government in the states.

The majority argues that "the Legislature" includes the people of Arizona, who have the power to pass laws, and who have delegated their legislative power to redistrict to the AIRC. It argues that "the Legislature" should be understood functionally, as we understand words like "search" in the Fourth Amendment. The dissent argues that the people of Arizona are not part of "the Legislature." A legislature must be a representative body, and by definition the people of Arizona are not representatives. (That conclusion is not completely obvious: the voters of Arizona actually do virtually represent everyone in the population who cannot vote, like children.)

But there also is a third possibility: that Arizona has more than one legislative body.

Despite the way the members of the Court discuss the case, *AIRC* does not have to be a case about whether the people can be part of "the Legislature" under the Elections Clause. Direct democracy matters to the case because the initiative was used to amend the Arizona state constitution to create a new governmental body to handle redistricting plans. Neither the majority nor the dissent denies that Arizona can use direct democracy to amend its state constitution. Rather, the question in the case is whether to consider this new body, the AIRC, to be part of "the Legislature" of the State of Arizona under the Elections Clause. That could be because the people of Arizona are part of "the Legislature" of the state and they have delegated some of their legislative power to the AIRC. But it could also be because the AIRC is itself a legislative body.

The paradigm case of a "legislature" is a representative body, elected directly or indirectly by the public, and usually much smaller in number than the voting public itself, just as the voting public is smaller in number than the group of people who live under and are bound by the state's laws. (Before the 17th Amendment, the Senate was indirectly representative, because Senators were elected by state legislatures. In Great Britain, the House of Lords was not even indirectly representative — its members were peers appointed by the King.)

The framers and adopters of the U.S. Constitution may not have expected the referendum or initiative, but they certainly did understand that different state constitutions might design the legislature in different ways. Some states might have one house or two. The members of the upper house might be elected or appointed by the members of the lower house. (That is, there could be indirect representation as well as direct representation.) There might be special-purpose legislatures that dealt with some topics but not others. There might be a power of veto by the governor or no veto, special supermajority rules for some subjects but not others, and so on. Accordingly, the Supreme Court held in Smiley v. Holm, 255 U.S. 355 (1932), that if the Governor's veto was part of the regular procedures for making binding laws in the state, it was also part of "the Legislature" for purposes of the Elections Clause.

The question in *AIRC* is how far this principle of allowing the state to design its own legislative institutions can be carried. Suppose, for example, that the state amends its Constitution so that bills on certain subjects — for example, redistricting and voting — do not become law unless ratified by the public in a referendum. The Court allowed a similar arrangement in Davis v. Hildebrant, 241 U.S. 565 (1916). In this case, the people hold a veto on certain kinds of bills, just as a Governor would.

Now suppose the state amends its constitution to create a second legislative body — which it calls "Legislature 2." Its members are appointed for fixed terms by the leaders of the older legislature (Legislature 1). Its members, in turn, can also appoint one additional member to break ties. The constitution gives Legislature 2 the power to pass all laws involving redistricting without the possibility of veto by either the Governor or by Legislature 1. Legislature 1 still handles all other issues of election law.

Is Legislature 2 part of the legislative power of the state under the Elections Clause? It is not identical with the people of the state, and its membership is much smaller than the state's voting population. It is indirectly representative because its members are appointed by members of Legislature 1, and it passes laws. It is not too much of a stretch to say that Legislature 2 is part of "the Legislature" of the state, along with Legislature 1.

Chief Justice Roberts emphasizes that the uses of the word "Legislature" in the rest of the Constitution generally refer to representative bodies, or indirectly representative bodies like the Senate before the 17th Amendment. But Legislature

2 satisfies these criteria. He also objects that the 17th Amendment distinguishes between the Legislature of the state and the people of the state. That is also not a problem: Legislature 2 is not the same as the people of the state.

Now suppose the state passes a new constitutional amendment. This amendment renames Legislature 2 and calls it the Arizona Independent Redistricting Commission. Should the name matter at all from the standpoint of the Elections Clause?

2. *What chumps! The puzzle of amendment versus interpretation.* Chief Justice Roberts ironically points out that if the majority's reasoning is correct, all proponents of the Seventeenth Amendment "had to do was interpret the constitutional term 'the Legislature' [in Art. I, §3,] to mean 'the people.'" He offers this remark as a *reductio ad absurdum*. If at one point in history people believed that a constitutional amendment was necessary to achieve a certain result, the result cannot legitimately be reached through subsequent judicial interpretation.

Looking over the history of constitutional interpretation, do you agree with this proposition as a general matter? Chief Justice Roberts may well be right that it might be very difficult to achieve the same result as the Seventeenth Amendment through interpretation. But what about contemporary Commerce Clause doctrine? Recall that in the 1920s Congress actually submitted a proposed amendment to the states designed to overturn *Hammer v. Dagenhart*. The New Deal revolution made this amendment superfluous. Does the fact that *United States v. Darby* achieved the same result as the proposed amendment mean that *Darby* is incorrect?

Also consider the Nineteenth Amendment. One reason why the suffragists spent decades pushing for an amendment guaranteeing women the right to vote is that they had been rebuffed in seeking an interpretation of the Fourteenth Amendment in *Minor v. Happersatt*. Since the courts seemed hostile to them, suffragists turned first to state governments, and then to the federal amendment process. By the 1970s, however, a guarantee of women's right to vote flowed easily from contemporary equal protection doctrine, including not only the sex equality cases but also Harper v. Virginia Board of Elections, 383 U.S. 663 (1966)(Casebook, p. 1799). See Sanford Levinson, How Many Times Has the United States Constitution Been Amended? (A) < 26; (B) 26; (C) 27; (D) > 27, 8 Constitutional Commentary 409 (1991). The reason for this, however was because of two great waves of public mobilization on behalf of women's rights, one of which had led to the Nineteenth Amendment, and the other of which led to the Equal Rights Amendment (ERA), proposed in 1972, and the sex equality decisions of the 1970s. Indeed, the sex equality decisions made the ERA largely superfluous. Does the fact that women's right to vote follows from modern equal protection clause doctrine mean that the sex equality decisions and *Harper* are wrongly decided?

Is there an easy way to decide, before the fact, whether proponents of a constitutional amendment are "chumps," in Chief Justice Roberts' words? That is, can one always tell in advance whether an amendment is necessary, or whether legislative workarounds or judicial interpretation would do the job? The answer may have to do with the form of the particular text at issue—does it state a "hard-wired" rule or a standard or a principle, like "equal protection of the laws"? But the answer also may have much to do with the political context in which the issue arises.

Today many people have argued for a constitutional amendment to overturn Justice Kennedy's opinion in Citizens United v. FEC, 558 U.S. 310 (2010). Are these people "chumps" because one could reverse *Citizens United* through litigation (assuming changes of membership on the Court, or changes of mind)? Or is the point that mobilizing for a new constitutional amendment to overturn *Citizens United* would significantly alter public opinion about the best interpretation of the First Amendment, thus making it easier for litigation to succeed? (Once again, compare the 1970s sex equality decisions.)

Add on p. 983 before section C:

Note: The constitutional controversy over Justice Scalia's replacement

Justice Antonin Scalia died on February 13, 2016. Within an hour of confirmation of Scalia's death, Senate Majority Leader Mitch McConnell stated that the Senate would not vote to confirm a replacement to fill the vacancy on the Supreme Court until after the 2016 election: "The American people should have a voice in the selection of their next Supreme Court Justice. Therefore, this vacancy should not be filled until we have a new president."[20] Republican leaders in the Senate quickly confirmed that there would be no hearings or vote on any nominee President Obama chose to replace Scalia. Nor would the Senators even meet with any Obama nominee as a courtesy, as they usually did. On February 23rd, 2016 the Chairman of the Senate Judiciary Committee, Charles Grassley, and all of the Republican members of the committee, signed a letter stating that "based on constitutional principle, and born of a necessity to protect the will of the American people, this Committee will not hold any hearings on any Supreme Court nominee until our next President is sworn in on January 20, 2017."[21]

President Obama responded by stating that he would make a nomination to replace Justice Scalia, and that the Senate had a constitutional duty to consider the nomination. Accordingly, on March 16, 2016, President Obama nominated Judge Merrick Garland, the Chief Judge of the U.S. Court of Appeals for

20. Burgess Everett and Glenn Thrush, McConnell throws down the gauntlet: No Scalia replacement under Obama, Politico, February 13, 2016, http://www.politico.com/story/2016/02/mitch-mcconnell-antonin-scalia-supreme-court-nomination-219248

21. Judiciary Committee Letter Opposing Supreme Court Hearings, New York Times, February 23, 2016, http://www.nytimes.com/interactive/2016/02/23/us/politics/document-Senate-SCOTUS-Letter.html

the D.C. Circuit, to the Supreme Court. At 63, Garland was older than most recent Supreme Court nominees, and generally considered relatively moderate; President Obama may have believed these features might attract Republican support. Even so, Senate Republicans reiterated their refusal to vote on or hold hearings on the nomination. Eventually a few Republican Senators agreed to meet with Garland as a courtesy, but stated their opposition to considering his nomination on the merits.

It was not difficult to discover the reason for this behavior. Before Scalia's death, the Supreme Court consisted of five conservative appointees, all appointed by Republicans, and four liberal appointees, all appointed by Democrats. One of the Republicans, Justice Anthony Kennedy, occasionally voted with the liberal Justices, so that the most controversial cases were often decided by 5-4 margins. Replacing Justice Scalia with a new Justice appointed by President Obama would likely result in a liberal majority on the Supreme Court for the first time since 1969. This would shift the median Justice from Anthony Kennedy, who usually, but not always, voted with his fellow conservatives on hotly contested issues, to the new Justice, or possibly Justice Stephen Breyer, who is widely regarded as the most moderate of the liberal Justices. Observers of the Court predicted that this shift might potentially have very significant effects on Supreme Court decisions and constitutional doctrine.

In the October 2015 Term, the Supreme Court had granted certiorari in a number of controversial and important cases involving affirmative action, voting rights, abortion, immigration, and the associational rights of non-union employees. Many observers hoped (or feared) that the results of these cases would shift Supreme Court doctrine further to the right. Now, with Justice Scalia's death, the Supreme Court might deadlock 4 to 4 on some or all of these cases. The result would be that the lower court's ruling would be affirmed, with no opinion from the Supreme Court and thus no nationwide effect on existing precedents.

Many of the most important cases decided in the October 2015 Term were directly or indirectly affected by Justice Scalia's death, as the Justices strove to reach compromises that would allow them to issue opinions instead of deadlocking. Justice Scalia's death also affected the Supreme Court's choice of cases for the next Term's docket. The Court now had incentives not to take too many high profile cases that might deadlock 4-4 along conservative/liberal lines.

The Republicans' decision to delay consideration of Scalia's replacement had important strategic elements. If the Democrats won the 2016 presidential election, then by waiting until January 2017 to consider a new Supreme Court nominee, Senate Republicans might prevent a new liberal majority from rendering decisions not only in the October 2015 Term, but also throughout most of the October 2016 Term as well. If confirmation hearings took several months, a new Justice might not be installed until April or May of 2017, making it too late for the new Justice to participate in any cases accepted for the October 2016 term. On the other hand, if the Republicans won the White House in 2017, they could attempt to speed up the confirmation process and install a new Justice as soon as possible, allowing the Justice to vote on some of the accepted cases.

The Republican strategy paid off, after Donald Trump won an electoral college victory in the 2016 presidential election. Shortly after taking office, on January 31, 2017, President Trump nominated Neil Gorsuch, a judge on the Tenth Circuit Court of Appeals, who, at age 49, was the youngest Supreme Court nominee since Clarence Thomas.

On March 23, at the close of committee hearings on Gorsuch's nomination, Senate Democrats announced that they would filibuster Gorsuch's nomination. President Trump called on Senate Republicans to use the "nuclear option" to alter the Senate's rules to eliminate the filibuster for Supreme Court appointments. (In 2013, when the Democrats controlled the Senate, Senate Majority Leader Harry Reid used the same procedure to eliminate the filibuster for executive branch appointments and judicial appointments other than the Supreme Court.)

On April 6, 2017, the Senate voted along party lines 52-48, to change the Senate rules and eliminate the filibuster for Supreme Court nominations. The next day, April 7, 2017, the Senate confirmed Gorusch's appointment by a vote of 55-45.

Discussion

Was the Senate's refusal to consider *any* Supreme Court nomination by President Obama constitutional? Does it matter that the nomination was to the Supreme Court rather than to a lower federal court?

1. *Arguments from text.* The text of the Constitution does not clearly forbid the Republican strategy. Article II, section 2 states that the President "shall nominate, and by and with the Advice and Consent of the Senate, shall appoint Ambassadors, other public Ministers and Consuls, Judges of the supreme Court, and all other Officers of the United States." Note that the text does not distinguish between Supreme Court nominations and nominations of other Officers of the United States, which include lower court judges.

Does the word "shall" in Article II, section 2 mean "is required to" or does the use of the word "shall" merely state the process by which appointments occur? If "shall" means "is required to," it would suggest that the President is constitutionally required to nominate someone for every Ambassadorship, and for every open position in his administration and in the federal judiciary. Does the fact that the *President* "shall appoint" with "the Advice and Consent of the Senate" mean that the *Senate* is required to hold hearings and vote on anyone the president nominates? Suppose that the Senate's advice is: "we advise you not to appoint anyone to this position"?

2. *Arguments from structure.* Are there structural reasons to require the Senate to consider Supreme Court nominations? Although there do not have to be lower federal courts, Article III contemplates that there has to be a Supreme Court. Does the Senate's refusal impede the functioning of the federal courts?

One reason might be that the Court is working at less than full strength. But does the Supreme Court have to have nine members? It has had a different number in the past. Note that in 2016 much of the concern about the Court's ability to do its job was premised on the fact that the Court had 4 conservative and 4 liberal members, who often disagreed. But if the balance were 5-3, the Court would not have deadlocked as often. Should a structural argument turn on the current composition of the Justices, or should it apply regardless of the current mix of personnel?

3. *Arguments from past practice.* A third approach is to look at the past practice of the representative branches of government. What kinds of precedents are there, and are they both relevant and legally binding?

Presidents usually have incentives to nominate as many people to the Supreme Court as they can. Therefore, it is not surprising that in the past, Presidents have often nominated Supreme Court justices in their last year in office, and even during the lame duck session following an election in which their party lost. (That is how John Marshall became Chief Justice, for example.)

What about the Senate's practices? Michael Gerhardt argues that there is little evidence of a practice of "shut[ing] down the Supreme Court confirmation process in presidential election years." He notes that the Senate Judiciary Committee had argued that "Not since 1932 has the Senate confirmed in a presidential election year a Supreme Court nominee to a vacancy arising in that year. And it is necessary to go even further back—to 1888—in order to find an election-year nominee who was nominated and confirmed under divided government, as we have now."[22] Gerhardt responds that "[t]his is true, but it hardly constitutes a tradition. Indeed, the Senate confirmed Frank Murphy in January 1940 and Anthony Kennedy in 1988, while it confirmed William Brennan in 1957, after Eisenhower had named him as a recess appointment and nominee to the Court in 1956."[23]

In 1968, President Johnson nominated Associate Justice Abe Fortas to replace Chief Justice Earl Warren. He then nominated Homer Thornberry to take Fortas's seat if Fortas were confirmed. However, neither was confirmed: Fortas withdrew his nomination before the 1968 election, and Thornberry was never confirmed. This example, Gerhardt explains, does not support a practice of refusing to consider a President's nominees at all. Quite the contrary: "the Senate actually held hearings – twenty-two, in fact – for the two nominations and Fortas was thwarted by a successful filibuster, which was based not on the fact it was an election year, but rather that Fortas, who had been confirmed as an Associate Justice a few years before, had committed several serious ethical breaches while on the Court."[24]

Finally, Gerhardt considers the argument that the Senate has begun to slow down consideration of lower court appointments in election years. Even if this is so, he argues, "it hasn't translated into the realm of Supreme Court

22. Judiciary Committee Letter Opposing Supreme Court Hearings, supra.
23. Michael Gerhardt, Getting the Senate's responsibilities on Supreme Court nominations right, SCOTUSblog, March 9th, 2016, http://www.scotusblog.com/2016/03/getting-the-senates-responsibilities-on-supreme-court-nominations-right/
24. Gerhardt, supra.

appointments."[25] Rather, Gerhardt argues, the Senate almost always confirms Supreme Court nominees—and it certainly doesn't refuse to give them even a hearing. He quotes Geoffrey Stone of the University of Chicago Law School, who points out that "*even when the Senate was controlled by the opposing party*, in the last 60 years every one of the eight nominees who was perceived to be both qualified and reasonably moderate was easily confirmed."[26] Gerhardt concludes that there is "no historical support for the claim that the Senate has a tradition of shutting down the Supreme Court appointment process in presidential election years. The tradition is the opposite, for the Senate to consider Supreme Court nominations, no matter the timing, and actually to confirm nominees when they are moderate and well qualified."[27]

Gerhardt argues that historical practice does not support the Senate Republicans' claim that the Senate has a tradition of shutting down the Supreme Court appointment process in presidential years. Assuming this is correct, what does it establish? Even if no political convention *supports* the Republicans' gambit, does the history of past practice establish a political convention that is legally binding and that *prohibits* what they are doing?

4. *Past practice and legal obligation.* Here it might be useful to distinguish (a) regularities of practice from (b) traditions and (c) conventions, and all three of these from (d) legal obligations. We might be able to identify certain *regularities of behavior* from the study of history, but that does not mean that people understood themselves to have a normative obligation to others to behave in a certain way. For example, every morning for the past five years, you might brush your teeth before you brush your hair, but it is probably not because you feel a normative obligation to others. There might be *prudential reasons* why people always tend to act in the same way—for example, in markets usually people try to buy low and sell high—but that is not because they owe an obligation to others to do so.

Some practices within a social group repeated long enough may become a *tradition*, which later members of the social group self-consciously accept as a tradition that should guide their behavior. People might argue, for example, that they should act in certain ways because their predecessors have always (or almost always) done things that way. They may even come up with justifications after the fact for retaining practices that others fell into for very different reasons. But even if a tradition exists, it does not necessarily create a binding legal obligation, much less a constitutional obligation. People often break with traditions, or alter or amend traditions, especially in politics.

Political *conventions* arise out of political practice because they helpfully establish mutual expectations, coordinate political action and lower the costs of

25. Id.

26. Geoffrey Stone, The Supreme Court Vacancy and the Responsibilities of the Senate, Huffington Post, February 24, 2016, http://www.huffingtonpost.com/geoffrey-r-stone/the-supreme-court-vacancy_b_9310498.html (emphasis in original).

27. Gerhardt, supra.

participating in politics. All parties abide by these conventions (or usually abide by them) because they fear that departing from them will harm them, either in the short run or the long run. In that case, the convention is self-enforcing for prudential reasons. But unless the convention is also legally binding, parties are legally free to depart from it if they are willing to accept the risk that the other party will retaliate. (Note that traditions may also be conventions, but they need not be. The tradition of wearing green on St. Patrick's Day, or singing carols at Christmas, for example, does not solve important coordination problems—that is, other than solving the problem of how to celebrate the holiday).

Arguments from political convention or tradition are a modality of constitutional argument. These arguments gloss the constitutional text by claiming that a particular political tradition or convention has become constitutionally obligatory. Opponents may disagree, arguing that past practice has not created such an obligation.

What is necessary for a tradition or a convention to become part of the Constitution, and therefore legally binding? Do all of the affected parties have to accept it? Is it enough that one party merely acquiesces for a period of time? Note that when we are speaking of inter-branch conventions, the people who begin to form a convention may not be the same people that are confronted with it later on. Why should earlier Presidents or Congresses be able to bind later ones?

What is the relationship between arguments from tradition or convention and other modalities of argument? For example, can tradition or convention overcome a text that is otherwise clear? (See the discussion in *Noel Canning v. NLRB*, in Chapter 6, *infra*.)

5. *Judicial enforcement.* Note that whether or not a tradition or convention becomes a legal obligation, it may not be judicially enforceable. There are many constitutional questions on which courts have not ruled and for institutional reasons are unlikely to do so. Examples include controversies involving foreign affairs, ratification of constitutional amendments, and the judicial appointments process. In these cases, members of the representative branches of government debate their constitutional prerogatives and obligations, and act accordingly. It may be very difficult to tell whether and how an obligation is binding, because different actors will disagree, or they may interpret the rules quite differently.

When courts are reticent to play a role in enforcing constitutional obligations, how if at all does the Constitution matter? Are claims that the President, or the members of the Senate, are violating the Constitution enforced by the voters rather than the courts? (On the electoral consequences of President Roosevelt's Court-packing plan, see Casebook, p. 632.[28]) Note, however, that the voters may care more about the current state of the economy than about the niceties of constitutional interpretation.

---

28. See also Curtis A. Bradley and Neil Siegel, Historical Gloss, Constitutional Conventions, and the Judicial Separation of Powers 105 Georgetown L. J. 255 (2016).

6. *Is there a political convention that requires the Senate to hold confirmation hearings?* Robin Bradley Kar and Jason Mazzone argue that that historical practice may have "ripened into a constitutional rule that informs the best interpretation of constitutional text and structure." Robin Bradley Kar & Jason Mazzone, The Garland Affair: What History and the Constitution Really Say About President Obama's Powers to Appoint a Replacement for Justice Scalia, 91 New York University Law Review Online 53 (2016). Although they stopped short of asserting that Senate Republicans clearly violated the Constitution, they believed that Senate Republicans should not have pressed the issue in order to avoid "difficult and unprecedented constitutional issues relating to separation of powers" as well as "pragmatic risks" to the constitutional system that might occur if the parties refuse to cooperate in the appointments process in the future.

Kar and Mazzone argue that "there have been 103 prior cases in which—as in the case of Obama's nomination of Garland—an elected President nominated someone to fill an actual Supreme Court vacancy and began the nomination process prior to the election of a successor. In all 103 cases, which go back all the way to the earliest days of the Republic, the sitting President was able to both nominate and appoint a replacement Justice—by and with the advice and consent of the Senate, and regardless of the senatorial rules and procedures in place."

The only exceptions, Kar and Mazzone explain, are situations in which the President made the appointment after the election of the next President, or the President who made the appointment had never been elected President but took office because of the death of the previous President. In the nineteenth century, there was debate about whether such accidental presidents should enjoy all of the powers of an elected president. (This question has been resolved by the Twenty-Fifth Amendment.) Kar and Mazzone argue that Abe Fortas's failed nomination in 1968 is not an exception to the rule. The Senate didn't refuse to consider President Johnson's proposed appointment of Fortas. It held hearings, but Senators objected to Fortas because, among other things, his reputation had been damaged by scandal.

Kar and Mazzone's argument, in short, was that Senate Republicans were improperly treating Obama as if he were not a fully legitimate President. Because he was fully legitimate—he had, after all, been elected not once, but twice— Senate Republicans had no right to refuse to consider Obama's nominations to the Supreme Court when a Supreme Court vacancy occurs. The fact that the vacancy falls within an election year in no way undermined Obama's democratic authority to perform the normal functions of his office; he was elected for a full term of four years expiring in January 2017. (If one wants to play that game, one might argue, along similar lines, that Senate Judiciary Chair Charles Grassley lacked democratic authority to hinder Obama because he was in the sixth year of his Senate term.)

Suppose that Kar and Mazzone's history is correct. What, exactly, does it prove? They might merely be pointing to a regularity of practice. One reason to think that they have not identified a political convention—much less one that is legally binding—is that their formula is rather complicated, and they seem to have been the first to come up with it. Political conventions, one might think, are those that are generally understood and expected by all of the relevant players in politics. Perhaps there is a convention about the Senate's role that most actors understand or assume, but Kar and Mazzone have incorrectly described it. For example, there might well be a convention that the Senate will consider the President's nominees unless it offers good reasons to the contrary. But if that is the relevant convention, Republican senators would insist that they had not violated it.

Moreover, even if Kar and Mazzone have identified a tradition or a convention, how do we know that it is legally enforceable, rather than just a product of prudence? Perhaps the Senate didn't have reasons to press the issue until 2016. (Compare the examples of recess appointments or the President's war powers.) Given the country's political polarization and the increasing power of the Supreme Court, the reasons that justified the convention may have changed. We are now seeing the emergence of a new set of behaviors better suited for a different political environment. Senators may have very good reasons to resist confirming a new Justice, who will sit for decades, if they have plausible reasons to delay in the hopes that their party will win the next presidential election.

7. *The argument from political dysfunction.* To be sure, the Senate's refusal to consider *any* nominations to the Supreme Court, no matter how qualified, is a particularly worrisome example of the increasing polarization of American politics. As noted above, one purpose of conventions is to help coordinate political action and prevent political dysfunction. Accordingly, one might object to the Senate's position because it is yet another example of an accelerating process that makes bi-partisan cooperation more difficult in the future. Even if the Supreme Court is not especially damaged by the Senate's actions, in the long run the national political process will be damaged because this kind of behavior helps accelerate the breakdown of a functioning government. In a presidential system with separation of powers, effective governance requires cooperation from both of the country's major political parties. If that cooperation breaks down, governance becomes increasingly difficult and the country is unable to respond to crises and long-term threats.

Does it follow from this argument that the Senate's action might have been acceptable if the other features of partisan polarization were not present? Or is the argument that the Senate would not have felt authorized to act in this way if other norms of bipartisan cooperation had not already broken down?

8. *The costs (and benefits) of intransigence.* What are the dangers of a strategy of intransigence on this particular issue? From one perspective, there aren't any downsides: The Republican strategy paid off—Neil Gorsuch now occupies Antonin Scalia's seat on the Supreme Court, and because he is relatively young, he will continue to serve for decades. On the other hand, it is possible that Democrats will find various ways to retaliate, because they feel they were cheated out of a Supreme Court appointment. This might lead to even further

escalations and a serious breakdown of the appointments process and of the political process generally. Does the risk that this might happen at some point in the future mean that the Republicans strategy was wrong? Or does it mean only that Senators always have to weigh costs and benefits in choosing a strategy?

After all, failing to block Garland had its own risks. Senate Republicans might have faced retaliation from the most conservative part of their political base, which despised President Obama and considers the appointment of conservative judges to be an important priority. Senate Republicans might well have decided that the political survival of the Republican majority in the Senate in the short run was far more important than the risk of retaliation down the road.

If this adequately describes the Republican calculus, the political convention Kar and Mazzone claim to have identified is no longer self-enforcing. Norms that are not self-enforcing will have to be enforced by some third party—for example, by the courts. Do you believe that this particular controversy was justiciable?

Insert on p. 1079 immediately before section E. Presidential Privileges and Immunities:

ZIVOTOFSKY v. KERRY
135 S.Ct. 2076 (2015)

[The petitioner, Menachem Binyamin Zivotofsky, was born in 2002 to United States citizens living in Jerusalem. In December 2002, Zivotofsky's mother visited the American Embassy in Tel Aviv to request both a passport and a consular report of birth abroad for her son. (A consular report of birth is used to establish U.S. citizenship for children of American parents born abroad.) Zivotofsky's mother asked that his place of birth be listed as "Jerusalem, Israel." The Embassy clerks explained that, pursuant to a long-standing State Department policy, the passport would list only "Jerusalem." Zivotofsky's parents, as his guardians, sued the Secretary of State. They argued that under §214(d) of the Foreign Relations Authorization Act (FRAA), Zivotofsky has the right to have "Israel" recorded as his place of birth in his passport. In Zivotofsky v. Clinton, 132 S.Ct. 1421 (2012), the Supreme Court held that this issue was not a political question. During the litigation, Zivotofsky focused on the passport claim, and waived any argument that his consular report of birth abroad should be treated differently than his passport. The Court therefore considered only the passport arguments, although Justice Thomas's separate opinion treated the passport and consular reports as presenting distinct legal issues.]

Justice KENNEDY delivered the opinion of the Court.

I

A

Jerusalem's political standing has long been, and remains, one of the most sensitive issues in American foreign policy, and indeed it is one of the most delicate issues in current international affairs. In 1948, President Truman formally recognized Israel in a signed statement of "recognition." That statement did not recognize Israeli sovereignty over Jerusalem. . . . [N]either President Truman nor any later United States President has issued an official statement or declaration acknowledging any country's sovereignty over Jerusalem. Instead, the Executive Branch has maintained that " 'the status of Jerusalem . . . should be decided not unilaterally but in consultation with all concerned.' " In a letter to Congress [during the Clinton Adminstration] then-Secretary of State Warren Christopher expressed the Executive's concern that "[t]here is no issue related to the Arab–Israeli negotiations that is more sensitive than Jerusalem." He further noted the Executive's opinion that "any effort . . . to bring it to the forefront" could be "very damaging to the success of the peace process."

The President's position on Jerusalem is reflected in State Department policy regarding passports and consular reports of birth abroad. Understanding that passports will be construed as reflections of American policy, the State Department's Foreign Affairs Manual instructs its employees, in general, to record the place of birth on a passport as the "country [having] present sovereignty over the actual area of birth." Dept. of State, 7 Foreign Affairs Manual (FAM) §1383.4 (1987). If a citizen objects to the country listed as sovereign by the State Department, he or she may list the city or town of birth rather than the country. The FAM, however, does not allow citizens to list a sovereign that conflicts with Executive Branch policy. Because the United States does not recognize any country as having sovereignty over Jerusalem, the FAM instructs employees to record the place of birth for citizens born there as "Jerusalem."

In 2002, Congress passed the . . . . the Foreign Relations Authorization Act, Fiscal Year 2003, 116 Stat. 1350. Section 214 of the Act is titled "United States Policy with Respect to Jerusalem as the Capital of Israel." . . . §214(d) addresses passports [and] seeks to override the FAM. . . . §214(d) states "[f]or purposes of the registration of birth, certification of nationality, or issuance of a passport of a United States citizen born in the city of Jerusalem, the Secretary shall, upon the request of the citizen or the citizen's legal guardian, record the place of birth as Israel."

When he signed the Act into law, President George W. Bush issued a statement declaring his position that §214 would, "if construed as mandatory rather than advisory, impermissibly interfere with the President's constitutional authority to formulate the position of the United States, speak for the Nation in international affairs, and determine the terms on which recognition is given to foreign states." The President concluded, "U.S. policy regarding Jerusalem has not changed."

Some parties were not reassured by the President's statement. A cable from the United States Consulate in Jerusalem noted that the Palestine Liberation Organization Executive Committee, Fatah Central Committee, and the Palestinian Authority Cabinet had all issued statements claiming that the Act " 'undermines the role of the U.S. as a sponsor of the peace process.' " In the Gaza Strip and elsewhere residents marched in protest.

In response the Secretary of State advised diplomats to express their understanding of "Jerusalem's importance to both sides and to many others around the world." He noted his belief that America's "policy towards Jerusalem" had not changed. . . .

II

In considering claims of Presidential power this Court refers to Justice Jackson's familiar tripartite framework from *Youngstown Sheet & Tube Co. v. Sawyer*, 343 U.S. 579, 635-38 (1952) (concurring opinion). The framework divides exercises of Presidential power into three categories: First, when "the President acts pursuant to an express or implied authorization of Congress, his authority is at its maximum, for it includes all that he possesses in his own right plus all that Congress can delegate." Second, "in absence of either a congressional grant or denial of authority" there is a "zone of twilight in which he and Congress may have concurrent authority," and where "congressional inertia, indifference or quiescence may" invite the exercise of executive power. Finally, when "the President takes measures incompatible with the expressed or implied will of Congress . . . he can rely only upon his own constitutional powers minus any constitutional powers of Congress over the matter." To succeed in this third category, the President's asserted power must be both "exclusive" and "conclusive" on the issue.

[T]he Secretary contends that §214(d) infringes on the President's exclusive recognition power by "requiring the President to contradict his recognition position regarding Jerusalem in official communications with foreign sovereigns." . . . [T]he Secretary acknowledges the President's power is "at its lowest ebb." Because the President's refusal to implement §214(d) falls into Justice Jackson's third category, his claim must be "scrutinized with caution," and he may rely solely on powers the Constitution grants to him alone. . . .

A

Recognition is a "formal acknowledgement" that a particular "entity possesses the qualifications for statehood" or "that a particular regime is the effective government of a state." It may also involve the determination of a state's territorial bounds. . . . Legal consequences follow formal recognition. Recognized sovereigns may sue in United States courts, and may benefit from sovereign immunity when they are sued. The actions of a recognized sovereign committed within its own territory also receive deference in domestic courts under the act of state doctrine. Recognition at international law, furthermore, is a precondition of regular diplomatic relations. Recognition is thus "useful, even necessary," to the existence of a state.

Despite the importance of the recognition power in foreign relations, the Constitution does not use the term "recognition," either in Article II or elsewhere. The Secretary asserts that the President exercises the recognition power based on the Reception Clause, which directs that the President "shall receive Ambassadors and other public Ministers." Art. II, §3. As Zivotofsky notes, the Reception Clause received little attention at the Constitutional Convention. In fact, during the ratification debates, Alexander Hamilton claimed that the power to receive ambassadors was "more a matter of dignity than of authority," a ministerial duty largely "without consequence." The Federalist No. 69.

At the time of the founding, however, prominent international scholars suggested that receiving an ambassador was tantamount to recognizing the sovereignty of the sending state. . . . It is a logical and proper inference, then, that a Clause directing the President alone to receive ambassadors would be understood to acknowledge his power to recognize other nations.

This in fact occurred early in the Nation's history when President Washington recognized the French Revolutionary Government by receiving its ambassador. See A. Hamilton, Pacificus No. 1, in The Letters of Pacificus and Helvidius 5, 13–14 (1845) (reprint 1976) (President "acknowledged the republic of France, by the reception of its minister"). After this incident the import of the Reception Clause became clear—causing Hamilton to change his earlier view. He wrote that the Reception Clause "includes th[e power] of judging, in the case of a revolution of government in a foreign country, whether the new rulers are competent organs of the national will, and ought to be recognised, or not." See *id.,* at 12; see also 3 J. Story, Commentaries on the Constitution of the United States §1560, p. 416 (1833) ("If the executive receives an ambassador, or other minister, as the representative of a new nation . . . it is an acknowledgment of the sovereign authority *de facto* of such new nation, or party"). As a result, the Reception Clause provides support, although not the sole authority, for the President's power to recognize other nations.

The inference that the President exercises the recognition power is further supported by his additional Article II powers. It is for the President, "by and with the Advice and Consent of the Senate," to "make Treaties, provided two thirds of the Senators present concur." Art. II, §2, cl. 2. In addition, "he shall nominate, and by and with the Advice and Consent of the Senate, shall appoint Ambassadors" as well as "other public Ministers and Consuls." *Ibid.*

As a matter of constitutional structure, these additional powers give the President control over recognition decisions. At international law, recognition may be effected by different means, but each means is dependent upon Presidential power. In addition to receiving an ambassador, recognition may occur on "the conclusion of a bilateral treaty," or the "formal initiation of diplomatic relations," including the dispatch of an ambassador. The President has the sole power to negotiate treaties, see *United States v. Curtiss–Wright Export Corp.,* 299 U.S. 304 (1936), and the Senate may not conclude or ratify a treaty without Presidential action. The President, too, nominates the Nation's ambassadors and dispatches other diplomatic agents. Congress may not send an ambassador without his involvement. Beyond that, the President himself has the power to open diplomatic channels simply by engaging in direct diplomacy with foreign heads of state and their ministers. The Constitution thus assigns the President means to effect recognition on his own initiative. Congress, by contrast, has no constitutional power that would enable it to initiate diplomatic relations with a foreign nation. Because these specific Clauses confer the recognition power on the President, the Court need not consider whether or to what extent the Vesting Clause, which provides that the "executive Power" shall be vested in the President, provides further support for the President's action here. Art. II, §1, cl. 1.

The text and structure of the Constitution grant the President the power to recognize foreign nations and governments. The question then becomes whether that power is exclusive. The various ways in which the President may unilaterally effect recognition—and the lack of any similar power vested in Congress—suggest that it is. So, too, do functional considerations. Put simply, the Nation must have a single policy regarding which governments are legitimate in the eyes of the United States and which are not. Foreign countries need to know, before entering into diplomatic relations or commerce with the United States, whether their ambassadors will be received; whether their officials will be immune from suit in federal court; and whether they may initiate lawsuits here to vindicate their rights. These assurances cannot be equivocal.

Recognition is a topic on which the Nation must "'speak . . . with one voice.'" *American Ins. Assn. v. Garamendi,* 539 U.S. 396 (2003) (quoting *Crosby v. National Foreign Trade Council,* 530 U.S. 363 (2000)). That voice must be the President's. Between the two political branches, only the Executive has the characteristic of unity at all times. And with unity comes the ability to exercise, to a greater degree, "[d]ecision, activity, secrecy, and dispatch." The Federalist No. 70 (A. Hamilton). The President is capable, in ways Congress is not, of engaging in the delicate and often secret diplomatic contacts that may lead to a decision on recognition. See, *e.g., United States v. Pink,* 315 U.S. 203 (1942). He is also better positioned to take the decisive, unequivocal action necessary to recognize other states at international law. These qualities explain why the Framers listed the traditional avenues of recognition—receiving ambassadors, making treaties, and sending ambassadors—as among the President's Article II powers.

[T]he President since the founding has exercised this unilateral power to recognize new states—and the Court has endorsed the practice. See *Banco Nacional de Cuba v. Sabbatino,* 376 U.S. 398 (1964); *Pink; Williams v. Suffolk Ins. Co.,* 13 Pet. 415, 420 (1839). Texts and treatises on international law treat the President's word as the final word on recognition. See, *e.g.,* Restatement (Third) of Foreign Relations Law §204, at 89 ("Under the Constitution of the United States the President has exclusive authority to recognize or not to recognize a foreign state or government"); see also L. Henkin, Foreign Affairs and the

U.S. Constitution 43 (2d ed. 1996) ("It is no longer questioned that the President does not merely perform the ceremony of receiving foreign ambassadors but also determines whether the United States should recognize or refuse to recognize a foreign government"). . . .

It remains true, of course, that many decisions affecting foreign relations—including decisions that may determine the course of our relations with recognized countries—require congressional action. Congress may "regulate Commerce with foreign Nations," "establish an uniform Rule of Naturalization," "define and punish Piracies and Felonies committed on the high Seas, and Offences against the Law of Nations," "declare War," "grant Letters of Marque and Reprisal," and "make Rules for the Government and Regulation of the land and naval Forces." U.S. Const., Art. I, §8. In addition, the President cannot make a treaty or appoint an ambassador without the approval of the Senate. Art. II, §2, cl. 2. The President, furthermore, could not build an American Embassy abroad without congressional appropriation of the necessary funds. Art. I, §8, cl. 1. Under basic separation-of-powers principles, it is for the Congress to enact the laws, including "all Laws which shall be necessary and proper for carrying into Execution" the powers of the Federal Government. §8, cl. 18.

In foreign affairs, as in the domestic realm, the Constitution "enjoins upon its branches separateness but interdependence, autonomy but reciprocity." *Youngstown* (Jackson, J., concurring). Although the President alone effects the formal act of recognition, Congress' powers, and its central role in making laws, give it substantial authority regarding many of the policy determinations that precede and follow the act of recognition itself. If Congress disagrees with the President's recognition policy, there may be consequences. Formal recognition may seem a hollow act if it is not accompanied by the dispatch of an ambassador, the easing of trade restrictions, and the conclusion of treaties. And those decisions require action by the Senate or the whole Congress.

In practice, then, the President's recognition determination is just one part of a political process that may require Congress to make laws. The President's exclusive recognition power encompasses the authority to acknowledge, in a formal sense, the legitimacy of other states and governments, including their territorial bounds. Albeit limited, the exclusive recognition power is essential to the conduct of Presidential duties. The formal act of recognition is an executive power that Congress may not qualify. If the President is to be effective in negotiations over a formal recognition determination, it must be evident to his counterparts abroad that he speaks for the Nation on that precise question.

A clear rule that the formal power to recognize a foreign government subsists in the President therefore serves a necessary purpose in diplomatic relations. All this, of course, underscores that Congress has an important role in other aspects of foreign policy, and the President may be bound by any number of laws Congress enacts. In this way ambition counters ambition, ensuring that the democratic will of the people is observed and respected in foreign affairs as in the domestic realm. See The Federalist No. 51 (J. Madison).

B

No single precedent resolves the question whether the President has exclusive recognition authority and, if so, how far that power extends. In part that is because, until today, the political branches have resolved their disputes over questions of recognition. The relevant cases, though providing important instruction, address the division of recognition power between the Federal Government and the States, or between the courts and the political branches—not between the President and Congress. As the parties acknowledge, some isolated statements in those cases lend support to the position that Congress has a role in the recognition process. In the end, however, a fair reading of the cases shows that the President's role in the recognition process is both central and exclusive.

During the administration of President Van Buren, in a case involving a dispute over the status of the Falkland Islands, the Court noted that "when the executive branch of the government" assumes "a fact in regard to the sovereignty of any island or country, it is conclusive on the judicial department." *Williams*. Once the President has made his determination, it "is enough to know, that in the exercise of his constitutional functions, he has decided the question. Having done this under the responsibilities which belong to him, it is obligatory on the people and government of the Union."

Later, during the 1930's and 1940's, the Court addressed issues surrounding President Roosevelt's decision to recognize the Soviet Government of Russia. In *United States v. Belmont,* 301 U.S. 324 (1937), and *Pink*, New York state courts declined to give full effect to the terms of executive agreements the President had concluded in negotiations over recognition of the Soviet regime. In particular the state courts, based on New York public policy, did not treat assets that had been seized by the Soviet Government as property of Russia and declined to turn those assets over to the United States. The Court stated that it "may not be doubted" that "recognition, establishment of diplomatic relations, . . . and agreements with respect thereto" are "within the competence of the President." *Belmont*. In these matters, "the Executive ha[s] authority to speak as the sole organ of th[e] government." The Court added that the President's authority "is not limited to a determination of the government to be recognized. It includes the power to determine the policy which is to govern the question of recognition." *Pink*; see also *Guaranty Trust Co.* (The "political department['s] . . . action in recognizing a foreign government and in receiving its diplomatic representatives is conclusive on all domestic courts"). Thus, New York state courts were required to respect the executive agreements.

It is true, of course, that *Belmont* and *Pink* are not direct holdings that the recognition power is exclusive. Those cases considered the validity of executive agreements, not the initial act of recognition. The President's determination in those cases did not contradict an Act of Congress. And the primary issue was whether the executive agreements could supersede state law. Still, the language in *Pink* and *Belmont,* which confirms the President's competence to determine questions of recognition, is strong support for the conclusion that it is for the President alone to determine which foreign governments are legitimate.

Banco Nacional de Cuba contains even stronger statements regarding the President's authority over recognition. There, the status of Cuba's Government and its acts as a sovereign were at issue. As the Court explained, "Political recognition is exclusively a function of the Executive." Because the Executive had recognized the Cuban Government, the Court held that it should be treated as sovereign and could benefit from the "act of state" doctrine. See also *Baker v. Carr,* 369 U.S. 186 (1962) ("[I]t is the executive that determines a person's status as representative of a foreign government"); *National City Bank of N.Y., [v. Republic of China*, 348 U.S. 356 (1955)] ("The status of the Republic of China in our courts is a matter for determination by the Executive and is outside the competence of this Court"). As these cases illustrate, the Court has long considered recognition to be the exclusive prerogative of the Executive.

The Secretary now urges the Court to define the executive power over foreign relations in even broader terms. He contends that under the Court's precedent the President has "exclusive authority to conduct diplomatic relations," along with "the bulk of foreign-affairs powers." In support of his submission that the President has broad, undefined powers over foreign affairs, the Secretary quotes *United States v. Curtiss–Wright Export Corp.,* which described the President as "the sole organ of the federal government in the field of international relations." This Court declines to acknowledge that unbounded power. A formulation broader than the rule that the President alone determines what nations to formally recognize as legitimate — and that he consequently controls his statements on matters of recognition — presents different issues and is unnecessary to the resolution of this case.

The *Curtiss–Wright* case does not extend so far as the Secretary suggests. In *Curtiss–Wright,* the Court considered whether a congressional delegation of power to the President was constitutional. Congress had passed a joint resolution giving the President the discretion to prohibit arms sales to certain militant powers in South America. The resolution provided criminal penalties for violation of those orders. The Court held that the delegation was constitutional, reasoning that Congress may grant the President substantial authority and discretion in the field of foreign affairs. Describing why such broad delegation may be appropriate, the opinion stated:

"In this vast external realm, with its important, complicated, delicate and manifold problems, the President alone has the power to speak or listen as a representative of the nation. He *makes* treaties with the advice and consent of the Senate; but he alone negotiates. Into the field of negotiation the Senate cannot intrude; and Congress itself is powerless to invade it. As Marshall said in his great argument of March 7, 1800, in the House of Representatives, 'The President is the sole organ of the nation in its external relations, and its sole representative with foreign nations.' [10 Annals of Cong.] 613."

This description of the President's exclusive power was not necessary to the holding of *Curtiss–Wright* — which, after all, dealt with congressionally authorized action, not a unilateral Presidential determination. Indeed, *Curtiss–Wright* did not hold that the President is free from Congress' lawmaking power in the

field of international relations. The President does have a unique role in com-
municating with foreign governments, as then-Congressman John Marshall
acknowledged. But whether the realm is foreign or domestic, it is still the
Legislative Branch, not the Executive Branch, that makes the law.

In a world that is ever more compressed and interdependent, it is essential
the congressional role in foreign affairs be understood and respected. For it
is Congress that makes laws, and in countless ways its laws will and should
shape the Nation's course. The Executive is not free from the ordinary controls
and checks of Congress merely because foreign affairs are at issue. See, *e.g.,
Medellín v. Texas,* 552 U.S. 491 (2008); *Youngstown*; *Little v. Barreme,* 2 Cranch
170 (1804). It is not for the President alone to determine the whole content of the
Nation's foreign policy.

That said, judicial precedent and historical practice teach that it is for the
President alone to make the specific decision of what foreign power he will
recognize as legitimate, both for the Nation as a whole and for the purpose of
making his own position clear within the context of recognition in discussions
and negotiations with foreign nations. Recognition is an act with immediate and
powerful significance for international relations, so the President's position must
be clear. Congress cannot require him to contradict his own statement regarding
a determination of formal recognition.

Zivotofsky's contrary arguments are unconvincing. . . . This Court's cases do
not hold that the recognition power is shared. [N]o one disputes that Congress
has a role in determining the status of United States territories. See U.S. Const.,
Art. IV, §3, cl. 2 (Congress may "dispose of and make all needful Rules and
Regulations respecting the Territory or other Property belonging to the United
States"). Other cases describing a shared power address the recognition of Indian
tribes — which is, similarly, a distinct issue from the recognition of foreign countries. See *Cherokee Nation v. Georgia,* 5 Pet. 1 (1831).

To be sure, the Court has mentioned both of the political branches in discussing international recognition, but it has done so primarily in affirming that the
Judiciary is not responsible for recognizing foreign nations. . . . This is consistent
with the fact that Congress, in the ordinary course, does support the President's
recognition policy, for instance by confirming an ambassador to the recognized
foreign government. Those cases do not cast doubt on the view that the Executive
Branch determines whether the United States will recognize foreign states and
governments and their territorial bounds.

C

Having examined the Constitution's text and this Court's precedent, it is
appropriate to turn to accepted understandings and practice. In separation-of-
powers cases this Court has often "put significant weight upon historical practice." *NLRB v. Noel Canning,* 573 U.S. ____,134 S.Ct. 2550 (2014) (emphasis
deleted). Here, history is not all on one side, but on balance it provides strong
support for the conclusion that the recognition power is the President's alone. As

Zivotofsky argues, certain historical incidents can be interpreted to support the position that recognition is a shared power. But the weight of historical evidence supports the opposite view, which is that the formal determination of recognition is a power to be exercised only by the President.

[E]ven a brief survey of the major historical examples, with an emphasis on those said to favor Zivotofsky, establishes no more than that some Presidents have chosen to cooperate with Congress, not that Congress itself has exercised the recognition power.

From the first Administration forward, the President has claimed unilateral authority to recognize foreign sovereigns. For the most part, Congress has acquiesced in the Executive's exercise of the recognition power. On occasion, the President has chosen, as may often be prudent, to consult and coordinate with Congress. As Judge Tatel noted in this case, however, "the most striking thing" about the history of recognition "is what is absent from it: a situation like this one," where Congress has enacted a statute contrary to the President's formal and considered statement concerning recognition.

The first debate over the recognition power arose in 1793, after France had been torn by revolution. Once the Revolutionary Government was established, Secretary of State Jefferson and President Washington, without consulting Congress, authorized the American Ambassador to resume relations with the new regime. Soon thereafter, the new French Government proposed to send an ambassador, Citizen Genet, to the United States. Members of the President's Cabinet agreed that receiving Genet would be a binding and public act of recognition. They decided, however, both that Genet should be received and that consultation with Congress was not necessary. Congress expressed no disagreement with this position, and Genet's reception marked the Nation's first act of recognition — one made by the President alone.

The recognition power again became relevant when yet another revolution took place — this time, in South America, as several colonies rose against Spain. In 1818, Speaker of the House Henry Clay announced he "intended moving the recognition of Buenos Ayres and probably of Chile." Clay thus sought to appropriate money " '[f]or one year's salary' " for " 'a Minister' " to present-day Argentina. President Monroe, however, did not share that view. Although Clay gave "one of the most remarkable speeches of his career," his proposed bill was defeated. That action has been attributed, in part, to the fact that Congress agreed the recognition power rested solely with the President. Four years later, after the President had decided to recognize the South American republics, Congress did pass a resolution, on his request, appropriating funds for "such missions to the independent nations on the American continent, as the President of the United States may deem proper."

A decade later, President Jackson faced a recognition crisis over Texas. In 1835, Texas rebelled against Mexico and formed its own government. But the President feared that recognizing the new government could ignite a war. After Congress urged him to recognize Texas, the President delivered a message to the Legislature. He concluded there had not been a "deliberate inquiry" into whether the President or Congress possessed the recognition power. He stated, however, "on the ground of expediency, I am disposed to concur" with Congress' preference regarding Texas. In response Congress appropriated funds for a "diplomatic agent to be sent to the Republic of Texas, whenever the President of the United States . . . shall deem it expedient to appoint such minister." Thus, although he cooperated with Congress, the President was left to execute the formal act of recognition.

President Lincoln, too, sought to coordinate with Congress when he requested support for his recognition of Liberia and Haiti. In his first annual message to Congress he said he could see no reason "why we should persevere longer in withholding our recognition of the independence and sovereignty of Hayti and Liberia." Nonetheless, he was "[u]nwilling" to "inaugurate a novel policy in regard to them without the approbation of Congress." In response Congress concurred in the President's recognition determination and enacted a law appropriating funds to appoint diplomatic representatives to the two countries — leaving, as usual, the actual dispatch of ambassadors and formal statement of recognition to the President.

Three decades later, the branches again were able to reach an accord, this time with regard to Cuba. In 1898, an insurgency against the Spanish colonial government was raging in Cuba. President McKinley determined to ask Congress for authorization to send armed forces to Cuba to help quell the violence. Although McKinley thought Spain was to blame for the strife, he opposed recognizing either Cuba or its insurgent government. At first, the House proposed a resolution consistent with McKinley's wishes. The Senate countered with a resolution that authorized the use of force but that did recognize both Cuban independence and the insurgent government. When the Senate's version reached the House, the House again rejected the language recognizing Cuban independence. The resolution went to Conference, which, after debate, reached a compromise. The final resolution stated "the people of the Island of Cuba are, and of right ought to be, free and independent," but made no mention of recognizing a new Cuban Government. Accepting the compromise, the President signed the joint resolution.

For the next 80 years, "[P]residents consistently recognized new states and governments without any serious opposition from, or activity in, Congress." The next debate over recognition did not occur until the late 1970's. It concerned China.

President Carter recognized the People's Republic of China (PRC) as the government of China, and derecognized the Republic of China, located on Taiwan. As to the status of Taiwan, the President "acknowledge[d] the Chinese position" that "Taiwan is part of China," but he did not accept that claim. The President proposed a new law defining how the United States would conduct business with Taiwan. After extensive revisions, Congress passed, and the President signed, the Taiwan Relations Act. The Act (in a simplified summary) treated Taiwan as if it were a legally distinct entity from China — an entity with which the United States intended to maintain strong ties.

Throughout the legislative process, however, no one raised a serious question regarding the President's exclusive authority to recognize the PRC—or to decline to grant formal recognition to Taiwan. Rather, Congress accepted the President's recognition determination as a completed, lawful act; and it proceeded to outline the trade and policy provisions that, in its judgment, were appropriate in light of that decision.

This history confirms the Court's conclusion in the instant case that the power to recognize or decline to recognize a foreign state and its territorial bounds resides in the President alone. For the most part, Congress has respected the Executive's policies and positions as to formal recognition. At times, Congress itself has defended the President's constitutional prerogative. Over the last 100 years, there has been scarcely any debate over the President's power to recognize foreign states. In this respect the Legislature, in the narrow context of recognition, on balance has acknowledged the importance of speaking "with one voice." *Crosby*. The weight of historical evidence indicates Congress has accepted that the power to recognize foreign states and governments and their territorial bounds is exclusive to the Presidency.

III

[S]ection 214(d) requires that, in a passport or consular report of birth abroad, "the Secretary shall, upon the request of the citizen or the citizen's legal guardian, record the place of birth as Israel" for a "United States citizen born in the city of Jerusalem." That is, §214(d) requires the President, through the Secretary, to identify citizens born in Jerusalem who so request as being born in Israel. But according to the President, those citizens were not born in Israel. As a matter of United States policy, neither Israel nor any other country is acknowledged as having sovereignty over Jerusalem. In this way, §214(d) "directly contradicts" the "carefully calibrated and longstanding Executive branch policy of neutrality toward Jerusalem."

If the power over recognition is to mean anything, it must mean that the President not only makes the initial, formal recognition determination but also that he may maintain that determination in his and his agent's statements. This conclusion is a matter of both common sense and necessity. If Congress could command the President to state a recognition position inconsistent with his own, Congress could override the President's recognition determination. Under international law, recognition may be effected by "written or oral declaration of the recognizing state." In addition an act of recognition must "leave no doubt as to the intention to grant it." Thus, if Congress could alter the President's statements on matters of recognition or force him to contradict them, Congress in effect would exercise the recognition power.

As Justice Jackson wrote in *Youngstown*, when a Presidential power is "exclusive," it "disabl[es] the Congress from acting upon the subject." Here, the subject is quite narrow: The Executive's exclusive power extends no further than his formal recognition determination. But as to that determination, Congress may not enact a law that directly contradicts it. This is not to say Congress may not express its disagreement with the President in myriad ways. For example, it may enact an embargo, decline to confirm an ambassador, or even declare war. But none of these acts would alter the President's recognition decision.

If Congress may not pass a law, speaking in its own voice, that effects formal recognition, then it follows that it may not force the President himself to contradict his earlier statement. That congressional command would not only prevent the Nation from speaking with one voice but also prevent the Executive itself from doing so in conducting foreign relations.

Although the statement required by §214(d) would not itself constitute a formal act of recognition, it is a mandate that the Executive contradict his prior recognition determination in an official document issued by the Secretary of State. See *Urtetiqui v. D'Arcy,* 9 Pet. 692 (1835) (a passport "from its nature and object, is addressed to foreign powers" and "is to be considered . . . in the character of a political document"). As a result, it is unconstitutional. This is all the more clear in light of the longstanding treatment of a passport's place-of-birth section as an official executive statement implicating recognition. The Secretary's position on this point has been consistent: He will not place information in the place-of-birth section of a passport that contradicts the President's recognition policy. If a citizen objects to the country listed as sovereign over his place of birth, then the Secretary will accommodate him by listing the city or town of birth rather than the country. But the Secretary will not list a sovereign that contradicts the President's recognition policy in a passport. Thus, the Secretary will not list "Israel" in a passport as the country containing Jerusalem.

The flaw in §214(d) is further underscored by the undoubted fact that the purpose of the statute was to infringe on the recognition power — a power the Court now holds is the sole prerogative of the President. The statute is titled "United States Policy with Respect to Jerusalem as the Capital of Israel." The House Conference Report proclaimed that §214 "contains four provisions related to the recognition of Jerusalem as Israel's capital." And, indeed, observers interpreted §214 as altering United States policy regarding Jerusalem — which led to protests across the region. From the face of §214, from the legislative history, and from its reception, it is clear that Congress wanted to express its displeasure with the President's policy by, among other things, commanding the Executive to contradict his own, earlier stated position on Jerusalem. This Congress may not do.

It is true, as Zivotofsky notes, that Congress has substantial authority over passports. See *Haig v. Agee,* 453 U.S. 280 (1981); *Zemel v. Rusk,* 381 U.S. 1 (1965); *Kent v. Dulles,* 357 U.S. 116 (1958). The Court does not question the power of Congress to enact passport legislation of wide scope. In *Kent v. Dulles,* for example, the Court held that if a person's " 'liberty' " to travel "is to be regulated" through a passport, "it must be pursuant to the law-making functions of the Congress." Later cases, such as *Zemel v. Rusk* and *Haig v. Agee,* also proceeded on the assumption that Congress must authorize the grounds on which passports may be approved or denied. This is consistent with the extensive lawmaking power the Constitution vests in Congress over the Nation's foreign affairs.

The problem with §214(d), however, lies in how Congress exercised its authority over passports. It was an improper act for Congress to "aggrandiz[e] its power at the expense of another branch" by requiring the President to contradict an earlier recognition determination in an official document issued by the Executive Branch. To allow Congress to control the President's communication in the context of a formal recognition determination is to allow Congress to exercise that exclusive power itself. As a result, the statute is unconstitutional.

3

In holding §214(d) invalid the Court does not question the substantial powers of Congress over foreign affairs in general or passports in particular. This case is confined solely to the exclusive power of the President to control recognition determinations, including formal statements by the Executive Branch acknowledging the legitimacy of a state or government and its territorial bounds. Congress cannot command the President to contradict an earlier recognition determination in the issuance of passports.

The judgment of the Court of Appeals for the District of Columbia Circuit is *Affirmed.*

Justice BREYER, concurring.

I continue to believe that this case presents a political question inappropriate for judicial resolution. See *Zivotofsky v. Clinton,* 566 U.S. ——,132 S.Ct. 1421, (2012) (BREYER, J., dissenting). But because precedent precludes resolving this case on political question grounds, I join the Court's opinion.

Justice THOMAS, concurring in the judgment in part and dissenting in part.

Our Constitution allocates the powers of the Federal Government over foreign affairs in two ways. First, it expressly identifies certain foreign affairs powers and vests them in particular branches, either individually or jointly. Second, it vests the residual foreign affairs powers of the Federal Government—*i.e.,* those not specifically enumerated in the Constitution—in the President by way of Article II's Vesting Clause.

Section 214(d) of the Foreign Relations Authorization Act, Fiscal Year 2003, ignores that constitutional allocation of power insofar as it directs the President, contrary to his wishes, to list "Israel" as the place of birth of Jerusalem-born citizens on their passports. The President has long regulated passports under his residual foreign affairs power, and this portion of §214(d) does not fall within any of Congress' enumerated powers.

By contrast, §214(d) poses no such problem insofar as it regulates consular reports of birth abroad. Unlike passports, these reports were developed to effectuate the naturalization laws, and they continue to serve the role of identifying persons who need not be naturalized to obtain U.S. citizenship. The regulation of these reports does not fall within the President's foreign affairs powers, but within Congress' enumerated powers under the Naturalization and Necessary and Proper Clauses.

Rather than adhere to the Constitution's division of powers, the Court relies on a distortion of the President's recognition power to hold both of these parts of §214(d) unconstitutional. Because I cannot join [the majority's] faulty analysis, I concur only in the portion of the Court's judgment holding §214(d) unconstitutional as applied to passports. I respectfully dissent from the remainder of the Court's judgment.

I

A

The Constitution specifies a number of foreign affairs powers and divides them between the political branches. . . . These specific allocations, however, cannot account for the entirety of the foreign affairs powers exercised by the Federal Government. Neither of the political branches is expressly authorized, for instance, to communicate with foreign ministers, to issue passports, or to repel sudden attacks. Yet the President has engaged in such conduct, with the support of Congress, since the earliest days of the Republic.

The President's longstanding practice of exercising unenumerated foreign affairs powers reflects a constitutional directive that "the President ha[s] primary responsibility—along with the necessary power—to protect the national security and to conduct the Nation's foreign relations." Specifically, the Vesting Clause of Article II provides that "[t]he executive Power shall be vested in a President of the United States." Art. II, §1. This Clause is notably different from the Vesting Clause of Article I, which provides only that "[a]ll legislative Powers *herein granted* shall be vested in a Congress of the United States," Art. I, §1 (emphasis added). By omitting the words "herein granted" in Article II, the Constitution indicates that the "executive Power" vested in the President is not confined to those powers expressly identified in the document. Instead, it includes all powers originally understood as falling within the "executive Power" of the Federal Government.

B

Founding-era evidence reveals that the "executive Power" included the foreign affairs powers of a sovereign State. John Locke's 17th-century writings laid the groundwork for this understanding of executive power. Locke described foreign affairs powers—including the powers of "war and peace, leagues and alliances, and all the transactions with all persons and communities without the commonwealth"—as "federative" power. Second Treatise of Civil Government §146, p. 73 (J. Gough ed. 1947). He defined the "executive" power as "comprehending the execution of the municipal laws of the society within itself upon all that are parts of it." Importantly, however, Locke explained that the federative and executive powers must be lodged together, lest "disorder and ruin" erupt from the division of the "force of the public."

Subsequent thinkers began to refer to both of these powers as aspects of "executive power." William Blackstone, for example, described the executive power in England as including foreign affairs powers, such as the "power of sending embassadors to foreign states, and receiving embassadors at home"; making "treaties, leagues, and alliances with foreign states and princes"; "making war and peace"; and "issu[ing] letters of marque and reprisal." 1 Commentaries on the Laws of England 245, 249, 250, 242–252 (1765) (Blackstone). Baron de Montesquieu similarly described executive power as including the power to "mak[e] peace or war, sen[d] or receiv[e] embassies, establis[h] the public security, and provid[e] against invasions." The Spirit of the Laws bk. XI, ch. 6, p. 151 (O. Piest ed., T. Nugent transl. 1949). In fact, "most writers of [Montesquieu's] tim[e] w[ere] inclined to think of the executive branch of government as being concerned nearly entirely with foreign affairs." W. Gwyn, The Meaning of the Separation of Powers 103 (1965).

That understanding of executive power prevailed in America. Following independence, Congress assumed control over foreign affairs under the Articles of Confederation. At that time, many understood that control to be an exercise of executive power. . . . This view of executive power was widespread at the time of the framing of the Constitution. . . . During the ratification debates, James Wilson . . . referred to the "executive powers of government" as including the external powers of a nation. 2 J. Elliot, The Debates in the Several State Conventions on the Adoption of the Federal Constitution 500–502 (1863). And Alexander Hamilton, writing as Publius, asserted that "[t]he actual conduct of foreign negotiations," "the arrangement of the army and navy, the directions of the operations of war . . . and other matters of a like nature" are "executive details" that "fal[l] peculiarly within the province of the executive department." The Federalist No. 72.

C

Early practice of the founding generation also supports this understanding of the "executive Power." . . . [T]he practices of the Washington administration and First Congress confirm that Article II's Vesting Clause was originally understood to include a grant of residual foreign affairs power to the Executive.

II

The statutory provision at issue implicates the President's residual foreign affairs power. . . . The President argues that [Section 214(d)] violates his foreign affairs powers generally and his recognition power specifically. Zivotofsky rejoins that Congress passed §214(d) pursuant to its enumerated powers and its action must therefore take precedence.

Neither has it quite right. The President is not constitutionally compelled to implement §214(d) as it applies to passports because passport regulation falls squarely within his residual foreign affairs power and Zivotofsky has identified no source of congressional power to require the President to list Israel as the place of birth for a citizen born in Jerusalem on that citizen's passport. Section 214(d) can, however, be constitutionally applied to consular reports of birth abroad because those documents do not fall within the President's foreign affairs authority but do fall within Congress' enumerated powers over naturalization.

[A]t every stage of the proceedings, Zivotofsky has pressed his claim that he is entitled to have his place of birth listed as "Israel" on *both* his passport and his consular report of birth abroad, and the consular report issue is fairly included in the question presented. Parties cannot waive the correct interpretation of the law simply by failing to invoke it. That the parties have argued the case as if the same analysis should apply to both documents does not relieve this Court of its responsibility to interpret the law correctly. [relocated footnote — eds.]

A

In the Anglo–American legal tradition, passports have consistently been issued and controlled by the body exercising executive power — in England, by the King; in the colonies, by the Continental Congress; and in the United States, by President Washington and every President since. . . . That the President has the power to regulate passports under his residual foreign affairs powers does not, however, end the matter, for Congress has repeatedly legislated on the subject of passports. These laws have always been narrow in scope. For example, Congress enacted laws prohibiting the issuance of passports to noncitizens, created an exception to that rule for "persons liable to military duty," and then eliminated that exception, It passed laws regulating the fees that the State Department should impose for issuance of the passports. It also enacted legislation addressing the duration for which passports may remain valid. And it passed laws imposing criminal penalties for false statements made when applying for passports, along with misuse of passports and counterfeiting or forgery of them. . . . Justice SCALIA, in his dissent, faults me for failing to identify the enumerated power under which these laws were permissible, but the question presented in *this* case is whether §214(d) is a constitutional exercise of Congress' power, and that is the question I address. [relocated footnote — eds.] As with any congressional action, however, [§214(d)] is constitutionally permissible only insofar as it is promulgated pursuant to one of Congress' enumerated powers.

The Constitution contains no Passport Clause, nor does it explicitly vest Congress with "plenary authority over passports." Because our Government is one of enumerated powers, "Congress has no power to act unless the Constitution authorizes it to do so." And "[t]he Constitution plainly sets forth the 'few and defined' powers that Congress may exercise." A "passport power" is not one of them.

Section 214(d)'s passport directive . . . does not fall within the power "[t]o regulate Commerce with foreign Nations." "At the time the original Constitution was ratified, 'commerce' consisted of selling, buying, and bartering, as well as transporting for these purposes." The listing of the place of birth of an applicant—whether born in Jerusalem or not—does not involve selling, buying, bartering, or transporting for those purposes.

True, a passport is frequently used by persons who may intend to engage in commerce abroad, but that use is insufficient to bring §214(d)'s passport directive within the scope of this power. The specific conduct at issue here—the listing of the birthplace of a U.S. citizen born in Jerusalem on a passport by the President—is not a commercial activity. Any commercial activities subsequently undertaken by the bearer of a passport are yet further removed from that regulation.

The power "[t]o establish an uniform Rule of Naturalization" is similarly unavailing. . . . A passport has never been issued as part of the naturalization process. It is—and has always been—a "travel document," issued for the same purpose it has always served: a request from one sovereign to another for the protection of the bearer.

For similar reasons, the Necessary and Proper Clause gives Congress no authority here. . . . As an initial matter, "Congress lacks authority to legislate [under this provision] if the objective is anything other than 'carrying into Execution' one or more of the Federal Government's enumerated powers." The "end [must] be legitimate" under our constitutional structure. *McCulloch v. Maryland.*

But even if the objective of a law is carrying into execution one of the Federal Government's enumerated powers, the law must be both necessary and proper to that objective. The "Clause is not a warrant to Congress to enact any law that bears some conceivable connection to the exercise of an enumerated power." Instead, "there must be a necessary and proper fit between the 'means' (the federal law) and the 'end' (the enumerated power or powers) it is designed to serve." The "means" chosen by Congress "will be deemed 'necessary' if they are 'appropriate' and 'plainly adapted' to the exercise of an enumerated power, and 'proper' if they are not otherwise 'prohibited' by the Constitution and not '[in]consistent' with its 'letter and spirit.'"

§214(d), as applied to passports, [cannot] be an exercise of Congress' power to carry into execution its foreign commerce or naturalization powers . . . because this aspect of §214(d) is directed at neither of the ends served by these powers. Although at a high level of generality, a passport could be related to foreign commerce and naturalization, that attenuated relationship is insufficient. The law in question must be "directly link[ed]" to the enumerated power. As applied to passports, §214(d) . . . does not "'carr[y] into Execution'" Congress' foreign commerce or naturalization powers. At most, it bears a tertiary relationship to an activity Congress is permitted to regulate: It directs the President's formulation of a document, which, in turn, may be used to facilitate travel, which, in turn, may facilitate foreign commerce. And the distinctive history of the passport as a travel rather than citizenship document makes its connection to naturalization even more tenuous.

Nor can this aspect of §214(d) be justified as an exercise of Congress' power to enact laws to carry into execution the President's residual foreign affairs powers. Simply put, §214(d)'s passport directive is not a "proper" means of carrying this power into execution. . . . [T]he best interpretation of "proper" is that a law must fall within the peculiar jurisdiction of Congress. . . . [T]o be "proper," a law "must be consistent with principles of separation of powers, principles of federalism, and individual rights." . . . If Congress could rely on the Necessary and Proper Clause to exercise power expressly allocated to the other branches or to prevent the exercise of such power by other branches, it could undermine the constitutional allocation of powers.

[Here] Congress seeks to facilitate the exercise of a power allocated to another branch. . . . First, a law could be "improper" if it purports to direct another branch's exercise of its power. Second, a law could be "improper" if it takes one of those actions *and* the branch to which the power is allocated objects to the action. . . . [T]he application of §214(d) to passports would be improper under either approach. The President has made a determination that the "place of birth" on a passport should list the country of present sovereignty. And the President has determined that no country is presently exercising sovereignty over the area of Jerusalem. Thus, the President has provided that passports for persons born in Jerusalem should list "Jerusalem" as the place of birth in the passport. Section 214(d) directs the President to exercise his power to issue and regulate the content of passports in a particular way, and the President has objected to that direction. Under either potential mechanism for evaluating the propriety of a law under the separation-of-powers limitation, this law would be improper. . . . Because §214(d) is not proper, I need not resolve whether such a law could be understood to "carry into execution" the President's power. [relocated footnote—eds.]

In support of his argument that the President must enforce §214(d), Zivotofsky relies heavily on a similar statute addressing the place of birth designation for persons born in Taiwan. That statute provided, "For purposes of the registration of birth or certification of nationality of a United States citizen born in Taiwan, the Secretary of State shall permit the place of birth to be recorded as Taiwan." The President has adopted that practice.

The President's decision to adopt that practice, however, says nothing about the constitutionality of the Taiwan provision in the first place. The constitutional allocation of powers "does not depend on the views of individual Presidents, nor on whether the encroached upon branch approves the encroachment." *Free Enterprise Fund v. Public Company Accounting Oversight Bd.,* 561 U.S. 477 (2010). And the argument from Presidential acquiescence here is particularly weak, given that the Taiwan statute is consistent with the President's longstanding policy on Taiwan. . . . Because the President otherwise treats Taiwan as a geographical area within the People's Republic of China, listing Taiwan as the place of birth did not directly conflict with the President's prevailing practices. Section 214(d) *does* so conflict, as it requires the President to list citizens born in Jerusalem as born in "Israel," even though the Foreign Affairs Manual has long prohibited that action.

. . .

Justice SCALIA characterizes my interpretation of the executive power, the naturalization power, and the Necessary and Proper Clause as producing "a presidency more reminiscent of George III than George Washington." But he offers no competing interpretation of either the Article II Vesting Clause or the Necessary and Proper Clause. And his decision about the Constitution's resolution of conflict among the branches could itself be criticized as creating a supreme legislative body more reminiscent of the Parliament in England than the Congress in America.

B

Although the consular report of birth abroad shares some features with a passport, it is historically associated with naturalization, not foreign affairs. In order to establish a "uniform Rule of Naturalization," Congress must be able to identify the categories of persons who are eligible for naturalization, along with the rules for that process. Congress thus has always regulated the "acquisition of citizenship by being born abroad of American parents . . . in the exercise of the power conferred by the Constitution to establish a uniform rule of naturalization." It has determined that children born abroad to U.S. parents, subject to some exceptions, are natural-born citizens who do not need to go through the naturalization process.

The consular report of birth abroad is well suited to carrying into execution the power conferred on Congress in the Naturalization Clause. The report developed in response to Congress' requirement that children born abroad to U.S. citizens register with the consulate or lose their citizenship. And it continues to certify the acquisition of U.S. citizenship at birth by a person born abroad to a U.S. citizen. . . . [A]lthough registration is no longer required to maintain birthright citizenship, the consular report of birth abroad remains the primary means by which children born abroad may obtain official acknowledgement of their citizenship. Once acknowledged as U.S. citizens, they need not pursue the naturalization process to obtain the rights and privileges of citizenship in this country. Regulation of the report is thus "appropriate" and "plainly adapted" to the exercise of the naturalization power.

By contrast, regulation of the report bears no relationship to the President's residual foreign affairs power. It has no historical pedigree uniquely associated with the President, contains no communication directed at a foreign power, and is primarily used for domestic purposes. To the extent that a citizen born abroad seeks a document to use as evidence of his citizenship abroad, he must obtain a passport.

Because regulation of the consular report of birth abroad is justified as an exercise of Congress' powers under the Naturalization and Necessary and Proper Clauses and does not fall within the President's foreign affairs powers, §214(d)'s treatment of that document is constitutional.

III

The majority . . . relies on a variation of the recognition power. . . . But I cannot join the majority's analysis because no act of recognition is implicated here. . . .

Assuming for the sake of argument that listing a non-recognized foreign sovereign as a citizen's place of birth on a U.S. passport could have the effect of recognizing that sovereign under international law, no such recognition would occur under the circumstances presented here. The United States has recognized Israel as a foreign sovereign since May 14, 1948. That the United States has subsequently declined to acknowledge Israel's sovereignty over Jerusalem has not changed its recognition of Israel as a sovereign state. And even if the United States were to acknowledge Israel's sovereignty over Jerusalem, that action would not change its recognition of Israel as a sovereign state. That is because the United States has already afforded Israel the rights and responsibilities attendant to its status as a sovereign State. Taking a different position on the Jerusalem question will have no effect on that recognition.

Perhaps recognizing that a formal recognition is not implicated here, the majority reasons that, if the Executive's exclusive recognition power "is to mean anything, it must mean that the President not only makes the initial, formal recognition determination but also that he may maintain that determination in his and his agent's statements." By "alter [ing] the President's statements on matters of recognition or forc[ing] him to contradict them," the majority reasons, "Congress in effect would exercise the recognition power." This argument stretches the recognition power beyond all recognition. Listing a Jerusalem-born citizen's place of birth as "Israel" cannot amount to recognition because the United States already recognizes Israel as an international person. . . .

Adhering to the Constitution's allocation of powers leads me to reach a different conclusion in this case from my colleagues: Section 214(d) can be constitutionally applied to consular reports of birth abroad, but not passports. I therefore respectfully concur in the judgment in part and dissent in part.

Chief Justice ROBERTS, with whom Justice ALITO joins, dissenting.

Today's decision is a first: Never before has this Court accepted a President's direct defiance of an Act of Congress in the field of foreign affairs. We have instead stressed that the President's power reaches "its lowest ebb" when he contravenes the express will of Congress, "for what is at stake is the equilibrium established by our constitutional system." *Youngstown Sheet & Tube Co. v. Sawyer* (Jackson, J., concurring).

Justice SCALIA's principal dissent, which I join in full, refutes the majority's unprecedented holding in detail. I write separately to underscore the stark nature of the Court's error on a basic question of separation of powers.

[T]he Executive may disregard "the expressed or implied will of Congress" only if the Constitution grants him a power "at once so conclusive and preclusive" as to "disabl[e] the Congress from acting upon the subject." *Youngstown* (Jackson, J., concurring).

Assertions of exclusive and preclusive power leave the Executive "in the least favorable of possible constitutional postures," and such claims have been "scrutinized with caution" throughout this Court's history. For our first 225 years, no President prevailed when contradicting a statute in the field of foreign affairs. See *Medellín v. Texas,* 552 U.S. 491 (2008); *Hamdan v. Rumsfeld,* 548 U.S. 557 (2006); *Youngstown* (majority opinion); *Little v. Barreme,* 2 Cranch 170 (1804).

In this case, the President claims the exclusive and preclusive power to recognize foreign sovereigns. The Court devotes much of its analysis to accepting the Executive's contention. I have serious doubts about that position. The majority places great weight on the Reception Clause, which directs that the Executive "shall receive Ambassadors and other public Ministers." Art. II, §3. But that provision, framed as an obligation rather than an authorization, appears alongside the *duties* imposed on the President by Article II, Section 3, not the *powers* granted to him by Article II, Section 2. Indeed, the People ratified the Constitution with Alexander Hamilton's assurance that executive reception of ambassadors "is more a matter of dignity than of authority" and "will be without consequence in the administration of the government." The Federalist No. 69. In short, at the time of the founding, "there was no reason to view the reception clause as a source of discretionary authority for the president."

The majority's other asserted textual bases are even more tenuous. The President does have power to make treaties and appoint ambassadors. Art. II, §2. But those authorities are *shared* with Congress, so they hardly support an inference that the recognition power is *exclusive*.

Precedent and history lend no more weight to the Court's position. The majority cites dicta suggesting an exclusive executive recognition power, but acknowledges contrary dicta suggesting that the power is shared. When the best you can muster is conflicting dicta, precedent can hardly be said to support your side.

As for history, the majority admits that it too points in both directions. Some Presidents have claimed an exclusive recognition power, but others have expressed uncertainty about whether such preclusive authority exists. Those in the skeptical camp include Andrew Jackson and Abraham Lincoln, leaders not generally known for their cramped conceptions of Presidential power. Congress has also asserted its authority over recognition determinations at numerous points in history. The majority therefore falls short of demonstrating that "Congress has accepted" the President's exclusive recognition power. In any event, we have held that congressional acquiescence is only "pertinent" when the President acts in the absence of express congressional authorization, not when he asserts power to disregard a statute, as the Executive does here. *Medellín*; see *Dames & Moore.*

In sum, although the President has authority over recognition, I am not convinced that the Constitution provides the "conclusive and preclusive" power required to justify defiance of an express legislative mandate. *Youngstown* (Jackson, J., concurring). As the leading scholar on this issue has concluded, the "text, original understanding, post-ratification history, and structure of the Constitution do not support the . . . expansive claim that this executive power is plenary." Reinstein, Is the President's Recognition Power Exclusive? 86 Temp. L. Rev. 1, 60 (2013).

But even if the President does have exclusive recognition power, he still cannot prevail in this case, because the statute at issue *does not implicate recognition*. The relevant provision, §214(d), simply gives an American citizen born in Jerusalem the option to designate his place of birth as Israel "[f]or purposes of" passports and other documents. The State Department itself has explained that "identification" — not recognition — "is the principal reason that U.S. passports require 'place of birth.'" Congress has not disputed the Executive's assurances that §214(d) does not alter the longstanding United States position on Jerusalem. And the annals of diplomatic history record no examples of official recognition accomplished via optional passport designation.

The majority acknowledges both that the "Executive's exclusive power extends no further than his formal recognition determination" and that §214(d) does "not itself constitute a formal act of recognition." Taken together, these statements come close to a confession of error. The majority attempts to reconcile its position by reconceiving §214(d) as a "mandate that the Executive contradict his prior recognition determination in an official document issued by the Secretary of State." But as just noted, neither Congress nor the Executive Branch regards §214(d) as a recognition determination, so it is hard to see how the statute could contradict any such determination.

At most, the majority worries that there may be a *perceived* contradiction based on a *mistaken* understanding of the effect of §214(d), insisting that some "observers interpreted §214 as altering United States policy regarding Jerusalem." To afford controlling weight to such impressions, however, is essentially to subject a duly enacted statute to an international heckler's veto.

Moreover, expanding the President's purportedly exclusive recognition power to include authority to avoid potential misunderstandings of legislative enactments proves far too much. Congress could validly exercise its enumerated powers in countless ways that would create more severe perceived contradictions with Presidential recognition decisions than does §214(d). If, for example, the President recognized a particular country in opposition to Congress's wishes, Congress could declare war or impose a trade embargo on that country. A neutral observer might well conclude that these legislative actions had, to put it mildly, created a perceived contradiction with the President's recognition decision. And yet each of them would undoubtedly be constitutional. So too would statements by nonlegislative actors that might be seen to contradict the President's recognition positions, such as the declaration in a political party platform that "Jerusalem is and will remain the capital of Israel." Landler, Pushed by Obama, Democrats Alter Platform Over Jerusalem, N.Y. Times, Sept. 6, 2012, p. A14.

Ultimately, the only power that could support the President's position is the one the majority purports to reject: the "exclusive authority to conduct diplomatic relations." The Government offers a single citation for this allegedly exclusive power: *United States v. Curtiss–Wright Export Corp.* But as the majority rightly acknowledges, *Curtiss–Wright* did not involve a claim that the Executive could contravene a statute; it held only that he could act pursuant to a legislative delegation.

The expansive language in *Curtiss–Wright* casting the President as the "sole organ" of the Nation in foreign affairs certainly has attraction for members of the Executive Branch. . . . But our precedents have never accepted such a sweeping understanding of executive power. See *Hamdan*; *Dames & Moore*; *Youngstown* (majority opinion); *id.* (Jackson, J., concurring); cf. *Little* [*v. Barreme*].

Just a few Terms ago, this Court rejected the President's argument that a broad foreign relations power allowed him to override a state court decision that contradicted U.S. international law obligations. *Medellín*. If the President's so-called general foreign relations authority does not permit him to countermand a State's lawful action, it surely does not authorize him to disregard an express statutory directive enacted by Congress, which—unlike the States—has extensive foreign relations powers of its own. Unfortunately, despite its protest to the contrary, the majority today allows the Executive to do just that.

Resolving the status of Jerusalem may be vexing, but resolving this case is not. Whatever recognition power the President may have, exclusive or otherwise, is not implicated by §214(d). It has not been necessary over the past 225 years to definitively resolve a dispute between Congress and the President over the recognition power. Perhaps we could have waited another 225 years. But instead the majority strains to reach the question based on the mere possibility that observers overseas might misperceive the significance of the birthplace designation at issue in this case. And in the process, the Court takes the perilous step—for the first time in our history—of allowing the President to defy an Act of Congress in the field of foreign affairs.

I respectfully dissent.

Justice SCALIA, with whom THE CHIEF JUSTICE and Justice ALITO join, dissenting.

. . . .

I

[B]efore turning to Presidential power under Article II, I think it well to establish the statute's basis in congressional power under Article I. Congress's power to "establish an uniform Rule of Naturalization," Art. I, §8, cl. 4, enables it to grant American citizenship to someone born abroad. The naturalization power also enables Congress to furnish the people it makes citizens with papers verifying their citizenship—say a consular report of birth abroad (which certifies citizenship of an American born outside the United States) or a passport (which certifies citizenship for purposes of international travel). As the Necessary and Proper Clause confirms, every congressional power "carries with it all those incidental powers which are necessary to its complete and effectual execution." *Cohens v. Virginia*, 6 Wheat. 264, 429, 5 L.Ed. 257 (1821). Even on a miserly understanding of Congress's incidental authority, Congress may make grants of citizenship "effectual" by providing for the issuance of certificates authenticating them.

One would think that if Congress may grant Zivotofsky a passport and a birth report, it may also require these papers to record his birthplace as "Israel." The birthplace specification promotes the document's citizenship-authenticating function by identifying the bearer, distinguishing people with similar names but different birthplaces from each other, helping authorities uncover identity fraud, and facilitating retrieval of the Government's citizenship records. To be sure, recording Zivotofsky's birthplace as "Jerusalem" rather than "Israel" would fulfill these objectives, but when faced with alternative ways to carry its powers into execution, Congress has the "discretion" to choose the one it deems "most beneficial to the people." *McCulloch v. Maryland.* It thus has the right to decide that recording birthplaces as "Israel" makes for better foreign policy. Or that regardless of international politics, a passport or birth report should respect its bearer's conscientious belief that Jerusalem belongs to Israel.

No doubt congressional discretion in executing legislative powers has its limits; Congress's chosen approach must be not only "necessary" to carrying its powers into execution, but also "proper." Congress thus may not transcend boundaries upon legislative authority stated or implied elsewhere in the Constitution. But as we shall see, §214(d) does not transgress any such restriction.

II

The Court frames this case as a debate about recognition. Recognition is a sovereign's official acceptance of a status under international law. A sovereign might recognize a foreign entity as a state, a regime as the other state's government, a place as part of the other state's territory, rebel forces in the other state as a belligerent power, and so on. President Truman recognized Israel as a state in 1948, but Presidents have consistently declined to recognize Jerusalem as a part of Israel's (or any other state's) sovereign territory.

The Court holds that the Constitution makes the President alone responsible for recognition and that §214(d) invades this exclusive power. I agree that the Constitution *empowers* the President to extend recognition on behalf of the United States, but I find it a much harder question whether it makes that power exclusive. The Court tells us that "the weight of historical evidence" supports exclusive executive authority over "the formal determination of recognition." But even with its attention confined to formal recognition, the Court is forced to admit that "history is not all on one side." To take a stark example, Congress legislated in 1934 to grant independence to the Philippines, which were then an American colony. 48 Stat. 456. In the course of doing so, Congress directed the President to "recognize the independence of the Philippine Islands as a separate and self-governing nation" and to "acknowledge the authority and control over the same of the government instituted by the people thereof." Constitutional? And if Congress may control recognition when exercising its power "to dispose of . . . the Territory or other Property belonging to the United States," Art. IV, §3, cl. 2, why not when exercising other enumerated powers? Neither text nor history nor precedent yields a clear answer to these questions. Fortunately, I have no need to confront these matters today — nor does the Court — because §214(d) plainly does not concern recognition.

Recognition is more than an announcement of a policy. Like the ratification of an international agreement or the termination of a treaty, it is a formal legal act with effects under international law. It signifies acceptance of an international status, and it makes a commitment to continued acceptance of that status and respect for any attendant rights. "Its legal effect is to create an estoppel. By granting recognition, [states] debar themselves from challenging in future whatever they have previously acknowledged." In order to extend recognition, a state must perform an act that unequivocally manifests that intention. That act can consist of an express conferral of recognition, or one of a handful of acts that by international custom imply recognition — chiefly, entering into a bilateral treaty, and sending or receiving an ambassador.

To know all this is to realize at once that §214(d) has nothing to do with recognition. Section 214(d) does not require the Secretary to make a formal declaration about Israel's sovereignty over Jerusalem. And nobody suggests that international custom infers acceptance of sovereignty from the birthplace designation on a passport or birth report, as it does from bilateral treaties or exchanges of ambassadors. Recognition would preclude the United States (as a matter of international law) from later contesting Israeli sovereignty over Jerusalem. But making a notation in a passport or birth report does not encumber the Republic with any international obligations. It leaves the Nation free (so far as international law is concerned) to change its mind in the future. That would be true even if the statute required *all* passports to list "Israel." But in fact it requires only those passports to list "Israel" for which the citizen (or his guardian) *requests* "Israel"; all the rest, under the Secretary's policy, list "Jerusalem." It is utterly impossible for this deference to private requests to constitute an act that unequivocally manifests an intention to grant recognition.

Section 214(d) performs a more prosaic function than extending recognition. Just as foreign countries care about what our Government has to say about their borders, so too American citizens often care about what our Government has to say about their identities. The State Department does not grant or deny recognition in order to accommodate these individuals, but it does make exceptions to its rules about how it records birthplaces. Although normal protocol requires specifying the bearer's country of birth in his passport, the State Department will, if the bearer protests, specify the city of birth instead — so that an Irish nationalist may have his birthplace recorded as "Belfast" rather than "United Kingdom," And although normal protocol requires specifying the country with *present* sovereignty over the bearer's place of birth, a special exception allows a bearer born before 1948 in what was then Palestine to have his birthplace listed as "Palestine." Section 214(d) requires the State Department to make a further accommodation. Even though the Department normally refuses to specify a country that lacks recognized sovereignty over the bearer's birthplace, it must suspend that policy upon the request of an American citizen born in Jerusalem. Granting a request to specify "Israel" rather than "Jerusalem" does not recognize Israel's sovereignty over Jerusalem, just as granting a request to specify "Belfast" rather than "United Kingdom" does not derecognize the United Kingdom's sovereignty over Northern Ireland.

The best indication that §214(d) does not concern recognition comes from the State Department's policies concerning Taiwan. According to the Solicitor General, the United States "acknowledges the Chinese position" that Taiwan is a part of China, but "does not take a position" of its own on that issue. Even so, the State Department has for a long time recorded the birthplace of a citizen born in Taiwan as "China." It indeed *insisted* on doing so until Congress passed a law (on which §214(d) was modeled) giving citizens the option to have their birthplaces recorded as "Taiwan." See §132, 108 Stat. 395, as amended by §1(r), 108 Stat. 4302. The Solicitor General explains that the designation "China" "involves a geographic description, not an assertion that Taiwan is . . . part of sovereign China." Quite so. Section 214(d) likewise calls for nothing beyond a "geographic description"; it does not require the Executive even to assert, never mind formally recognize, that Jerusalem is a part of sovereign Israel. Since birthplace specifications in citizenship documents are matters within Congress's control, Congress may treat Jerusalem as a part of Israel when regulating the recording of birthplaces, even if the President does not do so when extending recognition. Section 214(d), by the way, expressly directs the Secretary to "record the place of birth as Israel" "*[f]or purposes of* the registration of birth, certification of nationality, or issuance of a passport." (Emphasis added.) And the law bears the caption, "Record of Place of Birth as Israel *for Passport Purposes.*" (Emphasis added.) Finding recognition in this provision is rather like finding admission to the Union in a provision that treats American Samoa as a State for purposes of a federal highway safety program.

III

The Court complains that §214(d) requires the Secretary of State to issue official documents implying that Jerusalem is a part of Israel; that it appears in a section of the statute bearing the title "United States Policy with Respect to Jerusalem as the Capital of Israel"; and that foreign "observers interpreted [it] as altering United States policy regarding Jerusalem." But these features do not show that §214(d) recognizes Israel's sovereignty over Jerusalem. They show only that the law displays symbolic support for Israel's territorial claim. That symbolism may have tremendous significance as a matter of international diplomacy, but it makes no difference as a matter of constitutional law.

Even if the Constitution gives the President sole power to extend recognition, it does not give him sole power to make all decisions relating to foreign disputes over sovereignty. To the contrary, a fair reading of Article I allows Congress to decide for itself how its laws should handle these controversies. Read naturally, power to "regulate Commerce with foreign Nations," §8, cl. 3, includes power to regulate imports from Gibraltar as British goods or as Spanish goods. Read naturally, power to "regulate the Value . . . of foreign Coin," §8, cl. 5, includes power to honor (or not) currency issued by Taiwan. And so on for the other enumerated powers. These are not airy hypotheticals. A trade statute from 1800, for example, provided that "the whole of the island of Hispaniola" — whose status was then in controversy — "shall for purposes of [the] act be considered as a dependency of the French Republic." §7, 2 Stat. 10. In 1938, Congress allowed admission of the Vatican City's public records in federal courts, decades before the United States extended formal recognition. ch. 682, 52 Stat. 1163. The Taiwan Relations Act of 1979 grants Taiwan capacity to sue and be sued, even though the United States does not recognize it as a state. 22 U.S.C. §3303(b)(7). Section 214(d) continues in the same tradition.

The Constitution likewise does not give the President exclusive power to determine which claims to statehood and territory "are legitimate in the eyes of the United States." Congress may express its own views about these matters by declaring war, restricting trade, denying foreign aid, and much else besides. To take just one example, in 1991, Congress responded to Iraq's invasion of Kuwait by enacting a resolution authorizing use of military force. 105 Stat. 3. No doubt the resolution reflected Congress's views about the legitimacy of Iraq's territorial claim. The preamble referred to Iraq's "illegal occupation" and stated that "the international community has demanded . . . that Kuwait's independence and legitimate government be restored." These statements are far more categorical than the caption "United States Policy with Respect to Jerusalem as the Capital of Israel." Does it follow that the authorization of the use of military force invaded the President's exclusive powers? Or that it would have done so had the President recognized Iraqi sovereignty over Kuwait?

History does not even support an exclusive Presidential power to make what the Court calls "formal statements" about "the legitimacy of a state or government and its territorial bounds." For a long time, the Houses of Congress have made formal statements announcing their own positions on these issues, again without provoking constitutional objections. A recent resolution expressed the House of Representatives' "strong support for the legitimate, democratically-elected Government of Lebanon" and condemned an "illegitimate" and "unjustifiable" insurrection by "the terrorist group Hizballah." H. Res. 1194, 110th Cong, 2d Sess., 1, 4 (2008). An earlier enactment declared "the sense of the Congress that . . . Tibet . . . is an occupied country under the established principles of international law" and that "Tibet's true representatives are the Dalai Lama and the Tibetan Government in exile." §355, 105 Stat. 713 (1991). After Texas won independence from Mexico, the Senate resolved that "the State of Texas having established and maintained an independent Government, . . . it is expedient and proper . . . that the independent political existence of the said State be acknowledged by the Government of the United States." Cong. Globe, 24th Cong., 2d Sess., 83 (1837).

In the final analysis, the Constitution may well deny Congress power to recognize — the power to make an international commitment accepting a foreign entity as a state, a regime as its government, a place as a part of its territory, and so on. But whatever else §214(d) may do, it plainly does not make (or require the President to make) a commitment accepting Israel's sovereignty over Jerusalem.

IV

The Court does not try to argue that §214(d) extends recognition; nor does it try to argue that the President holds the exclusive power to make all nonrecognition decisions relating to the status of Jerusalem. As just shown, these arguments would be impossible to make with a straight face.

The Court instead announces a rule that is blatantly gerrymandered to the facts of this case. It concludes that, in addition to the exclusive power to make the "formal recognition determination," the President holds an ancillary exclusive power "to control . . . formal statements by the Executive Branch acknowledging the legitimacy of a state or government and its territorial bounds." It follows, the Court explains, that Congress may not "requir[e] the President to contradict an earlier recognition determination in an official document issued by the Executive Branch." So requiring imports from Jerusalem to be taxed like goods from Israel is fine, but requiring Customs to issue an official invoice to that effect is not? Nonsense.

Recognition is a type of legal act, not a type of statement. It is a leap worthy of the Mad Hatter to go from exclusive authority over making legal commitments about sovereignty to exclusive authority over making statements or issuing documents about national borders. The Court may as well jump from power over issuing declaratory judgments to a monopoly on writing law-review articles.

No consistent or coherent theory supports the Court's decision. At times, the Court seems concerned with the possibility of congressional interference with the President's ability to extend or withhold legal recognition. The Court concedes, as it must, that the notation required by §214(d) "would not itself constitute a formal act of recognition." It still frets, however, that Congress *could* try to regulate the President's "statements" in a way that "override[s] the President's recognition determination." But "[t]he circumstance, that . . . [a] power may be abused, is no answer. All powers may be abused." 2 J. Story, Commentaries on the Constitution of the United States §921, p. 386 (1833). What matters is whether *this* law interferes with the President's ability to withhold recognition. It would be comical to claim that it does. The Court identifies no reason to believe that the United States — or indeed any other country — uses the place-of-birth field in passports and birth reports as a forum for performing the act of recognition. That is why nobody thinks the United States withdraws recognition from Canada when it accommodates a Quebec nationalist's request to have his birthplace recorded as "Montreal."

To the extent doubts linger about whether the United States recognizes Israel's sovereignty over Jerusalem, §214(d) leaves the President free to dispel them by issuing a disclaimer of intent to recognize. A disclaimer always suffices to prevent an act from effecting recognition. Restatement (Second) of Foreign Relations Law of the United States §104(1) (1962). Recall that an earlier law grants citizens born in Taiwan the right to have their birthplaces recorded as "Taiwan." The State Department has complied with the law, but states in its Foreign Affairs Manual: "The United States does not officially recognize Taiwan as a 'state' or 'country,' although passport issuing officers may enter 'Taiwan' as a place of birth." Nothing stops a similar disclaimer here.

At other times, the Court seems concerned with Congress's failure to give effect to a recognition decision that the President has already made. The Court protests, for instance, that §214(d) "directly contradicts" the President's refusal to recognize Israel's sovereignty over Jerusalem. But even if the Constitution empowers the President alone to extend recognition, it nowhere obliges Congress to align its laws with the President's recognition decisions. Because the President and Congress are "perfectly co-ordinate by the terms of their common commission," The Federalist No. 49 (Madison), the President's use of the recognition power does not constrain Congress's use of its legislative powers.

Congress has legislated without regard to recognition for a long time and in a range of settings. For example, responding in 1817 and 1818 to revolutions in Latin America, Congress amended federal neutrality laws—which originally prohibited private military action for or against *recognized* states—to prohibit private hostilities against *unrecognized* states too. ch. 58, 3 Stat. 370; ch. 88, 3 Stat. 447; see *The Three Friends,* 166 U.S. 1, 52–59 (1897). Legislation from 90 years ago provided for the revision of national immigration quotas upon one country's surrender of territory to another, even if "the transfer . . . has not been recognized by the United States." §12(c), 43 Stat. 161 (1924). Federal law today prohibits murdering a foreign government's officials, 18 U.S.C. §1116, counterfeiting a foreign government's bonds, §478, and using American vessels to smuggle goods in violation of a foreign government's laws, §546—all "irrespective of recognition by the United States," §§11, 1116. Just as Congress may legislate independently of recognition in all of those areas, so too may it legislate independently of recognition when regulating the recording of birthplaces.

The Court elsewhere objects that §214(d) interferes with the autonomy and unity of the Executive Branch, setting the branch against itself. The Court suggests, for instance, that the law prevents the President from maintaining his neutrality about Jerusalem in "his and his agent's statements." That is of no constitutional significance. As just shown, Congress has power to legislate without regard to recognition, and where Congress has the power to legislate, the President has a duty to "take Care" that its legislation "be faithfully executed," Art. II, §3. It is likewise "the duty of the secretary of state to conform to the law"; where Congress imposes a responsibility on him, "he is so far the officer of the law; is amenable to the laws for his conduct; and cannot at his discretion sport away the vested rights of others." *Marbury v. Madison.* The Executive's involvement in carrying out this law does not affect its constitutionality; the Executive carries out every law.

The Court's error could be made more apparent by applying its reasoning to the President's power "to make Treaties," Art. II, §2, cl. 2. There is no question that Congress may, if it wishes, pass laws that openly flout treaties made by the President. *Head Money Cases,* 112 U.S. 580 (1884). Would anyone have dreamt that the President may refuse to carry out such laws—or, to bring the point closer to home, refuse to execute federal courts' judgments under such laws—so that the Executive may "speak with one voice" about the country's international obligations? To ask is to answer. Today's holding puts the implied power to recognize territorial claims (which the Court infers from the power to recognize states, which it infers from the responsibility to receive ambassadors) on a higher footing than the express power to make treaties. And this, even though the Federalist describes the making of treaties as a "delicate and important prerogative," but the reception of ambassadors as "more a matter of dignity than of authority," "a circumstance which will be without consequence in the administration of the government." The Federalist No. 69 (Hamilton).

In the end, the Court's decision does not rest on text or history or precedent. It instead comes down to "functional considerations"—principally the Court's perception that the Nation "must speak with one voice" about the status of Jerusalem. The vices of this mode of analysis go beyond mere lack of footing in the Constitution. Functionalism of the sort the Court practices today will *systematically* favor the unitary President over the plural Congress in disputes involving foreign affairs. It is possible that this approach will make for more effective foreign policy, perhaps as effective as that of a monarchy. It is certain that, in the long run, it will erode the structure of separated powers that the People established for the protection of their liberty.

V

Justice THOMAS's concurrence deems §214(d) constitutional to the extent it regulates birth reports, but unconstitutional to the extent it regulates passports. The concurrence finds no congressional power that would extend to the issuance or contents of passports. Including the power to regulate foreign commerce—even though passports facilitate the transportation of passengers, "a part of our commerce with foreign nations," *Henderson v. Mayor of New York,* 92 U.S. 259 (1876). Including the power over naturalization—even though passports issued to citizens, like birth reports, "have the same force and effect as proof of United States citizenship as certificates of naturalization," 22 U.S.C. §2705. Including the power to enforce the Fourteenth Amendment's guarantee that "[a]ll persons born or naturalized in the United States . . . are citizens of the United States"—even though a passport provides evidence of citizenship and so helps enforce this guarantee abroad. Including the power to exclude persons from the territory of the United States, see Art. I, §9, cl. 1—even though passports are the principal means of identifying citizens entitled to entry. Including the powers under which Congress has restricted the ability of various people to leave the country (fugitives from justice, for example, see 18 U.S.C. §1073)—even though passports are the principal means of controlling exit. Including the power to "make all needful Rules and Regulations respecting the Territory or other Property belonging to the United States," Art. IV, §3, cl. 2—even though "[a] passport remains at all times the property of the United States," 7 FAM §1317 (2013). The concurrence's stingy interpretation of the enumerated powers forgets that the Constitution does not "partake of the prolixity of a legal code," that "only its great outlines [are] marked, its important objects designated, and the minor ingredients which compose those objects [left to] be deduced from the nature of the objects themselves." *McCulloch*. It forgets, in other words, "that it is a *constitution* we are expounding." *Ibid.*

. . . .

[T]he concurrence says that passports have a "historical pedigree uniquely associated with the President." This statement overlooks the reality that, until Congress restricted the issuance of passports to the State Department in 1856, "passports were also issued by governors, mayors, and even . . . notaries public." To be sure, early Presidents granted passports without express congressional authorization. But this point establishes Presidential authority over passports in the face of congressional *silence,* not Presidential authority in the face of congressional *opposition.* Early in the Republic's history, Congress made it a crime for a consul to "grant a passport or other paper certifying that any alien, knowing him or her to be such, is a citizen of the United States." §8, 2 Stat. 205 (1803). Closer to the Civil War, Congress expressly authorized the granting of passports, regulated passport fees, and prohibited the issuance of passports to foreign citizens. §23, 11 Stat. 60–61 (1856). Since then, Congress has made laws about eligibility to receive passports, the duration for which passports remain valid, and even the type of paper used to manufacture passports. 22 U.S.C. §§212, 217a; §617(b), 102 Stat. 1755. (The concurrence makes no attempt to explain how these laws were supported by congressional powers other than those it rejects in the present case.) This Court has held that the President may not curtail a citizen's travel by withholding a passport, *except on grounds approved by Congress. Kent v. Dulles,* 357 U.S. 116 (1958). History and precedent thus refute any suggestion that the Constitution disables Congress from regulating the President's issuance and formulation of passports.

The concurrence adds that a passport "contains [a] communication directed at a foreign power." The "communication" in question is a message that traditionally appears in each passport (though no statute, to my knowledge, expressly requires its inclusion): "The Secretary of State of the United States of America hereby requests all whom it may concern to permit the citizen/national of the United States named herein to pass without delay or hindrance and in case of need to give all lawful aid and protection." I leave it to the reader to judge whether a request to "all whom it may concern" qualifies as a "communication directed at a foreign power." Even if it does, its presence does not affect §214(d)'s constitutionality. Requesting protection is only a "subordinate" function of a passport. *Kent* [*v. Dulles*]. This subordinate function has never been thought to invalidate other laws regulating the contents of passports; why then would it invalidate this one?

That brings me, in analytic crescendo, to the concurrence's suggestion that *even if* Congress's enumerated powers otherwise encompass §214(d), and *even if* the President's power to regulate the contents of passports is not exclusive, the law might *still* violate the Constitution, because it "conflict[s]" with the President's passport policy. It turns the Constitution upside-down to suggest that in areas of shared authority, it is the executive policy that preempts the law, rather than the other way around. Congress *may* make laws necessary and proper for carrying into execution the President's powers, Art. I, §8, cl. 18, but the President *must* "take Care" that Congress's legislation "be faithfully executed," Art. II, §3. And Acts of Congress made in pursuance of the Constitution are the "supreme Law of the Land"; acts of the President (apart from treaties) are not. Art. VI, cl. 2. That is why Chief Justice Marshall was right to think that a law prohibiting the seizure of foreign ships trumped a military order requiring it. *Little v. Barreme,* 2 Cranch 170 (1804). It is why Justice Jackson was right to think that a President who "takes measures incompatible with the expressed or implied will of Congress" may "rely only upon his own constitutional powers *minus any constitutional powers of Congress over the matter.*" *Youngstown Sheet & Tube Co. v. Sawyer,* 343 U.S. 579, 637 (1952) (concurring opinion) (emphasis added). And it is why Justice THOMAS is wrong to think that even if §214(d) operates in a field of shared authority the President might still prevail.

Whereas the Court's analysis threatens congressional power over foreign affairs with gradual erosion, the concurrence's approach shatters it in one stroke. The combination of (a) the concurrence's assertion of broad, unenumerated "residual powers" in the President; (b) its parsimonious interpretation of Congress's enumerated powers; and (c) its even more parsimonious interpretation of Congress's authority to enact laws "necessary and proper for carrying into Execution" the President's executive powers; produces (d) a presidency more reminiscent of George III than George Washington.

International disputes about statehood and territory are neither rare nor obscure. Leading foreign debates during the 19th century concerned how the United States should respond to revolutions in Latin America, Texas, Mexico, Hawaii, Cuba. During the 20th century, attitudes toward Communist governments in Russia and China became conspicuous subjects of agitation. Disagreements about Taiwan, Kashmir, and Crimea remain prominent today. A President empowered to decide all questions relating to these matters, immune from laws embodying congressional disagreement with his position, would have uncontrolled mastery of a vast share of the Nation's foreign affairs.

That is not the chief magistrate under which the American People agreed to live when they adopted the national charter. They believed that "[t]he accumulation of all powers, legislative, executive, and judiciary, in the same hands, . . . may justly be pronounced the very definition of tyranny." The Federalist No. 47 (Madison). For this reason, they did not entrust either the President or Congress with sole power to adopt uncontradictable policies about *any* subject—foreign-sovereignty disputes included. They instead gave each political department its own powers, and with that the freedom to contradict the other's policies. Under the Constitution they approved, Congress may require Zivotofsky's passport and birth report to record his birthplace as Israel, even if that requirement clashes with the President's preference for neutrality about the status of Jerusalem.

I dissent.

Discussion.

1. *How much does* Zivotofsky *increase executive power over foreign affairs?* In his dissent, Chief Justice Roberts emphasizes that *Zivotofsky* is a rare case: The Court upholds presidential power in the face of a contrary legislative decision by Congress. This is "box three" of Jackson's *Youngstown* framework, in which the President's power is "at its lowest ebb."

But the power upheld in *Zivotofsky* is not all that extensive. It is the power to formally acknowledge on behalf of the nation that a particular political "entity possesses the qualifications for statehood" or "that a particular regime is the effective government of a state." The President's power of recognition also extends to the "territorial bounds" of the state, including which government has sovereign authority over a particular piece of territory, or whether, as in the case of Jerusalem, the United States wants to avoid taking any official position on this question at all. Six Justices held that this power is exclusive with the President, while the dissenters — the Chief Justice and Justices Scalia and Alito — assume that the President can make these determinations in the absence of a decision by Congress.

At the same time, the majority opinion goes out of its way to emphasize that, outside of the recognition power, Congress is a full partner in foreign affairs. Eight Justices agree that Congress can substantially undermine the President's decisions on foreign affairs — for example, by refusing to pass laws, withholding appropriations, failing to appoint an ambassador, imposing trade sanctions, or enacting other regulations of foreign commerce at odds with the President's wishes. (Justice Thomas's opinion does not address this issue.) And all of the Justices except Justice Thomas agree that, outside of the recognition authority, the President must obey laws passed by Congress in the field of international relations.

The majority also goes out of its way to rebuff the Secretary of State's assertion that "the President has 'exclusive authority to conduct diplomatic relations,' along with 'the bulk of foreign-affairs powers.' " It reinterprets *Curtiss-Wright*, the standard cite of advocates of executive power in foreign affairs: "*Curtiss-Wright* did not hold that the President is free from Congress' lawmaking power in the field of international relations. . . . In a world that is ever more compressed and interdependent, it is essential the congressional role in foreign affairs be understood and respected. For it is Congress that makes laws, and in countless ways its laws will and should shape the Nation's course. The Executive is not free from the ordinary controls and checks of Congress merely because foreign affairs are at issue. . . . It is not for the President alone to determine the whole content of the Nation's foreign policy." Thus, although it supported presidential authority in a narrow class of cases, *Zivotofsky* contains far more language limiting executive power.

2. *Has Congress acquiesced? Two kinds of acquiescence.* The majority, reasoning from inter-branch convention, argues that "[t]he weight of historical evidence indicates Congress has accepted that the power to recognize foreign states and governments and their territorial bounds is exclusive to the Presidency." But there are two ways that a branch might acquiesce to the decisions of another

branch. First, Congress might agree with the President's *particular decision on the merits*, or it might defer to the President's judgment for prudential reasons. In the same way, the President might defer to Congress on the merits or for prudential reasons. The majority gives examples in which Presidents Jackson and Lincoln deferred to Congress's judgments about recognition. In the alternative, a branch might acquiesce in the other branch's *right to decide* the matter *in general*. How do we tell which kind of acquiescence has occurred? The mere fact that Congress has generally gone along with the President does not mean that it has surrendered its powers completely; after all, the majority does not believe that Jackson's and Lincoln's examples show that the president acquiesced to congressional power over recognition.

Is the case for congressional acquiescence weaker or stronger than the case for congressional acquiescence in *NLRB v. Noel Canning* (discussed in the Casebook, pp. 974-983)? On the general problem of how to interpret inter-branch conventions and acquiescence, see Curtis A. Bradley and Neil S. Siegel, After Recess: Historical Practice, Textual Ambiguity, and Constitutional Adverse Possession, 2014 Supreme Court Review 1 (2014).

3. *Did the Court need to hold that the president's recognition power is exclusive?* The strongest argument for the result in the case does not come from the history of inter-branch conventions or judicial precedents. It is structural. Successful conduct of international relations requires that the U.S government has the ability to make clear commitments to other nations. (See the discussion of the Treaty Power in *Bond v. United States*, Casebook, pp. 776-780.) For this reason, Congress does not have the power to force the President or his employees to contradict his previous statements about recognition; it can't force the President to muddy the waters through making contradictory claims about recognition. As Justice Kennedy puts it, "Congress may not enact a law that directly contradicts [the Executive's formal recognition determination]. Congress may . . . express its disagreement with the President in myriad ways. For example, it may enact an embargo, decline to confirm an ambassador, or even declare war. But none of these acts would alter the President's recognition decision. If Congress may not pass a law, speaking in its own voice, that effects formal recognition, then it follows that it may not force the President himself to contradict his earlier statement. That congressional command would not only prevent the Nation from speaking with one voice but also prevent the Executive itself from doing so in conducting foreign relations."

So far, so good. But does the law in *Zivotofsky* actually do this? None of the Justices argued that the law in question formally contradicted the president's recognition determination. At most we might that the law forces the President's agents to contradict his determination by issuing passports that say "Israel." Therefore, Marty Lederman suggests that the Court might easily have adopted a narrower holding. Whatever Congress's power to regulate foreign policy, or even to have a say on questions of recognition, "when its views contradict the President's, Congress does not have the power to control the Executive's conduct of *diplomacy*, that is, of deciding what to say to foreign officials. Or, even narrower than that, the Court could have held that Congress at a minimum cannot compel the President to *contradict* himself when engaged in diplomatic activity." Marty Lederman, Thoughts on *Zivotofsky*, Part Five: Why did the majority choose to decide whether the President's "recognition" power is exclusive?, Just Security, June 13, 2015, at http://justsecurity.org/23825/thoughts-zivotofsky-part-five-majority-choose-decide-presidents-recognition-power-exclusive/

4. *Two visions of the "unitary executive."* This narrower holding — and the structural reasoning behind it — makes particular sense against the backdrop of two contrasting visions of executive power, both of which are confusingly called the theory of the "unitary executive." The first theory concerns executive power to direct subordinates. Subject to Congressional statutes that organize the executive branch and create its departments, the President decides how to run the Executive branch and deploy executive power. The executive is "unitary" because all executive power rests in the President and in the President's agents, whom the President (ultimately) directs. (See the discussion in *Morrison v. Olson*, Casebook at pp. 950-969.) Lederman's approach is fully consistent with this model — Congress may not force the President's employees to take a different position on recognition than their boss.

The second theory that is sometimes called the "unitary executive" is most often associated with scholars like Professor John Yoo and with the George W. Bush Administration. This theory holds that when the President exercises express or implied executive powers granted under Article II, Congress may not interfere with those powers, and laws to the contrary are unconstitutional. Justice Thomas's opinion is closest to this model. Yet, as we have seen, the other eight Justices reject it.

5. *Broader and narrower structural arguments.* The most powerful argument for the result in *Zivotofsky* is a fairly narrow structural argument — Congress can't make the President's employees contradict him or her in diplomatic statements. However, the majority also makes a second, much broader structural argument — that the nation must speak with one voice and that the President is that voice. The very breadth of this argument may cause a few problems down the road.

Justice Kennedy argues that "[r]ecognition is a topic on which the Nation must "'speak . . . with one voice.'". He then insists that "[t]hat voice must be the President's." Why? Kennedy offers standard arguments about the special features of executive power:

> Between the two political branches, only the Executive has the characteristic of unity at all times. And with unity comes the ability to exercise, to a greater degree, "[d]ecision, activity, secrecy, and dispatch." The Federalist No. 70 (A. Hamilton). The President is capable, in ways Congress is not, of engaging in the delicate and often secret diplomatic contacts that may lead to a decision on recognition. . . . . He is also better positioned to take the decisive, unequivocal action necessary to recognize other states at international law. These qualities explain why the Framers listed the traditional avenues of recognition — receiving ambassadors, making treaties, and sending ambassadors — as among the President's Article II powers.

Stated in such broad strokes, however, this argument might simultaneously prove both too little and too much. It might prove too little because there could be situations in which Congress deliberates and makes a firm determination about recognition that is inconsistent with the President's, for example, by over-riding a presidential veto. In that case, it's not clear why the President's greater energy and dispatch matter all that much. The question would be definitively settled, and the nation would speak with a single voice — Congress's, as embodied in federal law.

The argument might prove too much because the same logic would seem to apply equally to a wide range of other foreign policy issues beyond formal recognition. In all of those areas, however, *Zivotofsky* holds that Congress has a say, and can even work to undermine the president's carefully planned foreign policy. The problem is that in virtually every other area of foreign affairs, one can point to the importance of "one voice," and emphasize the president's superior ability to work with "decision, activity, secrecy and dispatch." If those arguments don't win in all of the other contexts of foreign policy, why should they win only in the context of formal statements of recognition?

On the other hand, if *Zivotofsky* is just a case that tells Congress that it can't force presidents to talk out of both sides of their mouth in conducting diplomatic relations — or direct the President's subordinates to disagree with their boss on questions of diplomacy — these problems are greatly reduced, if not eliminated.

Add the following at the end of p. 1083

Note: The Emoluments Clauses

President Donald Trump is unique among modern American presidents for the vast financial holdings he had accumulated at the time he assumed office. In contrast to other modern chief executives such as Barack Obama, most of his wealth has not been in the form of holdings of securities and mutual funds, which could, in theory, be converted into holdings placed in a blind trust. Instead, much of President Trump's wealth comes from his leadership of a family business and its various real estate holdings and licensing deals around the globe.

Traditionally, incoming presidents have worked with ethics counsels to place their assets in a blind trust or to otherwise minimize conflicts of interest during the period they are in office. Shortly after the 2016 election, Trump brushed aside concerns about conflicts of interest, stating that "the law is totally on my side, meaning, the president can't have a conflict of interest."[32] Nevertheless, on January 11, 2017, President Trump promised to distance himself from his

---

32. The Editors, Donald Trump's New York Times Interview: Full Transcript, N.Y. Times (Nov. 23, 2016), https://www.nytimes.com/2016/11/23/us/politics/trump-new-york-times-interview-transcript.html.

businesses, and to hand over operations to his two sons (although he would retain ownership); he also promised that the Trump Organization would not engage in any new deals in foreign countries while he was in office. Even so, his business affairs continue to be carried on by members of his immediate family who are in constant contact with the President,[33] the no-new-foreign-deals pledge has turned out to be an empty promise,[34] and far from being unaware of his holdings and how they are doing, the President regularly visits many of his properties.[35] Perhaps unsurprisingly, a number of foreign states and officials have switched their business to Trump-owned or -branded properties.

The U.S. Constitution contains two clauses that are designed to prevent financial conflicts of interest and both the appearance and the reality of financial corruption. These are the Foreign and Domestic Emoluments Clauses of Article I, section 9, clause 8, and Article 2, section 1, clause 7.

The Foreign Emoluments Clause, Article I, section 9, clause 8, provides that "no Person holding any Office of Profit or Trust under [the United States], shall, without the Consent of the Congress, accept of any present, Emolument, Office, or Title, of any kind whatever, from any King, Prince, or foreign State."

During the Philadelphia Convention, on August 23, 1787, Charles Pinckney "urged the necessity of preserving foreign Ministers & other officers of the U.S. independent of external influence," and he moved to insert a provision which ultimately became Article I, section 9, clause 8.[36] This language was similar to that in Article VI of the Articles of Confederation, except that the new version applied only to federal officers, and allowed Congress to authorize exceptions.[37] The proposed language was adopted without objection.

At the Virginia ratifying convention, Governor Randolph explained that "[t]his restriction was provided to prevent corruption. . . . An accident, which actually happened, operated in producing the restriction. A box was presented to our ambassador by the king of our allies. It was thought proper, in order to exclude corruption and foreign influence, to prohibit any one in office from receiving or holding any emoluments from foreign states."[38] Randolph was

---

33. For a summary as of July 2017, see Kate Brannen, Trump Family's Endless Conflicts of Interest: Chapter and Verse, Newsweek, July 3, 2017, at http://www.newsweek.com/trump-familys-endless-conflicts-interest-chapter-and-verse-631216 .

34. See Jeremy Venook, Donald Trump's Conflicts of Interest: A Crib Sheet, The Atlantic, Jun 28, 2017, at https://www.theatlantic.com/business/archive/2017/06/donald-trump-conflicts-of-interests/508382/.

35. Sam Petulla, Tracking President Trump's Visits to Trump Properties, NBC News, Jul 3 2017, at http://www.nbcnews.com/politics/donald-trump/how-much-time-trump-spending-trump-properties-n753366.

36. 2 The Records of the Federal Convention of 1787 389 (Max Farrand ed., 1911).

37. Article VI provided: "[N]or shall any person holding any office of profit or trust under the United States, or any of them, accept any present, emolument, office or title of any kind whatever from any King, Prince or foreign State."

38. 2 The Debates of the Several State Conventions on the Adoption of the Federal Constitution 344 (Jonathan Elliot ed., 1937); 3 Farrand 327.

apparently referring to the gift of a very expensive diamond encrusted snuffbox, with a portrait of King Louis XVI, that had been given by the King to then-Ambassador Benjamin Franklin.[39]

The reason for prohibiting all such gifts in advance (at least without congressional "Consent"), Randolph explained, was that one could not rely on individual ministers to turn down such gifts when they were bestowed: "I believe, that if at that moment, when we were in harmony with the King of France, we had supposed that he was corrupting our ambassador, it might have disturbed that confidence, and diminished that mutual friendship, which contributed to carry us through the war."

In his commentaries on the Constitution, St. George Tucker, a Jeffersonian, pointed to the example of Charles II, who was said to be under the pay of Louis XIV: "In the reign of Charles the second of England, that prince, and almost all his officers of state were either actual pensioners of the court of France, or supposed to be under its influence, directly, or indirectly, from that cause. The reign of that monarch has been, accordingly, proverbially disgraceful to his memory." 1 St. George Tucker, Blackstone's Commentaries 295–96 & n.* (1803; reprint 1996). Tucker explained that "[t]he economy which ought to prevail in republican governments, with respects to salaries and other emoluments of office, might encourage the offer of presents from abroad, if the constitution and laws did not reprobate their acceptance."

The requirement of congressional consent serves two functions. First, it gives federal officials an excuse to turn down or donate gifts without offending foreign governments. Second, requiring Congress to consider the matter draws public attention to attempts to influence federal officials. Publicity gives federal officials incentives to avoid the appearance of impropriety. Moreover, even when Congress permits officials to accept foreign gifts or emoluments, the transparency that comes with congressional deliberation and approval makes it more likely that federal officials will not be influenced by a foreign state's generosity in their official conduct.

As of July 2017, Congress had not passed any resolutions with respect to Trump's holdings or income derived from them.

The Domestic Emoluments Clause of Article 2, section 1, clause 7, states that "The President shall, at stated Times, receive for his Services, a Compensation, which shall neither be increased nor diminished during the Period for which he shall have been elected, and he shall not receive within that Period any other Emolument from the United States, or any of them."

Unlike the Foreign Emoluments Clause, the Domestic Emoluments Clause applies only to the President, and Congress cannot make exceptions by giving its consent. In *The Federalist* 73, Alexander Hamilton explained that the requirement of fixed compensation was designed to prevent corruption of the President

---

39. Franklin requested and received permission to keep it, even though it is unclear from the text of the Articles of Confederation that Congress could give consent.

either by threats or temptations: Congress and the states "will have no power to alter it, either by increase or diminution, till a new period of service by a new election commences. They can neither weaken his fortitude by operating on his necessities, nor corrupt his integrity by appealing to his avarice. Neither the Union, nor any of its members, will be at liberty to give, nor will he be at liberty to receive, any other emolument than that which may have been determined by the first act."

Several lawsuits have been filed charging President Trump with violations of the Foreign and/or Domestic Emoluments Clause. One suit, *CREW v. Trump*, was brought by Citizens for Responsibility and Ethics in Washington (CREW), a progressive government-watchdog organization. They have been joined by an association of restaurants and restaurant workers and by a person who books events at various hotels that compete with Trump-branded properties for business from foreign guests and state officials staying in Washington, D.C. They allege that Trump's violations of the Foreign and Domestic Emoluments Clauses harm their economic interests.

A second suit, *District of Columbia v. Trump*, was brought by the Attorney Generals of the District of Columbia and Maryland, respectively. They argue that the President's Trump International Hotel in Washington, near the White House, draws business from taxpayer-financed convention centers and facilities in D.C. and Maryland. The hotel gives the President income both from foreign countries and officials, and from state and local government officials, who might be eager to please him.

D.C. and Maryland also argue that Trump's business practices generate pressure and competition among state and local governments to provide the Trump Organization with concessions and exemptions in taxation, environmental protection, land use, and zoning. This undermines their budgets, tax revenues, and regulatory authority. They argue that "the Domestic Emoluments Clause aims to prevent 'the United States, or any of them,' from feeling compelled (or being compelled) to confer private financial benefits on the President in order to compete for influence and favor."

A third suit, *Blumenthal v. Trump*, was brought by the Constitutional Accountability Center (CAC), a liberal public-interest organization devoted to constitutional issues. The plaintiffs in the suit include approximately 160 Congressmen and 30 senators, led by Connecticut Senator Richard Blumenthal and Michigan Congressman John Conyers. All are Democrats. The plaintiffs seek to enforce the Foreign Emoluments Clause. They argue that President Trump is receiving many different kinds of profits for his businesses from foreign governments and officials—many of whom wish to curry favor with him—but that the President has made no effort to seek Congress's permission or to provide Congress with the information necessary to judge whether he is in compliance with the Constitution. Their complaint argues that "[b]ecause Defendant has failed to come to Congress and seek consent before accepting foreign emoluments that have been confirmed through public reporting, it is impossible to know whether Defendant is accepting other foreign emoluments that have not yet been made public. Indeed, through his personal attorney, Defendant has indicated that he does not believe the Constitution requires him to seek or obtain Congress's consent before accepting benefits arising out of exchanges between foreign states and his businesses."

Discussion

1. *Standing.* All three suits raise important standing questions. Under the Supreme Court's modern doctrine, standing to bring suit under Article III of the Constitution requires that the plaintiff show three things: First, the plaintiff must have suffered an "injury in fact"—an invasion of a legally-protected interest which is (a) concrete and particularized, and (b) actual or imminent, not conjectural or hypothetical. Second, there must be a causal connection between the injury and the conduct complained of; the injury has to be fairly traceable to the challenged action of the defendant, and not the result of the independent action of some third party not before the court. Third, it must be likely, as opposed to merely speculative, that the injury will be redressed by a favorable decision. Lujan v. Defenders of Wildlife, 504 U. S. 555, 560-61 (1992). These three requirements are usually referred to for short as the requirements of (1) injury-in-fact, (2) causation and (3) redressability.

Do the *CREW* and *D.C.* plaintiffs have standing to challenge violations of the Foreign and Domestic Emoluments Clauses?

One might assume that the answer is yes, because the Emoluments Clauses are designed to benefit *all* Americans by ensuring that their elected officials are not unduly influenced by considerations that might conflict with the best interests of the nation as a whole. On this view, we are all injured if those officials are beholden to foreign powers or otherwise diverted from serving the public interest. The Supreme Court, however, has in recent decades repeatedly held that a "generalized grievance" in *seeing that officials obey the law*, suffered in common by all Americans, or by all taxpayers, is insufficient to establish Article III standing for any one of those aggrieved Americans. In such cases, the Court has reasoned, "the political process, rather than the judicial process, may provide the more appropriate remedy for a widely shared grievance."

Accordingly, the plaintiffs in the emoluments litigation would only have standing to challenge those violations that in some way affect them *personally*. So, for example, if the Philippines agrees to make it easier for the Trump Organization to build a new hotel in Manila that might produce lots of income, or Chinese officials decide to play on Trump golf courses in Scotland or New Jersey, it is not immediately apparent how such conduct would harm the plaintiffs personally and distinctly, even if President Trump's receipt of the income does violate the Foreign Emoluments Clause.

It is plausible to think that Trump's hotel in D.C. might hurt local businesses like the *CREW* plaintiffs because it draws away business from foreign and state officials eager to ingratiate themselves with the Trump Administration. But is the economic loss caused by Trump's acceptance of the extra profits? If a court required the Trump Organization to disgorge any profits from foreign and state officials, isn't it possible that at least some of these foreign and state officials would keep patronizing Trump's establishments anyway, just to please him? If so, then plaintiffs may not have shown causation and redressability. What is the plaintiffs' best response? (Hint: Consider changing the kind of remedy that plaintiffs seek.)[40] What do you make of D.C. and Maryland's other argument under the Domestic Emoluments Clause—that they are harmed by having to compete with other jurisdictions in offering tax breaks and regulatory concessions?[41]

Blumenthal v. Trump presents a different set of standing issues. Here the question is whether a group of individual members of Congress—not Congress as a whole or even one House—have standing to enforce the Foreign Emoluments Clause. In Raines v. Byrd, 521 U. S. 811 (1997), the Supreme Court held that six individual Members of Congress lacked standing to challenge the Line Item Veto Act. It "attach[ed] some importance to the fact that [the Raines plaintiffs had] not been authorized to represent their respective Houses of Congress." Id., at 829. "[I]ndeed," the Court observed, "both houses actively oppose[d] their suit." Id. Thus, the plaintiffs were asserting the institutional interests of Congress as a whole even though Congress did not want to assert those interests or did not believe that they were injured. By contrast, in Arizona Legislature v. Arizona Redistricting Commission, 135 S.Ct. 2652 (2015), the Supreme Court distinguished *Raines* and upheld the standing of the *entire* Arizona Legislature to protect its authority under the Elections Clause, Art. I, §4, cl. 1, to establish redistricting maps for federal House seats.[42] The Arizona legislature, the Court explained, "is an institutional plaintiff asserting an institutional injury, and it commenced this action after authorizing votes in both of its chambers." Is *Blumenthal v. Trump* closer to *Raines* or *Arizona Legislature*? Does the currently Republican-controlled Congress want to oversee Trump? If not, then does this mean that that the *Blumenthal* plaintiffs will have to wait until Trump's political opponents control both Houses of Congress?

2. *Political Question Doctrine.* The Supreme Court's 1962 decision in Baker v. Carr, 369 U.S. 186, 217 (1962) described six circumstances in which a legal issue might be nonjusticiable because it is a political question: (1) where the Constitution makes a textually demonstrable constitutional commitment of the

---

40. See Leah Littman, On Standing In CREW v. Trump Part I: Defining The Injury, Take Care, April 27, 2017, https://takecareblog.com/blog/on-standing-in-crew-v-trump-part-i-defining-the-injury.

41. There are additional theories of standing based on Maryland's sovereign and quasi-sovereign interests. For a discussion, see Laurence H. Tribe and Joshua Matz, Maryland and DC Have Standing to Sue Trump for Emoluments Violations, Take Care, June 12, 2017, https://takecareblog.com/blog/maryland-and-dc-have-standing-to-sue-trump-for-emoluments-violations.

42. See Art. I, §4, cl. 1 ("The Times, Places and Manner of holding Elections for Senators and Representatives, shall be prescribed in each State by the Legislature thereof"). The legislature argued that an Amendment to the Arizona Constitution by a statewide popular initiative, which had transferred the redistricting function to an expert commission, violated the Elections Clause.

issue to another branch of government; (2) where there is a lack of judicially dis-coverable and manageable standards for resolving it; (3) where the court would have to make a policy determination of a kind clearly for nonjudicial discretion; (4) where a decision would be disrespectful to coordinate branches of govern-ment; (5) where there is an unusual need to treat a political branch's decision as final; and (6) where it is necessary for the federal government to speak with one voice on an issue. In Zivotofsky v. Clinton, 132 S. Ct. 1421, 1427-28 (*Zivotofsky I*) (2012), the Court maintained that the first two of these six factors are virtually determinative, and emphasized that the political question doctrine is "a narrow exception to [the] rule" that "the Judiciary has a responsibility to decide cases properly before it, even those it 'would gladly avoid.'"

Whether a President has violated the Foreign Emoluments Clause may turn on whether Congress gives its consent. Therefore one might argue that the Constitution has assigned *to Congress* the exclusive power to decide whether something is an "emolument" and whether the President may accept it. Application of the Clause often implicates delicate foreign relations, which are inappropriate for courts to handle.

On the other hand, Congress's ability to bless what would otherwise be a vio-lation of the Emoluments Clause doesn't mean that Congress is the sole check on Presidential corruption. Moreover, Congress has by statute permitted a range of transactions for various federal officials, and cases construing these statutes are almost certainly justiciable.

In any case, this argument would not affect claims under the Domestic Emoluments Clause, under which congressional consent is immaterial. (Would it make sense if courts could adjudicate Domestic Emoluments Clause cases, but not those involving foreign enticements?)

A second and related argument for treating the clauses as non-justiciable is that, unless Congress specifically passes a statute governing gifts to Presidents, the sole remedy for violations of both clauses is impeachment and removal.

The problem with this theory is that it would give bad incentives to unscru-pulous Presidents.[43] If courts can rule on emoluments claims, presidents would have an incentive to get permission from both houses of Congress before accept-ing gifts from foreign governments. If the President does not wait, he or she will be subject to a lawsuit (assuming, of course, that someone has standing to sue). If the question is not justiciable, however, the incentives would work in the opposite direction. Presidents could accept gifts and dare Congress to impeach and remove (or they could just keep the income and gifts secret). It is politically very hard to impeach a president, and even harder to remove one. To be sure, Congress might try to pass a statute that limits the President's conduct and requires disclosure of income from foreign governments. But because the President can veto any such

---

43. Richard Primus, Two thoughts on the Government's Motion to Dismiss in the CREW emolu-ments case, Balkinization, June 9, 2017, https://balkin.blogspot.com/2017/06/two-thoughts-on-governments-motion-to.html .

law, Congress would have to obtain a two-thirds majority in both houses—a even larger majority in the House than is required for impeachment. In short, although the Clause contemplates that Presidents will not accept foreign gifts or emoluments unless both houses of Congress give permission, holding that the Clause is nonjusticiable would render this requirement effectively irrelevant.

3. *Does the Foreign Emoluments Clause apply to the President?* The text of the Domestic Emoluments Clause clearly applies to the President. It has long been assumed by Congress and the Executive Branch that the President holds an "Office of Profit or Trust under" the United States and therefore the Foreign Emoluments Clause applies to the President as well. Moreover, this reading is consistent with the central purpose of the Clause—to prevent foreign influence and corruption.

Nevertheless, Seth Barrett Tillman has recently argued that the Clause does not actually apply to the President, because although he is an "Officer," he does not hold an "Office of Profit or Trust under" the United States.[44] Tillman's view is that the latter group includes only appointed officials, not elected officials such as the President, Vice President, and members of Congress. Tillman points out that President George Washington received the key to the French Bastille and a portrait of Louis XVI from French officials without asking Congress's permission—apparently without anyone raising a constitutional objection. It is of course possible that Congress found it imprudent to object to Washington's probity; nevertheless these examples offer an argument from early practice that might gloss the text.

One difficulty with the argument is that it might prove too much.[45] If the President does not hold an "Office of Profit or Trust" under the United States, then the rest of the clause doesn't apply either. This means that foreign governments could hire the President as an employee, and give him or her foreign titles of nobility as well. The idea that the President could accept a foreign title from the King of England (for example) would have been unthinkable to the Framers. (Incidentally, the Titles of Nobility Clause, which immediately precedes the Foreign Emoluments Clause in Article I, section 9, clause 8, says only that "No Title of Nobility shall be granted by the *United States*." The ban on accepting foreign titles is in the Emoluments Clause.)

For this reason, the Justice Department has long taken the position that the President is bound by both the Foreign and the Domestic Emoluments Clauses. As a result, when President Barack Obama won the Nobel Prize in 2009 (along with an award of approximately 1.4 million dollars), it raised a Foreign Emoluments Clause question. The OLC issued an opinion explaining that he could keep the prize because the Nobel Committee that awards the Peace Prize was not a "King,

44. Seth Barrett Tillman, The Original Public Meaning Of The Foreign Emoluments Clause: A Reply To Professor Zephyr Teachout, 107 Nw. L. Rev. Colloquy 180 (2013).

45. See Marty Lederman, How the DOJ Brief in CREW v. Trump Reveals that Donald Trump is Violating the Foreign Emoluments Clause, Take Care, June 12, 2017, https://takecareblog.com/blog/how-the-doj-brief-in-crew-v-trump-reveals-that-donald-trump-is-violating-the-foreign-emoluments-clause.

Prince, or Foreign State" under the meaning of the Clause. Obama nevertheless donated the proceeds to charity.[46]

4. *What is an Emolument?* The final question is whether President Trump accepts an "emolument" when he benefits from profits flowing to Trump-owned and licensed businesses, or from concessions, benefits, and tax breaks to Trump-owned and licensed businesses.

John Mikhail has argued that the predominant meaning of the term "emolument" at the time of the founding was "anything of value," and that this is how the term was frequently used by Blackstone and by various Framers.[47] Under this definition, if the President receives anything of value from a foreign or state government, this violates the Foreign and Domestic Emoluments Clauses, respectively.

If one accepts this definition, however, it is still necessary to adopt some sort of limiting construction. Otherwise, the clauses would produce any number of implausible results. It would follow, for example, that federal officials could not, without congressional consent, own index or other mutual funds that included any companies that do business globally. A President could not own federal or state bonds because interest from the bonds would violate the Domestic Emoluments Clause. And officials could not receive royalties for books—even from books written and published before they took office—because some foreign or state government's library might have purchased the book. A simple reading of "emolument" as "anything of value" is too broad. Hence, the key substantive issue in *CREW* and other cases is what kind of limiting construction courts should adopt.

The employment theory. A relatively narrow construction would be that "emolument" refers only to compensation for services rendered in an employment or consulting relationship. Hence, the President violates the Foreign Emoluments Clause when he or she receives compensation for services arising out of an employment or consulting relationship with a foreign government. See Andy Grewal, The Foreign Emoluments Clause and the Chief Executive, SSRN, January 19, 2017, at https://papers.ssrn.com/sol3/papers.cfm?abstract_id=2902391. These situations, in which the President is directly in the pay of a foreign power, are likely to be very rare.

---

46. *See* Applicability of the Emoluments Clause and the Foreign Gifts and Decorations Act to the President's Receipt of the Nobel Peace Prize 33 Op. O.L.C. 1 (2009); Alister Bull and Mohammad Zargham, *Obama gives $1.4 million Nobel prize to 10 charities*, REUTERS, Mar 11th, 2010, http://www.reuters.com/article/us-obama-donation-idUSTRE62A5EN20100311.

47. John Mikhail, A Note on the Original Meaning of "Emolument," Balkinization, January 18, 2017, https://balkin.blogspot.com/2017/01/a-note-on-original-meaning-of-emolument.html; John Mikhail, Other uses of "emolument" in The Federalist (and the fallacy of affirming the consequent), Balkinization, January 25, 2017, https://balkin.blogspot.com/2017/01/other-uses-of-emolument-in-federalist.html ; John Mikhail, "Emolument" in Blackstone's Commentaries, May 28, 2017, https://balkin.blogspot.com/2017/05/emolument-in-blackstones-commentaries.html.

The nexus theory. In the *CREW* litigation, the Department of Justice has taken the view that an emolument need not require an employment or consulting relationship with a foreign government. It can also cover "benefits arising from services the President provides to [a] foreign state . . . as President (e.g., making executive decisions favorable to the paying foreign power)." "Neither the text nor the history of the Clauses," the DOJ explains, "shows that they were intended to reach benefits arising from a President's private business pursuits having nothing to do with his office or personal service to a foreign power." That is because "the evils sought to be prevented by the Clause are inducements in the forms of pecuniary compensation and other benefits for the President's services *as President*, as such benefits would pose the greatest danger of undermining the President's independence." Therefore, the DOJ argues, there must be a *nexus* between the payments or benefits that flow to the President and his or her office as President. Relying heavily on *one* definition in a handful of Founding-era dictionaries, the DOJ argues that an "emolument" includes any profit "*arising from* an office or employ" or the "receipt of value for services rendered or for a position held."

Under the DOJ's account, the fact that Trump obtains income from foreign officials staying at his hotels is not an emolument; nor is China's decision to authorize trademarks for Trump Organization businesses. The money does not flow to the President in his official capacity or because of any actions he has taken in his official capacity as President.

On the other hand, the CREW plaintiffs allege that foreign governments are shifting their business to Trump properties and that China has granted trademarks *in order to curry favor with the President*— that is, in the hope that he will use his official powers in ways that will benefit them (or not harm them). According to the CREW plaintiffs, then, the profits *do* "arise from" Trump's office, and thus satisfy even DOJ's definition, because the President receives these benefits as a result of his office, not in spite of it.[48]

To avoid this conclusion, the DOJ argues that plaintiffs must also show that the money flowed to Trump as compensation for *actions* he takes as President. It may be very difficult to prove that the President actually changed his decision-making because of the money flowing to his businesses from foreign governments. If the DOJ's nexus test requires this, it would make the Foreign Emoluments Clause largely unenforceable, absent proof of a deliberate quid pro quo.

The functional theory. A different view of the two clauses would be functional: an emolument is any income, gift or present that might have the potential of influencing or corrupting the integrity of the recipient, whether or not the income arises out of their actions as an officer.[49] This is the view that the Office

48. See Lederman, supra, note 9.
49. See Jane Chong, Reading the Office of Legal Counsel on Emoluments: Do Super-Rich Presidents Get a Pass?, Lawfare, July 1, 2017, https://lawfareblog.com/reading-office-legal-counsel-emoluments-do-super-rich-presidents-get-pass.

of Legal Counsel (OLC) took in a 1981 opinion about the Domestic Emoluments Clause.[50] It argued that President Reagan could receive California state retirement benefits arising from his service as governor of California because the income was already vested before he became President, and could not be withdrawn by the state. Therefore, there was no danger that it could influence his decisionmaking.

In 1993, the OLC held that the Foreign Emoluments Clause prevented members of the Administrative Conference (who are government officers operating in a federal agency) from drawing shares of their law firms' profits because those firms had clients who were foreign governments and money from client services went into the partnership pool.[51] The prohibition applied even though the officials "did not personally represent a foreign government, . . . had no personal contact with that client of the firm, [and] could not be said to be subject to the foreign government's 'control' in his or her activities on behalf of the partnership." Rather, the OLC argued, "[m]ore important . . . is the fact that the Conference member would draw a proportionate share of the partnership's pooled profits, which would include any profits the firm earned from representing its foreign governmental client. Because the amount the Conference member would receive from the partnership's profits would be a function of the amount paid to the firm by the foreign government, the partnership would in effect be a conduit for that government. Thus, some portion of the member's income could fairly be attributed to a foreign government." Presumably, the practical concern was that if a foreign government were unhappy with the Conference's work, it could switch law firms, affecting the partnership pool, and creating indirect pressure on the official from the partnership.

Which of these accounts best serves the purposes of the two Clauses? Which is likely to produce the most coherent and administrable doctrine?

Add the following at the end of p. 1091, Note: Presidential Impeachment

The materials on presidential impeachment have been moved to http://jackbalkin.yale.edu/sites/default/files/files/impeachmentmaterials1.pdf

---

50. President Reagan's Ability to Receive Retirement Benefits from the State of California, 5 Op. O.L.C. 187 (1981).

51. Applicability of the Emoluments Clause to Non-Government Members of ACUS, 17 Op. O.L.C. 114, 119 (1993).

Chapter 7

Race and the Equal Protection Clause

Insert the following on p. 1193 before Note: The Rise and Fall of the Political Process Doctrine:

TEXAS DEPARTMENT OF HOUSING AND COMMUNITY AFFAIRS V. INCLUSIVE COMMUNITIES PROJECT, INC., 135 S.Ct. 2507 (2015): [The Supreme Court, by a vote of 5-4, held that plaintiffs could bring disparate impact claims under the Fair Housing Act of 1968 (FHA), 82 Stat. 81, as amended, 42 U.S.C. §3601 *et seq.* The Fair Housing Act was the third of the great 1960s civil rights statutes. It was enacted in the wake of the assassination of Martin Luther King, Jr., and the Kerner Commission Report of 1968 that warned that "[o]ur Nation is moving toward two societies, one black, one white — separate and unequal."

The Inclusive Communities Project (ICP) sued the Texas Department of Housing and Community Affairs, alleging that alleging that the Department and its officers had caused continued segregated housing patterns by allocating too many tax credits to developers for housing in predominantly black inner-city areas and too few for housing in predominantly white suburban neighborhoods. Justice Kennedy's majority opinion argued that the language of the FHA was sufficiently similar to that of §703(a) of Title VII of the Civil Rights Act of 1964, and Section 4(a) of the Age Discrimination in Employment Act of 1967 (ADEA), 81 Stat. 602 *et seq.,* as amended. Disparate impact claims were available under both statutes. Justice Kennedy then went on to discuss the purposes of disparate impact liability and potential constitutional limitations.]

KENNEDY, J: Recognition of disparate-impact claims is consistent with the FHA's central purpose. *Griggs.* The FHA, like Title VII and the ADEA, was enacted to eradicate discriminatory practices within a sector of our Nation's economy. See 42 U.S.C. §3601 ("It is the policy of the United States to provide, within constitutional limitations, for fair housing throughout the United States"). These unlawful practices include zoning laws and other housing restrictions that function unfairly to exclude minorities from certain neighborhoods without any sufficient justification. Suits targeting such practices reside at the heartland of disparate-impact liability. See, *e.g., Huntington* [v. *Huntington Branch, NAACP,* 488 U.S. 15 (1988)] (invalidating zoning law preventing construction of multi-family rental units); [*United States v.*] *Black Jack,* [508 F.2d 1179 (C.A.8 1974)] (invalidating ordinance prohibiting construction of new multifamily dwellings);

Greater New Orleans Fair Housing Action Center v. St. Bernard Parish, 641 F.Supp.2d 563 (E.D.La.2009) (invalidating post-Hurricane Katrina ordinance restricting the rental of housing units to only " 'blood relative[s]' " in an area of the city that was 88.3% white and 7.6% black). The availability of disparate-impact liability, furthermore, has allowed private developers to vindicate the FHA's objectives and to protect their property rights by stopping municipalities from enforcing arbitrary and, in practice, discriminatory ordinances barring the construction of certain types of housing units. Recognition of disparate-impact liability under the FHA also plays a role in uncovering discriminatory intent: It permits plaintiffs to counteract unconscious prejudices and disguised animus that escape easy classification as disparate treatment. In this way disparate-impact liability may prevent segregated housing patterns that might otherwise result from covert and illicit stereotyping.

[D]isparate-impact liability has always been properly limited in key respects that avoid the serious constitutional questions that might arise under the FHA, for instance, if such liability were imposed based solely on a showing of a statistical disparity. Disparate-impact liability mandates the "removal of artificial, arbitrary, and unnecessary barriers," not the displacement of valid governmental policies. *Griggs.* The FHA is not an instrument to force housing authorities to reorder their priorities. Rather, the FHA aims to ensure that those priorities can be achieved without arbitrarily creating discriminatory effects or perpetuating segregation."

Unlike the heartland of disparate-impact suits targeting artificial barriers to housing, the underlying dispute in this case involves a novel theory of liability. This case, on remand, may be seen simply as an attempt to second-guess which of two reasonable approaches a housing authority should follow in the sound exercise of its discretion in allocating tax credits for low-income housing.

An important and appropriate means of ensuring that disparate-impact liability is properly limited is to give housing authorities and private developers leeway to state and explain the valid interest served by their policies. This step of the analysis is analogous to the business necessity standard under Title VII and provides a defense against disparate-impact liability. As the Court explained in *Ricci,* an entity "could be liable for disparate-impact discrimination only if the [challenged practices] were not job related and consistent with business necessity." Just as an employer may maintain a workplace requirement that causes a disparate impact if that requirement is a "reasonable measure[ment] of job performance," *Griggs,* so too must housing authorities and private developers be allowed to maintain a policy if they can prove it is necessary to achieve a valid interest. To be sure, the Title VII framework may not transfer exactly to the fair-housing context, but the comparison suffices for present purposes.

It would be paradoxical to construe the FHA to impose onerous costs on actors who encourage revitalizing dilapidated housing in our Nation's cities merely because some other priority might seem preferable. Entrepreneurs must be given latitude to consider market factors. Zoning officials, moreover, must often make decisions based on a mix of factors, both objective (such as cost and traffic patterns) and, at least to some extent, subjective (such as preserving historic architecture). These factors contribute to a community's quality of life and are legitimate concerns for housing authorities. The FHA does not decree a particular vision of urban development; and it does not put housing authorities and private developers in a double bind of liability, subject to suit whether they choose to rejuvenate a city core or to promote new low-income housing in suburban communities. As HUD itself recognized in its recent rulemaking, disparate-impact liability "does not mandate that affordable housing be located in neighborhoods with any particular characteristic."

In a similar vein, a disparate-impact claim that relies on a statistical disparity must fail if the plaintiff cannot point to a defendant's policy or policies causing that disparity. A robust causality requirement ensures that "[r]acial imbalance . . . does not, without more, establish a prima facie case of disparate impact" and thus protects defendants from being held liable for racial disparities they did not create. *Wards Cove Packing Co. v. Atonio,* 490 U.S. 642 (1989), superseded by statute on other grounds, 42 U.S.C. §2000e–2(k). Without adequate safeguards at the prima facie stage, disparate-impact liability might cause race to be used and considered in a pervasive way and "would almost inexorably lead" governmental or private entities to use "numerical quotas," and serious constitutional questions then could arise.

The litigation at issue here provides an example. From the standpoint of determining advantage or disadvantage to racial minorities, it seems difficult to say as a general matter that a decision to build low-income housing in a blighted inner-city neighborhood instead of a suburb is discriminatory, or vice versa. If those sorts of judgments are subject to challenge without adequate safeguards, then there is a danger that potential defendants may adopt racial quotas — a circumstance that itself raises serious constitutional concerns.

Courts must therefore examine with care whether a plaintiff has made out a prima facie case of disparate impact and prompt resolution of these cases is important. A plaintiff who fails to allege facts at the pleading stage or produce statistical evidence demonstrating a causal connection cannot make out a prima facie case of disparate impact. For instance, a plaintiff challenging the decision of a private developer to construct a new building in one location rather than another will not easily be able to show this is a policy causing a disparate impact because such a one-time decision may not be a policy at all. It may also be difficult to establish causation because of the multiple factors that go into investment decisions about where to construct or renovate housing units. And as Judge Jones observed below, if the ICP cannot show a causal connection between the Department's policy and a disparate impact — for instance, because federal law substantially limits the Department's discretion — that should result in dismissal of this case.

The FHA imposes a command with respect to disparate-impact liability. Here, that command goes to a state entity. In other cases, the command will go to a private person or entity. Governmental or private policies are not contrary to the disparate-impact requirement unless they are "artificial, arbitrary, and unnecessary barriers." *Griggs*. Difficult questions might arise if disparate-impact liability under the FHA caused race to be used and considered in a pervasive and explicit manner to justify governmental or private actions that, in fact, tend to perpetuate race-based considerations rather than move beyond them. Courts should avoid interpreting disparate-impact liability to be so expansive as to inject racial considerations into every housing decision.

The limitations on disparate-impact liability discussed here are also necessary to protect potential defendants against abusive disparate-impact claims. If the specter of disparate-impact litigation causes private developers to no longer construct or renovate housing units for low-income individuals, then the FHA would have undermined its own purpose as well as the free-market system. And as to governmental entities, they must not be prevented from achieving legitimate objectives, such as ensuring compliance with health and safety codes. The Department's *amici,* in addition to the well-stated principal dissenting opinion in this case [by Justice Alito], call attention to the decision by the Court of Appeals for the Eighth Circuit in *Gallagher v. Magner,* 619 F.3d 823 (2010). Although the Court is reluctant to approve or disapprove a case that is not pending, it should be noted that *Magner* was decided without the cautionary standards announced in this opinion and, in all events, the case was settled by the parties before an ultimate determination of disparate-impact liability.

Were standards for proceeding with disparate-impact suits not to incorporate at least the safeguards discussed here, then disparate-impact liability might displace valid governmental and private priorities, rather than solely "remov[ing] . . . artificial, arbitrary, and unnecessary barriers." *Griggs*. And that, in turn, would set our Nation back in its quest to reduce the salience of race in our social and economic system.

It must be noted further that, even when courts do find liability under a disparate-impact theory, their remedial orders must be consistent with the Constitution. Remedial orders in disparate-impact cases should concentrate on the elimination of the offending practice that "arbitrar [ily] . . . operate[s] invidiously to discriminate on the basis of rac[e]." *Ibid.* If additional measures are adopted, courts should strive to design them to eliminate racial disparities through race-neutral means. See *Richmond v. J.A. Croson Co.,* 488 U.S. 469, 510 (1989) (plurality opinion) ("[T]he city has at its disposal a whole array of race-neutral devices to increase the accessibility of city contracting opportunities to small entrepreneurs of all races"). Remedial orders that impose racial targets or quotas might raise more difficult constitutional questions.

While the automatic or pervasive injection of race into public and private transactions covered by the FHA has special dangers, it is also true that race may be considered in certain circumstances and in a proper fashion. Cf. *Parents Involved in Community Schools v. Seattle School Dist. No. 1,* 551 U.S. 701, 789 (2007) (KENNEDY, J., concurring in part and concurring in judgment) ("School boards may pursue the goal of bringing together students of diverse backgrounds and races through other means, including strategic site selection of new schools;

[and] drawing attendance zones with general recognition of the demographics of neighborhoods"). Just as this Court has not "question[ed] an employer's affirmative efforts to ensure that all groups have a fair opportunity to apply for promotions and to participate in the [promotion] process," *Ricci,* it likewise does not impugn housing authorities' race-neutral efforts to encourage revitalization of communities that have long suffered the harsh consequences of segregated housing patterns. When setting their larger goals, local housing authorities may choose to foster diversity and combat racial isolation with race-neutral tools, and mere awareness of race in attempting to solve the problems facing inner cities does not doom that endeavor at the outset.

The Court holds that disparate-impact claims are cognizable under the Fair Housing Act upon considering its results-oriented language, the Court's interpretation of similar language in Title VII and the ADEA, Congress' ratification of disparate-impact claims in 1988 against the backdrop of the unanimous view of nine Courts of Appeals, and the statutory purpose.

THOMAS, J., dissenting:

We should drop the pretense that *Griggs'* interpretation of Title VII was legitimate. . . . *Griggs'* disparate-impact doctrine defies not only the statutory text, but reality itself. In their quest to eradicate what they view as institutionalized discrimination, disparate-impact proponents doggedly assume that a given racial disparity at an institution is a product of that institution rather than a reflection of disparities that exist outside of it. That might be true, or it might not. Standing alone, the fact that a practice has a disparate impact is not conclusive evidence, as the *Griggs* Court appeared to believe, that a practice is "discriminatory." "Although presently observed racial imbalance *might* result from past [discrimination], racial imbalance can also result from any number of innocent private decisions." We should not automatically presume that any institution with a neutral practice that happens to produce a racial disparity is guilty of discrimination until proved innocent.

As best I can tell, the reason for this wholesale inversion of our law's usual approach is the unstated — and unsubstantiated — assumption that, in the absence of discrimination, an institution's racial makeup would mirror that of society. But the absence of racial disparities in multi-ethnic societies has been the exception, not the rule. When it comes to "proportiona[l] represent[ation]" of ethnic groups, "few, if any, societies have ever approximated this description." "All multi-ethnic societies exhibit a tendency for ethnic groups to engage in different occupations, have different levels (and, often, types) of education, receive different incomes, and occupy a different place in the social hierarchy."

Racial imbalances do not always disfavor minorities. At various times in history, "racial or ethnic minorities . . . have owned or directed more than half of whole industries in particular nations." These minorities "have included the Chinese in Malaysia, the Lebanese in West Africa, Greeks in the Ottoman Empire, Britons in Argentina, Belgians in Russia, Jews in Poland, and Spaniards in Chile — among many others." "In the seventeenth century Ottoman Empire," this phenomenon was seen in the palace itself, where the "medical staff consisted of 41 Jews and 21 Muslims." And in our own country, for roughly a quarter-century now, over 70 percent of National Basketball Association players have been black. To presume that these and all other measurable disparities are products of racial discrimination is to ignore the complexities of human existence.

Yet, if disparate-impact liability is not based on this assumption and is instead simply a way to correct for imbalances that do not result from any unlawful conduct, it is even less justifiable. This Court has repeatedly reaffirmed that " 'racial balancing' " by state actors is " 'patently unconstitutional,' " even when it supposedly springs from good intentions. *Fisher v. University of Tex. at Austin,* 570 U.S. _____,133 S.Ct. 2411 (2013). And if that "racial balancing" is achieved through disparate-impact claims limited to only some groups—if, for instance, white basketball players cannot bring disparate-impact suits—then we as a Court have constructed a scheme that parcels out legal privileges to individuals on the basis of skin color. A problem with doing so should be obvious: "Government action that classifies individuals on the basis of race is inherently suspect." *Schuette v. BAMN,* 572 U.S. _____,134 S.Ct. 1623 (2014) (plurality opinion). That is no less true when judges are the ones doing the classifying. Disparate-impact liability is thus a rule without a reason, or at least without a legitimate one. . . .

Whatever deference is due *Griggs* as a matter of *stare decisis,* we should at the very least confine it to Title VII. We should not incorporate it into statutes such as the Fair Housing Act and the ADEA, which were passed years before Congress had any reason to suppose that this Court would take the position it did in *Griggs.* And we should certainly not allow it to spread to statutes like the Fair Housing Act, whose operative text, unlike that of the ADEA's, does not even mirror Title VII's.

ALITO, J, joined by ROBERTS, C.J., SCALIA and THOMAS, JJ.:

No one wants to live in a rat's nest. Yet in *Gallagher v. Magner,* 619 F.3d 823 (2010), a case that we agreed to review several Terms ago, the Eighth Circuit held that the Fair Housing Act could be used to attack St. Paul, Minnesota's efforts to combat "rodent infestation" and other violations of the city's housing code. The court agreed that there was no basis to "infer discriminatory intent" on the part of St. Paul. Even so, it concluded that the city's "aggressive enforcement of the Housing Code" was actionable because making landlords respond to "rodent infestation, missing dead-bolt locks, inadequate sanitation facilities, inadequate heat, inoperable smoke detectors, broken or missing doors," and the like increased the price of rent. Since minorities were statistically more likely to fall into "the bottom bracket for household adjusted median family income," they were disproportionately affected by those rent increases, *i.e.,* there was a "disparate impact." The upshot was that even St. Paul's good-faith attempt to ensure minimally acceptable housing for its poorest residents could not ward off a disparate-impact lawsuit.

We granted certiorari in *Magner.* Before oral argument, however, the parties settled. The same thing happened again in *Township of Mount Holly v. Mt. Holly*

Gardens Citizens in Action, Inc., 571 U.S. ____, 133 S.Ct. 2824 (2013). [relocated footnote — eds.]

Today, the Court embraces the same theory that drove the decision in *Magner*. This is a serious mistake. The Fair Housing Act does not create disparate-impact liability, nor do this Court's precedents. And today's decision will have unfortunate consequences for local government, private enterprise, and those living in poverty. Something has gone badly awry when a city can't even make slumlords kill rats without fear of a lawsuit. . . . .

Not only is the decision of the Court inconsistent with what the FHA says and our precedents, it will have unfortunate consequences. Disparate-impact liability has very different implications in housing and employment cases.

Disparate impact puts housing authorities in a very difficult position because programs that are designed and implemented to help the poor can provide the grounds for a disparate-impact claim. As *Magner* shows, when disparate impact is on the table, even a city's good-faith attempt to remedy deplorable housing conditions can be branded "discriminatory." Disparate-impact claims thus threaten "a whole range of tax, welfare, public service, regulatory, and licensing statutes." *Washington v. Davis,* 426 U.S. 229 (1976).

This case illustrates the point. The Texas Department of Housing and Community Affairs (the Department) has only so many tax credits to distribute. If it gives credits for housing in lower income areas, many families — including many minority families — will obtain better housing. That is a good thing. But if the Department gives credits for housing in higher income areas, some of those families will be able to afford to move into more desirable neighborhoods. That is also a good thing. Either path, however, might trigger a disparate-impact suit.

This is not mere speculation. Here, one respondent has sued the Department for not allocating enough credits to higher income areas. See Brief for Respondent Inclusive Communities Project, Inc., 23. But *another* respondent argues that giving credits to wealthy neighborhoods violates "the moral imperative to improve the substandard and inadequate affordable housing in many of our inner cities." This latter argument has special force because a city can build more housing where property is least expensive, thus benefiting more people. In fact, federal law often favors projects that revitalize low-income communities.

No matter what the Department decides, one of these respondents will be able to bring a disparate-impact case. And if the Department opts to compromise by dividing the credits, both respondents might be able to sue. Congress surely did not mean to put local governments in such a position.

The Solicitor General's answer to such problems is that HUD will come to the rescue. In particular, HUD regulations provide a defense against disparate-impact liability if a defendant can show that its actions serve "substantial, legitimate, nondiscriminatory interests" that "necessar[ily]" cannot be met by "another practice that has a less discriminatory effect." 24 CFR §100.500(b) (2014). (There is, of course, no hint of anything like this defense in the text of the FHA. But then, there is no hint of disparate-impact liability in the text of the FHA either.)

The effect of these regulations, not surprisingly, is to confer enormous discretion on HUD — without actually solving the problem. What is a "substantial" interest? Is there a difference between a "legitimate" interest and a "nondiscriminatory" interest? To what degree must an interest be met for a practice to be "necessary"? How are parties and courts to measure "discriminatory effect"?

These questions are not answered by the Court's assurance that the FHA's disparate-impact "analysis 'is analogous to the Title VII requirement that an employer's interest in an employment practice with a disparate impact be job related.'" The business-necessity defense is complicated enough in employment cases; what it means when plopped into the housing context is anybody's guess. What is the FHA analogue of "job related"? Is it "housing related"? But a vast array of municipal decisions affect property values and thus relate (at least indirectly) to housing. And what is the FHA analogue of "business necessity"? "Housing-policy necessity"? What does that mean?

Compounding the problem, the Court proclaims that "governmental entities . . . must not be prevented from achieving legitimate objectives, such as ensuring compliance with health and safety codes." But what does the Court mean by a "legitimate" objective? And does the Court mean to say that there can be no disparate-impact lawsuit if the objective is "legitimate"? That is certainly not the view of the Government, which takes the position that a disparate-impact claim may be brought to challenge actions taken with such worthy objectives as improving housing in poor neighborhoods and making financially sound lending decisions.

Because HUD's regulations and the Court's pronouncements are so "hazy," courts — lacking expertise in the field of housing policy — may inadvertently harm the very people that the FHA is meant to help. Local governments make countless decisions that may have some disparate impact related to housing. Certainly Congress did not intend to "engage the federal courts in an endless exercise of second-guessing" local programs.

Even if a city or private entity named in a disparate-impact suit believes that it is likely to prevail if a disparate-impact suit is fully litigated, the costs of litigation, including the expense of discovery and experts, may "push cost-conscious defendants to settle even anemic cases." *Bell Atlantic Corp. v. Twombly,* 550 U.S. 544 (2007). Defendants may feel compelled to "abandon substantial defenses and . . . pay settlements in order to avoid the expense and risk of going to trial." And parties fearful of disparate-impact claims may let race drive their decision-making in hopes of avoiding litigation altogether. Cf. *Ricci.* All the while, similar dynamics may drive litigation against private actors.

. . . .

At last I come to the "purpose" driving the Court's analysis: The desire to eliminate the "vestiges" of "residential segregation by race." We agree that all Americans should be able "to buy decent houses without discrimination . . . *because of* the color of their skin." 114 Cong. Rec. 2533 (remarks of Sen. Tydings) (emphasis added). See 42 U.S.C. §§3604(a), 3605(a) ("because of race"). But this Court has no license to expand the scope of the FHA to beyond what Congress enacted.

When interpreting statutes, " '[w]hat the legislative intention was, can be derived only from the words . . . used; and we cannot speculate beyond the reasonable import of these words.' " "[I]t frustrates rather than effectuates legislative intent simplistically to assume that *whatever* furthers the statute's primary objective must be the law."

Here, privileging purpose over text also creates constitutional uncertainty. The Court acknowledges the risk that disparate impact may be used to "perpetuate race-based considerations rather than move beyond them." And it agrees that "racial quotas . . . rais[e] serious constitutional concerns." Yet it still reads the FHA to authorize disparate-impact claims. We should avoid, rather than invite, such "difficult constitutional questions." By any measure, the Court today makes a serious mistake.

Discussion

1. Inclusive Communities *and colorblindness*. In what sense is disparate impact liability race conscious, and in what sense is it race neutral? (Consider the concrete examples presented by *Griggs*, *Ricci*, and *Inclusive Communities*.) Does it matter whether the context is housing or employment?

How is disparate impact liability like affirmative action and how is it different? Disparate impact liability intervenes in housing policies to ensure that such policies do not reflect covert (and hard-to-prove) intentional discrimination or "unconscious prejudice," past or present. In deciding whether a law creates a racial preference, one has to have a baseline for comparison. What is the relevant baseline in housing discrimination? In employment?

2. Inclusive Communities *and the anti-balkanization principle*. Justice Kennedy's opinion, while upholding disparate impact, also attempts to cabin it to avoid constitutional problems: "Difficult questions might arise if disparate-impact liability under the FHA caused race to be used and considered in a pervasive and an explicit manner to justify governmental or private actions that, in fact, tend to perpetuate race-based considerations rather than move beyond them." What kinds of state action might "tend to perpetuate race-based considerations rather than move beyond them"?

Consider Reva B. Siegel, *Meador Lecture: Race-Conscious but Race-Neutral: The Constitutionality of Disparate Impact in the Roberts Court*, 66 Ala. L. Rev. 663, 686 n. 150 (2015): "[An] antibalkanization reading emphasizes . . . that Justice Kennedy's opinions in *Ricci*, *Parents Involved*, and *Fisher* all affirm, as well as limit, race-conscious state action promoting equal opportunity. . . . [A] central theme of Justice Kennedy's equal protection opinions is that government may intervene in race-conscious ways to heal social division, but should strive to do so in ways that do not aggravate social division."

How might disparate impact liability heal social divisions? What are the sources of these social divisions, according to the majority? How might disparate impact liability, or remedies for it, exacerbate social divisions? What factors make this more likely to occur? What limits on disparate impact suits might reduce this risk and allay Justice Kennedy's concerns?

Note that Justice Kennedy once again quotes his limiting concurrence in *Parents Involved*. What does this language tell us about the current Court's views on race-conscious but formally race-neutral approaches, like the ten percent plan discussed in *Fisher*?

3. *Damned if you do, damned if you don't.* Justice Alito argues that disparate impact liability is inappropriate in housing discrimination cases, because many housing policies will have disparate impacts on minority groups. In some cases, no matter what a government housing agency does, somebody might point to a disparate impact on some racial or ethnic group. *Griggs* limits disparate impact by the concept of business necessity. Can this be applied to private decisionmaking about housing policy? What about government decisionmaking about housing policy of the kind challenged in *Inclusive Communities*? The government is not attempting to make profits, so a test of business necessity is not apposite. What is the functional equivalent of the business necessity test in the housing context? Justice Alito argues that any test one might come up with will be too vague and will not give government officials fair warning. Is he correct?

4. Inclusive Communities *and "racial balancing."* Justice Thomas argues that disparate impact liability is ultimately an attempt at racial balancing, which is unconstitutional. Note that the Court's statements against "racial balancing" have generally come in affirmative action cases like *Croson*. In affirmative action cases governments use classifications that treat individuals differently based on their race in order to integrate workforces, enhance opportunities in government contracting, or increase minority participation in education. Do disparate impact remedies distinguish among individuals by race in the same way? Does the use of formally-race neutral methods to increase minority participation in employment, contracting, or education constitute "racial balancing" under the Court's decisions?

Why does Thomas believe that race-conscious attention to numbers is constitutionally problematic? Paying attention to numbers may be necessary to detect and remedy intentional discrimination, but that does not make the prohibition on intentional race discrimination constitutionally suspect. Suppose that we have abundant social science evidence showing that unconscious race discrimination persists and is a pervasive part of social life? Is attention to numbers permissible to remedy *that* kind of discrimination?

In *Inclusive Communities*, Justice Thomas explains why he is opposed to any attempts at "racial balancing." He criticizes the "assumption that, in the absence of discrimination, an institution's racial makeup would mirror that of society." He objects to " 'proportiona[l] represent[ation]' of ethnic groups" on the ground that " 'few, if any, societies have ever approximated this description.' 'All multi-ethnic societies exhibit a tendency for ethnic groups to engage in different occupations, have different levels (and, often, types) of education, receive different incomes, and occupy a different place in the social hierarchy.' " (Similar passages appear in Justice O'Connor's opinion in *Croson*.)

In sum, Justice Thomas asserts (1) that, absent discrimination, racial and ethnic groups would still differ and occupy different places in the social hierarchy—presumably because of group differences in culture, taste, and abilities; and (2) that federal courts and the Constitution should act to protect those differences from civil rights laws that might diminish them. Do you agree? Are these beliefs and commitments about racial and ethnic groups "colorblind"?

Add following note 2 on p. 1335:

FISHER

v.

UNIVERSITY OF TEXAS AT AUSTIN

[*FISHER II*]

136 S.Ct. 2198 (2016)

[The University of Texas at Austin uses an undergraduate admissions system containing two components. First, because of the State's Top Ten Percent Law, it offers admission to any students who graduate from a Texas high school in the top 10% of their class. This policy was adopted by the Texas Legislature in wake of the 1996 decision in *Hopwood v. Texas*, 78 F. 3d. 932 (5th Cir. 1996), which held that any consideration of race in admissions violates the Equal Protection Clause.

Second, the University of Texas fills the remainder of its incoming freshman class, some 25%, by combining an applicant's 'Academic Index'—the student's SAT score and high school academic performance—with the applicant's 'Personal Achievement Index,' a holistic review containing numerous factors, including race. The University adopted its current admissions process in 2004, after a year-long-study of its admissions process—undertaken in the wake of *Grutter* and *Gratz*—led it to conclude that its prior race-neutral system did not reach its goal of providing the educational benefits of diversity to its undergraduate students.

Petitioner Abigail Fisher, who was not in the top 10% of her high school class, was denied admission to the University's 2008 freshman class. She filed suit, alleging that the University's consideration of race as part of its holistic-review process disadvantaged her and other Caucasian applicants, in violation of the Equal Protection Clause. The District Court entered summary judgment in the University's favor, and the Fifth Circuit affirmed. The Supreme Court vacated the judgment, *Fisher v. University of Texas at Austin*, 570 U. S. ___ (*Fisher I*), and remanded the case to the Fifth Circuit, so the lower court could evaluate the University's program under the proper strict scrutiny standard. On remand, the Fifth Circuit again affirmed the entry of summary judgment for the University. The Supreme Court affirmed, 4-3, with Justice Kagan not participating.]

KENNEDY, J., delivered the opinion of the Court, in which GINSBURG, BREYER, and SOTOMAYOR, JJ., joined:

. . . .

II

Fisher I set forth three controlling principles relevant to assessing the constitutionality of a public university's affirmative-action program. First, "[r]ace may not be considered [by a university] unless the admissions process can withstand strict scrutiny," Strict scrutiny requires the university to demonstrate with clarity that its "purpose or interest is both constitutionally permissible and substantial, and that its use of the classification is necessary . . . to the accomplishment of its purpose." Second, *Fisher I* confirmed that "the decision to pursue 'the educational benefits that flow from student body diversity' . . . is, in substantial measure, an academic judgment to which some, but not complete, judicial deference is proper." A university cannot impose a fixed quota or otherwise "define diversity as 'some specified percentage of a particular group merely because of its race or ethnic origin.'" Once, however, a university gives "a reasoned, principled explanation" for its decision, deference must be given "to the University's conclusion, based on its experience and expertise, that a diverse student body would serve its educational goals." Third, *Fisher I* clarified that no deference is owed when determining whether the use of race is narrowly tailored to achieve the university's permissible goals. A university, *Fisher I* explained, bears the burden of proving a "nonracial approach" would not promote its interest in the educational benefits of diversity "about as well and at tolerable administrative expense." Though "[n]arrow tailoring does not require exhaustion of every conceivable race-neutral alternative" or "require a university to choose between maintaining a reputation for excellence [and] fulfilling a commitment to provide educational opportunities to members of all racial groups," *Grutter*, it does impose "on the university the ultimate burden of demonstrating" that "race-neutral alternatives" that are both "available" and "workable" "do not suffice." *Fisher I.*

III

The University's program is *sui generis* [because] it combines holistic review with a percentage plan. . . . The component of the University's admissions policy that had the largest impact on petitioner's chances of admission was not the school's consideration of race under its holistic-review process but rather the Top Ten Percent Plan. Because petitioner did not graduate in the top 10 percent of her high school class, she was categorically ineligible for more than three-fourths of the slots in the incoming freshman class. It seems quite plausible, then, to think that petitioner would have had a better chance of being admitted to the University if the school used race-conscious holistic review to select its entire incoming class, as was the case in *Grutter*. Despite the Top Ten Percent Plan's outsized effect on petitioner's chances of admission, she has not challenged it. . . . [hence the] record . . . is almost devoid of information about . . .

how students admitted solely based on their class rank differ in their contribution to diversity from students admitted through holistic review.

In an ordinary case, this evidentiary gap perhaps could be filled by a remand to the district court for further factfinding. When petitioner's application was rejected, however, the University's . . . approach to admission had been in effect for just three years. . . . Furthermore, . . . the University lacks any authority to alter the role of the Top Ten Percent Plan . . . [which] was mandated by the Texas Legislature. . . . If the University had no reason to think that it could deviate from the Top Ten Percent Plan, it similarly had no reason to keep extensive data on the Plan or the students admitted under it. . . . Under the circumstances of this case, then, a remand would do nothing more than prolong a suit that has already persisted for eight years and cost the parties on both sides significant resources. Petitioner long since has graduated from another college, and the University's policy--and the data on which it first was based--may have evolved or changed in material ways. . . . [All of] [t]hese circumstances refute any criticism that the University did not make good-faith efforts to comply with the law.

That does not diminish, however, the University's continuing obligation to satisfy the burden of strict scrutiny in light of changing circumstances. The University engages in periodic reassessment of the constitutionality, and efficacy, of its admissions program. Going forward, that assessment must be undertaken in light of the experience the school has accumulated and the data it has gathered since the adoption of its admissions plan. . . . Through regular evaluation of data and consideration of student experience, the University must tailor its approach in light of changing circumstances, ensuring that race plays no greater role than is necessary to meet its compelling interest. The University's examination of the data it has acquired in the years since petitioner's application, for these reasons, must proceed with full respect for the constraints imposed by the Equal Protection Clause. The type of data collected, and the manner in which it is considered, will have a significant bearing on how the University must shape its admissions policy to satisfy strict scrutiny in the years to come. Here, however, the Court is necessarily limited to the narrow question before it: whether, drawing all reasonable inferences in her favor, petitioner has shown by a preponderance of the evidence that she was denied equal treatment at the time her application was rejected.

IV

[P]etitioner makes four arguments. First, she argues that the University has not articulated its compelling interest with sufficient clarity. According to petitioner, the University must set forth more precisely the level of minority enrollment that would constitute a "critical mass." . . . . As this Court's cases have made clear, however, the compelling interest that justifies consideration of race in college admissions is not an interest in enrolling a certain number of minority students. Rather, a university may institute a race-conscious admissions program as a means of obtaining "the educational benefits that flow from student body diversity." *Fisher I*; see also *Grutter*. As this Court has said, enrolling a diverse student body "promotes cross-racial understanding, helps to break down racial stereotypes, and enables students to better understand persons of different races." Equally important, "student body diversity promotes learning outcomes, and better prepares students for an increasingly diverse workforce and society."

Increasing minority enrollment may be instrumental to these educational benefits, but it is not, as petitioner seems to suggest, a goal that can or should be reduced to pure numbers. Indeed, since the University is prohibited from seeking a particular number or quota of minority students, it cannot be faulted for failing to specify the particular level of minority enrollment at which it believes the educational benefits of diversity will be obtained.

On the other hand, asserting an interest in the educational benefits of diversity writ large is insufficient. A university's goals cannot be elusory or amorphous — they must be sufficiently measurable to permit judicial scrutiny of the policies adopted to reach them.

The record reveals that in first setting forth its current admissions policy, the University articulated concrete and precise goals. On the first page of its 2004 'Proposal to Consider Race and Ethnicity in Admissions,' the University identifies the educational values it seeks to realize through its admissions process: the destruction of stereotypes, the "promot[ion of] cross-racial understanding," "the preparation of a student body 'for an increasingly diverse workforce and society,' and the "cultivat[ion of] a set of leaders with legitimacy in the eyes of the citizenry." Later in the proposal, the University explains that it strives to provide an "academic environment" that offers a "robust exchange of ideas, exposure to differing cultures, preparation for the challenges of an increasingly diverse workforce, and acquisition of competencies required of future leaders." All of these objectives, as a general matter, mirror the "compelling interest" this Court has approved in its prior cases.

The University has provided in addition a "reasoned, principled explanation" for its decision to pursue these goals. The University's 39-page proposal was written following a year-long study, which concluded that "[t]he use of race-neutral policies and programs ha[d] not been successful" in [achieving these goals]. Further support for the University's conclusion can be found in the depositions and affidavits from various admissions officers, all of whom articulate the same, consistent "reasoned, principled explanation." Petitioner's contention that the University's goal was insufficiently concrete is rebutted by the record.

Second, petitioner argues that the University has no need to consider race because it had already "achieved critical mass" by 2003 using the Top Ten Percent Plan and race-neutral holistic review. Petitioner is correct that a university bears a heavy burden in showing that it had not obtained the educational benefits of diversity before it turned to a race-conscious plan. The record reveals, however, that, at the time of petitioner's application, the University could not be faulted on this score. Before changing its policy the University conducted "months of study and deliberation, including retreats, interviews, [and] review of data," and concluded that "[t]he use of race-neutral policies and programs ha[d] not been successful in achieving" sufficient racial diversity at the University. At no stage in this litigation has petitioner challenged the University's good faith in conducting its studies, and the Court properly declines to consider the extra-record materials the dissent relies upon, many of which are tangential to this case at best and none of which the University has had a full opportunity to respond to.

The record itself contains significant evidence, both statistical and anecdotal, in support of the University's position. To start, the demographic data the University has submitted show consistent stagnation in terms of the percentage of minority students enrolling at the University from 1996 to 2002. In 1996, for example, 266 African-American freshmen enrolled, a total that constituted 4.1 percent of the incoming class. In 2003, the year *Grutter* was decided, 267 African-American students enrolled--again, 4.1 percent of the incoming class. The numbers for Hispanic and Asian-American students tell a similar story. Although demographics alone are by no means dispositive, they do have some value as a gauge of the University's ability to enroll students who can offer underrepresented perspectives.

In addition to this broad demographic data, the University put forward evidence that minority students admitted under the *Hopwood* regime [which required race-neutral admissions] experienced feelings of loneliness and isolation.

This anecdotal evidence is, in turn, bolstered by further, more nuanced quantitative data. In 2002, 52 percent of undergraduate classes with at least five students had no African-American students enrolled in them, and 27 percent had only one African-American student. In other words, only 21 percent of undergraduate classes with five or more students in them had more than one African-American student enrolled. Twelve percent of these classes had no Hispanic students, as compared to 10 percent in 1996. Though a college must continually reassess its need for race-conscious review, here that assessment appears to have been done with care, and a reasonable determination was made that the University had not yet attained its goals.

Third, petitioner argues that considering race was not necessary because such consideration has had only a " 'minimal impact' in advancing the [University's] compelling interest." Again, the record does not support this assertion. In 2003, 11 percent of the Texas residents enrolled through holistic review were Hispanic and 3.5 percent were African-American. In 2007, by contrast, 16.9 percent of the Texas holistic-review freshmen were Hispanic and 6.8 percent were African-American. Those increases — of 54 percent and 94 percent, respectively — show that consideration of race has had a meaningful, if still limited, effect on the diversity of the University's freshman class.

In any event, it is not a failure of narrow tailoring for the impact of racial consideration to be minor. The fact that race consciousness played a role in only a small portion of admissions decisions should be a hallmark of narrow tailoring, not evidence of unconstitutionality.

Petitioner's final argument is that "there are numerous other available race-neutral means of achieving" the University's compelling interest. A review of the record reveals, however, that, at the time of petitioner's application, none of her proposed alternatives was a workable means for the University to attain the benefits of diversity it sought. For example, petitioner suggests that the University could intensify its outreach efforts to African-American and Hispanic applicants. But the University submitted extensive evidence of the many ways in which it already had intensified its outreach efforts to those students. . . . Perhaps more significantly, in the wake of *Hopwood*, the University spent seven years attempting to achieve its compelling interest using race-neutral holistic review. None of these efforts succeeded, and petitioner fails to offer any meaningful way in which the University could have improved upon them at the time of her application.

Petitioner also suggests altering the weight given to academic and socioeconomic factors in the University's admissions calculus. This proposal ignores the fact that the University tried, and failed, to increase diversity through enhanced consideration of socioeconomic and other factors. And it further ignores this Court's precedent making clear that the Equal Protection Clause does not force universities to choose between a diverse student body and a reputation for academic excellence. *Grutter*.

Petitioner's final suggestion is to uncap the Top Ten Percent Plan, and admit more—if not all—the University's students through a percentage plan. As an initial matter, petitioner overlooks the fact that the Top Ten Percent Plan, though facially neutral, cannot be understood apart from its basic purpose, which is to boost minority enrollment. Percentage plans are "adopted with racially segregated neighborhoods and schools front and center stage." *Fisher I*, (GINSBURG, J., dissenting). "It is race consciousness, not blindness to race, that drives such plans." *Ibid.* Consequently, petitioner cannot assert simply that increasing the University's reliance on a percentage plan would make its admissions policy more race neutral.

Even if, as a matter of raw numbers, minority enrollment would increase under such a regime, petitioner would be hard-pressed to find convincing support for the proposition that college admissions would be improved if they were a function of class rank alone. That approach would sacrifice all other aspects of diversity in pursuit of enrolling a higher number of minority students. A system that selected every student through class rank alone would exclude the star athlete or musician whose grades suffered because of daily practices and training. It would exclude a talented young biologist who struggled to maintain above-average grades in humanities classes. And it would exclude a student whose freshman-year grades were poor because of a family crisis but who got herself back on track in her last three years of school, only to find herself just outside of the top decile of her class.

These are but examples of the general problem. Class rank is a single metric, and like any single metric, it will capture certain types of people and miss others. This does not imply that students admitted through holistic review are necessarily more capable or more desirable than those admitted through the Top Ten Percent Plan. It merely reflects the fact that privileging one characteristic above all others does not lead to a diverse student body. Indeed, to compel universities to admit students based on class rank alone is in deep tension with the goal of educational diversity as this Court's cases have defined it. At its center, the Top Ten Percent Plan is a blunt instrument that may well compromise the University's own definition of the diversity it seeks.

In addition to these fundamental problems, an admissions policy that relies exclusively on class rank creates perverse incentives for applicants. Percentage plans "encourage parents to keep their children in low-performing segregated schools, and discourage students from taking challenging classes that might lower their grade point averages."

For all these reasons, although it may be true that the Top Ten Percent Plan in some instances may provide a path out of poverty for those who excel at schools lacking in resources, the Plan cannot serve as the admissions solution that petitioner suggests. Wherever the balance between percentage plans and holistic review should rest, an effective admissions policy cannot prescribe, realistically, the exclusive use of a percentage plan.

In short, none of petitioner's suggested alternatives—nor other proposals considered or discussed in the course of this litigation—have been shown to be "available" and "workable" means through which the University could have met its educational goals, as it understood and defined them in 2008. *Fisher I*. The University has thus met its burden of showing that the admissions policy it used at the time it rejected petitioner's application was narrowly tailored.

* * *

[I]t remains an enduring challenge to our Nation's education system to reconcile the pursuit of diversity with the constitutional promise of equal treatment and dignity. In striking this sensitive balance, public universities, like the States themselves, can serve as "laboratories for experimentation." The University of Texas at Austin has a special opportunity to learn and to teach. The University now has at its disposal valuable data about the manner in which different approaches to admissions may foster diversity or instead dilute it. The University must continue to use this data to scrutinize the fairness of its admissions program; to assess whether changing demographics have undermined the need for a race-conscious policy; and to identify the effects, both positive and negative, of the affirmative-action measures it deems necessary.

The Court's affirmance of the University's admissions policy today does not necessarily mean the University may rely on that same policy without refinement. It is the University's ongoing obligation to engage in constant deliberation and continued reflection regarding its admissions policies.

The judgment of the Court of Appeals is affirmed.

It is so ordered.

JUSTICE THOMAS, dissenting.

I join JUSTICE ALITO's dissent. As JUSTICE ALITO explains, the Court's decision today is irreconcilable with strict scrutiny, rests on pernicious assumptions about race, and departs from many of our precedents.

I write separately to reaffirm that "a State's use of race in higher education admissions decisions is categorically prohibited by the Equal Protection
Clause." *Fisher I* (THOMAS, J., concurring). "The Constitution abhors classifications based on race because every time the government places citizens on
racial registers and makes race relevant to the provision of burdens or benefits,
it demeans us all." *Id.* That constitutional imperative does not change in the face
of a "faddish theor[y]" that racial discrimination may produce "educational benefits." *Id..* The Court was wrong to hold otherwise in. I would overrule *Grutter*
and reverse the Fifth Circuit's judgment.

JUSTICE ALITO, with whom THE CHIEF JUSTICE and JUSTICE
THOMAS join, dissenting.

Something strange has happened since our prior decision in this case. In
[*Fisher I,*] we held that strict scrutiny requires the University of Texas at Austin
to show that its use of race and ethnicity in making admissions decisions serves
compelling interests and that its plan is narrowly tailored to achieve those ends.
Rejecting the argument that we should defer to UT's judgment on those matters,
we made it clear that UT was obligated (1) to identify the interests justifying its
plan with enough specificity to permit a reviewing court to determine whether
the requirements of strict scrutiny were met, and (2) to show that those requirements were in fact satisfied. On remand, UT failed to do what our prior decision
demanded. The University has still not identified with any degree of specificity
the interests that its use of race and ethnicity is supposed to serve. Its primary
argument is that merely invoking "the educational benefits of diversity" is sufficient and that it need not identify any metric that would allow a court to determine whether its plan is needed to serve, or is actually serving, those interests.
This is nothing less than the plea for deference that we emphatically rejected in
our prior decision. Today, however, the Court inexplicably grants that request.

To the extent that UT has ever moved beyond a plea for deference and identified the relevant interests in more specific terms, its efforts have been shifting,
unpersuasive, and, at times, less than candid. When it adopted its race-based
plan, UT said that the plan was needed to promote classroom diversity. It pointed
to a study showing that African-American, Hispanic, and Asian-American students were underrepresented in many classes. But UT has never shown that its
race-conscious plan actually ameliorates this situation. The University presents
no evidence that its admissions officers, in administering the "holistic" component of its plan, make any effort to determine whether an African-American,
Hispanic, or Asian-American student is likely to enroll in classes in which
minority students are underrepresented. And although UT's records should permit it to determine without much difficulty whether holistic admittees are any
more likely than students admitted through the Top Ten Percent Law, to enroll
in the classes lacking racial or ethnic diversity, UT either has not crunched those
numbers or has not revealed what they show. Nor has UT explained why the
underrepresentation of Asian-American students in many classes justifies its
plan, which discriminates *against* those students.

At times, UT has claimed that its plan is needed to achieve a "critical mass" of African-American and Hispanic students, but it has never explained what this term means. According to UT, a critical mass is neither some absolute number of African-American or Hispanic students nor the percentage of African-Americans or Hispanics in the general population of the State. The term remains undefined, but UT tells us that it will let the courts know when the desired end has been achieved. This is a plea for deference--indeed, for blind deference--the very thing that the Court rejected in *Fisher I*.

UT has also claimed at times that the race-based component of its plan is needed because the Top Ten Percent Plan admits *the wrong kind* of African-American and Hispanic students, namely, students from poor families who attend schools in which the student body is predominantly African-American or Hispanic. As UT put it in its brief in *Fisher I*, the race-based component of its admissions plan is needed to admit "[t]he African-American or Hispanic child of successful professionals in Dallas."

After making this argument in its first trip to this Court, UT apparently had second thoughts, and in the latest round of briefing UT has attempted to disavow ever having made the argument. But it did, and the argument turns affirmative action on its head. Affirmative-action programs were created to help *disadvantaged* students.

Although UT now disowns the argument that the Top Ten Percent Plan results in the admission of the wrong kind of African-American and Hispanic students, the Fifth Circuit majority bought a version of that claim. As the panel majority put it, the Top Ten African-American and Hispanic admittees cannot match the holistic African-American and Hispanic admittees when it comes to "records of personal achievement," a "variety of perspectives" and "life experiences," and "unique skills." All in all, according to the panel majority, the Top Ten Percent students cannot "enrich the diversity of the student body" in the same way as the holistic admittees. As Judge Garza put it in dissent, the panel majority concluded that the Top Ten Percent admittees are "somehow more homogenous, less dynamic, and more undesirably stereotypical than those admitted under holistic review." (Garza, J., dissenting).

The Fifth Circuit reached this conclusion with little direct evidence regarding the characteristics of the Top Ten Percent and holistic admittees. Instead, the assumption behind the Fifth Circuit's reasoning is that most of the African-American and Hispanic students admitted under the race-neutral component of UT's plan were able to rank in the top decile of their high school classes only because they did not have to compete against white and Asian-American students. This insulting stereotype is not supported by the record. African-American and Hispanic students admitted under the Top Ten Percent Plan receive higher college grades than the African-American and Hispanic students admitted under the race-conscious program.

It should not have been necessary for us to grant review a second time in this case, and I have no greater desire than the majority to see the case drag on. But that need not happen. When UT decided to adopt its race-conscious plan, it had every reason to know that its plan would have to satisfy strict scrutiny and that this meant that it would be *its burden* to show that the plan was narrowly tailored to serve compelling interests. UT has failed to make that showing. By all rights, judgment should be entered in favor of petitioner.

But if the majority is determined to give UT yet another chance, we should reverse and send this case back to the District Court. What the majority has now done—awarding a victory to UT in an opinion that fails to address the important issues in the case—is simply wrong.

[Justice Alito criticized the argument from critical mass:]

[W]ithout knowing in reasonably specific terms what critical mass is or how it can be measured, a reviewing court cannot conduct the requisite "careful judicial inquiry" into whether the use of race was "necessary." *Fisher I*. . . . Because UT has failed to explain "with clarity," *Fisher I*, why it needs a race-conscious policy and how it will know when its goals have been met, the narrow tailoring analysis cannot be meaningfully conducted. UT therefore cannot satisfy strict scrutiny. . . .

According to the majority, however, UT has articulated the following "concrete and precise goals": "the destruction of stereotypes, the promot[ion of] cross-racial understanding, the preparation of a student body for an increasingly diverse workforce and society, and the cultivat[ion of] a set of leaders with legitimacy in the eyes of the citizenry." These are laudable goals, but they are not concrete or precise, and they offer no limiting principle for the use of racial preferences. For instance, how will a court ever be able to determine whether stereotypes have been adequately destroyed? Or whether cross-racial understanding has been adequately achieved? If a university can justify racial discrimination simply by having a few employees opine that racial preferences are necessary to accomplish these nebulous goals, then the narrow tailoring inquiry is meaningless. Courts will be required to defer to the judgment of university administrators, and affirmative-action policies will be completely insulated from judicial review.

By accepting these amorphous goals as sufficient for UT to carry its burden, the majority violates decades of precedent rejecting blind deference to government officials defending "inherently suspect" classifications. . . . Most troublingly, the majority's uncritical deference to UT's self-serving claims blatantly contradicts our decision in the prior iteration of this very case, in which we faulted the Fifth Circuit for improperly "deferring to the University's good faith in its use of racial classifications." *Fisher I*. As we emphasized just three years ago, our precedent "ma[kes] clear that it is for the courts, not for university administrators, to ensure that" an admissions process is narrowly tailored. . . .

[N]either UT nor the majority is clear about the relationship between Texas demographics and UT's interest in obtaining a critical mass. Does critical mass depend on the relative size of a particular group in the population of a State? For example, is the critical mass of African-Americans and Hispanics in Texas, where African-Americans are about 11.8% of the population and Hispanics are about 37.6%, different from the critical mass in neighboring New Mexico, where the African-American population is much smaller (about 2.1%) and the Hispanic population constitutes a higher percentage of the State's total (about 46.3%)?

UT's answer to this question has veered back and forth. At oral argument in *Fisher I*, UT's lawyer indicated that critical mass "could" vary "from group to group" and from "state to state." And UT initially justified its race-conscious plan at least in part on the ground that "significant differences between the racial and ethnic makeup of the University's undergraduate population and the state's population prevent the University from fully achieving its mission." UT's extensive reliance on state demographics is also revealed by its substantial focus on increasing the representation of Hispanics, but not Asian-Americans, because Hispanics, but not Asian-Americans, are underrepresented at UT when compared to the demographics of the State. . . . .

To the extent that UT is pursuing parity with Texas demographics, that is nothing more than 'outright racial balancing,' which this Court has time and again held 'patently unconstitutional.' *Fisher I* ; see *Grutter, Croson, Bakke*. . . . . Although UT claims an interest in the educational benefits of diversity, it appears to have paid little attention to anything other than the number of minority students on its campus and in its classrooms. UT's 2004 Proposal illustrates this approach by repeatedly citing numerical assessments of the racial makeup of the student body and various classes as the justification for adopting a race-conscious plan. Instead of focusing on the benefits of diversity, UT seems to have resorted to a simple racial census.

The majority, for its part, claims that "[a]lthough demographics alone are by no means dispositive, they do have some value as a gauge of the University's ability to enroll students who can offer underrepresented perspectives." But even if UT merely "view[s] the demographic disparity as cause for concern," and is seeking only to reduce—rather than eliminate—the disparity, that undefined goal cannot be properly subjected to strict scrutiny. In that case, there is simply no way for a court to know what specific demographic interest UT is pursuing, why a race-neutral alternative could not achieve that interest, and when that demographic goal would be satisfied. If a demographic discrepancy can serve as "a gauge" that justifies the use of racial discrimination, then racial discrimination can be justified on that basis until demographic parity is reached. There is no logical stopping point short of patently unconstitutional racial balancing. Demographic disparities thus cannot be used to satisfy strict scrutiny here. See *Croson* (rejecting a municipality's assertion that its racial set-aside program was justified in light of past discrimination because that assertion had "no logical stopping point" and could continue until the percentage of government contracts awarded to minorities "mirrored the percentage of minorities in the population as a whole").

The other major explanation UT offered in the Proposal was its desire to promote classroom diversity. The Proposal stressed that UT "has not reached a critical mass at the *classroom level*." . . . UT concluded that it had a "compelling educational interest" in employing racial preferences to ensure that it did not 'have large numbers of classes in which there are no students—or only a single student—of a given underrepresented race or ethnicity.

UT now equivocates, disclaiming any discrete interest in classroom diversity. Instead, UT has taken the position that the lack of classroom diversity was merely a 'red flag that UT had not yet fully realized "the constitutionally permissible educational benefits of diversity."' But UT has failed to identify the level of classroom diversity it deems sufficient, again making it impossible to apply strict scrutiny. A reviewing court cannot determine whether UT's race-conscious program was necessary to remove the so-called "red flag" without understanding the precise nature of that goal or knowing when the "red flag" will be considered to have disappeared.

[M]oreover, if UT is truly seeking to expose its students to a diversity of ideas and perspectives, its policy is poorly tailored to serve that end. UT's own study—which the majority touts as the best "nuanced quantitative data" supporting UT's position—demonstrated that classroom diversity was more lacking for students classified as Asian-American than for those classified as Hispanic. But the UT plan discriminates *against* Asian-American students. UT is apparently unconcerned that Asian-Americans "may be made to feel isolated or may be seen as . . . 'spokesperson[s]' of their race or ethnicity." And unless the University is engaged in unconstitutional racial balancing based on Texas demographics (where Hispanics outnumber Asian-Americans), it seemingly views the classroom contributions of Asian-American students as less valuable than those of Hispanic students. In UT's view, apparently, "Asian Americans are not worth as much as Hispanics in promoting 'cross-racial understanding,' breaking down 'racial stereotypes,' and enabling students to 'better understand persons of different races.'" . . . . This reasoning, which the majority implicitly accepts by blessing UT's reliance on the classroom study, places the Court on the "tortuous" path of "decid[ing] which races to favor." And the Court's willingness to allow this "discrimination against individuals of Asian descent in UT admissions is particularly troubling, in light of the long history of discrimination against Asian Americans, especially in education." . . . .

The majority's assertion that UT's race-based policy does not discriminate against Asian-American students, defies the laws of mathematics. UT's program is clearly designed to increase the number of African-American and Hispanic students by giving them an admissions boost vis-a-vis other applicants. Given a "limited number of spaces," providing a boost to African-Americans and Hispanics inevitably harms students who do not receive the same boost by decreasing their odds of admission. [relocated footnote—eds.]

Perhaps the majority finds discrimination against Asian-American students benign, since Asian-Americans are *"overrepresented"* at UT. But "[h]istory should teach greater humility." "'[B]enign' carries with it no independent meaning, but reflects only acceptance of the current generation's conclusion that a politically acceptable burden, imposed on particular citizens on the basis of race, is reasonable." Where, as here, the government has provided little explanation for why it needs to discriminate based on race, "there is simply no way of determining what classifications are 'benign' . . . and what classifications are in fact motivated by illegitimate notions of racial inferiority or simple racial politics." *Parents Involved*, 551 U. S., at 783 (opinion of KENNEDY, J.) By accepting the classroom study as proof that UT satisfied strict scrutiny, the majority "move[s] us from 'separate but equal' to 'un-equal but benign.' " *Metro Broadcasting*, (KENNEDY, J., dissenting).

In addition to demonstrating that UT discriminates against Asian-American students, the classroom study also exhibits UT's use of a few crude, overly simplistic racial and ethnic categories. . . . . For example, students labeled "Asian American," seemingly include "individuals of Chinese, Japanese, Korean, Vietnamese, Cambodian, Hmong, Indian and other backgrounds comprising roughly 60% of the world's population." It would be ludicrous to suggest that all of these students have similar backgrounds and similar ideas and experiences to share. So why has UT lumped them together and concluded that it is appropriate to discriminate against Asian-American students because they are "over-represented" in the UT student body? UT has no good answer. And UT makes no effort to ensure that it has a critical mass of, say, "Filipino Americans" or "Cambodian Americans." As long as there are a sufficient number of "Asian Americans," UT is apparently satisfied.

UT's failure to provide any definition of the various racial and ethnic groups is also revealing. UT does not specify what it means to be "African-American," "Hispanic," "Asian American," "Native American," or "White." And UT evidently labels each student as falling into only a single racial or ethnic group, without explaining how individuals with ancestors from different groups are to be characterized. As racial and ethnic prejudice recedes, more and more students will have parents (or grandparents) who fall into more than one of UT's five groups. According to census figures, individuals describing themselves as members of multiple races grew by 32% from 2000 to 2010. A recent survey reported that 26% of Hispanics and 28% of Asian-Americans marry a spouse of a different race or ethnicity. UT's crude classification system is ill suited for the more integrated country that we are rapidly becoming. UT assumes that if an applicant describes himself or herself as a member of a particular race or ethnicity, that applicant will have a perspective that differs from that of applicants who describe themselves as members of different groups. But is this necessarily so? If an applicant has one grandparent, great-grandparent, or great-great-grandparent who was a member of a favored group, is that enough to permit UT to infer that this student's classroom contribution will reflect a distinctive perspective or set of experiences associated with that group? UT does not say. It instead relies on applicants to "classify themselves." This is an invitation for applicants to game the system.

Finally, it seems clear that the lack of classroom diversity is attributable in good part to factors other than the representation of the favored groups in the UT student population. UT offers an enormous number of classes in a wide range of subjects, and it gives undergraduates a very large measure of freedom to choose their classes. UT also offers courses in subjects that are likely to have special appeal to members of the minority groups given preferential treatment under its challenged plan, and this of course diminishes the number of other courses in which these students can enroll. Having designed an undergraduate program that virtually ensures a lack of classroom diversity, UT is poorly positioned to argue that this very result provides a justification for racial and ethnic discrimination, which the Constitution rarely allows.

. . . .

UT also alleges—and the majority embraces—an interest in avoiding "feelings of loneliness and isolation" among minority students. In support of this argument, they cite only demographic data and anecdotal statements by UT officials that some students (we are not told how many) feel "isolated." This vague interest cannot possibly satisfy strict scrutiny.

If UT is seeking demographic parity to avoid isolation, that is impermissible racial balancing. And linking racial loneliness and isolation to state demographics is illogical. Imagine, for example, that an African-American student attends a university that is 20% African-American. If racial isolation depends on a comparison to state demographics, then that student is more likely to feel isolated if the school is located in Mississippi (which is 37.0% African-American) than if it is located in Montana (which is 0.4% African-American). In reality, however, the student may feel—if anything—*less* isolated in Mississippi, where African-Americans are more prevalent in the population at large.

If, on the other hand, state demographics are not driving UT's interest in avoiding racial isolation, then its treatment of Asian-American students is hard to understand. As the District Court noted, "the gross number of Hispanic students attending UT exceeds the gross number of Asian-American students." In 2008, for example, UT enrolled 1,338 Hispanic freshmen and 1,249 Asian-American freshmen. UT never explains why the Hispanic students—but not the Asian-American students—are isolated and lonely enough to receive an admissions boost, notwithstanding the fact that there are more Hispanics than Asian-Americans in the student population. The anecdotal statements from UT officials certainly do not indicate that Hispanics are somehow lonelier than Asian-Americans.

Ultimately, UT has failed to articulate its interest in preventing racial isolation with any clarity, and it has provided no clear indication of how it will know when such isolation no longer exists. Like UT's purported interests in demographic parity, classroom diversity, and intraracial diversity, its interest in avoiding racial isolation cannot justify the use of racial preferences.

Even assuming UT is correct that, under *Grutter*, it need only cite a generic interest in the educational benefits of diversity, its plan still fails strict scrutiny because it is not narrowly tailored. Narrow tailoring requires "a careful judicial inquiry into whether a university could achieve sufficient diversity without using racial classifications." *Fisher I.* Here, there is no evidence that race-blind, holistic review would not achieve UT's goals at least "about as well" as UT's race-based policy. In addition, UT could have adopted other approaches to further its goals, such as intensifying its outreach efforts, uncapping the Top Ten Percent Law, or placing greater weight on socioeconomic factors.

The majority argues that none of these alternatives is "a workable means for the University to attain the benefits of diversity it sought." Tellingly, however, the majority devotes only a single, conclusory sentence to the most obvious race-neutral alternative: race-blind, holistic review that considers the applicant's unique characteristics and personal circumstances. Under a system that combines the Top Ten Percent Plan with race-blind, holistic review, UT could still admit "the star athlete or musician whose grades suffered because of daily practices and training," the "talented young biologist who struggled to maintain above-average grades in humanities classes," and the "student whose freshman-year grades were poor because of a family crisis but who got herself back on track in her last three years of school." All of these unique circumstances can be considered without injecting race into the process. Because UT has failed to provide any evidence whatsoever that race-conscious holistic review will achieve its diversity objectives more effectively than race-blind holistic review, it cannot satisfy the heavy burden imposed by the strict scrutiny standard. . . . .

Because UT has failed to satisfy strict scrutiny, I respectfully dissent.

Discussion

1. Fisher *and* Grutter. Justice Kennedy dissented in *Grutter*, objecting that the majority's framework for reviewing challenges to affirmative action programs was too deferential to educators. He also wrote *Fisher I*, which seemed to strengthen strict scrutiny requirements in affirmative action cases. Nevertheless, in *Fisher II*, Justice Kennedy wrote the majority opinion upholding the University of Texas' affirmative action program. This is the first time since Justice Kennedy joined the Court in 1988 that he has voted to uphold a race-conscious affirmative action program, much less written an opinion justifying it.

Note how, in *Fisher II*, Justice Kennedy adopts much of the reasoning of *Grutter*, which allowed race-conscious affirmative action in order to foster the "promot[ion of] cross-racial understanding," "the preparation of a student body 'for an increasingly diverse workforce and society,' and the "cultivat[ion of] a set of leaders with legitimacy in the eyes of the citizenry."

Justice Kennedy also seems to accept Justice Ginsburg's argument, dissenting in *Fisher I*, that it is misleading to call the Texas Ten Percent Plan race-neutral, because it is transparently motivated by a purpose to increase minority enrollments. Nevertheless, he assumes that the Ten Percent Plan is constitutional under the Equal Protection Clause. Compare his opinion in *Fisher II* with his opinion in *Inclusive Communities*, in which he assumed the constitutionality of disparate impact liability. Although disparate impact liability can be understood as a method of smoking out invidious motivation, it also helps remedy past segregative effects and promotes racial integration of workforces and neighborhoods. What has changed in Justice Kennedy's approach to affirmative action, and what seems constant? What might account for these developments?

2. *Continuing obligations.* Justice Kennedy makes clear that universities like UT have continuing obligations to monitor their student bodies to decide whether their admissions standards comport with strict scrutiny: "The University must continue to use [its] data to scrutinize the fairness of its admissions program [and] to assess whether changing demographics have undermined the need for a race-conscious policy . . . The Court's affirmance of the University's admissions policy today does not necessarily mean the University may rely on that same policy without refinement." The Court concludes: "It is the University's ongoing obligation to engage in constant deliberation and continued reflection regarding its admissions policies." According to Justice Kennedy, why is this obligation required by the Constitution?

Does *Fisher II* make state universities vulnerable to periodic suits from opponents of affirmative action? If you were serving as university counsel, what practical steps would you advise the university to take to discharge its "ongoing obligation to engage in constant deliberation and continued reflection regarding its admissions policies"?

3. *Critical mass.* Justice Alito's dissent reiterates Chief Justice Rehnquist's critique in *Grutter* of "critical mass" as a justification for diversity. Alito argues that using race conscious affirmative action to achieve a critical mass of minorities is a disguised form of racial balancing designed to make Texas's admissions roughly reflect the demographics of the state. How does the majority respond to this argument?

Suppose the Court acknowledged that state universities are trying to achieve a rough relationship between the percentage of particular minorities of college age in their state and the number of minority applicants they accept, but that this practice is nevertheless legitimate, building on Justice O'Connor's arguments in *Grutter* that educational institutions must "cultivate a set of leaders with legitimacy in the eyes of the citizenry." Would such candor be appropriate? If the Court wanted to adopt this approach, how would it have to change its affirmative action doctrines?

4. *Multiracial identity and discrimination against Asian Americans.* Justice Alito's dissent makes two moves that we are likely to see in future challenges to affirmative action programs.

First, Justice Alito does not object, as previous Justices have, that affirmative action programs unfairly discriminate against whites, that they will stir up white resentment against minorities, or that they harm the minorities they purport to help. Instead, he argues that affirmative action programs discriminate against another minority, Asian-Americans. This criticism recalls arguments in the early years of affirmative action that race-conscious admissions policies were unfair to another minority, Jews, because they were reminiscent of quotas that had previously limited the admission of Jews to elite institutions. Should affirmative action programs be permitted to increase enrollments for only some minority groups, but not for others? How does your answer connect to the diversity rationale? To Justice O'Connor's arguments in *Grutter* about legitimacy in the eyes of the citizenry?

Second, Justice Alito argues that the country has become increasingly mixed race, that it is increasingly difficult to identify who is a member of which race or ethnic group, and that a mixed race population undermines the arguments for diversity. This argument puts a new spin on Justice Powell's argument in *Bakke* that the United States is a nation of minorities and that it is unfair to disadvantage whites because whites themselves contain many groups. Do the arguments for affirmative action and for educational diversity become stronger or weaker as minority and multi-racial populations increase in the United States?

Insert at the end of p. 1372:

Note: The Travel Ban Cases

During the 2016 Presidential campaign, Donald Trump ran on a platform of restricting illegal immigration, deporting undocumented aliens, and preventing the United States from being invaded by radical Islamists. He strongly opposed receiving refugees from Syria fleeing that country's civil war. On December 7, 2015, following a mass shooting in San Bernadino, California, candidate Trump gave a speech in which he called for "a total and complete shutdown of Muslims entering the United States until our country's representatives can figure out what is going on."[1] The proposal for what became known as a "Muslim ban" was posted on Trump's campaign website until March 2017. During the 2016 campaign Trump and his surrogates alternatively described the proposal as a ban on people coming from countries known to produce terrorism, along with a call for "extreme vetting" of people entering the United States.[2]

Shortly after taking office, on January 27, 2017, President Trump signed Executive Order No. 13769, entitled Protecting the Nation From Foreign Terrorist Entry Into the United States. 82 Fed.Reg. 8977 (EO–1). Section 3(c) of EO–1 suspended the entry of foreign nationals of seven countries identified as presenting heightened terrorism risks — Iran, Iraq, Libya, Somalia, Sudan, Syria, and Yemen — for 90 days. The asserted purpose of the 90-day suspension was to allow executive branch officials to review the adequacy of current practices for visa adjudications. In addition, §5 of EO–1 also modified refugee policy. It suspended the United States Refugee Admissions Program (USRAP) for 120 days and reduced the number of refugees eligible to be admitted to the United States during fiscal year 2017 from 110,000 to 50,000.

1. Jessica Taylor, Trump calls for total and complete shutdown of muslims, NPR, December 7, 2015, http://www.npr.org/2015/12/07/458836388/trump-calls-for-total-and-complete-shutdown-of-muslims-entering-u-s

2. Ali Vitali, Donald Trump Shifts on Muslim Ban, Calls for 'Extreme Vetting', NBC News, July 17, 2016, http://www.nbcnews.com/politics/2016-election/donald-trump-shifts-muslim-ban-calls-extreme-vetting-n611276.

EO–1 created enormous confusion at airports around the United States, in part because it was not immediately clear—even to federal officials—whether the order applied to permanent residents of the United States (green card holders) who were also nationals of the seven countries. On January 28, protests against the order began around the country and at various airports. A week after EO-1 was issued, a Federal District Court entered a nationwide temporary restraining order enjoining enforcement of several of its key provisions. *Washington v. Trump,* 2017 WL 462040 (W.D.Wash., Feb.3, 2017). Six days later, the Ninth Circuit denied the Government's emergency motion to stay the order pending appeal. *Washington v. Trump,* 847 F.3d 1151 (2017).

Rather than continue to litigate EO–1, the Government announced that it would revoke the order and issue a new one. On March 6, 2017, the Trump Administration issued Executive Order No. 13780, Protecting the Nation From Foreign Terrorist Entry Into the United States, 82 Fed.Reg. 13209 (EO–2). EO–2 eliminated Iraq from the seven countries. It stated that conditions in the remaining six countries "demonstrate [that] nationals [of those countries] continue to present heightened risks to the security of the United States," §1(e), and that "some of those who have entered the United States through our immigration system have proved to be threats to our national security," §1(h).

EO–2 also modified features of the entry and refugee suspensions in EO–1. These are the four most important features:

1. Global review program. First, Section 2 of EO–2 directs the Secretary of Homeland Security to conduct a global review to determine whether foreign governments provide adequate information about nationals applying for United States visas. §2(a). It also directs the Secretary to report his findings to the President within 20 days of the order's "effective date," at which point those nations identified as deficient in providing necessary information will be given 50 days to alter their practices. §§2(b), (d).[3]

2. 90-day suspension of entry from six Muslim-majority countries. Second, in addition to the global review requirement, Section 2 of EO–2 featured a revised version of the entry suspension. The entry of nationals of six of the seven countries designated in EO–1—Iran, Libya, Somalia, Sudan, Syria, and Yemen—is "suspended for 90 days from the effective date" of the order. §2(c). EO–2 explains that the 90-day suspension is necessary to ensure that dangerous individuals do not enter the United States while the Executive is working to establish

---

3. Thereafter, federal agencies are directed to recommend new vetting procedures and entry limitations to the President: "[T]he Secretary of Homeland Security, in consultation with the Secretary of State and the Attorney General, shall submit to the President a list of countries recommended for inclusion in a Presidential proclamation that would prohibit the entry of appropriate categories of foreign nationals of countries that have not provided the information requested until they do so or until the Secretary of Homeland Security certifies that the country has an adequate plan to do so, or has adequately shared information through other means. The Secretary of State, the Attorney General, or the Secretary of Homeland Security may also submit to the President the names of additional countries for which any of them recommends other lawful restrictions or limitations deemed necessary for the security or welfare of the United States." §2(e).

"adequate standards . . . to prevent infiltration by foreign terrorists" pursuant to Section 2. In addition, the 90-day suspension will "temporarily reduce investigative burdens on agencies" during the Secretary's 20–day review. Section 3(c) of EO–2 provides for case-by-case waivers of the entry bar.

3. 120-day suspension of USRAP refugee program. Third, §6(a) of EO–2 suspends "decisions on applications for refugee status" and "travel of refugees into the United States under the USRAP" for 120 days following the effective date of the executive order. During the 120-day period, the order directs the Secretary of State to review the adequacy of USRAP application and adjudication procedures and implement whatever additional procedures are necessary "to ensure that individuals seeking admission as refugees do not pose a threat" to national security.

4. Limitation of refugees during Fiscal Year 2017. Fourth, citing President Trump's determination that "the entry of more than 50,000 refugees in fiscal year 2017 would be detrimental to the interests of the United States," §6(b) of EO–2 "suspend[s] any entries in excess of that number" for this fiscal year.

Section 14 of EO–2 established the order's effective date as March 16, 2017.

Litigation challenging EO-2 quickly proceeded in many courts, including district courts in Hawaii and Maryland. The challengers argued that the entry bans and limits in EO-2 violated the Establishment Clause because they were motivated by anti-Muslim animus. They also argued that the President lacked authority to promulgate those bans and limits under the Immigration and Nationality Act (INA). The Hawaii and Maryland courts issued sweeping injunctions, which the government appealed.

INTERNATIONAL REFUGEE ASSISTANCE PROJECT V. TRUMP, 857 F.3d 554 (4th Cir. 2017)(May 25, 2017): [John Doe # 1, a lawful permanent resident whose Iranian wife sought entry to the United States, challenged §2(c) of EO–2 — the provision temporarily suspending entry from six countries. A federal district court in Maryland concluded that respondents were likely to succeed on their Establishment Clause claim with respect to §2(c) and entered a nationwide preliminary injunction barring the Government from enforcing §2(c) against any foreign national seeking entry to the United States. The Fourth Circuit, sitting en banc, upheld (by a vote of 10-3) the district court's preliminary injunction on the ground that EO-2 was motivated by anti-Muslim animus and violated the Establishment Clause. Three of the ten judges in the majority also concluded that the President lacked statutory authority to promulgate the ban and limits (a question that the other judges did not reach).]

GREGORY, Chief Judge:

The question for this Court, distilled to its essential form, is whether the Constitution, as the Supreme Court declared in *Ex parte Milligan*, 71 U.S. (4 Wall.) 2 (1866), remains "a law for rulers and people, equally in war and in peace." And if so, whether it protects Plaintiffs' right to challenge an Executive Order that in text speaks with vague words of national security, but in context drips with religious intolerance, animus, and discrimination. Surely the Establishment Clause of the First Amendment yet stands as an untiring sentinel for the protection of one of our most cherished founding principles — that government shall not establish any religious orthodoxy, or favor or disfavor one religion over another. Congress granted the President broad power to deny entry to aliens, but that power is not absolute. It cannot go unchecked when, as here, the President wields it through an executive edict that stands to cause irreparable harm to individuals across this nation. Therefore, for the reasons that follow, we affirm in substantial part the district court's issuance of a nationwide preliminary injunction as to Section 2(c) of the challenged Executive Order. . . . .

For a district court to grant a preliminary injunction, "a plaintiff 'must establish [1] that he is likely to succeed on the merits, [2] that he is likely to suffer irreparable harm in the absence of preliminary relief, [3] that the balance of equities tips in his favor, and [4] that an injunction is in the public interest.'" The district court found that Plaintiffs satisfied all four requirements as to their Establishment Clause claim, and it enjoined Section 2(c) of EO-2. We evaluate the court's findings for abuse of discretion, reviewing its factual findings for clear error and its legal conclusions de novo. . . .

The Government argues that the court erroneously applied [standard Establishment Clause doctrine] instead of the more deferential test [in immigration law] set forth in *Kleindienst v. Mandel*, 408 U.S. 753 (1972). In *Mandel*, American university professors had invited Mandel, a Belgian citizen and revolutionary Marxist and professional journalist, to speak at a number of conferences in the United States. But Mandel's application for a nonimmigrant visa was denied under a then-existing INA provision that barred the entry of aliens "who advocate the economic, international, and governmental doctrines of world communism.". . . . The American professors sued, alleging, among other things, that the denial of Mandel's visa violated their First Amendment rights to "hear his views and engage him in a free and open academic exchange."

The Supreme Court, citing "Congress' 'plenary power to make rules for the admission of aliens and to exclude those who possess those characteristics which Congress has forbidden,'" found that the longstanding principle of deference to the political branches in the immigration context limited its review of plaintiffs' challenge. The Court held that "when the Executive exercises this power [to exclude an alien] on the basis of a facially legitimate and bona fide reason, the courts will neither look behind the exercise of that discretion, nor test it by balancing its justification against the [plaintiffs'] First Amendment interests." The Court concluded that the Attorney General's stated reason for denying Mandel's visa — that he had violated the terms of prior visas — satisfied this test. It therefore did not review plaintiffs' First Amendment claim.

Courts have continuously applied *Mandel*'s "facially legitimate and bona fide" test to challenges to individual visa denials. . . . But in another more recent line of cases, the Supreme Court has made clear that despite the political branches' plenary power over immigration, that power is still "subject to important constitutional limitations," *Zadvydas v. Davis*, 533 U.S. 678 (2001), and that it is the judiciary's responsibility to uphold those limitations. [INS v.] *Chadha*, 462 U.S. at 941 (stating that Congress and the Executive must "cho[ose] a constitutionally permissible means of implementing" their authority over immigration). These cases instruct that the political branches' power over immigration is not tantamount to a constitutional blank check, and that vigorous judicial review is required when an immigration action's constitutionality is in question.

We are bound to give effect to both lines of cases, meaning that we must enforce constitutional limitations on immigration actions while also applying *Mandel's* deferential test to those actions as the Supreme Court has instructed. For the reasons that follow, however, we find that these tasks are not mutually exclusive, and that *Mandel's* test still contemplates meaningful judicial review of constitutional challenges in certain, narrow circumstances, as we have here.

[Under *Mandel*,] [t]he government need only show that the challenged action is "facially legitimate and bona fide" to defeat a constitutional challenge. These are separate and quite distinct requirements. To be "facially legitimate," there must be a valid reason for the challenged action stated on the face of the action. *Kerry v. Din*, 135 S.Ct. 2128, 2140–41 (2015) (Kennedy, J., concurring in the judgment). . . . [The court explained that Justice Kennedy's concurrence is the controlling opinion in *Din*.]

And as the name suggests, the "bona fide" requirement concerns whether the government issued the challenged action in good faith. . . . Here, the burden is on the plaintiff. Justice Kennedy explained that where a plaintiff makes "an affirmative showing of bad faith" that is "plausibly alleged with sufficient particularity," courts may "look behind" the challenged action to assess its "facially legitimate" justification. *Id.* (suggesting that if plaintiff had sufficiently alleged that government denied visa in bad faith, court should inquire whether the government's stated statutory basis for denying the visa was the actual reason for the denial). In the typical case, it will be difficult for a plaintiff to make an affirmative showing of bad faith with plausibility and particularity. And absent this affirmative showing, courts must defer to the government's "facially legitimate" reason for the action.

Mandel therefore clearly sets a high bar for plaintiffs seeking judicial review of a constitutional challenge to an immigration action. But although *Mandel* 's "facially legitimate and bona fide" test affords significant deference to the political branches' decisions in this area, it does not completely insulate those decisions from *any* meaningful review. Where plaintiffs have seriously called into question whether the stated reason for the challenged action was provided in good faith, we understand *Mandel*, as construed by Justice Kennedy in his controlling concurrence in *Din*, to require that we step away from our deferential posture and look behind the stated reason for the challenged action. In other words, *Mandel's* requirement that an immigration action be "bona fide" may in some instances compel more searching judicial review. . . .

EO-2's stated purpose is "to protect the Nation from terrorist activities by foreign nationals admitted to the United States." We find that this stated national security interest is, on its face, a valid reason for Section 2(c)'s suspension of entry. EO-2 therefore satisfies *Mandel* 's first requirement. . . . But in this case, Plaintiffs have alleged that EO-2's stated purpose was given in bad faith. . . .

Plaintiffs must "plausibly allege[ ] with sufficient particularity" that the reason for the government action was provided in bad faith. Plaintiffs here claim that EO-2 invokes national security in bad faith, as a pretext for what really is an anti-Muslim religious purpose. Plaintiffs point to ample evidence that national security is not the true reason for EO-2, including, among other things, then-candidate Trump's numerous campaign statements expressing animus towards the Islamic faith; his proposal to ban Muslims from entering the United States; his subsequent explanation that he would effectuate this ban by targeting "territories" instead of Muslims directly; the issuance of EO-1, which targeted certain majority-Muslim nations and included a preference for religious minorities; an advisor's statement that the President had asked him to find a way to ban Muslims in a legal way; and the issuance of EO-2, which resembles EO-1 and which President Trump and his advisors described as having the same policy goals as EO-1. Plaintiffs also point to the comparably weak evidence that EO-2 is meant to address national security interests, including the exclusion of national security agencies from the decisionmaking process, the post hoc nature of the national security rationale, and evidence from DHS that EO-2 would not operate to diminish the threat of potential terrorist activity.

Based on this evidence, we find that Plaintiffs have more than plausibly alleged that EO-2's stated national security interest was provided in bad faith, as a pretext for its religious purpose. And having concluded that the "facially legitimate" reason proffered by the government is not "bona fide," we no longer defer to that reason and instead may "look behind" EO-2.

Since Justice Kennedy's concurrence in *Din*, no court has confronted a scenario where, as here, plaintiffs have plausibly alleged with particularity that an immigration action was taken in bad faith. We therefore have minimal guidance on what "look[ing] behind" a challenged immigration action entails. . . . [But] in the Establishment Clause context, our normal constitutional tool for reviewing facially neutral government actions is the test in *Lemon v. Kurtzman*, 403 U.S. 602 (1971). . . . Because Plaintiffs have made a substantial and affirmative showing that the government's national security purpose was proffered in bad faith, we find it appropriate to apply our longstanding Establishment Clause doctrine. Applying this doctrine harmonizes our duty to engage in the substantial deference required by *Mandel* and its progeny with our responsibility to ensure that the political branches choose constitutionally permissible means of exercising their immigration power. We therefore proceed to "look behind" EO-2 using the framework developed in *Lemon* to determine if EO-2 was motivated by a primarily religious purpose, rather than its stated reason of promoting national security.

To prevail under the *Lemon* test, the Government must show that the challenged action (1) "ha[s] a secular legislative purpose," (2) that "its principal or primary effect [is] one that neither advances nor inhibits religion," and (3) that it does "not foster 'an excessive government entanglement with religion.' " The Government must satisfy all three prongs of *Lemon* to defeat an Establishment Clause challenge. *Edwards v. Aguillard*, 482 U.S. 578 (1987). The dispute here centers on *Lemon* 's first prong. . . . [T] he Government must show that the challenged action "ha[s] a secular legislative purpose" . . . that is "genuine, not a sham, and not merely secondary to a religious objective." The government cannot meet this requirement by identifying *any* secular purpose for the challenged action. *McCreary County v. ACLU of Ky.*, 545 U.S. 844 (2005). Rather, the government must show that the challenged action's *primary* purpose is secular.

When a court considers whether a challenged government action's primary purpose is secular, it attempts to discern the "official objective . . . from readily discoverable fact, without any judicial psychoanalysis of a drafter's heart of hearts." *McCreary*. The court acts as a reasonable, "objective observer," taking into account "the traditional external signs that show up in the 'text, legislative history, and implementation of the statute,' or comparable official act." It also considers the action's "historical context" and "the specific sequence of events leading to [its] passage." *Edwards*. And as a reasonable observer, a court has a "reasonable memor[y]," and it cannot " 'turn a blind eye to the context in which [the action] arose.' " *McCreary*.

The evidence in the record, viewed from the standpoint of the reasonable observer, creates a compelling case that EO-2's primary purpose is religious. Then-candidate Trump's campaign statements reveal that on numerous occasions, he expressed anti-Muslim sentiment, as well as his intent, if elected, to ban Muslims from the United States. For instance, on December 7, 2015, Trump posted on his campaign website a "Statement on Preventing Muslim Immigration," in which he "call[ed] for a total and complete shutdown of Muslims entering the United States until our representatives can figure out what is going on" and remarked, "[I]t is obvious to anybody that the hatred is beyond comprehension . . . . [O]ur country cannot be the victims of horrendous attacks by people that believe only in Jihad, and have no sense of reason or respect for human life." In a March 9, 2016 interview, Trump stated that "Islam hates us," and that "[w]e can't allow people coming into this country who have this hatred," Less than two weeks later, in a March 22 interview, Trump again called for excluding Muslims, because "we're having problems with the Muslims, and we're having problems with Muslims coming into the country." And on December 21, 2016, when asked whether recent attacks in Europe affected his proposed Muslim ban, President-Elect Trump replied, "You know my plans. All along, I've proven to be right. 100% correct."

As a candidate, Trump also suggested that he would attempt to circumvent scrutiny of the Muslim ban by formulating it in terms of nationality, rather than religion. On July 17, 2016, in response to a tweet stating, "Calls to ban Muslims from entering the U.S. are offensive and unconstitutional," Trump said, "So you call it territories. OK? We're gonna do territories." One week later, Trump asserted that entry should be "immediately suspended [ed] . . . from any nation that has been compromised by terrorism." When asked whether this meant he was "roll[ing]back" his call for a Muslim ban, he said his plan was an "expansion" and explained that "[p]eople were so upset when I used the word Muslim," so he was instead "talking territory instead of Muslim."

Significantly, the First Executive Order appeared to take this exact form, barring citizens of seven predominantly Muslim countries from entering the United

States. And just before President Trump signed EO-1 on January 27, 2017, he stated, "This is the 'Protection of the Nation from Foreign Terrorist Entry into the United States.' We all know what that means." The next day, presidential advisor and former New York City Mayor Giuliani appeared on Fox News and asserted that "when [Trump] first announced it, he said, 'Muslim ban.' He called me up. He said, 'Put a commission together. Show me the right way to do it legally.'"

Shortly after courts enjoined the First Executive Order, President Trump issued EO-2, which the President and members of his team characterized as being substantially similar to EO-1. EO-2 has the same name and basic structure as EO-1, but it does not include a preference for religious-minority refugees and excludes Iraq from its list of Designated Countries. EO-2, §1(e). It also exempts certain categories of nationals from the Designated Countries and institutes a waiver process for qualifying individuals. EO-2, §3(b), (c). Senior Policy Advisor Miller described the changes to EO-2 as "mostly minor technical differences," and said that there would be "the same basic policy outcomes for the country." White House Press Secretary Spicer stated that "[t]he principles of the [second] executive order remain the same." And President Trump, in a speech at a rally, described EO-2 as "a watered down version of the first order." These statements suggest that like EO-1, EO-2's purpose is to effectuate the promised Muslim ban, and that its changes from EO-1 reflect an effort to help it survive judicial scrutiny, rather than to avoid targeting Muslims for exclusion from the United States.

These statements, taken together, provide direct, specific evidence of what motivated both EO-1 and EO-2: President Trump's desire to exclude Muslims from the United States. The statements also reveal President Trump's intended means of effectuating the ban: by targeting majority-Muslim nations instead of Muslims explicitly. And after courts enjoined EO-1, the statements show how President Trump attempted to preserve its core mission: by issuing EO-2 — a "watered down" version with "the same basic policy outcomes." These statements are the exact type of "readily discoverable fact[s]" that we use in determining a government action's primary purpose. *McCreary*. They are explicit statements of purpose and are attributable either to President Trump directly or to his advisors. We need not probe anyone's heart of hearts to discover the purpose of EO-2, for President Trump and his aides have explained it on numerous occasions and in no uncertain terms. EO-2 cannot be read in isolation from the statements of planning and purpose that accompanied it, particularly in light of the sheer number of statements, their nearly singular source, and the close connection they draw between the proposed Muslim ban and EO-2 itself. The reasonable observer could easily connect these statements to EO-2 and understand that its primary purpose appears to be religious, rather than secular.

The Government argues, without meaningfully addressing Plaintiffs' proffered evidence, that EO-2's primary purpose is in fact secular because it is facially neutral and operates to address the risks of potential terrorism without targeting any particular religious group. That EO-2's stated objective is religiously neutral is not dispositive; the entire premise of our review under *Lemon* is that even facially neutral government actions can violate the Establishment Clause. . . .

The Government's argument that EO-2's primary purpose is related to national security, is belied by evidence in the record that President Trump issued the First Executive Order without consulting the relevant national security agencies, and that those agencies only offered a national security rationale after EO-1 was enjoined. Furthermore, internal reports from DHS contradict this national security rationale, with one report stating that "most foreign-born, US-based violent extremists likely radicalized several years after their entry to the United States, limiting the ability of screening and vetting officials to prevent their entry because of national security concerns." According to former National Security Officials, Section 2(c) serves "no legitimate national security purpose," given that "not a single American has died in a terrorist attack on U.S. soil at the hands of citizens of these six nations in the last forty years" and that there is no evidence of any new security risks emanating from these countries. Corrected Brief for Former National Security Officials as Amici Curiae Supporting Appellees 5–8, ECF No. 126-1. Like the district court, we think this strong evidence that any national security justification for EO-2 was secondary to its primary religious purpose and was offered as more of a "litigating position" than as the actual purpose of EO-2. And EO-2's text does little to bolster any national security rationale: the only examples it provides of immigrants born abroad and convicted of terrorism-related crimes in the United States include two Iraqis — Iraq is not a designated country in EO-2 — and a Somalian refugee who entered the United States as a child and was radicalized here as an adult. EO-2, §1(h). The Government's asserted national security purpose is therefore no more convincing as applied to EO-2 than it was to EO-1.

Relatedly, the Government argues that EO-2's operation "confirms its stated purpose." "[I]t applies to six countries based on risk, not religion; and in those six countries, the suspension applies irrespective of any alien's religion." *Id.* In support of its argument that EO-2 does not single out Muslims, the Government notes that these six countries are either places where ISIS has a heavy presence (Syria), state sponsors of terrorism (Iran, Sudan, and Syria), or safe havens for terrorists (Libya, Somalia, and Yemen). The Government also points out that the six Designated Countries represent only a small proportion of the world's majority-Muslim nations, and EO-2 applies to everyone in those countries, even non-Muslims. This shows, the Government argues, that EO-2's primary purpose is secular. The trouble with this argument is that EO-2's practical operation is not severable from the myriad statements explaining its operation as intended to bar Muslims from the United States. And that EO-2 is underinclusive by targeting only a small percentage of the world's majority-Muslim nations and overinclusive for targeting all citizens, even non-Muslims, in the Designated Countries, is not responsive to the purpose inquiry. This evidence might be relevant to our analysis under *Lemon*'s second prong, which asks whether a government act has the primary *effect* of endorsing or disapproving of religion, *see Lynch v. Donnelly*, 465 U.S. 668 (1984) (O'Connor, J., concurring), but it does not answer whether the government acted with a primarily religious purpose to begin with. If we limited our purpose inquiry to review of the operation of a facially neutral order, we would be caught in an analytical loop, where the order would always survive scrutiny. It is for this precise reason that when we attempt to discern purpose, we look to more than just the challenged action itself. And here, when we consider the full context of EO-2, it is evident that it is likely motivated primarily by religion. We do not discount that there may be a national security concern motivating EO-2; we merely find it likely that any such purpose is secondary to EO-2's religious purpose.

The Government separately contends that our purpose inquiry should not extend to "extrinsic evidence" that is beyond EO-2's relevant context. The Government first argues that we should not look beyond EO-2's "text and operation." But this is clearly incorrect, as the Supreme Court has explicitly stated that we review more than just the face of a challenged action. *See, e.g., Bd. of Educ. of Kiryas Joel Vill. Sch. Dist. v. Grumet*, 512 U.S. 687 (1994). . . .

[F]inally, the Government argues that even if we could consider unofficial acts and statements, we should not rely on campaign statements. Those statements predate President Trump's constitutionally significant "transition from private life to the Nation's highest public office," and as such, they are less probative than official statements, the Government contends. We recognize that in many cases, campaign statements may not reveal all that much about a government actor's purpose. But we decline to impose a bright-line rule against considering campaign statements, because as with any evidence, we must make an individualized determination as to a statement's relevancy and probative value in light of all the circumstances. The campaign statements here are probative of purpose because they are closely related in time, attributable to the primary decision-maker, and specific and easily connected to the challenged action. *See Village of Arlington Heights v. Metro. Hous. Dev. Corp.*, 429 U.S. 252 (1977) (explaining that in the equal protection context, "[w]hen there is [ ] proof that a discriminatory purpose has been a motivating factor in the decision," a court may consider "contemporary statements by members of the decisionmaking body").

Just as the reasonable observer's "world is not made brand new every morning," *McCreary*, nor are we able to awake without the vivid memory of these statements. We cannot shut our eyes to such evidence when it stares us in the face, for "there's none so blind as they that won't see." If and when future courts are confronted with campaign or other statements proffered as evidence of governmental purpose, those courts must similarly determine, on a case-by-case basis, whether such statements are probative evidence of governmental purpose. Our holding today neither limits nor expands their review. . . . . . This finding comports with the *McCreary* Court's observation that "past actions [do not] forever taint" a government action. Whether a statement continues to taint a government action is a fact-specific inquiry for the court evaluating the statement. [relocated footnote — eds.]

The Government argues that reviewing campaign statements here would encourage scrutiny of all religious statements ever made by elected officials, even remarks from before they assumed office. But our review creates no such sweeping implications, because as the Supreme Court has counseled, our purpose analysis "demands a sensitive inquiry into such circumstantial and direct evidence of intent as may be available." Just as a reasonable observer would not understand general statements of religious conviction to inform later government action, nor would we look to such statements as evidence of purpose. A person's particular religious beliefs, her college essay on religious freedom, a speech she gave on the Free Exercise Clause — rarely, if ever, will such evidence reveal anything about that person's actions once in office. For a past statement to be relevant to the government's purpose, there must be a substantial, specific connection between it and the challenged government action. And here, in this highly unique set of circumstances, there is a direct link between the President's numerous campaign statements promising a Muslim ban that targets territories, the discrete action he took only one week into office executing that exact plan, and EO-2, the "watered down" version of that plan that "get[s] just about everything," and "in some ways, more."

For similar reasons, we reject the Government's argument that our review of these campaign statements will "inevitably 'chill political debate during campaigns.'" Not all—not even most—political debate will have any relevance to a challenged government action. Indeed, this case is unique not because we are considering campaign statements, but because we have such directly relevant and probative statements of government purpose at all. *See Smith v. Town of Clarkton*, 682 F.2d 1055, 1064 (4th Cir. 1982) (observing that government actors "seldom, if ever, announce on the record that they are pursuing a particular course of action because of their desire to discriminate"). To the extent that our review chills campaign promises to condemn and exclude entire religious groups, we think that a welcome restraint.

Lastly, the Government contends that we are ill-equipped to "attempt[ ] to assess what campaign statements reveal about the motivation for later action." The Government argues that to do so would "mire [us] in a swamp of unworkable litigation," and "forc[e us] to wrestle with intractable questions," such as "the level of generality at which a statement must be made, by whom, and how long after its utterance the statement remains probative." But discerning the motives behind a challenged government action is a well-established part of our purpose inquiry. As part of this inquiry, courts regularly evaluate decisionmakers' statements that show their purpose for acting. And the purpose inquiry is not limited to Establishment Clause challenges; we conduct this analysis in a variety of contexts. *See, e.g., United States v. Windsor*, ____ U.S. ____, 133 S.Ct. 2675 (2013) (striking down federal statute based in part on "strong evidence" that "the congressional purpose [was] to influence or interfere with state sovereign choices about who may be married"); *Pers. Adm'r of Mass. v. Feeney*, 442 U.S. 256 (1979) (upholding public hiring preferences based in part on finding that government had not created preferences with purpose of discriminating on the basis of sex); *N.C. State Conference of NAACP v. McCrory*, 831 F.3d 204, 219 (4th Cir. 2016) (concluding that challenged voting restrictions were unconstitutional because they were motivated by racially discriminatory intent). We therefore see nothing "intractable" about evaluating a statement's probative value based on the identity of the speaker and how specifically the statement relates to the challenged government action, for this is surely a routine part of constitutional analysis. And this analysis is even more straightforward here, because we are not attempting to discern motive from many legislators' statements . . . but rather are looking primarily to one person's statements to discern that person's motive for taking a particular action once in office.

The Government has repeatedly asked this Court to ignore evidence, circumscribe our own review, and blindly defer to executive action, all in the name of the Constitution's separation of powers. We decline to do so, not only because it is the particular province of the judicial branch to say what the law is, but also because we would do a disservice to our constitutional structure were we to let its mere invocation silence the call for meaningful judicial review. The deference we give the coordinate branches is surely powerful, but even it must yield in certain circumstances, lest we abdicate our own duties to uphold the Constitution.

EO-2 cannot be divorced from the cohesive narrative linking it to the animus that inspired it. In light of this, we find that the reasonable observer would likely conclude that EO-2's primary purpose is to exclude persons from the United States on the basis of their religious beliefs. We therefore find that EO-2 likely fails *Lemon*'s purpose prong in violation of the Establishment Clause. Accordingly, we hold that the district court did not err in concluding that Plaintiffs are likely to succeed on the merits of their Establishment Clause claim.

THACKER, Circuit Judge, concurring:

I concur in the majority's opinion but write separately for three reasons: (1) I would not consider remarks made by candidate Trump before he took his presidential oath of office; (2) I would nonetheless find that Appellees have demonstrated a likelihood of success on the merits of their argument that Section 2(c) of the Second Executive Order ("EO-2") violates the Establishment Clause, based solely on remarks made or sentiments expressed after January 20, 2017 . . . . [T]he judiciary's ability to probe official, presidential conduct is related to his discharge of official power. . . . It follows that a president's conduct after he takes office, but not before, carries the imprimatur of official "government" action, and can only then be considered "government interference" under the Establishment Clause.

For more practical reasons, we should also hesitate to attach constitutional significance to words a candidate utters on the campaign trail. Campaign speeches are inevitably scattered with bold promises, but once the dust settles after an election — when faced with the reality of the office and with benefit of wise counsel — a newly inducted public official may act with a different philosophy. Presidents throughout history have dialed back or even reversed campaign promises. To be sure, the President's statements regarding Islam before assuming office reveal religious animus that is deeply troubling. Nonetheless, I do not adhere to the view that we should magnify our analytical lens simply because doing so would support our conclusion, particularly when we need not do so. . . .

Given that they were made on the campaign trail, I do not consider as part of my analysis the President's campaign website's archived statements about the plan to ban all Muslims from entering the United States. However, I must note it is peculiar that those statements were removed shortly before we began hearing arguments in this case. *See* Dan Merica, *Trump campaign removes controversial Muslim ban language from website*, CNN (May 8, 2017, 3:37 PM), http://www.cnn.com/2017/05/08/politics/trump-muslim-ban-campaign-website/ (saved as ECF opinion attachment) [relocated footnote—eds.]

NIEMEYER, CIRCUIT JUDGE, with whom JUDGE SHEDD and JUDGE AGEE join, dissenting:

In affirming the district court's ruling based on the Establishment Clause, the majority looks past the face of the Order's statements on national security and immigration, which it concedes are neutral in terms of religion, and considers campaign statements made by candidate Trump to conclude that the Order denigrates Islam, in violation of the Establishment Clause. This approach (1) plainly violates the Supreme Court's directive in *Mandel*; (2) adopts a *new rule of law* that uses campaign statements to recast the plain, unambiguous, and religiously neutral text of an executive order; and (3) radically extends the Supreme Court's Establishment Clause holdings. I address these legal errors in turn.

[In *Mandel*] [t]he Court forbade judges from interfering with the executive's "facially legitimate and bona fide" exercise of its immigration authority or balancing that exercise against constitutional rights. Specifically, it recognized that "Congress has delegated conditional exercise of this power [of exclusion] to the Executive" and declined to apply more scrutiny to executive exercise of that power than it would to Congress's own actions. It concluded:

> We hold that when the Executive exercises this power negatively on the basis of a facially legitimate and bona fide reason, *the courts will neither look behind the exercise of that discretion, nor test it by balancing its justification against the First Amendment interests* of those who seek personal communication with the applicant.

Id. (emphasis added). . . . In *Fiallo v. Bell*, 430 U.S. 787 (1977), the Court declined to scrutinize a statute that gave different immigration status to a child born out of wedlock depending on whether it was the child's mother or father who was a citizen or lawful permanent resident. Although that statute involved two suspect classifications—gender and legitimacy—the Court, citing *Mandel*, nonetheless concluded that "it is not the judicial role in cases of this sort to probe and test the justifications" of immigration policies. Accordingly, in response to the plaintiffs' arguments that the distinction was based "on an overbroad and outdated stereotype," the Court indicated that "this argument should be addressed to the Congress rather than the courts."

And both *Mandel* and *Fiallo* were reaffirmed more recently in Justice Kennedy's opinion in *Kerry v. Din*, ____ U.S. ___, 135 S.Ct. 2128 (2015) (Kennedy, J., concurring in the judgment). In *Din*, the Court considered a suit by a United States citizen who alleged that the government deprived her of a liberty interest protected under the Due Process Clause by denying her husband's visa application without adequate explanation, providing only a citation to the provision under which the visa was denied. Justice Kennedy, writing for himself and Justice Alito to provide the fourth and fifth votes in favor of the government, stated that "[t]he reasoning and the holding in *Mandel* control here" and that the reasoning of *Mandel* "has particular force in the area of national security." He concluded that "respect for the political branches' broad power over the creation and administration of the immigration system" meant that, because the government had provided Din with a facially legitimate and bona fide reason for its action, Din had no viable constitutional claim. . . .

To reach its conclusion, the majority does not adopt the plaintiffs' broad argument that *Mandel* does not even apply. Instead, in its attempt to escape *Mandel*'s clear holding, it asserts that "[w]here plaintiffs have seriously called into question whether the stated reason for the challenged action was provided in good faith," the court may "step away from our deferential posture and look behind the stated reason for the challenged action" to attempt to discern the action's purpose. This approach, which totally undermines *Mandel*, is the foundation of its new rule that campaign statements may be considered to recast an unambiguous, later-adopted executive order on immigration. The majority states that even though the Order is on its face legitimate and provides reasons rooted in national security, because the plaintiffs "have more than plausibly alleged" bad faith, "we no longer defer" to the Order's stated purpose "and instead may 'look behind' [the Order]" in an attempt to discern whether the national security reason was *in fact* provided as a pretext for its religious purpose. . . . If the majority's understanding had been shared by the Supreme Court, it would have compelled different results in each of *Mandel*, *Fiallo*, and *Din*, as in each of those cases the plaintiffs alleged bad faith with at least as much particularity as do the plaintiffs here. In *Mandel*, the allegations were such that Justice Marshall, writing in dissent, observed that "[e]ven the briefest peek behind the Attorney General's reason for refusing a waiver in this case would reveal that it is a sham." In *Fiallo*, Justice Marshall, again writing in dissent, pointed to the fact that the statute in question relied on "invidious classifications." And in *Din*, the plaintiffs argued that the consular decision should be reviewed because it fell within the "limited circumstances where the government provides no reason, or where the reason on its face is illegitimate." But, as those cases hold, a lack of good faith must appear on the face of the government's action, not from looking behind it. . . . .

In looking behind the face of the government's action for facts to show the alleged bad faith, rather than looking for bad faith on the face of the executive action itself, the majority grants itself the power to conduct an extratextual search for evidence suggesting bad faith, which is exactly what three Supreme Court opinions have prohibited. *Mandel*, *Fiallo*, and *Din* have for decades been entirely clear that courts are not free to look behind these sorts of exercises of executive discretion in search of circumstantial evidence of alleged bad faith.

The majority, now for the first time, rejects these holdings in favor of its politically desired outcome.

B

Considering the Order on its face, as we are required to do by *Mandel, Fiallo,* and *Din*, it is entirely without constitutional fault. The Order was a valid exercise of the President's authority under 8 U.S.C. §§1182(f) and 1185(a) to suspend the entry of "any aliens" or "any class of aliens" and to prescribe "reasonable rules, regulations, and orders" regarding entry, so long as the President finds that the aliens' admission would be "detrimental to the interests of the United States." Moreover, the particular reasons given for the issuance of the Executive Order respond directly to the described risk of terrorism from six countries, justifying the imposition of a 90-day pause in the admission of nationals from those countries while the Administration determines whether existing screening and vetting procedures are adequate.

The Executive Order begins by noting that the previous Administration, in conjunction with Congress, identified seven countries — Iran, Iraq, Libya, Somalia, Sudan, Syria, and Yemen — "as presenting heightened concerns about terrorism and travel to the United States," specifically noting that the previous Administration's Secretary of Homeland Security designated Libya, Somalia, and Yemen as countries of concern for travel purposes based on terrorism and national security. And finally it notes that Members of Congress had expressed concerns about "screening and vetting procedures" following terrorist attacks in 2016 in Europe, as well as in this country.

Adding to the historical assessment of those risks, the Executive Order continues with its conclusions, based on additional data, that the conditions in the countries previously identified had worsened, at least with respect to six of the seven countries (excepting Iraq), noting that some of those countries were state sponsors of terrorism or were significantly compromised by terrorist organizations. Several of the countries were unwilling or unable to share or validate information about nationals seeking to travel to the United States, and in some, the conditions increasingly enabled "terrorist operatives or sympathizers to travel to the United States."

Finally, the Order addresses the particular circumstances of each of the six countries covered by the Order, noting for example, that Iran, Sudan, and Syria were state sponsors of terrorism; that the governments in Libya, Somalia, and Syria were rendered partially or entirely unable to resist terrorist organizations because of the organizations' activities; and that Iran, Libya, Syria, and Yemen either were not cooperating with the United States in its counterterrorism efforts or were unable to do so.

None of the facts or conditions recited as reasons for the issuance of the Executive Order have been challenged as untrue or illegitimate. Indeed, the plaintiffs conceded during oral argument that if another candidate had won the presidential election in November 2016 and thereafter entered this same

Executive Order, they would have had no problem with the Order. As counsel for the plaintiffs stated, "I think in that case [the Order] could be constitutional." Similarly, the district court found the face of the Order to be neutral in terms of religion. And the majority too so concludes.

Moreover, these reasons amply support the modest action taken by the Executive Order, which imposes only a temporary pause of 90 days to assess whether the screening and vetting procedures that are applied to nationals from these high-risk countries are adequate to identify and exclude terrorists. Even this pause is accompanied by an authorization to issue waivers designed to limit any harmful impact without compromising national security.

While the legitimate justifications for the Order are thoroughly established, its supposed ills are nowhere present on its face. Far from containing the sort of religious advocacy or disparagement that can violate the Establishment Clause, the Order contains no reference to religion whatsoever. Nor is there any trace of discriminatory animus. In short, under *Mandel* and its progeny, Executive Order 13,780 comfortably survives our review.

The majority's new rule, which considers statements made by candidate Trump during the presidential campaign to conclude that the Executive Order does not mean what it says, is fraught with danger and impracticability. Apart from violating all established rules for construing unambiguous texts—whether statutes, regulations, executive orders, or, indeed, contracts—reliance on campaign statements to impose a new meaning on an unambiguous Executive Order is completely strange to judicial analysis.

The Supreme Court has repeatedly warned against "judicial psychoanalysis of a drafter's heart of hearts." *McCreary Cty., Ky. v. Am. Civil Liberties Union of Ky.*, 545 U.S. 844, 862 (2005). And consistent with that warning, the Court has never, "in evaluating the legality of executive action, deferred to comments made by such officials to the media." *Hamdan v. Rumsfeld*, 548 U.S. 557, 623–24 n.52 (2006). The Court's reluctance to consider statements made in the course of campaigning derives from good sense and a recognition of the pitfalls that would accompany such an inquiry.

Because of their nature, campaign statements are unbounded resources by which to find intent of various kinds. They are often short-hand for larger ideas; they are explained, modified, retracted, and amplified as they are repeated and as new circumstances and arguments arise. And they are often ambiguous. A court applying the majority's new rule could thus have free reign to select whichever expression of a candidate's developing ideas best supports its desired conclusion.

Moreover, opening the door to the use of campaign statements to inform the text of later executive orders has no rational limit. If a court, dredging through the myriad remarks of a campaign, fails to find material to produce the desired outcome, what stops it from probing deeper to find statements from a previous campaign, or from a previous business conference, or from college?

And how would use of such statements take into account intervening acts, events, and influences? When a candidate wins the election to the presidency, he takes an oath of office to abide by the Constitution and the laws of the Nation;

he appoints officers of the government and retains advisors, usually specialized in their field. Is there not the possibility that a candidate might have different intentions than a President in office? And after taking office, a President faces new external events that may prompt new approaches altogether. How would a court assess the effect of these intervening events on presidential intent without conducting judicial psychoanalysis?

The foibles of such a rule are unbounded and its adoption would have serious implications for the democratic process. As Judge Kozinski said well when he wrote about the Ninth Circuit's use of the same campaign statements:

> Even if a politician's past statements were utterly clear and consistent, using them to yield a specific constitutional violation would suggest an absurd result — namely, that the policies of an elected official can be forever held hostage by the unguarded declarations of a candidate. If a court were to find that campaign skeletons prevented an official from pursuing otherwise constitutional policies, what could he do to cure the defect? Could he stand up and recant it all ("just kidding!") and try again? Or would we also need a court to police the sincerity of that mea culpa — piercing into the public official's "heart of hearts" to divine whether he really changed his mind, just as the Supreme Court has warned us not to? . . .

Washington v. Trump, No. 17-35105 (9th Cir. March 17, 2017) (Kozinski, J., dissenting from the denial of reconsideration en banc).

The danger of the majority's new rule is that it will enable any court to justify its decision to strike down any executive action with which it disagrees. It need only find one statement that contradicts the stated reasons for a subsequent executive action and thereby pronounce that reasons for the executive action are a pretext. This, I submit, is precisely what the majority opinion does.

Moreover, the unbounded nature of the majority's new rule will leave the President and his Administration in a clearly untenable position for future action. It is undeniable that President Trump will need to engage in foreign policy regarding majority-Muslim nations, including those designated by the Order. And yet the majority now suggests that at least some of those future actions might also be subject to the same challenges upheld today. Presumably, the majority does not intend entirely to stop the President from creating policies that address these nations, but it gives the President no guidelines for "cleansing" himself of the "taint" they have purportedly identified.

Finally, the new rule would by itself chill political speech directed at voters seeking to make their election decision. It is hard to imagine a greater or more direct chill on campaign speech than the knowledge that any statement made may be used later to support the inference of some nefarious intent when official actions are inevitably subjected to legal challenges. Indeed, the majority does not even deny that it employs an approach that will limit communication to voters. Instead, it simply opines remarkably that such chilling is "a welcome restraint."

The Supreme Court surely will shudder at the majority's adoption of this new rule that has no limits or bounds — one that transforms the majority's criticisms of a candidate's various campaign statements into a constitutional violation.

Finally, it is readily apparent that the plaintiffs' attempt to use campaign statements to transform a facially neutral executive action into an Establishment Clause violation would, in any event, be unlikely to succeed on the merits. . . . [T]he Supreme Court has never applied the Establishment Clause to matters of national security and foreign affairs. And of the few government actions that the Supreme Court has invalidated based on a religious purpose, each is manifestly distinguishable from the Order here.

[In] *McCreary*, . . . the Court there confronted a *facially religious* government action—the display of the Ten Commandments in two county courthouses. The Court in *McCreary* thus began with a *presumption* that the display was intended to promote religion. . . . In stark contrast, the district court here concluded, and the majority agrees, that nothing on the face of the Executive Order speaks to religion. Under *McCreary*, we should therefore begin with the presumption that the Order is neutral toward religion.

To be sure, the Supreme Court in "unusual cases" will find a religious purpose even where the government action contains no facial reference to religion. . . . [But] [i]n each case, the Court found the government action inexplicable *but for* a religious purpose, and it looked to extrinsic evidence only to confirm its suspicion, prompted by the face of the action, that it had religious origins. . . . The Executive Order in this case . . . is framed and enforced without reference to religion, and the government's proffered national security justifications, which are consistent with the stated purposes of the Order, withstand scrutiny. Conflicting extrinsic statements made prior to the Order's enactment surely cannot supplant its facially legitimate national security purpose. . . .

The government here, by contrast, provides ample nonreligious justification for the Order and actively contests that it has any religious purpose. Far from running "counter" to typical national security practice, each of the Order's six affected countries was previously designated as "a state sponsor of terrorism, has been significantly compromised by terrorist organizations, or contains active conflict zones." And an Order that affects all nationals of six countries, irrespective of their religion, is not so precisely hewn to religious lines that we can infer, based on its operation alone, a predominantly religious purpose. . . .

The majority's intense factual inquiry is particularly inappropriate where the government's secular purpose is related to national security—a subject, as the majority recognizes, on which we owe the executive significant deference.

Unless corrected by the Supreme Court, the majority's new approach, which is unsupported by any Supreme Court case, will become a sword for plaintiffs to challenge facially neutral government actions, particularly those affecting regions dominated by a single religion. Government officials will avoid speaking about religion, even privately, lest a court discover statements that could be used to ascribe a religious motivation to their future actions. And, in the more immediate future, our courts will be faced with the unworkable task of determining when this President's supposed religious motive has sufficiently dissipated so as to allow executive action toward these or other majority-Muslim countries. The

Establishment Clause demands none of these unfortunate and unprecedented results.

* * *

For all of the foregoing reasons, I would reject the plaintiffs' and the district court's Establishment Clause arguments and vacate the district court's injunction.

SHEDD, Circuit Judge, with whom Judge NIEMEYER and Judge AGEE join, dissenting:

National security is a complex business with potentially grave consequences for our country. Recognizing this fact, the Supreme Court has observed that "it is obvious and unarguable that no governmental interest is more compelling than the security of the Nation." This observation is especially true in today's world, where we face threats from radical terrorists who seek to cross our borders for the purpose of harming us and destroying our way of life. Although we often are quick to forget the fact, "the real risks, the real threats, of terrorist attacks are constant and not likely soon to abate;" therefore, "the Government's interest in combating terrorism is an urgent objective of the highest order." Given the multitude of critical factors involved in protecting national security, including the delicacy of foreign relations and the worldwide intelligence information that is constantly generated, combined with the ever-changing threatening circumstances, "questions of national security . . . do not admit of easy answers, especially not as products of the necessarily limited analysis undertaken in a single case," and "they are and should be undertaken only by those directly responsible to the people whose welfare they advance or imperil."

Every President has the "constitutional responsibility for the security of the Nation as the Chief Executive and as Commander in Chief of our Armed forces." In this role, a President and his national security advisors (unlike federal judges at all levels, lawyers, and commentators) have constant access to information "that may describe new and serious threats to our Nation and its people." For these reasons and more, "courts traditionally have been reluctant to intrude upon the authority of the Executive in military and national security affairs."

This case involves the President's attempt to impose a *temporary pause* on the entry of nationals from six countries that indisputably present national security concerns. "It is pertinent to observe that any policy toward aliens is vitally and intricately interwoven with contemporaneous policies in regard to the conduct of foreign relations, the war power, and the maintenance of a republican form of government. Such matters are so exclusively entrusted to the political branches of government as to be largely immune from judicial inquiry or interference." Along this line, the Supreme Court has noted that "the Government's interest in preventing the entry of unwanted persons and effects is at its zenith at the international border," and has explained that the President is not obligated to disclose his reasons "for deeming nationals of a particular country a special threat . . . and even if [he] did disclose them a court would be ill equipped to determine their authenticity and utterly unable to assess their adequacy," *Reno v. American-Arab Anti-Discrimination Comm.*, 525 U.S. 471, 491 (1999).

One thing is certain: to whatever extent it is permissible to examine the President's national security decision in this case, where the President has acted "pursuant to an express or implied authorization from Congress," the President's decision is entitled to "the strongest of presumptions and the widest latitude of judicial interpretation, and the burden of persuasion would rest heavily upon any who might attack it." *Dames & Moore v. Regan*, 453 U.S. 654 (1981). This is especially true when, as here, plaintiffs seek preliminary injunctive relief to stop the President from executing a national security policy, for in even the most routine cases, which this certainly is not, a preliminary injunction "is a drastic and extraordinary remedy, which should not be granted as a matter of course."

The obvious rationale underlying these important principles has been discussed many times by the Supreme Court, this Court, and others, but the district court totally failed to respect them. Rather than giving any deference to the President (or his national security advisors) regarding his national security assessment, or imposing a heavy burden on the plaintiffs to overcome the President's decision, or showing any sense of restraint in wielding the extraordinary remedy of injunctive relief, the district court simply cast aside the President's decision as nothing more than a sham based on its own ideas concerning the wisdom of the Executive Order. In doing so, the district court made the extraordinary finding — based on a *preliminary* evidentiary record — that the President exercised his otherwise lawful authority to effect the temporary pause primarily because he bears animus towards Muslims and wants to impose a "Muslim ban." Remarkably, the district court made this finding while also acknowledging that the Executive Order is facially neutral, that there are heightened security risks with the countries listed in the Executive Order, and that national security interests would be served by the travel pause.

The shortcomings inherent in the district court's fact-finding are obvious. It is primarily based on the district court's selectively negative interpretation of political campaign statements made before the President swore his oath of office, its acceptance of the national security assessment of *former* government officials (many of whom openly oppose this President), its failure to account for the national security assessment of the *current* Attorney General and Secretary of Homeland Security, its misplaced conclusion regarding the President's decision not to submit the Executive Order to the Executive bureaucracy for "inter-agency review," and the purported novelty of the temporary travel pause. Moreover, despite its express recognition of the dangers posed by the designated countries and the national security interests served by the temporary travel pause, the district court — with no access to intelligence information — criticized the President for failing to identify any instances of individuals who came from the designated countries having engaged in terrorist activity in the United States, faulted the President for not explaining why the temporary travel pause is the necessary response to the existing risks, and ultimately found that the President failed to prove that national security cannot be maintained without the temporary travel pause. As if all of this is not enough, the President's supposed goal of "banning Muslims" from the United States is not remotely served by the temporary travel pause, a fact that makes the district court's factual finding even more dubious.

The district court's questionable fact-finding is sufficient (among other reasons) to vacate the injunction, but there is ultimately a more obvious fatal flaw in the injunction order: the court's complete failure to actually account for the public interest. In addition to the general restraint courts must show when considering injunctive relief, courts "should be particularly cautious when contemplating relief that implicates public interests." Although the public interest generally favors the protection of constitutional rights, that interest must sometimes yield to the public interest in national security, because "unless a society has the capability and will to defend itself from the aggressions of others, constitutional protections of any sort have little meaning," This is such a case. . . .

[T]herefore, the relevant point is not whether the temporary travel pause is the *only* way, or even the best way, to protect national security. The simple fact of the matter is that regardless of any ulterior motive one might ascribe to the President, the record still conclusively establishes that the temporary travel pause will in fact promote an important national security objective.

Undoubtedly, protection of constitutional rights is important, but there are often times in the federal system when constitutional rights must yield for the public interest. As we have explained, for example, in applying the state secrets doctrine, a plaintiff with a plausibly viable constitutional claim can be barred from pursuing it "not through any fault of his own, but because his personal interest in pursuing his civil claim is subordinated to the collective interest in national security." In my view, the very serious national security interest served by the temporary travel pause (as determined by those who are duly empowered to make the decision and who have access to current intelligence information) greatly outweighs the alleged temporary and relatively minor harm that will befall these few plaintiffs. The district court abused its discretion by failing to strike this balance.

Today's decision may be celebrated by some as a victory for individual civil rights and justice, and by others as a political defeat for this President. Yet, it is shortsighted to ignore the larger ramifications of this decision. Regrettably, at the end of the day, the real losers in this case are the millions of individual Americans whose security is threatened on a daily basis by those who seek to do us harm. Even if the district court's instinct is correct and no tangible harm directly results from its order enjoining the President from attempting to protect American citizens, the injunction prohibits the government from addressing a serious risk identified by the Attorney General and Homeland Security Secretary; therefore, the security of our nation is indisputably lessened as a result of the injunction. Moreover, the President and his national security advisors (and perhaps future Presidents) will be seriously hampered in their ability to exercise their constitutional duty to protect this country. . . . At oral argument, several judges (including myself) questioned when, if ever, the President could free himself from the stigma of bias that the district court has enshrined by its preliminary "factfinding." Notably, no one has provided a satisfactory response. [relocated footnote — eds.]

HAWAII V. TRUMP, 2017 WL 2529640 (9th Cir., June 12, 2017): [The State of Hawaii and Dr. Ismail Elshikh, an American citizen and imam whose Syrian mother-in-law sought entry into the United States, challenged §2 and §6 of EO-2. A district court in Hawaii not only issued a categorical injunction against implementation of the entry bans and refugee limit, but also enjoined the internal agency review of procedures that Sections 2 and 6 prescribed. A three-judge panel of the Ninth Circuit upheld most of the Hawaii federal district court's preliminary injunction against EO-2, including the injunction against the §2(c) entry suspension, the §6(a) suspension of refugee admissions, and the §6(b) refugee cap. The Ninth Circuit narrowed the injunction, however, so that it would not bar the Government from undertaking the internal executive reviews directed by EO–2. Accordingly, the internal review began in June. Although the district court based its opinion on the Establishment Clause, the Ninth Circuit did not address that question, but concluded instead that the President lacked statutory authority to promulgate the bans and limits under the Immigration and Naturalization Act (INA), a holding that avoided the need to reach the constitutional questions.]

PER CURIAM:
Under Article I of the Constitution, the power to make immigration laws "is entrusted exclusively to Congress." . . .
In the INA of 1952, Congress delegated some of its power to the President through Section 212(f), which provides:

> Whenever the President finds that the entry of any aliens or of any class of aliens into the United States would be detrimental to the interests of the United States, he may by proclamation, and for such period as he shall deem necessary, suspend the entry of all aliens or any class of aliens as immigrants or nonimmigrants, or impose on the entry of aliens any restrictions he may deem to be appropriate.

8 U.S.C. §1182(f).
In Section 2(c) of the Order, the President invokes this power . . . to suspend for 90 days the entry of nationals from the six designated countries. . . . [I]n Section 6(b), the President invokes §1182(f) to cap refugee admissions at 50,000 for the 2017 fiscal year.
The parties dispute whether EO2 falls clearly within the President's congressionally delegated authority. To be sure, §1182(f) gives the President broad authority to suspend the entry of aliens or classes of aliens. However, this authority is not unlimited. Section 1182(f) requires that the President *find* that the entry of a class of aliens into the United States *would be detrimental* to the interests of the United States. This section requires that the President's findings support the conclusion that entry of all nationals from the six designated countries, all refugees, and refugees in excess of 50,000 would be harmful to the national interest.

There is no sufficient finding in EO2 that the entry of the excluded classes would be detrimental to the interests of the United States.

i

Section 2(c) declares that "the unrestricted entry into the United States of nationals of Iran, Libya, Somalia, Sudan, Syria, and Yemen would be detrimental to the interests of the United States" and directs that the entry of nationals from those designated countries be barred for 90 days. The provision bans more than 180 million people from entry based on their national origin, including nationals who may have never been physically present in those countries.

Section 2(c) [gives four reasons justifications for the ban]: "[1] To temporarily reduce investigative burdens on relevant agencies during the review period [of the United States' vetting procedures], [2] to ensure the proper review and maximum utilization of available resources for the screening and vetting of foreign nationals, [3] to ensure that adequate standards are established to prevent infiltration by foreign terrorists, and [4] in light of the national security concerns." The Government explains that the Order's objective "is to address the risk that potential terrorists might exploit possible weaknesses in the Nation's screening and vetting procedures while the review of those procedures is underway."

We reject the first three reasons provided in Section 2(c) because they relate to preservation of government resources to review existing procedures and ensure adequate vetting procedures. There is no finding that present vetting standards are inadequate, and no finding that absent the improved vetting procedures there likely will be harm to our national interests. These identified reasons do not support the conclusion that the entry of nationals from the six designated countries would be harmful to our national interests.

[T]he fourth reason [given is] national security concerns . . . Section 1(d) of the Order explains that nationals from Iran, Libya, Somalia, Sudan, Syria, and Yemen warrant additional scrutiny because:

> Each of these *countries* is a state sponsor of terrorism, has been significantly compromised by terrorist organizations, or contains active conflict zones. Any of these circumstances diminishes the foreign government's willingness or ability to share or validate important information about individuals seeking to travel to the United States. Moreover, the significant presence in each of these *countries* of terrorist organizations, their members, and others exposed to those organizations increases the chance that conditions will be exploited to enable terrorist operatives or sympathizers to travel to the United States. Finally, once foreign nationals from these countries are admitted to the United States, it is often difficult to remove them, because many of these *countries* typically delay issuing, or refuse to issue, travel documents.

Because of these country conditions, the Order concludes that "the risk of erroneously permitting entry of a national of one of these countries who intends to commit terrorist acts or otherwise harm the national security of the United

States is unacceptably high." The Order further indicates that "hundreds of persons born abroad have been convicted of terrorism-related crimes in the United States[,]" but does not identify the number of nationals from the six designated countries who have been so convicted.

The Order makes no finding that nationality alone renders entry of this broad class of individuals a heightened security risk to the United States. . . . The Order does not tie these nationals in any way to terrorist organizations within the six designated countries. It does not identify these nationals as contributors to active conflict or as those responsible for insecure country conditions. It does not provide any link between an individual's nationality and their propensity to commit terrorism or their inherent dangerousness. In short, the Order does not provide a rationale explaining why permitting entry of nationals from the six designated countries under current protocols would be detrimental to the interests of the United States.

The Order's discussion of country conditions fails to bridge the gap. Indeed, its use of nationality as the sole basis for suspending entry means that nationals without significant ties to the six designated countries, such as those who left as children or those whose nationality is based on parentage alone, should be suspended from entry. Yet, nationals of other countries who do have meaningful ties to the six designated countries — and may be contributing to the very country conditions discussed — fall outside the scope of Section 2(c). Consequently, EO2's focus on nationality "could have the paradoxical effect of barring entry by a Syrian national who has lived in Switzerland for decades, but not a Swiss national who has immigrated to Syria during its civil war."

Although the Order explains that country conditions in the six designated countries lessen their governments' ability to share information about nationals seeking to travel to our country, the Order specifically avoids making any finding that the current screening processes are inadequate. As the law stands, a visa applicant bears the burden of showing that the applicant is eligible to receive a visa or other document for entry and is not inadmissible. The Government already can exclude individuals who do not meet that burden. The Order offers no further reason explaining how this individualized adjudication process is flawed such that permitting entry of an entire class of nationals is injurious to the interests of the United States.

Finally, the Order relies on 8 U.S.C. §1187(a)(12) to explain why the six countries have been designated. In §1187(a)(12), Congress prevented use of the Visa Waiver Program by dual nationals of, or those who have visited in the last six years, (1) Iraq and Syria, (2) any country designated by the Secretary of State as a state sponsor of terrorism, and (3) any other country designated as a country of concern by the Secretary of Homeland Security, in consultation with the Secretary of State and the Director of National Intelligence. Rather than setting an outright ban on entry of nationals from these countries, Congress restricted access to the tourist Visa Waiver Program and instead required that persons who are nationals of or have recently traveled to these countries enter the United States with a visa. This provision reflects Congress's considered view on similar security concerns that the Order seeks to address. The Order identifies no new information to justify Section 2(c)'s blanket ban as contrasted with §1187(a)(12)'s restriction from the Visa Waiver Program. Moreover, relying on §1187(a)(12) alone, which requires that aliens from these countries undergo vetting through visa procedures, does not explain why their *entry* would be detrimental to the interests of the United States. [T]he Order's state[s] . . . —that the "*unrestricted* entry into the United States of nationals [of the six designated countries] would be detrimental to the interests of the United States." [But] Section 1187(a)(12) dictates that the entry of individuals covered by the Order is never "unrestricted."

In conclusion, the Order does not offer a sufficient justification to suspend the entry of more than 180 million people on the basis of nationality. National security is not a "talismanic incantation" that, once invoked, can support any and all exercise of executive power under §1182(f). *Korematsu v. United States,* 323 U.S. 214, 235, 65 S.Ct. 193, 89 L.Ed. 194 (1944) (Murphy, J., dissenting) ("[T]he exclusion order necessarily must rely for its reasonableness upon the assumption that all persons of Japanese ancestry may have a dangerous tendency to commit sabotage and espionage and to aid our Japanese enemy in other ways. It is difficult to believe that reason, logic or experience could be marshalled in support of such an assumption."). Section 1182(f) requires that the President exercise his authority only after meeting the precondition of finding that entry of an alien or class of aliens *would be* detrimental to the interests of the United States. Here, the President has not done so.

ii

Section 6(a) suspends travel of refugees into the United States under USRAP and suspends decisions on applications for refugee status for 120 days but does not specifically announce that the entry of refugees would be detrimental to the interests of the United States. . . . .

EO2 does not reveal any threat or harm to warrant suspension of USRAP for 120 days and does not support the conclusion that the entry of refugees in the interim time period would be harmful. Nor does it provide any indication that present vetting and screening procedures are inadequate. Instead, EO2 justifies the 120-day suspension as a review period of USRAP application and adjudication processes. The Government reiterates that the President directed the suspension "in order to allow the Secretary of State to review application and adjudication processes." These explanations do not support a finding that the travel and admission of refugees would be detrimental to the interests of the United States. . . . . Refugees receive the most thorough vetting of all travelers to the United States in a process that takes eighteen to twenty-four months. By the time refugees are approved for resettlement in the United States, they have been reviewed by the United Nations High Commissioner for Refugees, the National Counterterrorism Center, the Federal Bureau of Investigation, the Department of Homeland Security, the Department of Defense, the Department of State, and the U.S. intelligence community. [relocated footnote—eds.]

iii

Section 6(b) of EO2 restricts entry of refugees to no more than 50,000 in the 2017 fiscal year because entry in excess of 50,000 "would be detrimental to the interests of the United States." But in accordance with 8 U.S.C. §1157, President Obama previously determined that the admission of 110,000 refugees to the United States during fiscal year 2017 was justified by humanitarian concerns or otherwise in the national interest. . . . To the extent that 60,000 additional refugees can be considered a class of aliens, EO2 makes *no* findings to justify barring entry in excess of 50,000 as detrimental to the interests of the United States. EO2 gives no explanation for why the 50,001st to the 110,000th refugee would be harmful to the national interest, nor does it specify any further threat to national security. And there is not any rationale explaining why the previous target admission of 110,000 refugees this fiscal year was justified by humanitarian concerns or otherwise in the national interest, but that the entry of more than 50,000 refugees this same fiscal year would be detrimental to the national interest. Here too, the President did not meet the statutory precondition of exercising his authority under §1182(f) to cap refugee admissions.

The actions taken in Sections 2 and 6 require the President first to make sufficient findings that the entry of nationals from the six designated countries and the entry of all refugees would be detrimental to the interests of the United States. We conclude that the President did not satisfy this precondition before exercising his delegated authority. Plaintiffs have shown a likelihood of success on the merits of their claim that the President exceeded his [statutory] authority . . . .

2

Plaintiffs [also] contend that Section 2(c) of the Order violates the INA because it discriminates on the basis of nationality, thus violating the non-discrimination mandate of §1152(a)(1)(A) of the INA. They argue that although the President is given broad authority under §1182(f), this authority is restrained by §1152(a)(1)(A).

Contemporaneous to enacting the Civil Rights Act of 1964 and the Voting Rights Act of 1965, Congress passed the INA of 1965 to eliminate the "national origins system as the basis for the selection of immigrants to the United States." H.R. Rep. No. 89-745, at 8 (1965). Section 1152(a)(1)(A) was enacted as part of that act, and provides:

> [N]o person shall receive any preference or priority or be discriminated against in the issuance of an immigrant visa because of the person's race, sex, *nationality*, place of birth, or place of residence.

8 U.S.C. §1152(a)(1)(A) (emphasis added). Section 1152(a)(1)(A) contains specific exemptions, and §1182(f) is not among them.

The Government tries to reconcile the Order's Section 2(c) with §1152(a)(1)(A) by arguing that Section 2(c) bars *entry* of nationals from the six designated countries but does not deny the *issuance of immigrant visas* based on nationality. EO2's suspension of entry on the basis of nationality, however, in substance operates as a ban on visa issuance on the basis of nationality. The Order's text confirms as much. Its primary purpose is to evaluate screening and vetting procedures associated with the visa issuance process. . . . The Government also stresses that it should not be required to issue visas for aliens who are validly barred from entry, explaining that "[r]equiring that such aliens be issued visas permitting them to travel to this country, only to be denied entry upon arrival, would create needless difficulties and confusion." Indeed, the Government clarified at oral argument that as a practical matter, the entry ban would be implemented through visa denials. . . .

We cannot blind ourselves to the fact that, for nationals of the six designated countries, EO2 is effectively a ban on the issuance of immigrant visas. If allowed to stand, EO2 would bar issuance of visas based on nationality in violation of §1152(a)(1)(A). The Government did not dispute this point at oral argument, and it stands to reason that the whole system of the visa issuance would grind to a halt for nationals of the six designated countries whose entry is barred from the United States. Issuance of visas will automatically stop for those who are banned based on nationality. Yet Congress could not have used "more explicit language" in "unambiguously direct[ing] that no nationality-based discrimination shall occur." . . . .

Our conclusion that §1152(a)(1)(A)'s non-discrimination mandate cabins the President's authority under §1182(f) is reinforced by other canons of statutory construction. First, a later enacted, more specific statute generally governs over an earlier, more general one. Here, §1152(a)(1)(A) was enacted in 1965, after §1182(f) was enacted in 1952. Section 1152(a)(1)(A) is also more specific, and sets a limitation on the President's broad authority to exclude aliens—he may do so, but not in a way that discriminates based on nationality. . . . .

The Government contends that §§1182(f) "[has] long been understood to permit the president to draw nationality-based distinctions." However . . . prior executive orders and proclamations did not suspend classes of aliens on the basis of national origin, but instead on the basis of affiliation or culpable conduct. . . . To be clear, Presidents have invoked §§1182(f) . . . to restrict certain aliens or classes of aliens from entering the United States, but EO2 is unprecedented in its scope, purpose, and breadth. . . . .

Having considered the President's authority under §1182(f) and the non-discrimination mandate of §1152(a)(1)(A), we also conclude that Plaintiffs have shown a likelihood of success on the merits of their claim that Section 2(c) of the Order, in suspending the issuance of immigrant visas and denying entry based on nationality, exceeds the restriction of §1152(a)(1)(A) and the overall statutory scheme intended by Congress.

3

[The Ninth Circuit also held that the INA limited the President's ability to reduce the number of refugees in fiscal year 2017, because the act requires the President, after consulting with Congress, to "set the annual admission of refugees before the beginning of every fiscal year." 8 U.S.C. §1157(a)(2). President Obama followed the statutorily required methods for consultation with Congress in setting a figure of 110,000 refugees during fiscal year 2017. Because President Trump acted unilaterally and without consulting Congress in changing the numbers during the fiscal year, he violated these provisions of the INA. The Ninth Circuit also noted that there is an explicit statutory provision allowing the President to increase the number of admitted refugees mid-year after appropriate consultation with Congress; but there is no explicit provision authorizing the President to decrease them. *See id.* §1157(b).] Congress prescribed specific actions the President must take before setting the number of refugees who may be admitted as justified by humanitarian concerns or as otherwise in the national interest. *See generally* 8 U.S.C. §1157. The President relied on §1182(f)—an earlier and more general provision—to conclude that admission of refugees above 50,000 is detrimental to the interest of the United States. But §1157, a "narrow, precise, and specific" statutory provision, may not be overridden by §1182(f), a provision "covering a more generalized spectrum" of issues. As a result, Plaintiffs have also shown a likelihood of success on the merits for their argument that Section 6(b) of EO2 conflicts with 8 U.S.C. §1157. . . . .

5

Finally, we note that in considering the President's authority, we are cognizant of Justice Jackson's tripartite framework in *Youngstown Sheet & Tube Co. v. Sawyer. See* 343 U.S. 579, 635–38 (1952) (Jackson, J., concurring). Section 1182(f) ordinarily places the President's authority at its maximum. "When the President acts pursuant to an express or implied authorization of Congress, his authority is at its maximum, for it includes all that he possesses in his own right plus all that Congress can delegate." *Id.* at 635, 72 S.Ct. 863. However, given the express will of Congress through §1152(a)(1)(A)'s non-discrimination mandate, [and] §1157's procedure for refugee admissions to this country, ... the President took measures that were incompatible with the expressed will of Congress, placing his power "at its lowest ebb." In this zone, "Presidential claim to a power at once so conclusive and preclusive must be scrutinized with caution, for what is at stake is the equilibrium established by our constitutional system." We have based our decision holding the entry ban unlawful on statutory considerations, and nothing said herein precludes Congress and the President from reaching a new understanding and confirming it by statute. If there were such consensus between Congress and the President, then we would view Presidential power at its maximum, and not in the weakened state based on conflict with statutory law.

In sum, we conclude that Plaintiffs have shown a likelihood of success on the merits at least as to their arguments that EO2 contravenes the INA by exceeding the President's authority under §1182(f), discriminating on the basis of nationality, and disregarding the procedures for setting annual admissions of refugees.

[The Ninth Circuit concluded that "Plaintiffs are likely to suffer irreparable harm in the absence of preliminary relief" and that the balance of harms weighed in favor of a preliminary injunction.]

* * *

In the early morning hours of June 5th, while the Ninth Circuit was still considering the case, the President of the United States commented on the case and complained about his own Justice Department's legal strategy in a series of tweets:

"The Justice Dept. should have stayed with the original Travel Ban, not the watered down, politically correct version they submitted to S.C." Donald J. Trump (@realDonaldTrump), Twitter (June 5, 2017, 3:29 AM), https://twitter.com/realdonaldtrump/status/871675245043888128?lang=en

"The Justice Dept. should ask for an expedited hearing of the watered down Travel Ban before the Supreme Court - & seek much tougher version!" Donald J. Trump (@realDonaldTrump), Twitter (June 5, 2017, 3:37 AM), https://twitter.com/realDonaldTrump/status/871677472202477568?lang=en

"In any event we are EXTREME VETTING people coming into the U.S. in order to help keep our country safe. The courts are slow and political!" Donald J. Trump (@realDonaldTrump), Twitter (June 5, 2017, 3:44 AM), https://twitter.com/realDonaldTrump/status/871679061847879682?lang=en

The government appealed to the Supreme Court for grants of certiorari to reverse the Fourth and Ninth Circuits. The government also asked the Supreme Court to stay the injunctions "pending appeal."[4]

TRUMP v. INTERNATIONAL REFUGEE ASSISTANCE PROJECT, 2017 WL 2722580: [The Supreme Court, in a per curiam opinion, granted the petitions for certiorari, and set the cases to be argued in October 2017, after the internal review procedures should be completed. The more pressing and immediate question, however, was whether the Court would stay the injunctions over the course of the summer, while the review was ongoing. A 6-3 majority of the Court refused to stay the preliminary injunctions, but modified them to exclude "foreign nationals abroad who have no connection to the United States at all."]

PER CURIAM:

---

4. There was an additional procedural skirmish about mootness. The respondents in *IRAP* argued that the suspension of entry in §2(c) would expire on June 14 because Section 2(c) directs that entry "be suspended for 90 days from the effective date of" EO–2, which was March 16. Therefore, by June 14, the entry suspension would expire, which would render the dispute over §2(c) moot. On June 14, President Trump issued a memorandum to Executive Branch officials, declaring that the effective date of each enjoined provision of EO–2 is the date on which the injunctions in these cases "are lifted or stayed with respect to that provision." Presidential Memorandum for the Secretary of State, the Attorney General, the Secretary of Homeland Security, and the Director of National Intelligence (June 14, 2017). The memorandum further provided that, to the extent necessary, it "should be construed to amend the Executive Order." *Ibid.* The Government took the position that, if any mootness problem existed previously, the President's memorandum cured it.

A

To begin, we grant both of the Government's petitions for certiorari and consolidate the cases for argument. The Clerk is directed to set a briefing schedule that will permit the cases to be heard during the first session of October Term 2017. (The Government has not requested that we expedite consideration of the merits to a greater extent.) In addition to the issues identified in the petitions, the parties are directed to address the following question: "Whether the challenges to §2(c) became moot on June 14, 2017."

B

[W]e grant the Government's applications to stay the injunctions, to the extent the injunctions prevent enforcement of §2(c) with respect to foreign nationals who lack any bona fide relationship with a person or entity in the United States. We leave the injunctions entered by the lower courts in place with respect to respondents and those similarly situated, as specified in this opinion.

Crafting a preliminary injunction is an exercise of discretion and judgment, often dependent as much on the equities of a given case as the substance of the legal issues it presents. The purpose of such interim equitable relief is not to conclusively determine the rights of the parties, but to balance the equities as the litigation moves forward. In awarding a preliminary injunction a court must also "conside[r] . . . the overall public interest." In the course of doing so, a court "need not grant the total relief sought by the applicant but may mold its decree to meet the exigencies of the particular case."

Here, of course, we are not asked to grant a preliminary injunction, but to stay one. In assessing the lower courts' exercise of equitable discretion, we bring to bear an equitable judgment of our own. Before issuing a stay, "[i]t is ultimately necessary . . . to balance the equities — to explore the relative harms to applicant and respondent, as well as the interests of the public at large." This Court may, in its discretion, tailor a stay so that it operates with respect to only "some portion of the proceeding."

The courts below took account of the equities in fashioning interim relief, focusing specifically on the concrete burdens that would fall on Doe, Dr. Elshikh, and Hawaii if §2(c) were enforced. They reasoned that §2(c) would "directly affec[t]" Doe and Dr. Elshikh by delaying entry of their family members to the United States. The Ninth Circuit concluded that §2(c) would harm the State by preventing students from the designated nations who had been admitted to the University of Hawaii from entering this country. These hardships, the courts reasoned, were sufficiently weighty and immediate to outweigh the Government's interest in enforcing §2(c). Having adopted this view of the equities, the courts approved injunctions that covered not just respondents, but parties similarly situated to them — that is, people or entities in the United States who have relationships with foreign nationals abroad, and whose rights might be affected if those foreign nationals were excluded. See *Mandel*, 408 U.S., at 763–765 (permitting

American plaintiffs to challenge the exclusion of a foreign national on the ground that the exclusion violated their own First Amendment rights).

But the injunctions reach much further than that: They also bar enforcement of §2(c) against foreign nationals abroad who have no connection to the United States at all. The equities relied on by the lower courts do not balance the same way in that context. Denying entry to such a foreign national does not burden any American party by reason of that party's relationship with the foreign national. And the courts below did not conclude that exclusion in such circumstances would impose any legally relevant hardship on the foreign national himself. See [*Mandel,* 408 U.S.,] at 762 ("[A]n unadmitted and nonresident alien . . . ha[s] no constitutional right of entry to this country"). So whatever burdens may result from enforcement of §2(c) against a foreign national who lacks any connection to this country, they are, at a minimum, a good deal less concrete than the hardships identified by the courts below.

At the same time, the Government's interest in enforcing §2(c), and the Executive's authority to do so, are undoubtedly at their peak when there is no tie between the foreign national and the United States. Indeed, EO–2 itself distinguishes between foreign nationals who have some connection to this country, and foreign nationals who do not, by establishing a case-by-case waiver system primarily for the benefit of individuals in the former category. The interest in preserving national security is "an urgent objective of the highest order." To prevent the Government from pursuing that objective by enforcing §2(c) against foreign nationals unconnected to the United States would appreciably injure its interests, without alleviating obvious hardship to anyone else.

We accordingly grant the Government's stay applications in part and narrow the scope of the injunctions as to §2(c). The injunctions remain in place only with respect to parties similarly situated to Doe, Dr. Elshikh, and Hawaii. In practical terms, this means that §2(c) may not be enforced against foreign nationals who have a credible claim of a bona fide relationship with a person or entity in the United States. All other foreign nationals are subject to the provisions of EO–2.

The facts of these cases illustrate the sort of relationship that qualifies. For individuals, a close familial relationship is required. A foreign national who wishes to enter the United States to live with or visit a family member, like Doe's wife or Dr. Elshikh's mother-in-law, clearly has such a relationship. As for entities, the relationship must be formal, documented, and formed in the ordinary course, rather than for the purpose of evading EO–2. The students from the designated countries who have been admitted to the University of Hawaii have such a relationship with an American entity. So too would a worker who accepted an offer of employment from an American company or a lecturer invited to address an American audience. Not so someone who enters into a relationship simply to avoid §2(c): For example, a nonprofit group devoted to immigration issues may not contact foreign nationals from the designated countries, add them to client lists, and then secure their entry by claiming injury from their exclusion. [relocated footnote — eds.]

In light of the June 12 decision of the Ninth Circuit vacating the injunction as to §2(a), the executive review directed by that subsection may proceed promptly, if it is not already underway. EO–2 instructs the Secretary of Homeland Security to complete this review within 20 days, after which time foreign governments will be given 50 days further to bring their practices into line with the Secretary's directives. Given the Government's representations in this litigation concerning the resources required to complete the 20–day review, we fully expect that the relief we grant today will permit the Executive to conclude its internal work and provide adequate notice to foreign governments within the 90–day life of §2(c).

C

The *Hawaii* injunction extends beyond §2(c) to bar enforcement of the §6(a) suspension of refugee admissions and the §6(b) refugee cap. In our view, the equitable balance struck above applies in this context as well. An American individual or entity that has a bona fide relationship with a particular person seeking to enter the country as a refugee can legitimately claim concrete hardship if that person is excluded. As to these individuals and entities, we do not disturb the injunction. But when it comes to refugees who lack any such connection to the United States, for the reasons we have set out, the balance tips in favor of the Government's compelling need to provide for the Nation's security.

The Government's application to stay the injunction with respect to §§6(a) and (b) is accordingly granted in part. Section 6(a) may not be enforced against an individual seeking admission as a refugee who can credibly claim a bona fide relationship with a person or entity in the United States. Nor may §6(b); that is, such a person may not be excluded pursuant to §6(b), even if the 50,000–person cap has been reached or exceeded. As applied to all other individuals, the provisions may take effect.

* * *

Accordingly, the petitions for certiorari are granted, and the stay applications are granted in part.

It is so ordered.

Justice THOMAS, with whom Justice ALITO and Justice GORSUCH join, concurring in part and dissenting in part.

I agree with the Court that the preliminary injunctions entered in these cases should be stayed, although I would stay them in full. The decision whether to stay the injunctions is committed to our discretion, but our discretion must be "guided by sound legal principles." The two "most critical" factors we must consider in deciding whether to grant a stay are "(1) whether the stay applicant has made a strong showing that [it] is likely to succeed on the merits" and "(2) whether the applicant will be irreparably injured absent a stay." Where a party seeks a stay pending certiorari, as here, the applicant satisfies the first factor only if it can show both "a reasonable probability that certiorari will be granted" and "a significant possibility that the judgment below will be reversed." When we determine that those critical factors are satisfied, we must "balance the equities" by "explor[ing] the relative harms to applicant and respondent, as well as the interests of the public at large."

The Government has satisfied the standard for issuing a stay pending certiorari. We have, of course, decided to grant certiorari. And I agree with the Court's implicit conclusion that the Government has made a strong showing that it is likely to succeed on the merits—that is, that the judgments below will be reversed. The Government has also established that failure to stay the injunctions will cause irreparable harm by interfering with its "compelling need to provide for the Nation's security." Finally, weighing the Government's interest in preserving national security against the hardships caused to respondents by temporary denials of entry into the country, the balance of the equities favors the Government. I would thus grant the Government's applications for a stay in their entirety.

Reasonable minds may disagree on where the balance of equities lies as between the Government and respondents in these cases. It would have been reasonable, perhaps, for the Court to have left the injunctions in place only as to respondents themselves. But the Court takes the additional step of keeping the injunctions in place with regard to an unidentified, unnamed group of foreign nationals abroad. No class has been certified, and neither party asks for the scope of relief that the Court today provides. . . .

Moreover, I fear that the Court's remedy will prove unworkable. Today's compromise will burden executive officials with the task of deciding—on peril of contempt—whether individuals from the six affected nations who wish to enter the United States have a sufficient connection to a person or entity in this country. The compromise also will invite a flood of litigation until this case is finally resolved on the merits, as parties and courts struggle to determine what exactly constitutes a "bona fide relationship," who precisely has a "credible claim" to that relationship, and whether the claimed relationship was formed "simply to avoid §2(c)". . . . And litigation of the factual and legal issues that are likely to arise will presumably be directed to the two District Courts whose initial orders in these cases this Court has now—unanimously—found sufficiently questionable to be stayed as to the vast majority of the people potentially affected.

Discussion

1. *A Trump discount?* Judge Shedd's dissent in *IRAP* emphasizes that courts normally defer to executive branch officials in matters of national security, in part because "a President and his national security advisors (unlike federal judges at all levels, lawyers, and commentators) have constant access to information 'that may describe new and serious threats to our Nation and its people.'" Did the Fourth and Ninth Circuits give the Trump Administration less deference than other recent Administrations? If so, is that because they believed that the decision-makers who devised the executive order were less competent, or less informed than decision-makers in previous Administrations? If there really is a

"Trump discount" at work, why is it legitimate for courts to make such assessments of the quality of decisionmaking by executive branch officials? What do these decisions portend for how much courts will defer to decisions by future Administrations not headed by Donald Trump?

There are two different accounts of why courts should defer to the political branches in questions of foreign policy. The first justification is that the political branches have greater *democratic authority*. But if so, why does this distinguish foreign policy from domestic policy, where courts intervene all the time? A second justification for special deference in the area of foreign policy is *comparative expertise*. (Why, if at all, does foreign policy call for greater expertise than domestic policy?) Courts presume that the people in charge of foreign policy decisionmaking are competent, have significant expertise, pay careful to intelligence reports, seek advice from career civil servants, engage in appropriate interagency consultation, and therefore are likely to make prudent judgments in most cases.

The first reason for deference to Executive Branch officials would apply no matter who is president. The second reason for deference offers only a strong, albeit rebuttable, presumption; if the court suspects that decisionmakers are venal or incompetent, the courts will defer less.

2. *The plenary power doctrine and immigration exceptionalism.* One cannot understand the issues in the travel ban cases apart from immigration law's unique status in the constitutional order. The current understanding of the federal government's power to regulate immigration stems from the plenary power doctrine that originated in the 19th century Chinese Exclusion Case, Chae Chan Ping v. United States, 130 U.S. 581, 609 (1889).

The plenary power doctrine is associated with two different ideas. The first is that Congress's power to regulate immigration does not come from any enumerated power in Article I, but rather is an "an incident of sovereignty belonging to the government of the United States." Id. at 609. The second is that — with a few notable exceptions — courts have largely refrained from enforcing constitutional constraints on the federal government's enactment and enforcement of immigration laws. See, e.g., Fiallo v. Bell, 430 U.S. 787, 792 (1977) ("Our cases have long recognized the power to expel or exclude aliens as a fundamental sovereign attribute exercised by the Government's political departments largely immune from judicial control.") The first idea does not necessarily imply the second; the mere fact that federal power is unenumerated does not mean that it is beyond judicial scrutiny. What joins the two ideas is that control over immigration is a matter of national sovereignty.

Federal courts have often allowed the political branches to make classifications and distinctions in immigration enforcement that would almost certainly be unconstitutional if made by the states, or even if made by the federal government outside of the immigration context. See generally Gabriel J. Chin, Segregation's Last Stronghold: Race Discrimination and the Constitutional Law of Immigration, 46 UCLA L. Rev. 1 (1998). In addition, the Court has not generally used the Bill of Rights to protect the rights of noncitizens who live outside the United States. See United States v. Verdugo–Urquidez, 494 U.S. 259, 269 (1990)(holding that the Fifth Amendment's protections do not extend to aliens outside the territorial boundaries of the United States). The travel ban cases arise in this difficult context for the protection of the rights of aliens.

For this reason, plaintiffs attempting to chip away at the plenary power doctrine have tried two different strategies. First, they have used federal statutory claims and procedural objections to protect constitutional norms. The Ninth Circuit challenge in *Hawaii v. Trump* is an example.

Second, plaintiffs have tried to protect the rights of aliens through protecting the constitutional rights of citizens and permanent residents who are affected by the immigration laws. In *IRAP v. Trump*, for example, the 4th Circuit argued that plaintiff Doe #1 (a permanent resident) had standing to raise an Establishment Clause challenge to EO-2 because he suffered a distinct personal injury: "Doe #1 has . . . asserted two distinct injuries stemming from his "personal contact" with the alleged establishment of religion [in] EO-2. First, EO-2 will bar his wife's entry into the United States and prolong their separation. And second, EO-2 sends a state-sanctioned message condemning his religion and causing him to feel excluded and marginalized in his community."

Although the plenary power doctrine is still very much alive, social change, political mobilization, globalization, and litigation strategies have put it under increasing pressure. The travel ban cases exemplify how constitutional doctrine in this area is being contested and reshaped in an era of globalization.

3. *The scope of the plenary power doctrine and the role of judicial scrutiny in immigration law.* There are at least two different explanations for judicial deference in immigration law. The stronger version holds that the Constitution's equality norms simply do not constrain the distinctions the political branches use in deciding who can enter the country. The federal government has broad power to make virtually any distinctions it wants about who gains entry to the country and who must leave—including, for example, on the basis of religion or national origin. The Justice Department has not adopted this position in the travel ban litigation. In oral arguments before the courts of appeals, DOJ lawyers have effectively conceded that it would be unconstitutional for the government to exclude Muslims, as such, from entering the United States.

The second version of the "plenary power" doctrine focuses on the role of courts: Although the Constitution may impose substantive constraints on the immigration power, the judiciary should not attempt to oversee the political branches or decide whether the political branches have violated the Constitution. Instead, courts must apply a "presumption of regularity" and they must accept at face value the Executive's representations of the basis for immigration restrictions. In the words of *Kleindienst v. Mandel*—which has been at the center of the travel ban dispute—"when the Executive exercises th[e] power [to exclude an alien] on the basis of a facially legitimate and bona fide reason, the courts will [not] look behind the exercise of that discretion."

The Executive branch has placed a great deal of weight on this second version of the "plenary power" doctrine; it argues that courts cannot look behind the *facially* legitimate reasons the President has cited for the entry bans and refugee limitations. Nevertheless, both the Fourth and Ninth Circuits concluded that, in this particular context, it is permissible for the courts to question the President's stated reasons for the immigration limits. As a result, although courts do not apply standard-form equal protection doctrine, both circuits invoked equality norms in other ways.

The Fourth Circuit brought equality norms into the discussion through the Establishment Clause. The guarantee against government establishment of religion has important overlaps with equality doctrines under the Fourteenth and Fifth Amendments.. First, it forbids the government from preferring one religion over another, or religion over nonreligion; it also forbids signaling that some people are disfavored because of their religious identity, beliefs or practices. Second, as in equal protection law, one can show a violation of these norms by showing an intent to discriminate on the basis of religion. Third, modern Establishment Clause doctrine often focuses on the social meaning of government action, by asking whether a reasonable observer would view the government as endorsing (or disfavoring) a particular religion or religion in general. This inquiry is similar to the way the Court has treated animus doctrine in gay rights cases like *Romer v. Evans* and *United States v. Windsor*.

The Ninth Circuit, by contrast, rested solely on statutory grounds. But an important part of the argument — as well as the arguments of Judges Keenan and Wynn in the Fourth Circuit — rested on an antidiscrimination provision in the 1965 Act. This provision, the court argued, reflected Congress's decision to limit the President's otherwise broad discretion to restrict entry; it forbade distinctions based upon *either* religion *or* national origin. Note as well how the court draws a connection between the 1965 Immigration and Naturalization Act and the 1964 Civil Rights Act and the 1965 Voting Act.[5] Finally, although the Ninth Circuit does not engage directly in an animus analysis, it repeatedly argues that the Trump Administration has not offered factual findings to justify its Executive Order, and it points out that the process by which the decision was made was procedurally irregular. Demonstrating a poor fit between means and ends, noting lack of adequate explanation, and emphasizing procedural irregularities are standard ways that courts show invidious motivation, or otherwise establish impermissible distinctions, in equal protection doctrine.

4. *Taking Trump seriously but not literally.* The dissenters in the 4th Circuit argue that courts should not consider campaign statements as evidence of unlawful intention. What distinguishes campaign statements from other kinds of statements? One possibility is that campaign statements are unreliable evidence of intentions. Perhaps candidates will say things they don't really believe to get

---

5. See Cristina M. Rodriguez, Immigration and the Civil Rights Agenda, 6 Stan. J. C.R. & C.L. 125, 127 (2010) ("The 1965 reforms of the INA that finally abolished [racially discriminatory immigration] quotas emerged from the political and cultural milieu that produced the Civil Rights Act of 1964 and the Voting Rights Act of 1965 and were defended by members of Congress as realizations of the anti-discrimination aspirations of the era.")

power but once they take office they will reveal their actual beliefs. A second possibility is that campaign statements do not reflect the views of the Administration as a whole. (Why is this relevant if the President is the head of the Executive Branch?) A third possibility has nothing to do with the reliability of the evidence. Instead, it argues that campaigns are often messy, dirty affairs, and politicians should get a fresh start once they take office, so that they are not hamstrung by what they had to say to get into office. As before, an important question is how much turns — or should turn — on the exceptional nature of Trump's presidency. Whatever doctrines courts make will presumably apply to future presidents.

5. *Youngstown analysis.* Near the end of its opinion in *Hawaii v. Trump*, the Ninth Circuit invokes *Youngstown*. This might seem surprising, given that the case concerns statutory interpretation, and not constitutional limits on presidential power. Nevertheless, a central question in *Youngstown* analysis is whether the President is acting by express or implicit delegation from Congress, or against Congress's wishes. Courts decide this question by determining Congress's purposes, using standard tools of statutory interpretation. (We saw this, for example, in *Hamdan v. Rumsfeld*, which is also nominally a statutory decision, but turns on whether President Bush had complied with the statutory framework for military tribunals set out by Congress.) How does the Ninth Circuit demonstrate that the Trump Administration has acted contrary to Congress's purposes in the INA? Could one argue in precisely the opposite direction, and show that the President has done nothing other than exercise the authority that Congress willingly gave him?

6. *Discretion is the better part of valor.* The Supreme Court's per curiam opinion in *IRAP* is carefully written to leave open as much as possible. Justice Thomas's dissent argues that the per curiam implicitly accepts the likelihood that the government will eventually win on appeal, but that inference by no means follows from anything in the per curiam opinion. Indeed, if the Court had determined that the government is likely to win on the merits, and the respondents are likely to lose, presumably the Court would have stayed the injunction completely.

Perhaps more interesting is the Court's statement that "The Clerk is directed to set a briefing schedule that will permit the cases to be heard during the first session of October Term 2017. (The Government has not requested that we expedite consideration of the merits to a greater extent.)" EO-2 went into effect on June 29th, 2017; ninety days expire at the end of September, before the October Term begins. Unless the Administration issues a new executive order, the controversy may become moot before the Justices can hear the case on the merits. On the other hand, if the Administration does issue a new executive order, based on new findings of fact, the controversy will likely head back to the lower federal courts. Either way, the Supreme Court may not resolve the constitutional questions, if at all, for some time.

7. *Bona fide relationships and credible claims.* Isn't Justice Thomas correct that the Court's "compromise . . . will invite a flood of litigation until this case is finally resolved on the merits, as parties and courts struggle to determine what exactly constitutes a 'bona fide relationship,' who precisely has a 'credible claim'

to that relationship, and whether the claimed relationship was formed 'simply to avoid §2(c)' "? If the Trump Administration takes a narrow view of these terms, there will likely be more litigation in the lower federal courts before the Supreme Court gets around to hearing the merits. (And in fact, a new round of litigation had already begun as this supplement went to press.) Is the majority's test too vague? Why do you think the Court did not draw its distinctions more precisely, perhaps based upon existing categories of aliens in the Immigration Act itself?

Chapter 8

Sex Equality

Insert the following before section III on p. 1453:

SESSIONS v. MORALES–SANTANA
2017 WL 2507339

Justice GINSBURG delivered the opinion of the Court.

[The Immigration and Nationality Act provides when people born abroad gain U.S. citizenship when only one of their parents is a U.S. citizen. The relevant rule for married couples at the time of respondent's birth is 8 U.S.C. §1401(a)(7) (1958 ed.), which requires the U.S.-citizen parent to have ten years' physical presence in the United States prior to the child's birth, "at least five of which were after attaining" age 14. Section 1409(a) makes this rule applicable to unwed U.S.-citizen fathers, but §1409(c) creates an exception for an unwed U.S.-citizen mother. Her citizenship can be transmitted to a child born abroad if she has lived continuously in the United States for just one year prior to the child's birth.

Respondent Luis Ramón Morales–Santana, who has lived in the United States since he was 13, asserts U.S. citizenship at birth based on the U.S. citizenship of his biological father, José Morales. José moved to the Dominican Republic 20 days short of his 19th birthday. He therefore fell short of §1401(a)(7)'s requirement of five years' physical presence after age 14. In the Dominican Republic, he lived with the Dominican woman who gave birth to Morales–Santana. José accepted parental responsibility and included Morales–Santana in his household; he married Morales–Santana's mother and his name was then added to hers on Morales–Santana's birth certificate.

In 2000, the Government sought to remove respondent Morales–Santana based on several criminal convictions, treating him as an alien because, at his time of birth, his father did not satisfy the requirement of five years' physical presence after age 14. An immigration judge rejected Morales–Santana's citizenship claim and ordered his removal. Morales–Santana later moved to reopen the proceedings, asserting that the Government's refusal to recognize that he derived citizenship from his U.S.-citizen father violated the Constitution's equal protection guarantee.

The Board of Immigration Appeals denied the motion, but the Second Circuit reversed. It held that the differential treatment of unwed mothers and fathers was unconstitutional under the equal protection component of the Fifth Amendment's Due Process Clause, and held that Morales–Santana derived citizenship through his father, just as he would were his mother the U.S. citizen.]

II

Because §1409 treats sons and daughters alike, Morales–Santana does not suffer discrimination on the basis of *his* gender. He complains, instead, of gender-based discrimination against his father, who was unwed at the time of Morales–Santana's birth and was not accorded the right an unwed U.S.-citizen mother would have to transmit citizenship to her child. . . . . . Ordinarily, a party "must assert his own legal rights" and "cannot rest his claim to relief on the legal rights . . . of third parties." But we recognize an exception where, as here, "the party asserting the right has a close relationship with the person who possesses the right [and] there is a hindrance to the possessor's ability to protect his own interests." José Morales' ability to pass citizenship to his son, respondent Morales–Santana, easily satisfies the "close relationship" requirement. So, too, is the "hindrance" requirement well met. . . . José died in 1976, Record 140, many years before the current controversy arose. Morales–Santana is thus the "obvious claimant," the "best available proponent," of his father's right to equal protection.

III

Sections 1401 and 1409 . . . date from an era when the lawbooks of our Nation were rife with overbroad generalizations about the way men and women are. Today, laws of this kind are subject to review under the heightened scrutiny that now attends "all gender-based classifications." . . . Prescribing one rule for mothers, another for fathers, §1409 is of the same genre as the classifications we declared unconstitutional in *Reed, Frontiero, Wiesenfeld, Goldfarb,* and *Westcott.* As in those cases, heightened scrutiny is in order. Successful defense of legislation that differentiates on the basis of gender, we have reiterated, requires an "exceedingly persuasive justification." [*United States v.*] *Virginia.*

A

The defender of legislation that differentiates on the basis of gender must show "at least that the [challenged] classification serves important governmental objectives and that the discriminatory means employed are substantially related to the achievement of those objectives." *Virginia.* Moreover, the classification must substantially serve an important governmental interest *today,* for "in interpreting the [e]qual [p]rotection [guarantee], [we have] recognized that new insights and societal understandings can reveal unjustified inequality . . . that once passed unnoticed and unchallenged." *Obergefell v. Hodges,* 576 U.S. —— ,135 S.Ct. 2584 (2015). Here, the Government has supplied no "exceedingly persuasive justification," for §1409(a) and (c)'s "gender-based" and "gender-biased" disparity.

1

History reveals what lurks behind §1409. Enacted in the Nationality Act of 1940 (1940 Act), see 54 Stat. 1139–1140, §1409 ended a century and a half of congressional silence on the citizenship of children born abroad to unwed parents. During this era, two once habitual, but now untenable, assumptions pervaded our Nation's citizenship laws and underpinned judicial and administrative rulings: In marriage, husband is dominant, wife subordinate; unwed mother is the natural and sole guardian of a nonmarital child.

Under the once entrenched principle of male dominance in marriage, the husband controlled both wife and child. "[D]ominance [of] the husband," this Court observed in 1915, "is an ancient principle of our jurisprudence." *Mackenzie v. Hare,* 239 U.S. 299 (1915). Through the early 20th century, a male citizen automatically conferred U.S. citizenship on his alien wife. Act of Feb. 10, 1855, ch. 71, §2, 10 Stat. 604. A female citizen, however, was incapable of conferring citizenship on her husband; indeed, she was subject to expatriation if she married an alien. . . . . In 1907, Congress codified several judicial decisions and prevailing State Department views by providing that a female U.S. citizen automatically lost her citizenship upon marriage to an alien. Act of Mar. 2, 1907, ch. 2534, §3, 34 Stat. 1228 [relocated footnote—eds.]

The family of a citizen or a lawfully admitted permanent resident enjoyed statutory exemptions from entry requirements, but only if the citizen or resident was male. See, *e.g.,* Act of Mar. 3, 1903, ch. 1012, §37, 32 Stat. 1221 (wives and children entering the country to join permanent-resident aliens and found to have contracted contagious diseases during transit shall not be deported if the diseases were easily curable or did not present a danger to others); S.Rep. No. 1515, 81st Cong., 2d Sess., 415–417 (1950) (wives exempt from literacy and quota requirements). And from 1790 until 1934, the foreign-born child of a married couple gained U.S. citizenship only through the father. . . . . In 1934, Congress moved in a new direction by allowing a married mother to transmit her citizenship to her child. Act of May 24, 1934, ch. 344, §1, 48 Stat. 797. [relocated footnote—eds.]

For unwed parents, the father-controls tradition never held sway. Instead, the mother was regarded as the child's natural and sole guardian. At common law, the mother, and only the mother, was "bound to maintain [a nonmarital child] as its natural guardian." 2 J. Kent, Commentaries on American Law *215–*216 (8th ed. 1854). In line with that understanding, in the early 20th century, the State Department sometimes permitted unwed mothers to pass citizenship to their children, despite the absence of any statutory authority for the practice.

In the 1940 Act, Congress discarded the father-controls assumption concerning married parents, but codified the mother-as-sole-guardian perception regarding unmarried parents. The Roosevelt administration, which proposed §1409, explained: "[T]he mother [of a nonmarital child] stands in the place of the father . . . [,] has a right to the custody and control of such a child as against the putative father, and is bound to maintain it as its natural guardian."

This unwed-mother-as-natural-guardian notion renders §1409's gender-based residency rules understandable. Fearing that a foreign-born child could turn out "more alien than American in character," the administration believed that a citizen parent with lengthy ties to the United States would counteract the influence of the alien parent. Concern about the attachment of foreign-born children to the United States explains the treatment of unwed citizen fathers, who, according to the familiar stereotype, would care little about, and have scant contact with, their nonmarital children. For unwed citizen mothers, however, there was no need for a prolonged residency prophylactic: The alien father, who might transmit foreign ways, was presumptively out of the picture.

2

For close to a half century . . . this Court has viewed with suspicion laws that rely on "overbroad generalizations about the different talents, capacities, or preferences of males and females." *Virginia*. In particular, we have recognized that if a "statutory objective is to exclude or 'protect' members of one gender" in reliance on "fixed notions concerning [that gender's] roles and abilities," the "objective itself is illegitimate." *Mississippi Univ. for Women [v. Hogan]*. . . . [T]he Court has held that no "important [governmental] interest" is served by laws grounded, as §1409(a) and (c) are, in the obsolescing view that "unwed fathers [are] invariably less qualified and entitled than mothers" to take responsibility for nonmarital children. *Caban v. Mohammed*, 441 U.S. 380 (1979).

Lehr v. Robertson, 463 U.S. 248 (1983), on which the Court relied in *Tuan Anh Nguyen v. INS*, 533 U.S. 53 (2001), recognized that laws treating fathers and mothers differently "may not constitutionally be applied . . . where the mother and father are in fact similarly situated with regard to their relationship with the child." The "similarly situated" condition was not satisfied in *Lehr*, however, for the father in that case had "never established any custodial, personal, or financial relationship" with the child. Here, there is no dispute that José Morales formally accepted parental responsibility for his son during Morales–Santana's childhood. [relocated footnote—eds.]

Overbroad generalizations of that order, the Court has come to comprehend, have a constraining impact, descriptive though they may be of the way many people still order their lives. . . . . Even if stereotypes frozen into legislation have "statistical support," our decisions reject measures that classify unnecessarily and overbroadly by gender when more accurate and impartial lines can be drawn. In fact, unwed fathers assume responsibility for their children in numbers already large and notably increasing. See Brief for Population and Family Scholars as *Amici Curiae* 3, 5–13 (documenting that nonmarital fathers "are [often] in a parental role at the time of their child's birth," and "most . . . formally acknowledge their paternity either at the hospital or in the birthing center just after the child is born"); Brief for American Civil Liberties Union et al. as *Amici Curiae* 22 (observing, *inter alia,* that "[i]n 2015, fathers made up 16 percent of single parents with minor children in the United States"). [relocated footnote—eds.]

Laws according or denying benefits in reliance on "[s]tereotypes about women's domestic roles," the Court has observed, may "creat[e] a self-fulfilling cycle of discrimination that force[s] women to continue to assume the role of primary family caregiver." *Nevada Dept. of Human Resources v. Hibbs,* 538 U.S. 721 (2003). Correspondingly, such laws may disserve men who exercise responsibility for raising their children. In light of the equal protection jurisprudence this Court has developed since 1971, §1409(a) and (c)'s discrete duration-of-residence requirements for unwed mothers and fathers who have accepted parental responsibility is stunningly anachronistic.

B

In urging this Court nevertheless to reject Morales–Santana's equal protection plea, the Government cites three decisions of this Court: *Fiallo v. Bell,* 430 U.S. 787 (1977); *Miller v. Albright,* 523 U.S. 420 (1998); and *Nguyen v. INS,* 533 U.S. 53 (2001). None controls this case.

The 1952 Act provision at issue in *Fiallo* [*v. Bell,* 430 U.S. 787 (1977)] gave special immigration preferences to alien children of citizen (or lawful-permanent-resident) mothers, and to alien unwed mothers of citizen (or lawful-permanent-resident) children. Unwed fathers and their children, asserting their right to equal protection, sought the same preferences. Applying minimal scrutiny (rational-basis review), the Court upheld the provision, relying on Congress' "exceptionally broad power" to admit or exclude aliens. This case, however, involves no entry preference for aliens. Morales–Santana claims he is, and since birth has been, a U.S. citizen.

The provision challenged in *Miller*[*v. Albright* and *Nguyen* as violative of equal protection requires unwed U.S.-citizen fathers, but not mothers, to formally acknowledge parenthood of their foreign-born children in order to transmit their U.S. citizenship to those children. See §1409(a)(4) (2012 ed.). After *Miller* produced no opinion for the Court, we took up the issue anew in *Nguyen.* There, the Court held that imposing a paternal-acknowledgment requirement on fathers was a justifiable, easily met means of ensuring the existence of a biological parent-child relationship, which the mother establishes by giving birth. Morales–Santana's challenge does not renew the contest over §1409's paternal-acknowledgment requirement . . . and the Government does not dispute that Morales–Santana's father, by marrying Morales–Santana's mother, satisfied that requirement.

Unlike the paternal-acknowledgment requirement at issue in *Nguyen* and *Miller,* the physical-presence requirements now before us relate solely to the duration of the parent's prebirth residency in the United States, not to the parent's filial tie to the child. As the Court of Appeals observed in this case, a man needs no more time in the United States than a woman "in order to have assimilated citizenship-related values to transmit to [his] child." And unlike *Nguyen*'s parental-acknowledgment requirement, §1409(a)'s age-calibrated physical-presence requirements cannot fairly be described as "minimal."

C

[T]he Government maintains that the statute serves two important objectives: (1) ensuring a connection between the child to become a citizen and the United States and (2) preventing "statelessness," *i.e.,* a child's possession of no citizenship at all. Even indulging the assumption that Congress intended §1409 to serve these interests, . . . neither rationale survives heightened scrutiny.

1

[T]he Government does not contend, nor could it, that unmarried men take more time to absorb U.S. values than unmarried women do. Instead, [it argues that] [a]n unwed mother . . . is the child's only "legally recognized" parent at the time of childbirth. An unwed citizen father enters the scene later, as a second parent. A longer physical connection to the United States is warranted for the unwed father, the Government maintains, because of the "competing national influence" of the alien mother. Congress, the Government suggests, designed the statute to bracket an unwed U.S.-citizen mother with a married couple in which both parents are U.S. citizens, and to align an unwed U.S.-citizen father with a married couple, one spouse a citizen, the other, an alien.

Underlying this apparent design is the assumption that the alien father of a nonmarital child born abroad to a U.S.-citizen mother will not accept parental responsibility . . . . Hardly gender neutral, see *id.,* at 9, that assumption conforms to the long-held view that unwed fathers care little about, indeed are strangers to, their children. Lump characterization of that kind, however, no longer passes equal protection inspection.

Accepting, *arguendo,* that Congress intended the diverse physical-presence prescriptions to serve an interest in ensuring a connection between the foreign-born nonmarital child and the United States, the gender-based means scarcely serve the posited end. The scheme permits the transmission of citizenship to children who have no tie to the United States so long as their mother was a U.S. citizen continuously present in the United States for one year at any point in her life *prior* to the child's birth. The transmission holds even if the mother marries the child's alien father immediately after the child's birth and never returns with the child to the United States. At the same time, the legislation precludes citizenship transmission by a U.S.-citizen father who falls a few days short of meeting §1401(a)(7)'s longer physical-presence requirements, even if the father acknowledges paternity on the day of the child's birth and raises the child in the United States. One cannot see in this driven-by-gender scheme the close means-end fit required to survive heightened scrutiny.

2

The Government maintains that Congress established the gender-based residency differential in §1409(a) and (c) to reduce the risk that a foreign-born child of a U.S. citizen would be born stateless. This risk, according to the Government, was substantially greater for the foreign-born child of an unwed U.S.-citizen mother than it was for the foreign-born child of an unwed U.S.-citizen father. But [based on the legislative history] there is little reason to believe that a statelessness concern prompted the diverse physical-presence requirements. Nor has the Government shown that the risk of statelessness disproportionately endangered the children of unwed mothers. . . . It will not do to "hypothesiz[e] or inven[t]" governmental purposes for gender classifications "*post hoc* in response to litigation." *Virginia*.

Infecting the Government's risk-of-statelessness argument is an assumption without foundation. . . . Experts who have studied the issue report that . . . "the risk of parenting stateless children abroad was, as of [1940 and 1952], and remains today, substantial for unmarried U.S. fathers, a risk perhaps greater than that for unmarried U.S. mothers." One can hardly characterize as gender neutral a scheme allegedly attending to the risk of statelessness for children of unwed U.S.-citizen mothers while ignoring the same risk for children of unwed U.S.-citizen fathers. . . .

IV

While the equal protection infirmity in retaining a longer physical-presence requirement for unwed fathers than for unwed mothers is clear, this Court is not equipped to grant the relief Morales–Santana seeks, *i.e.,* extending to his father (and, derivatively, to him) the benefit of the one-year physical-presence term §1409(c) reserves for unwed mothers. . . . [W]hen the 'right invoked is that to equal treatment,' the appropriate remedy is a mandate of equal treatment, a result that can be accomplished by withdrawal of benefits from the favored class as well as by extension of benefits to the excluded class." *Heckler v. Mathews,* 465 U.S. 728 (1984). . . . The choice between these outcomes is governed by the legislature's intent, as revealed by the statute at hand. . . .

Ordinarily, we have reiterated, "extension, rather than nullification, is the proper course." [I] n a series of cases involving federal financial assistance benefits, the Court struck discriminatory exceptions denying benefits to discrete groups, which meant benefits previously denied were extended. See, *e.g., Goldfarb* (survivors' benefits) *Jimenez v. Weinberger,* 417 U.S. 628 (1974) (disability benefits); *Department of Agriculture v. Moreno,* 413 U.S. 528 (1973) (food stamps); *Frontiero* (military spousal benefits). Here, however, the discriminatory exception consists of *favorable* treatment for a discrete group (a shorter physical-presence requirement for unwed U.S.-citizen mothers giving birth abroad). Following the same approach as in those benefits cases—striking the discriminatory exception—leads here to extending the general rule of longer physical-presence requirements to cover the previously favored group.

The Court has looked to Justice Harlan's concurring opinion in *Welsh v. United States,* 398 U.S., 333, 361–367 (1970) in considering whether the legislature would have struck an exception and applied the general rule equally to all, or instead, would have broadened the exception to cure the equal protection violation. In making this assessment, a court should " 'measure the intensity of commitment to the residual policy' "—the main rule, not the exception—"'and consider the degree of potential disruption of the statutory scheme that would occur by extension as opposed to abrogation.' ".

The residual policy here, the longer physical-presence requirement stated in §§1401(a)(7) and 1409, evidences Congress' recognition of "the importance of residence in this country as the talisman of dedicated attachment." And the potential for "disruption of the statutory scheme" is large. For if §1409(c)'s one-year dispensation were extended to unwed citizen fathers, would it not be irrational to retain the longer term when the U.S.-citizen parent is married? Disadvantageous treatment of marital children in comparison to nonmarital children is scarcely a purpose one can sensibly attribute to Congress.

Although extension of benefits is customary in federal benefit cases, all indicators in this case point in the opposite direction. Put to the choice, Congress, we believe, would have abrogated §1409(c)'s exception, preferring preservation of the general rule.

V

[W] e must adopt the remedial course Congress likely would have chosen "had it been apprised of the constitutional infirmity." Although the preferred rule in the typical case is to extend favorable treatment, this is hardly the typical case. Extension here would render the special treatment Congress prescribed in §1409(c), the one-year physical-presence requirement for U.S.-citizen mothers, the general rule, no longer an exception. Section 1401(a)(7)'s longer physical-presence requirement, applicable to a substantial majority of children born abroad to one U.S.-citizen parent and one foreign-citizen parent, therefore, must hold sway. Going forward, Congress may address the issue and settle on a uniform prescription that neither favors nor disadvantages any person on the basis of gender. In the interim, as the Government suggests, §1401(a)(7)'s now-five-year requirement should apply, prospectively, to children born to unwed U.S.-citizen mothers.

Justice THOMAS, joined by Justice ALITO, sees our equal protection ruling as "unnecessary," given our remedial holding. But, "as we have repeatedly emphasized, discrimination itself . . . perpetuat[es] 'archaic and stereotypic notions' " incompatible with the equal treatment guaranteed by the Constitution.. [relocated footnote—eds.]

The judgment of the Court of Appeals for the Second Circuit is affirmed in part and reversed in part, and the case is remanded for further proceedings consistent with this opinion.

It is so ordered.

Justice GORSUCH took no part in the consideration or decision of this case.

Justice THOMAS, with whom Justice ALITO joins, concurring in the judgment in part.

[T]he Court's remedial holding resolves this case. Because respondent cannot obtain relief in any event, it is unnecessary for us to decide whether the 1952 version of the INA was constitutional, whether respondent has third-party standing to raise an equal protection claim on behalf of his father, or whether other immigration laws (such as the current versions of §§1401(g) and 1409) are constitutional. I therefore concur only in the judgment reversing the Second Circuit.

Discussion

1. *Did Morales-Santana win or lose his case?* The Court holds that the provisions challenged by Morales-Santana discriminate unconstitutionally based on sex, but then holds that the proper remedy is that both citizen mothers and fathers alike must satisfy the five-year rule. Because Morales-Santana's father fell short by 20 days, his son, the respondent in this case, is not a citizen. Why doesn't Justice Ginsburg "level up" instead of "leveling down?"

What is at stake in the remedial decision to level up or level down? One important consideration is that courts should try to do what the legislature would have done if it was not able to pursue the discriminatory policy. Should courts always follow legislative intentions, even if they are tinged by unconstitutional motivations? A second consideration is the coherence and fairness of the larger statutory scheme. How important is it that in this case, leveling up would put unwed citizen fathers in a better position than married fathers? A third consideration is the area of law in which courts are intervening. Is it relevant that this is an immigration case, and the Supreme Court might want to avoid interfering with Congress's decisions about who gets to be a U.S. citizen?

If the Court cannot give Morales-Santana the remedy he seeks, is the Court's entire discussion dicta, as Justice Thomas suggests? Or should it be relevant in how the Board of Immigration Appeals exercises prosecutorial discretion?[1]

2. *Discrimination against non-marital fathers.* One of the most important consequences of *Morales-Santana* may be in family law outside of the immigration context. Justice Ginsburg criticizes "the obsolescing view that 'unwed fathers [are] invariably less qualified and entitled than mothers' to take responsibility for nonmarital children," and her opinion suggests that family law doctrines that make overbroad and stereotypical generalizations about unwed fathers are constitutionally suspect.

3. *Sex discrimination and nationality.* Historically, as Justice Ginsburg explains, immigration law proceeded on two tracks. Married couples were governed by coverture rules, under which the child's (and originally, the wife's) nationality was subsumed into the husband's. Children of unmarried couples,

---

1. See Mark Tushnet, Did Morales-Santana (the person) Win or Lose in the Supreme Court?, Balkinization, June 12, 2017, https://balkin.blogspot.com/2017/06/did-morales-santana-person-win-or-lose.html .

by contrast, were assigned the mother's nationality, based on assumptions about maternal closeness and paternal irresponsibility. Gradually, Congress eliminated the discriminatory treatment of husbands and wives, but provisions treating men and women differently remained for unmarried couples. The Court upheld such a provision in *Nguyen v. INS*, but struck down a different one in *Morales-Santana*. Do you agree with Justice Ginsburg that *Nguyen* is distinguishable from *Morales-Santana*?

Chapter 9

Liberty, Equality, and Fundamental Rights: The Constitution, the Family, and the Body

Insert on p. 1530 before Note: The Reach of Griswold:

For a discussion of Griswold's contemporary relevance, see the Yale Law Journal Forum Symposium, *Griswold at 50*, and related articles: Reva B. Siegel, How Conflict Entrenched the Right to Privacy, 124 Yale L. J. Forum 316 (2015); Melissa Murray, Overlooking Equality on the Road to Griswold, 124 Yale L. J. Forum 324 (2015); Cary Franklin, Griswold and the Public Dimension of the Right to Privacy, 124 Yale L. J. Forum 332 (2015); Douglas NeJaime, Griswold's Progeny: Assisted Reproduction, Procreative Liberty, and Sexual Orientation Equality, 124 Yale L. J. Forum 340 (2015); Neil S. Siegel & Reva B. Siegel, Contraception as a Sex Equality Right, 124 Yale L. J. Forum 349 (2015).

Add on p. 1630 before Section IV:

WHOLE WOMAN'S HEALTH v. HELLERSTEDT
136 S.Ct. 2292 (2016)

JUSTICE BREYER delivered the opinion of the Court.

In *Planned Parenthood of Southeastern Pa. v. Casey*, 505 U. S. 833, 878 (1992), a plurality of the Court concluded that there "exists" an "undue burden" on a woman's right to decide to have an abortion, and consequently a provision of law is constitutionally invalid, if the *"purpose or effect"* of the provision *"is to place a substantial obstacle* in the path of a woman seeking an abortion before the fetus attains viability." (Emphasis added.) The plurality added that "[u]nnecessary health regulations that have the purpose or effect of presenting a substantial obstacle to a woman seeking an abortion impose an undue burden on the right." *Ibid*.

We must here decide whether two provisions of Texas' House Bill 2 [(H. B. 2)] violate the Federal Constitution as interpreted in *Casey*. The first provision, which we shall call the *"admitting-privileges requirement,"* says that "[a] physician performing or inducing an abortion . . . must, on the date the abortion is performed or induced, have active admitting privileges at a hospital that . . . is located not further than 30 miles from the location at which the abortion is performed or induced." Tex. Health & Safety Code Ann. §171.0031(a) (West Cum. Supp. 2015). [Previously, Texas had] required an abortion facility to maintain a written protocol "for managing medical emergencies and the transfer of patients requiring further emergency care to a hospital."

The second provision, which we shall call the "*surgical-center requirement*," says that "the minimum standards for an abortion facility must be equivalent to the minimum standards adopted under [the Texas Health and Safety Code section] for ambulatory surgical centers." Tex. Health & Safety Code Ann. §245.010(a).

We conclude that neither of these provisions offers medical benefits sufficient to justify the burdens upon access that each imposes. Each places a substantial obstacle in the path of women seeking a previability abortion, each constitutes an undue burden on abortion access, *Casey*, and each violates the Federal Constitution.

I

[The Texas Legislature enacted House Bill 2 in July 2013. In September, before the new law took effect, a group of Texas abortion providers filed a facial challenge to the admitting privileges provision; it was ultimately rejected by the Fifth Circuit Court of Appeals, in *Planned Parenthood of Greater Tex. Surgical Health Servs. v. Abbott*, 748 F. 3d 583, 592 (2014) (*Abbott*). After the law went into effect, petitioners, another group of abortion providers (including some *Abbott* plaintiffs), filed the current lawsuit, claiming that both the admitting-privileges and the surgical-center requirements violated *Casey*. They sought injunctions preventing enforcement of the admitting-privileges provision as applied to physicians at one abortion facility in McAllen and one in El Paso and prohibiting enforcement of the surgical-center requirement throughout Texas.]

The District Court . . . conducted a 4-day bench trial. . . . [and] reached the following conclusions:

Prior to the enactment of H. B. 2, there were more than 40 licensed abortion facilities in Texas. [That] "number dropped by almost half [to about 20] leading up to and in the wake of enforcement of the admitting-privileges requirement that went into effect in late-October 2013." . . . "[T]he decrease in geographical distribution of abortion facilities" has meant that the number of women of reproductive age living more than 50 miles from a clinic has doubled (from 800,000 to over 1.6 million); those living more than 100 miles [away] has increased by 150% (from 400,000 to 1 million); those living more than 150 miles [away] has increased by more than 350% (from 86,000 to 400,000); and those living more than 200 miles [away] has increased by about 2,800% (from 10,000 to 290,000).

[If the surgical-center requirement were allowed to take effect, the number of abortion facilities, after September 1, 2014, would be reduced further, so that "only seven facilities and a potential eighth will exist in Texas." In addition,] the number of women of reproductive age living significant distances from an abortion provider will increase as follows: 2 million women of reproductive age will live more than 50 miles from an abortion provider; 1.3 million will live more than 100 miles from an abortion provider; 900,000 will live more than 150 miles from an abortion provider; and 750,000 more than 200 miles from an abortion provider.

"Based on historical data pertaining to Texas's average number of abortions, and assuming perfectly equal distribution among the remaining seven or eight providers, this would result in each facility serving between 7,500 and 10,000 patients per year. Accounting for the seasonal variations in pregnancy rates and a slightly unequal distribution of patients at each clinic, it is foreseeable that over 1,200 women per month could be vying for counseling, appointments, and follow-up visits at some of these facilities. [The district court found that] [t]he suggestion "that these seven or eight providers could meet the demand of the entire state stretches credulity." . . . The [admitting privileges and surgical center requirements] "erect a particularly high barrier for poor, rural, or disadvantaged women."

[The district court found that] "[t]he great weight of evidence demonstrates that, before the act's passage, abortion in Texas was extremely safe with particularly low rates of serious complications and virtually no deaths occurring on account of the procedure. . . . Abortion, as regulated by the State before the enactment of House Bill 2, has been shown to be much safer, in terms of minor and serious complications, than many common medical procedures not subject to such intense regulation and scrutiny," [including] . . . colonoscopies . . . vasectomy and endometrial biopsy . . . [and] plastic surgery.

[The district court also found that] "risks are not appreciably lowered for patients who undergo abortions at ambulatory surgical centers as compared to nonsurgical-center facilities," [and that] "[w]omen will not obtain better care or experience more frequent positive outcomes at an ambulatory surgical center as compared to a previously licensed facility." [Despite the lack of additional benefits,] [t]he "cost of coming into compliance" with the surgical-center requirement "for existing clinics is significant," "undisputedly approach[ing] 1 million dollars," and "most likely exceed[ing] 1.5 million dollars," with "[s]ome . . . clinics" unable to "comply due to physical size limitations of their sites." The "cost of acquiring land and constructing a new compliant clinic will likely exceed three million dollars." [The district court compared these requirements to those facing the existing] "433 licensed ambulatory surgical centers in Texas," of which "336 . . . are apparently either 'grandfathered' or enjo[y] the benefit of a waiver of some or all" of the surgical-center "requirements."

On the basis of these and other related findings, the District Court determined that the surgical-center requirement "imposes an undue burden on the right of women throughout Texas to seek a previability abortion," and that the "admitting-privileges requirement, . . . in conjunction with the ambulatory-surgical-center requirement, imposes an undue burden on the right of women in the Rio Grande Valley, El Paso, and West Texas to seek a previability abortion." The District Court concluded that the "two provisions" would cause "the closing of almost all abortion clinics in Texas that were operating legally in the fall of 2013," and thereby create a constitutionally "impermissible obstacle as applied to all women seeking a previability abortion" by "restricting access to previously available legal facilities."

[The district court enjoined the admitting privileges and surgical center requirement, but the Fifth Circuit Court of Appeals reversed in most respects.] With minor exceptions, it found both provisions constitutional and allowed them to take effect. . . . The Court of Appeals concluded [that res judicata barred the District Court from holding the admitting-privileges requirement unconstitutional statewide and that res judicata also barred the challenge to the surgical-center provision. It held that] a state law "regulating previability abortion is constitutional if: (1) it does not have the purpose or effect of placing a substantial obstacle in the path of a woman seeking an abortion of a nonviable fetus; and (2) it is reasonably related to (or designed to further) a legitimate state interest." . . . "[B]oth the admitting privileges requirement and" the surgical-center requirement "were rationally related to a legitimate state interest," namely, "rais[ing] the standard and quality of care for women seeking abortions and . . . protect[ing] the health and welfare of women seeking abortions." . . . . [T]he Court of Appeals said that women in El Paso wishing to have an abortion could use abortion providers in nearby New Mexico.

II

[The Court held that petitioners were not barred by res judicata from bringing their constitutional challenges.]

III

Undue Burden—Legal Standard

We begin with the standard, as described in *Casey*. We recognize that the "State has a legitimate interest in seeing to it that abortion, like any other medical procedure, is performed under circumstances that insure maximum safety for the patient." *Roe v. Wade*. But, we added, "a statute which, while furthering [a] valid state interest, has the effect of placing a substantial obstacle in the path of a woman's choice cannot be considered a permissible means of serving its legitimate ends." *Casey*. Moreover, "[u]nnecessary health regulations that have the purpose or effect of presenting a substantial obstacle to a woman seeking an abortion impose an undue burden on the right." *Id*.

The [Fifth Circuit] Court of Appeals wrote that a state law is "constitutional if: (1) it does not have the purpose or effect of placing a substantial obstacle in the path of a woman seeking an abortion of a nonviable fetus; and (2) it is reasonably related to (or designed to further) a legitimate state interest." [It held that] "the district court erred by substituting its own judgment for that of the legislature" when it conducted its "undue burden inquiry," in part because "medical uncertainty underlying a statute is for resolution by legislatures, not the courts." (citing *Gonzales v. Carhart*, 550 U. S. 124, 163 (2007)).

The Court of Appeals' articulation of the relevant standard is incorrect. The first part of [its] test may be read to imply that a district court should not consider the existence or nonexistence of medical benefits when considering whether a regulation of abortion constitutes an undue burden. The rule announced in *Casey*, however, requires that courts consider the burdens a law imposes on abortion access together with the benefits those laws confer See *Casey* (performing this balancing with respect to a spousal notification provision); id. (same balancing with respect to a parental notification provision). And the second part of the test is wrong to equate the judicial review applicable to the regulation of a constitutionally protected personal liberty with the less strict review applicable where, for example, economic legislation is at issue. See, *e.g., Williamson v. Lee Optical*. The Court of Appeals' approach simply does not match the standard that this Court laid out in *Casey*, which asks courts to consider whether any burden imposed on abortion access is "undue."

The statement that legislatures, and not courts, must resolve questions of medical uncertainty is also inconsistent with this Court's case law. Instead, the Court, when determining the constitutionality of laws regulating abortion procedures, has placed considerable weight upon evidence and argument presented in judicial proceedings. In *Casey*, for example, we relied heavily on the District Court's factual findings and the research-based submissions of *amici* in declaring [the spousal notification provision] unconstitutional. And, in *Gonzales* the Court, while pointing out that we must review legislative "factfinding under a deferential standard," added that we must not "place dispositive weight" on those "findings." *Gonzales* went on to point out that the "*Court retains an independent constitutional duty to review factual findings where constitutional rights are at stake.*" (emphasis added). Although there we upheld a statute regulating abortion, we did not do so solely on the basis of legislative findings explicitly set forth in the statute, noting that "evidence presented in the District Courts contradicts" some of the legislative findings. In these circumstances, we said, "[u]ncritical deference to Congress' factual findings . . . is inappropriate."

Unlike in *Gonzales*, the relevant statute here does not set forth any legislative findings. Rather, one is left to infer that the legislature sought to further a constitutionally acceptable objective (namely, protecting women's health). For a district court to give significant weight to evidence in the judicial record in these circumstances is consistent with this Court's case law. . . . [T]he District Court did so here. It did not simply substitute its own judgment for that of the legislature. It considered the evidence in the record—including expert evidence, presented in stipulations, depositions, and testimony. It then weighed the asserted benefits against the burdens. We hold that, in so doing, the District Court applied the correct legal standard.

IV

Undue Burden—Admitting-Privileges Requirement

. . .

The purpose of the admitting-privileges requirement is to help ensure that women have easy access to a hospital should complications arise during an abortion procedure. But the District Court found that it brought about no such health-related benefit. The court found that "[t]he great weight of evidence demonstrates that, before the act's passage, abortion in Texas was extremely safe with particularly low rates of serious complications and virtually no deaths occurring on account of the procedure." Thus, there was no significant health-related problem that the new law helped to cure.

The evidence upon which the court based this conclusion included, among other things: Expert testimony . . .

[1] that complications rarely require hospital admission, much less immediate transfer to a hospital from an outpatient clinic[;]

[2] that "it is extremely unlikely that a patient will experience a serious complication at the clinic that requires emergent hospitalization" and "in the rare case in which [one does], the quality of care that the patient receives is not affected by whether the abortion provider has admitting privileges at the hospital[;]"

[3] that [when] surgical abortion patients . . . do suffer complications requiring hospitalization, most of these complications occur in the days after the abortion, not on the spot[; and]

[4] that a delay before the onset of complications is also expected for medical abortions, as "abortifacient drugs take time to exert their effects, and thus the abortion itself almost always occurs after the patient has left the abortion facility." Some experts added that, if a patient needs a hospital in the day or week following her abortion, she will likely seek medical attention at the hospital nearest her home.

We have found nothing in Texas' record evidence that shows that, compared to prior law (which required [only] a "working arrangement" with a doctor with admitting privileges), the new law advanced Texas' legitimate interest in protecting women's health. We add that, when directly asked at oral argument whether Texas knew of a single instance in which the new requirement would have helped even one woman obtain better treatment, Texas admitted that there was no evidence in the record of such a case. This answer is consistent with the findings of the other Federal District Courts that have considered the health benefits of other States' similar admitting-privileges laws.

At the same time, the record evidence indicates that the admitting-privileges requirement places a "substantial obstacle in the path of a woman's choice." *Casey.* The District Court found, as of the time the admitting-privileges requirement began to be enforced, the number of facilities providing abortions dropped in half, from about 40 to about 20. Eight abortion clinics closed in the months leading up to the requirement's effective date. Eleven more closed on the day the admitting-privileges requirement took effect.

Other evidence helps to explain why the new requirement led to the closure of clinics. [It is] undisputed . . . that "hospitals often condition admitting privileges on reaching a certain number of admissions per year." . . . [I]n direct testimony, the president of Nova Health Systems . . . pointed out that it would be difficult for doctors regularly performing abortions at the El Paso clinic to obtain admitting privileges at nearby hospitals because "[d]uring the past 10 years, over

17,000 abortion procedures were performed at the El Paso clinic [and n]ot a single one of those patients had to be transferred to a hospital for emergency treatment, much less admitted to the hospital." In a word, doctors would be unable to maintain admitting privileges or obtain those privileges for the future, because the fact that abortions are so safe meant that providers were unlikely to have any patients to admit.

[O]ther common prerequisites to obtaining admitting privileges . . . have nothing to do with ability to perform medical procedures. . . . The admitting-privileges requirement does not serve any relevant credentialing function.

In our view, the record contains sufficient evidence that the admitting-privileges requirement led to the closure of half of Texas' clinics, or thereabouts. Those closures meant fewer doctors, longer waiting times, and increased crowding. Record evidence also supports the finding that after the admitting-privileges provision went into effect, the "number of women of reproductive age living in a county . . . more than 150 miles from a provider increased from approximately 86,000 to 400,000 . . . and the number of women living in a county more than 200 miles from a provider from approximately 10,000 to 290,000." We recognize that increased driving distances do not always constitute an "undue burden." See *Casey*. But here, those increases are but one additional burden, which, when taken together with others that the closings brought about, and when viewed in light of the virtual absence of any health benefit, lead us to conclude that the record adequately supports the District Court's "undue burden" conclusion.

The dissent's only argument [in response to this evidence is that although] "H. B. 2 caused the closure of *some* clinics," (emphasis added), other clinics may have closed for other reasons (so we should not "actually count" the burdens resulting from those closures against H. B. 2). But petitioners satisfied their burden to present evidence of causation by presenting direct testimony as well as plausible inferences to be drawn from the timing of the clinic closures. The District Court credited that evidence and concluded from it that H. B. 2 in fact led to the clinic closures. The dissent's speculation that perhaps other evidence, not presented at trial or credited by the District Court, might have shown that some clinics closed for unrelated reasons does not provide sufficient ground to disturb the District Court's factual finding on that issue.

In the same breath, the dissent suggests that one benefit of H. B. 2's requirements would be that they might "force unsafe facilities to shut down." . . . [T]he dissent points to the Kermit Gosnell scandal. Gosnell, a physician in Pennsylvania, was convicted of first-degree murder and manslaughter. He "staffed his facility with unlicensed and indifferent workers, and then let them practice medicine unsupervised" and had "[d]irty facilities; unsanitary instruments; an absence of functioning monitoring and resuscitation equipment; the use of cheap, but dangerous, drugs; illegal procedures; and inadequate emergency access for when things inevitably went wrong." Gosnell's behavior was terribly wrong. But there is no reason to believe that an extra layer of regulation would have affected that behavior. Determined wrongdoers, already ignoring existing statutes and safety measures, are unlikely to be convinced to adopt safe practices by a new overlay of regulations. Regardless, Gosnell's deplorable crimes could escape detection only because his facility went uninspected for more than 15 years. Pre-existing Texas law already contained numerous detailed regulations covering abortion facilities, including a requirement that facilities be inspected at least annually. The record contains nothing to suggest that H. B. 2 would be more effective than pre-existing Texas law at deterring wrongdoers like Gosnell from criminal behavior.

V

Undue Burden—Surgical-Center Requirement

The second challenged provision of Texas' new law sets forth the surgical-center requirement. Prior to enactment of the new requirement, Texas law required abortion facilities to meet a host of health and safety requirements. . . . policed by random and announced inspections, at least annually, as well as adminis-trative penalties, injunctions, civil penalties, and criminal penalties for certain violations.

H. B. 2 added the requirement that an "abortion facility" meet the "minimum standards . . . for ambulatory surgical centers" under Texas law. . . . . There is considerable evidence in the record supporting the District Court's findings indicating that the statutory provision requiring all abortion facilities to meet all surgical-center standards does not benefit patients and is not necessary. The District Court found that "risks are not appreciably lowered for patients who undergo abortions at ambulatory surgical centers as compared to nonsurgical-center facilities." [and] that women "will not obtain better care or experience more frequent positive outcomes at an ambulatory surgical center as compared to a previously licensed facility." And these findings are well supported.

The record makes clear that the surgical-center requirement provides no bene-fit when complications arise in the context of an abortion produced through med-ication. That is because, in such a case, complications would almost always arise only after the patient has left the facility. The record also contains evidence indi-cating that abortions taking place in an abortion facility are safe—indeed, safer than numerous procedures that take place outside hospitals and to which Texas does not apply its surgical-center requirements. The total number of deaths in Texas from abortions was five in the period from 2001 to 2012, or about one every two years (that is to say, one out of about 120,000 to 144,000 abortions). Nationwide, childbirth is 14 times more likely than abortion to result in death, but Texas law allows a midwife to oversee childbirth in the patient's own home. Colonoscopy, a procedure that typically takes place outside a hospital (or surgi-cal center) setting, has a mortality rate 10 times higher than an abortion. [and] the mortality rate for liposuction, another outpatient procedure, is 28 times higher than the mortal ity rate for abortion. Medical treatment after an incomplete mis-carriage often involves a procedure identical to that involved in a nonmedical abortion, but it often takes place outside a hospital or surgical center. And Texas partly or wholly grandfathers (or waives in whole or in part the surgical-center requirement for) about two-thirds of the facilities to which the surgical-center standards apply. But it neither grandfathers nor provides waivers for any of the facilities that perform abortions. These facts indicate that the surgical-center provision imposes "a requirement that simply is not based on differences" between abortion and other surgical procedures "that are reasonably related to" preserving women's health, the asserted "purpos[e] of the Act in which it is found." *Doe* [*v. Bolton*].

Moreover, many surgical-center requirements are inappropriate as applied to surgical abortions. Requiring scrub facilities; maintaining a one-way traffic pattern through the facility; having ceiling, wall, and floor finishes; separating soiled utility and sterilization rooms; and regulating air pressure, filtration, and humidity control can help reduce infection where doctors conduct procedures that penetrate the skin. But abortions typically involve either the administration of medicines or procedures performed through the natural opening of the birth canal, which is itself not sterile. Nor do provisions designed to safeguard heavily sedated patients (unable to help themselves) during fire emergencies provide any help to abortion patients, as abortion facilities do not use general anesthesia or deep sedation. Further, since the few instances in which serious complications do arise following an abortion almost always require hospitalization, not treatment at a surgical center, surgical-center standards will not help in those instances either.

The upshot is that this record evidence, along with the absence of any evidence to the contrary, provides ample support for the District Court's conclusion that "[m]any of the building standards mandated by the act and its implementing rules have such a tangential relationship to patient safety in the context of abortion as to be nearly arbitrary." That conclusion, along with the supporting evidence, provides sufficient support for the more general conclusion that the surgical-center requirement "will not [provide] better care or . . . more frequent positive outcomes." The record evidence thus supports the ultimate legal conclusion that the surgical-center requirement is not necessary.

At the same time, the record provides adequate evidentiary support for the District Court's conclusion that the surgical-center requirement places a substantial obstacle in the path of women seeking an abortion. The parties stipulated that the requirement would further reduce the number of abortion facilities available to seven or eight facilities, located in Houston, Austin, San Antonio, and Dallas/ Fort Worth. In the District Court's view, the proposition that these "seven or eight providers could meet the demand of the entire State stretches credulity." We take this statement as a finding that these few facilities could not "meet" that "demand."

The Court of Appeals held that this finding was "clearly erroneous." [because] the finding rested upon the "*ipse dixit*" of one expert, Dr. Grossman [who testified that the requirement would cause the number of abortions that clinics would have to provide to rise by a factor of 5. It argued] that there was no evidence that the current surgical centers (*i.e.*, the seven or eight) are operating at full capacity or could not increase capacity. . . . [But] [t]he Federal Rules of Evidence state that an expert may testify in the 'form of an opinion' as long as that opinion rests upon "sufficient facts or data" and "reliable principles and methods." Rule 702. In this case Dr. Grossman's opinion rested upon his participation, along with other university researchers, in research that tracked "the number of open facilities providing abortion care in the state by . . . requesting information from the Texas Department of State Health Services . . . [, t]hrough interviews with clinic staff[,] and review of publicly available information." The District Court acted within its legal authority in determining that Dr. Grossman's testimony was admissible. [Moreover,]

common sense suggests that, more often than not, a physical facility that satisfies a certain physical demand will not be able to meet five times that demand without expanding or otherwise incurring significant costs. Suppose that we know only that a certain grocery store serves 200 customers per week, that a certain apartment building provides apartments for 200 families, that a certain train station welcomes 200 trains per day. While it is conceivable that the store, the apartment building, or the train station could just as easily provide for 1,000 customers, families, or trains at no significant additional cost, crowding, or delay, most of us would find this possibility highly improbable. The dissent takes issue with this general, intuitive point by arguing that many places operate below capacity and that in any event, facilities could simply hire additional providers. We disagree that, according to common sense, medical facilities, well known for their wait times, operate below capacity as a general matter. And the fact that so many facilities were forced to close by the admitting-privileges requirement means that hiring more physicians would not be quite as simple as the dissent suggests. Courts are free to base their findings on commonsense inferences drawn from the evidence. And that is what the District Court did here. . . .

Texas suggests that the seven or eight remaining clinics could expand sufficiently to provide abortions for the 60,000 to 72,000 Texas women who sought them each year. Because petitioners had satisfied their burden, the obligation was on Texas, if it could, to present evidence rebutting that issue to the District Court. Texas admitted that it presented no such evidence [that expansion was possible]. . . .

More fundamentally, in the face of no threat to women's health, Texas seeks to force women to travel long distances to get abortions in crammed-to-capacity superfacilities. Patients seeking these services are less likely to get the kind of individualized attention, serious conversation, and emotional support that doctors at less taxed facilities may have offered. Healthcare facilities and medical professionals are not fungible commodities. Surgical centers attempting to accommodate sudden, vastly increased demand, may find that quality of care declines. Another commonsense inference that the District Court made is that these effects would be harmful to, not supportive of, women's health.

Finally, the District Court found that the costs that a currently licensed abortion facility would have to incur to meet the surgical-center requirements were considerable, ranging from $1 million per facility (for facilities with adequate space) to $3 million per facility (where additional land must be purchased). This evidence supports the conclusion that more surgical centers will not soon fill the gap when licensed facilities are forced to close.

We agree with the District Court that the surgical-center requirement, like the admitting-privileges requirement, provides few, if any, health benefits for women, poses a substantial obstacle to women seeking abortions, and constitutes an "undue burden" on their constitutional right to do so.

VI

. . . Texas claims that the provisions at issue here do not impose a substantial obstacle because the women affected by those laws are not a "large fraction" of Texan women "of reproductive age," which Texas reads *Casey* to have required. But *Casey* used the language "large fraction" to refer to "a large fraction of cases in which [the provision at issue] is *relevant*," a class narrower than "all women," "pregnant women," or even "the class of *women seeking abortions* identified by the State." (emphasis added). Here, as in *Casey*, the relevant denominator is "those [women] for whom [the provision] is an actual rather than an irrelevant restriction."

Texas [also] looks for support to *Simopoulos v. Virginia*, 462 U. S. 506 (1983), . . . in which this Court upheld a surgical-center requirement as applied to second-trimester abortions. This case, however, unlike *Simopoulos,* involves restrictions applicable to all abortions, not simply to those that take place during the second trimester. Most abortions in Texas occur in the first trimester, not the second. More importantly, in *Casey* we discarded the trimester framework, and we now use "viability" as the relevant point at which a State may begin limiting women's access to abortion for reasons unrelated to maternal health. Because the second trimester includes time that is both previability and postviability, *Simopoulos* cannot provide clear guidance. Further, the Court in *Simopoulos* found that the petitioner in that case, unlike petitioners here, had waived any argument that the regulation did not significantly help protect women's health.

* * *

For these reasons the judgment of the Court of Appeals is reversed, and the case is remanded for further proceedings consistent with this opinion.

It is so ordered.

JUSTICE GINSBURG, concurring.

The Texas law called H. B. 2 inevitably will reduce the number of clinics and doctors allowed to provide abortion services. Texas argues that H. B. 2's restrictions are constitutional because they protect the health of women who experience complications from abortions. In truth, "complications from an abortion are both rare and rarely dangerous." See Brief for American College of Obstetricians and Gynecologists et al. as *Amici Curiae* 6-10 (collecting studies and concluding '[a] bortion is one of the safest medical procedures performed in the United States'); Brief for Social Science Researchers as *Amici Curiae* 5-9 (compiling studies that

show '[c]omplication rates from abortion are very low'). Many medical procedures, including childbirth, are far more dangerous to patients, yet are not subject to ambulatory-surgical-center or hospital admitting-privileges requirements.
See also Brief for Social Science Researchers 9-11 (comparing statistics on risks
for abortion with tonsillectomy, colonoscopy, and in-office dental surgery); Brief
for American Civil Liberties Union et al. as *Amici Curiae* 7 (all District Courts
to consider admitting-privileges requirements found abortion "is at least as safe
as other medical procedures routinely performed in outpatient settings"). Given
those realities, it is beyond rational belief that H. B. 2 could genuinely protect the
health of women, and certain that the law "would simply make it more difficult
for them to obtain abortions." When a State severely limits access to safe and
legal procedures, women in desperate circumstances may resort to unlicensed
rogue practitioners, *faute de mieux*, at great risk to their health and safety. So
long as this Court adheres to *Roe* and *Casey*, Targeted Regulation of Abortion
Providers laws like H. B. 2 that "do little or nothing for health, but rather strew
impediments to abortion," cannot survive judicial inspection.

JUSTICE THOMAS, dissenting.
[T]oday's opinion . . . reimagines the undue-burden standard used to assess
the constitutionality of abortion restrictions. . . . *Casey* . . . instructed courts
to look to whether a law substantially impedes women's access to abortion,
and whether it is reasonably related to legitimate state interests. As the Court
explained, "[w]here it has a rational basis to act, and it does not impose an undue
burden, the State may use its regulatory power" to regulate aspects of abortion
procedures, "all in furtherance of its legitimate interests in regulating the medical profession in order to promote respect for life, including life of the unborn."
Gonzales v. Carhart.

I remain fundamentally opposed to the Court's abortion jurisprudence. Even
taking *Casey* as the baseline, however, the majority radically rewrites the undue-
burden test in three ways. First, today's decision requires courts to "consider the
burdens a law imposes on abortion access together with the benefits those laws
confer." Second, today's opinion tells the courts that, when the law's justifications are medically uncertain, they need not defer to the legislature, and must
instead assess medical justifications for abortion restrictions by scrutinizing the
record themselves. Finally, even if a law imposes no "substantial obstacle" to
women's access to abortions, the law now must have more than a "reasonabl[e]
relat[ion] to . . . a legitimate state interest." These precepts are nowhere to be
found in *Casey* or its successors, and transform the undue-burden test to something much more akin to strict scrutiny.

. . . When assessing Pennsylvania's recordkeeping requirements for abortion
providers, for instance, *Casey* did not weigh its benefits and burdens. Rather,
Casey held that the law had a legitimate purpose because data collection advances
medical research, "so it cannot be said that the requirements serve no purpose
other than to make abortions more difficult." The opinion then asked whether the
recordkeeping requirements imposed a "substantial obstacle," and found none.

Contrary to the majority's statements, *Casey* did not balance the benefits and burdens of Pennsylvania's spousal and parental notification provisions, either. Pennsylvania's spousal notification requirement, the plurality said, imposed an undue burden because findings established that the requirement would "likely . . . prevent a significant number of women from obtaining an abortion"—not because these burdens outweighed its benefits. And *Casey* summarily upheld parental notification provisions because even pre-*Casey* decisions had done so. [Similarly,] . . . [t]he Court in *Mazurek v. Armstrong*, 520 U. S. 968 (1997) (*per curiam*), had no difficulty upholding a Montana law authorizing only physicians to perform abortions—even though no legislative findings supported the law, and the challengers claimed that "all health evidence contradict[ed] the claim that there is any health basis for the law." *Mazurek* also deemed objections to the law's lack of benefits "squarely foreclosed by *Casey* itself." Instead, the Court explained, "the Constitution gives the States broad latitude to decide that particular functions may be performed only by licensed professionals, *even if an objective assessment might suggest that those same tasks could be performed by others*." (quoting *Casey*; emphasis in original). . . . .

Before today, this Court had "given state and federal legislatures wide discretion to pass legislation in areas where there is medical and scientific uncertainty." *Gonzales*. This Court emphasized that this "traditional rule" of deference "is consistent with *Casey*." This Court underscored that legislatures should not be hamstrung "if some part of the medical community were disinclined to follow the proscription." And this Court concluded that "[c]onsiderations of marginal safety, including the balance of risks, are within the legislative competence when the regulation is rational and in pursuit of legitimate ends." This Court could not have been clearer: When-ever medical justifications for an abortion restriction are debatable, that "provides a sufficient basis to conclude in [a] facial attack that the [law] does not impose an undue burden." *Gonzales*. Otherwise, legislatures would face "too exacting" a standard. *Id.*

Today, however, the majority refuses to leave disputed medical science to the legislature because past cases "placed considerable weight upon the evidence and argument presented in judicial proceedings." But while *Casey* relied on record evidence to uphold Pennsylvania's spousal-notification requirement, that requirement had nothing to do with debated medical science. And while *Gonzales* observed that courts need not blindly accept all legislative findings, that does not help the majority. *Gonzales* refused to accept Congress' finding of "a medical consensus that the prohibited procedure is never medically necessary" because the procedure's necessity was debated within the medical community. Having identified medical uncertainty, *Gonzales* explained how courts should resolve conflicting positions: by respecting the legislature's judgment.

Finally, the majority overrules another central aspect of *Casey* by requiring laws to have more than a rational basis even if they do not substantially impede access to abortion. "Where [the State] *has a rational basis to act* and it does not impose an undue burden," this Court previously held, "the State may use its regulatory power" to impose regulations "in furtherance of its legitimate interests in regulating the medical profession in order to promote respect for life, including life of the unborn." *Gonzales* (emphasis added). No longer. Though the majority declines to say how substantial a State's interest must be, one thing is clear: The State's burden has been ratcheted to a level that has not applied for a quarter century. . . . .

The majority's undue-burden test looks far less like our post-*Casey* precedents and far more like the strict-scrutiny standard that *Casey* rejected, under which only the most compelling rationales justified restrictions on abortion. One searches the majority opinion in vain for any acknowledgment of the 'premise central' to *Casey*'s rejection of strict scrutiny: "that the government has a legitimate and substantial interest in preserving and promoting fetal life" from conception, not just in regulating medical procedures. *Gonzales*. Meanwhile, the majority's undue-burden balancing approach risks ruling out even minor, previously valid infringements on access to abortion. Moreover, by second-guessing medical evidence and making its own assessments of "quality of care" issues, the majority reappoints this Court as "the country's *ex officio* medical board with powers to disapprove medical and operative practices and standards throughout the United States." *Gonzales*. And the majority seriously burdens States, which must guess at how much more compelling their interests must be to pass muster and what "commonsense inferences" of an undue burden this Court will identify next.

JUSTICE ALITO, with whom THE CHIEF JUSTICE and JUSTICE THOMAS join, dissenting.

[Justice Alito argued first, that the plaintiff's claims were precluded by res judicata; and second, that even if the Court properly reached the merits, it should have held unconstitutional only those portions of H. B. 2 that actually imposed a substantial burden. Finally, he argued that plaintiffs had not demonstrated that H.B. 2 actually caused an undue burden on women seeking abortions in Texas].

[I]n order to obtain the sweeping relief they seek—facial invalidation of those provisions—[petitioners] must show, at a minimum, that these provisions have an unconstitutional impact on at least a "large fraction" of Texas women of reproductive age.

The proper standard for facial challenges is unsettled in the abortion context. Like the Court in *Gonzales*, I do not decide the question, and use the more plaintiff-friendly "large fraction" formulation only because petitioners cannot meet even that test. The Court, by contrast, applies the "large fraction" standard without even acknowledging the open question. In a similar vein, it holds that the fraction's "relevant denominator is 'those [women] for whom [the provision] is an actual rather than an irrelevant restriction.'" I must confess that I do not understand this holding. The purpose of the large-fraction analysis, presumably, is to compare the number of women *actually* burdened with the number *potentially* burdened. Under the Court's holding, we are supposed to use the same figure (women actually burdened) as both the numerator and the denominator.

By my math, that fraction is always "1," which is pretty large as fractions go. [relocated footnote—eds.]

[There could be an unconstitutional impact] if the clinics able to comply with the new requirements either lacked the requisite overall capacity or were located too far away to serve a "large fraction" of the women in question.

Petitioners did not make that showing. Instead of offering direct evidence, they relied on two crude inferences. First, they pointed to the number of abortion clinics that closed after the enactment of H. B. 2, and asked that it be inferred that all these closures resulted from the two challenged provisions. They made little effort to show why particular clinics closed. Second, they pointed to the number of abortions performed annually at ASCs [ambulatory surgical centers] before H. B. 2 took effect and, because this figure is well below the total number of abortions performed each year in the State, they asked that it be inferred that ASC-compliant clinics could not meet the demands of women in the State. Petitioners failed to provide any evidence of the actual capacity of the facilities that would be available to perform abortions in compliance with the new law—even though they provided this type of evidence in their first case to the District Court at trial and then to this Court in their application for interim injunctive relief. . . .

I do not dispute the fact that H. B. 2 caused the closure of some clinics. Indeed, it seems clear that H. B. 2 was intended to force unsafe facilities to shut down. The law was one of many enacted by States in the wake of the Kermit Gosnell scandal, in which a physician who ran an abortion clinic in Philadelphia was convicted for the first-degree murder of three infants who were born alive and for the manslaughter of a patient. Gosnell had not been actively supervised by state or local authorities or by his peers, and the Philadelphia grand jury that investigated the case recommended that the Commonwealth adopt a law requiring abortion clinics to comply with the same regulations as ASCs. If Pennsylvania had had such a requirement in force, the Gosnell facility may have been shut down before his crimes. And if there were any similarly unsafe facilities in Texas, H. B. 2 was clearly in-tended to put them out of business.

While there can be no doubt that H. B. 2 caused some clinics to cease operation, the absence of proof regarding the reasons for particular closures is a problem because some clinics have or may have closed for at least four reasons other than the two H. B. 2 requirements at issue here. These are:

1. *H. B. 2's restriction on medication abortion.* In their first case, petitioners challenged the provision of H. B. 2 that regulates medication abortion, but that part of the statute was upheld by the Fifth Circuit and not relitigated in this case. The record in this case indicates that in the first six months after this restriction took effect, the number of medication abortions dropped by 6,957 (compared to the same period the previous year).

2. *Withdrawal of Texas family planning funds.* In 2011, Texas passed a law preventing family planning grants to providers that perform abortions and their affiliates. In the first case, petitioners' expert admitted that some clinics closed "as a result of the defunding," and as discussed below, this withdrawal appears specifically to have caused multiple clinic closures in West Texas.

3. *The nationwide decline in abortion demand.* Petitioners' expert testimony relies on a study from the Guttmacher Institute which concludes that "[t]he national abortion rate has resumed its decline, and *no evidence was found that the overall drop in abortion incidence was related to the decrease in providers or to restrictions implemented between 2008 and 2011*" emphasis in testimony). . . .

4. *Physician retirement (or other localized factors).* Like everyone else, most physicians eventually retire, and the retirement of a physician who performs abortions can cause the closing of a clinic or a reduction in the number of abortions that a clinic can perform. When this happens, the closure of the clinic or the reduction in capacity cannot be attributed to H. B. 2 unless it is shown that the retirement was caused by the admitting privileges or surgical center requirements as opposed to age or some other factor.

At least nine Texas clinics may have ceased performing abortions (or reduced capacity) for one or more of the reasons having nothing to do with the provisions challenged here. . . . Neither petitioners nor the District Court properly addressed these complexities in assessing causation—and for no good reason. The total number of abortion clinics in the State was not large. Petitioners could have put on evidence about the challenged provisions' role in causing the closure of each clinic, and the court could have made a factual finding as to the cause of each closure.

Precise findings are important because the key issue here is not the number or percentage of clinics affected, but the effect of the closures on women seeking abortions, *i.e.*, on the capacity and geographic distribution of clinics used by those women. To the extent that clinics closed (or experienced a reduction in capacity) for any reason unrelated to the challenged provisions of H. B. 2, the corresponding burden on abortion access may not be factored into the access analysis. Because there was ample reason to believe that some closures were caused by these other factors, the District Court's failure to ascertain the reasons for clinic closures means that, on the record before us, there is no way to tell which closures actually count. Petitioners—who, as plaintiffs, bore the burden of proof—cannot simply point to temporal correlation and call it causation. . . .

Even if the District Court had properly filtered out immaterial closures, its analysis would have been incomplete for a second reason. Petitioners offered scant evidence on the capacity of the clinics that are able to comply with the admitting privileges and ASC requirements, or on those clinics' geographic distribution. . . . [I]t is not unassailable "common sense" to hold that current utilization equals capacity; if all we know about a grocery store is that it currently serves 200 customers per week, that fact alone does not tell us whether it is an overcrowded minimart or a practically empty supermarket. Faced with increased demand, ASCs could potentially increase the number of abortions performed without prohibitively expensive changes. Among other things, they might hire more physicians who perform abortions, utilize their facilities more intensively or efficiently, or shift the mix of services provided. [W]hat matters for present purposes is not the capacity of just those ASCs that performed abortions prior to the enactment of H. B. 2 but the capacity of those that would be available to perform abortions after the statute took effect. And since the enactment of H. B. 2, the number of ASCs performing abortions has increased by 50%—from six in 2012 to nine today. . . .

The other potential obstacle to abortion access is the distribution of facilities throughout the State. This might occur if the two challenged H. B. 2 requirements, by causing the closure of clinics in some rural areas, led to a situation in which a "large fraction" of women of reproductive age live too far away from any open clinic. Based on the Court's holding in *Casey*, it appears that the need to travel up to 150 miles is not an undue burden, and the evidence in this case shows that if the only clinics in the State were those that would have remained open if the judgment of the Fifth Circuit had not been enjoined, roughly 95% of the women of reproductive age in the State would live within 150 miles of an open facility (or lived outside that range before H. B. 2). Because the record does not show why particular facilities closed, the real figure may be even higher than 95%.

We should decline to hold that these statistics justify the facial invalidation of the H. B. 2 requirements. The possibility that the admitting privileges requirement *might* have caused a closure in Lubbock is no reason to issue a facial injunction exempting Houston clinics from that requirement. I do not dismiss the situation of those women who would no longer live within 150 miles of a clinic as a result of H. B. 2. But under current doctrine such localized problems can be addressed by narrow as-applied challenges. . . .

When we decide cases on particularly controversial issues, we should take special care to apply settled procedural rules in a neutral manner. The Court has not done that here.

I therefore respectfully dissent.

Discussion

1. *A new approach to the "undue burden" test. Whole Woman's Health* was the Supreme Court's most important statement on abortion rights since its 1992 decision in *Planned Parenthood of Southeastern Pennsylvania v. Casey*. It responded to an increasingly pressing question: when the state purports to regulate abortion not in order to protect *unborn life* but to protect women's *health*, what is an undue burden under *Casey*? Although *Casey* primarily concerned fetal protection measures, it did consider regulations of abortion premised on women's health. It held that the undue burden test applied to these regulations as well, and it explained that "[u]nnecessary health regulations that have the purpose or effect of presenting a substantial obstacle to a woman seeking an abortion impose an undue burden on the right."

This raised the obvious question of how one knew that a regulation was "unnecessary." In 2007, Gonzales v. Carhart did not provide a clear answer. It held that, in the face of genuine medical uncertainty or scientific dispute, Congress could decide what it believed best protected women's health, and courts should generally defer to its judgment.

Pro-life groups took *Gonzales* as a sign that state legislatures could pass new regulations of abortion clinics officially premised on protecting women's health, but that also constricted women's access to abortion. Because many abortion clinics could not afford to meet the new regulatory standards in state abortion laws, some or all of them would close their doors. Slowly but surely, abortion opponents hoped to limit access to abortion in substantial parts of the country by imposing successive sets of health regulations on abortion providers. Pro-life advocates argued that, even if there was a dispute about the health benefits of the new regulations, under *Gonzales*, courts should defer to legislative judgments if they were rationally related to women's health and if women could still obtain abortions in the state. This incrementalist approach eventually led to Texas's ambitious gambit in H.B. 2, which looked to close most clinics in a very large state.

Whole Woman's Health made clear that *Casey* did not permit this strategy. It applied a balancing test derived from *Casey*.

2. *Considering both costs and benefits.* First, *Whole Woman's Health* reads *Casey's* "undue burden" standard to consider *both* the degree of health protection an abortion regulation actually affords as well as the practical effects of the regulation on women's access to abortion. Perhaps a burden on women's access to abortion might be justified by a regulation that seriously improved women's health, but a different regulation might be "undue" if it imposed a similar burden but the health benefits were minor or non-existent. The less plausible the health benefits, the more likely it is that the burden is "undue." Where the legislation does not improve women's health at all, burdens on the ability of women to obtain abortion are likely to be unconstitutional, as Justice Ginsburg points out in her concurrence.

The Fifth Circuit — and the dissenting Justices — read *Gonzales* to require a different test. The Fifth Circuit held that the question whether a health-justified restriction on abortion provided benefits to women's health was subject to rational basis review. The question of health benefits, and the evidence for them, was for democratic determination, the Circuit reasoned, and it held that the district court was prohibited from scrutinizing the factual basis of the state's claims. So long as the legislature had any reason to believe a law advanced health to any degree, judges were obliged to defer to the legislature's reasoning. As the Fifth Circuit had explained, "[i]n our circuit we do not balance the wisdom or effectiveness of a law against the burdens the law imposes." It was therefore inappropriate, for example, for the lower court to inquire into whether the ambulatory surgical center provision would actually improve women's health and safety. Then, assuming that the health regulation passed rational basis scrutiny, the court would inquire into whether it imposed an undue burden on women's ability to obtain abortions.

However, as *Whole Women's Health* explains, *Casey* and *Gonzales* do not actually employ rational basis review. Rather, it was the *dissenting* judges in *Casey* who argued for rational basis review. Judges must scrutinize the factual record to determine whether laws impose an undue burden on women's right to decide whether to carry a pregnancy to term.

3. Whole Woman's Health *and judicial review of medical justifications*. In order to decide whether the health benefits of the state's regulation are sufficiently substantial, *Whole Woman's Health* holds that courts should not simply defer to legislative assertions. Following *Casey* and *Gonzales*, *Whole Woman's Health* holds that courts must engage in their own independent fact finding. Thus *Whole Woman's Health* gives courts authority to review the evidence and balance gains in women's health against burdens on women's access to abortion. That is because too deferential a standard of review would have allowed determined state legislatures gradually to eliminate most access to abortion within their borders.

Gonzales recognized that legislatures had some leeway in making judgments about medical safety where evidence was disputed. Nevertheless, Justice Kennedy, the author of *Gonzales*, joined in *Whole Woman's Health*. In hindsight, it is possible that his remarks about judicial deference in *Gonzales* were directed primarily to the precise issue before the Court—partial birth abortion—which Justice Kennedy believed was both morally upsetting and medically unnecessary. Outside of that context, Justice Kennedy may have been much less willing to defer to legislative findings about women's health.

4. *Health-Justified Restrictions on Abortion and Women's Dignity*. Why do *Casey* (and now *Whole Woman's Health*) require courts to scrutinize the facts supporting health-justified restrictions on abortion? Linda Greenhouse and Reva Siegel argue that scrutiny of this kind is necessary to secure constitutional protections for women's dignity:

> *Casey* gave states more latitude to protect potential life but only so long as states employed means that respect women's dignity: "[T]he means chosen by the State to further the interest in potential life must be calculated to inform the woman's free choice, not hinder it"and cannot impose an "undue burden" on the abortion decision. These values at *Casey*'s core should guide review of health-justified restrictions on abortion. When states single out abortion for burdensome health regulations, courts must confirm that the laws actually serve health-related ends and do not instead provide a backdoor way of protecting potential life. Scrutinizing the facts that justify laws targeting abortion for onerous health restrictions thus . . . ensures that legislatures do not employ health restrictions on abortion to protect unborn life by unconstitutional means. Preserving the distinction between abortion restrictions that protect women's health and abortion restrictions that protect unborn life secures constitutional protection for women's dignity.

Linda Greenhouse & Reva B. Siegel, "*Casey* and the Clinic Closings: When 'Protecting Health' Obstructs Choice" 125 Yale. L.J. 1428, 1432 (2016).

5. Whole Woman's Health *and fetal protective regulations*. *Whole Woman's Health* applies a balancing test to health protective regulations. The less justified the regulation in actually promoting women's health, the more likely it is that the burden on women is undue. Does the same balancing test apply to fetal protective regulations, in which the state is permitted to persuade women not to have

abortions? When the majority cites *Casey* for the proposition that balancing benefits and burdens is required, it actually cites to *Casey*'s evaluation of two fetal protection laws—the spousal notification provision (which it struck down) and the parental notification provision (which it upheld). How, if at all, is the process of balancing different when a judge reviews a fetal–protective versus a woman-protective restriction on abortion? Can you think of burdens a state might impose on pregnant women that actually do little to inform women's choices?

6. *The tone of* Whole Woman's Health. *Casey* invoked the constitutional values at stake in protecting women's decisions about abortion right and in regulating them. The joint opinion acknowledged the deep conflict dividing the country and called for national unity on the abortion question. *Whole Woman's Health*, by contrast, is written in an unemotional, technocratic style. The majority does not discuss the ground or purpose of the abortion right, or say anything about the connection between reproductive rights and women's equality. The majority demonstrates that the health-case for a law like Texas' is weak and, indeed, nonexistent. Yet it does not accuse the state of having the unconstitutional purpose of deliberately attempting to obstruct women's access to abortion.

Part of the reason for this reticence may be due to Justice Breyer's approach to judging, which tends to focus on facts, public policy, and scientific studies. But the silences in the opinion may be intentional. In writing an opinion that completely rejects the state's justifications for the admitting privileges and surgical center law, Justice Breyer nonetheless refrained from calling the state's good faith into question. Justice Breyer may have intentionally written a restrained, factually oriented opinion in an effort to avoid exacerbating the abortion conflict any more than a decision rejecting one side's claims already would.

Are there reasons to prefer the decisional style of *Whole Women's Health* over that of the *Casey* decision? What if anything is lost? In what contexts might it matter that the Court is silent about the constitutional values at stake in protecting women's decisions about abortion, or the state's efforts to restrict them?

7. *The fate of TRAP laws.* Despite the decision's generally unassuming tone, *Whole Woman's Health* significantly changes the legal landscape for TRAP (targeted regulation of abortion providers) laws. In order to ensure that nobody misses the point, Justice Ginsburg states clearly in her concurrence that scientific studies show that abortion is a very safe procedure for women and that laws that try to single out abortion for special regulatory burdens that do not apply to equally safe or (even more risky) procedures are unlikely to pass constitutional muster. Why is singling out abortion for onerous regulation presumptively unconstitutional under *Casey* and *Whole Woman's Health*?

Whole Woman's Health directs judges to examine the facts carefully and independently as they weigh the benefits and burdens of health-justified restrictions on abortion. This means, however, that plaintiffs challenging TRAP laws may have to hold lengthy trials, which may be costly. Moreover, defenders of TRAP laws will have multiple ways of distinguishing the laws of other states from Texas' law, which was particularly burdensome.

8. *Muted dissents.* Justice Thomas and Justice Alito's dissents do not attempt to relitigate the legitimacy of *Roe* or *Casey*. Instead, they object to the majority opinion on rather technical grounds. Justice Thomas argues that *Gonzales* requires greater deference to legislatures. Justice Alito argues that the plaintiffs' arguments are barred by res judicata. He also engages in his own fact-specific inquiry designed to cast doubt on whether Texas' law really did limit women's ability to obtain abortions. Perhaps, he suggested, any limitations were caused by other factors. Moreover, perhaps after H.B. 2 goes into effect, the remaining abortion clinics in Texas will expand to meet increased demand. Why do you think that the dissents focus on technical questions rather than attack the legitimacy of the abortion right head on, as occurred in many of the cases from *Roe* to *Casey*?

9. *The elephant in the room—unconstitutional purpose. Casey's* undue burden test actually has two prongs. State abortion regulations are unconstitutional if they have *either* the purpose *or* the effect of placing a substantial obstacle in the past of a woman seeking abortion of a fetus before viability. Nevertheless, as noted above, Justice Breyer's opinion focuses only on the effect of Texas's law and says nothing about its likely purpose. Yet it would not be at all surprising—indeed, it is fairly likely—that then-Texas Governor Rick Perry and many state legislators supported H.B. 2 because they wanted to reduce the number of abortions in Texas, if not eliminate abortion completely. In fact, during litigation the law's supporters talked candidly about their interest in protecting unborn life, as well as women.[1] Texas Governor Greg Abbott objected to the Supreme Court's decision in just these terms: "The decision erodes states' lawmaking authority to safeguard the health and safety of women, and subjects more innocent life to being lost." He added that "Texas' goal is to protect innocent life, while ensuring the highest health and safety standards for women."[2]

Moreover, TRAP laws like H.B. 2 were developed by pro-life organizations as part of their long-term strategy to protect unborn life and eventually outlaw abortion in the United States. Although Texas politicians repeatedly asserted that their goal was to protect women's health from the harms of abortion, it does not take very much imagination to conclude that this was not the only—or even the central—purpose of laws like H.B. 2. (For his part, Justice Alito's does his best to suggest that any reduction in access to abortion is accidental or inconsequential and not the result of any opposition to the right to abortion on Texas's part.)

Why do you think Justice Breyer said nothing about the likely purposes behind H.B. 2? First, *Whole Woman's Health* is the first Supreme Court case in a quarter century to strike down an abortion law—and it called into question the

---

1. Reva Siegel and Linda Greenhouse, When "protecting health" obstructs choice, SCOTUSBlog, January 5th, 2016, at http://www.scotusblog.com/2016/01/symposium-when-protecting-health-obstructs-choice/ (quoting state officials statements that their goals were protection of unborn life and closing abortion clinics in Texas). For many other examples, see Greenhouse & Siegel, *Casey* and the Clinic Closings, supra at 1451-53.

2. Jess Bravin, Supreme Court Rejects Texas Abortion Law as 'Undue Burden,' Wall Street Journal, June 27, 2016, http://www.wsj.com/articles/supreme-court-voids-texas-abortion-regulations-1467036610

constitutionality of many other state laws. It is possible that the members of the *Whole Woman's Health* majority wanted to write in a non-accusatory fashion. It might not be a good idea to accuse state legislatures of acting in bad faith, especially if the Court wants their cooperation in the future. (Compare Earl Warren's opinion in *Brown v. Board of Education*, through which he hoped to induce acceptance by Southern states).

Second, it is difficult to prove unconstitutional intention by multimember legislatures without significant direct evidence of unlawful purpose. On the other hand, the Supreme Court apparently has had no difficulty in holding that Colorado voters acted with animus in *Romer v. Evans*, or that Congress demeaned gay couples in *United States v. Windsor*. (In fact, the same Justices were in the majority in *Whole Woman's Health* and *Windsor*).Why do you think that the majority saw the issue of gay rights differently from the issue of abortion?

Third, Justice Breyer's fact-based approach tends to make purpose inquiries superfluous. If one can show that TRAP laws like H.B. 2 don't really promote women's health, it's a fair inference that they were passed for other reasons—i.e., to make it difficult for women to get abortions. But since one has proved the effect prong of *Casey*, there's no need to go on to infer purpose and argue for the other prong of the test.

This is one way of reading Justice Ginsburg's brief concurrence. She points out that "it is beyond rational belief that H. B. 2 could genuinely protect the health of women, and certain that the law 'would simply make it more difficult for them to obtain abortions.'" If it is "beyond rational belief" that Texas was protecting women's health, the inference as to purpose is obvious.

Insert on p. 1716 following the notes to Windsor v. United States:

OBERGEFELL v. HODGES
135 S.Ct. 2584 (2015)

[Michigan, Kentucky, Ohio, and Tennessee defined marriage as a union between one man and one woman. The petitioners, 14 same-sex couples and two men whose same-sex partners are deceased, challenged the state laws, arguing that the Fourteenth Amendment gave them the right to marry or the right to have to have same-sex marriages lawfully performed in another State given full recognition.]

Justice KENNEDY delivered the opinion of the Court.

The Constitution promises liberty to all within its reach, a liberty that includes certain specific rights that allow persons, within a lawful realm, to define and express their identity. The petitioners in these cases seek to find that liberty by marrying someone of the same sex and having their marriages deemed lawful on the same terms and conditions as marriages between persons of the opposite sex. . . .

II

Before addressing the principles and precedents that govern these cases, it is appropriate to note the history of the subject now before the Court.

A

From their beginning to their most recent page, the annals of human history reveal the transcendent importance of marriage. The lifelong union of a man and a woman always has promised nobility and dignity to all persons, without regard to their station in life. Marriage is sacred to those who live by their religions and offers unique fulfillment to those who find meaning in the secular realm. Its dynamic allows two people to find a life that could not be found alone, for a marriage becomes greater than just the two persons. Rising from the most basic human needs, marriage is essential to our most profound hopes and aspirations.

The centrality of marriage to the human condition makes it unsurprising that the institution has existed for millennia and across civilizations. Since the dawn of history, marriage has transformed strangers into relatives, binding families and societies together. Confucius taught that marriage lies at the foundation of government. This wisdom was echoed centuries later and half a world away by Cicero, who wrote, "The first bond of society is marriage; next, children; and then the family." There are untold references to the beauty of marriage in religious and philosophical texts spanning time, cultures, and faiths, as well as in art and literature in all their forms. It is fair and necessary to say these references were based on the understanding that marriage is a union between two persons of the opposite sex.

That history is the beginning of these cases. The respondents say it should be the end as well. To them, it would demean a timeless institution if the concept and lawful status of marriage were extended to two persons of the same sex. Marriage, in their view, is by its nature a gender-differentiated union of man and woman. This view long has been held — and continues to be held — in good faith by reasonable and sincere people here and throughout the world.

The petitioners acknowledge this history but contend that these cases cannot end there. Were their intent to demean the revered idea and reality of marriage, the petitioners' claims would be of a different order. But that is neither their purpose nor their submission. To the contrary, it is the enduring importance of marriage that underlies the petitioners' contentions. This, they say, is their whole point. Far from seeking to devalue marriage, the petitioners seek it for themselves because of their respect — and need — for its privileges and responsibilities. And their immutable nature dictates that same-sex marriage is their only real path to this profound commitment.

Recounting the circumstances of three of these cases illustrates the urgency of the petitioners' cause from their perspective. Petitioner James Obergefell, a plaintiff in the Ohio case, met John Arthur over two decades ago. They fell in love and started a life together, establishing a lasting, committed relation. In 2011, however, Arthur was diagnosed with amyotrophic lateral sclerosis, or ALS. This debilitating disease is progressive, with no known cure. Two years ago, Obergefell and Arthur decided to commit to one another, resolving to marry before Arthur died. To fulfill their mutual promise, they traveled from Ohio to Maryland, where same-sex marriage was legal. It was difficult for Arthur to move, and so the couple were wed inside a medical transport plane as it remained on the tarmac in Baltimore. Three months later, Arthur died. Ohio law does not permit Obergefell to be listed as the surviving spouse on Arthur's death certificate. By statute, they must remain strangers even in death, a state-imposed separation Obergefell deems "hurtful for the rest of time." He brought suit to be shown as the surviving spouse on Arthur's death certificate.

April DeBoer and Jayne Rowse are co-plaintiffs in the case from Michigan. They celebrated a commitment ceremony to honor their permanent relation in 2007. They both work as nurses, DeBoer in a neonatal unit and Rowse in an emergency unit. In 2009, DeBoer and Rowse fostered and then adopted a baby boy. Later that same year, they welcomed another son into their family. The new baby, born prematurely and abandoned by his biological mother, required around-the-clock care. The next year, a baby girl with special needs joined their family. Michigan, however, permits only opposite-sex married couples or single individuals to adopt, so each child can have only one woman as his or her legal parent. If an emergency were to arise, schools and hospitals may treat the three children as if they had only one parent. And, were tragedy to befall either DeBoer or Rowse, the other would have no legal rights over the children she had not been permitted to adopt. This couple seeks relief from the continuing uncertainty their unmarried status creates in their lives.

Army Reserve Sergeant First Class Ijpe DeKoe and his partner Thomas Kostura, co-plaintiffs in the Tennessee case, fell in love. In 2011, DeKoe received orders to deploy to Afghanistan. Before leaving, he and Kostura married in New York. A week later, DeKoe began his deployment, which lasted for almost a year. When he returned, the two settled in Tennessee, where DeKoe works full-time for the Army Reserve. Their lawful marriage is stripped from them whenever they reside in Tennessee, returning and disappearing as they travel across state lines. DeKoe, who served this Nation to preserve the freedom the Constitution protects, must endure a substantial burden.

The cases now before the Court involve other petitioners as well, each with their own experiences. Their stories reveal that they seek not to denigrate marriage but rather to live their lives, or honor their spouses' memory, joined by its bond.

B

The ancient origins of marriage confirm its centrality, but it has not stood in isolation from developments in law and society. The history of marriage is one of both continuity and change. That institution—even as confined to opposite-sex relations—has evolved over time.

For example, marriage was once viewed as an arrangement by the couple's parents based on political, religious, and financial concerns; but by the time of the Nation's founding it was understood to be a voluntary contract between a man and a woman. See N. Cott, Public Vows: A History of Marriage and the Nation 9–17 (2000); S. Coontz, Marriage, A History 15–16 (2005). As the role and status of women changed, the institution further evolved. Under the centuries-old doctrine of coverture, a married man and woman were treated by the State as a single, male-dominated legal entity. See 1 W. Blackstone, Commentaries on the Laws of England 430 (1765). As women gained legal, political, and property rights, and as society began to understand that women have their own equal dignity, the law of coverture was abandoned. These and other developments in the institution of marriage over the past centuries were not mere superficial changes. Rather, they worked deep transformations in its structure, affecting aspects of marriage long viewed by many as essential.

These new insights have strengthened, not weakened, the institution of marriage. Indeed, changed understandings of marriage are characteristic of a Nation where new dimensions of freedom become apparent to new generations, often through perspectives that begin in pleas or protests and then are considered in the political sphere and the judicial process.

This dynamic can be seen in the Nation's experiences with the rights of gays and lesbians. Until the mid–20th century, same-sex intimacy long had been condemned as immoral by the state itself in most Western nations, a belief often embodied in the criminal law. For this reason, among others, many persons did not deem homosexuals to have dignity in their own distinct identity. A truthful declaration by same-sex couples of what was in their hearts had to remain unspoken. Even when a greater awareness of the humanity and integrity of homosexual persons came in the period after World War II, the argument that gays and lesbians had a just claim to dignity was in conflict with both law and widespread social conventions. Same-sex intimacy remained a crime in many States. Gays and lesbians were prohibited from most government employment, barred from military service, excluded under immigration laws, targeted by police, and burdened in their rights to associate.

For much of the 20th century, moreover, homosexuality was treated as an illness. When the American Psychiatric Association published the first Diagnostic and Statistical Manual of Mental Disorders in 1952, homosexuality was classified as a mental disorder, a position adhered to until 1973. Only in more recent years have psychiatrists and others recognized that sexual orientation is both a normal expression of human sexuality and immutable.

In the late 20th century, following substantial cultural and political developments, same-sex couples began to lead more open and public lives and to establish families. This development was followed by a quite extensive discussion of the issue in both governmental and private sectors and by a shift in public attitudes toward greater tolerance. As a result, questions about the rights of gays and lesbians soon reached the courts, where the issue could be discussed in the formal discourse of the law.

This Court first gave detailed consideration to the legal status of homosexuals in *Bowers v. Hardwick,* 478 U.S. 186 (1986). There it upheld the constitutionality of a Georgia law deemed to criminalize certain homosexual acts. Ten years later, in *Romer v. Evans,* 517 U.S. 620 (1996), the Court invalidated an amendment to Colorado's Constitution that sought to foreclose any branch or political subdivision of the State from protecting persons against discrimination based on sexual orientation. Then, in 2003, the Court overruled *Bowers,* holding that laws making same-sex intimacy a crime "demea[n] the lives of homosexual persons." *Lawrence v. Texas,* 539 U.S. 558 [(2003)].

Against this background, the legal question of same-sex marriage arose. In 1993, the Hawaii Supreme Court held Hawaii's law restricting marriage to opposite-sex couples constituted a classification on the basis of sex and was therefore subject to strict scrutiny under the Hawaii Constitution. Although this decision did not mandate that same-sex marriage be allowed, some States were concerned by its implications and reaffirmed in their laws that marriage is defined as a union between opposite-sex partners. So too in 1996, Congress passed the Defense of Marriage Act (DOMA), 110 Stat. 2419, defining marriage for all federal-law purposes as "only a legal union between one man and one woman as husband and wife." 1 U.S.C. §7.

The new and widespread discussion of the subject led other States to a different conclusion. In 2003, the Supreme Judicial Court of Massachusetts held the State's Constitution guaranteed same-sex couples the right to marry. After that ruling, some additional States granted marriage rights to same-sex couples, either through judicial or legislative processes. . . . Two Terms ago, in *United States v. Windsor,* 570 U.S. _____ (2013), this Court invalidated DOMA to the extent it barred the Federal Government from treating same-sex marriages as valid even when they were lawful in the State where they were licensed. DOMA, the Court held, impermissibly disparaged those same-sex couples "who wanted to affirm their commitment to one another before their children, their family, their friends, and their community."

Numerous cases about same-sex marriage have reached the United States Courts of Appeals in recent years. In accordance with the judicial duty to base their decisions on principled reasons and neutral discussions, without scornful or disparaging commentary, courts have written a substantial body of law considering all sides of these issues. That case law helps to explain and formulate the underlying principles this Court now must consider. With the exception of the opinion here under review and one other [from the Eighth Circuit decided in 2006], the Courts of Appeals have held that excluding same-sex couples from marriage violates the Constitution. There also have been many thoughtful District Court decisions addressing same-sex marriage — and most of them, too, have concluded same-sex couples must be allowed to marry. In addition the highest courts of many States have contributed to this ongoing dialogue in decisions interpreting their own State Constitutions.

After years of litigation, legislation, referenda, and the discussions that attended these public acts, the States are now divided on the issue of same-sex marriage.

III

Under the Due Process Clause of the Fourteenth Amendment, no State shall "deprive any person of life, liberty, or property, without due process of law." The fundamental liberties protected by this Clause include most of the rights enumerated in the Bill of Rights. In addition these liberties extend to certain personal choices central to individual dignity and autonomy, including intimate choices that define personal identity and beliefs. See, *e.g., Eisenstadt v. Baird,* 405 U.S. 438 (1972); *Griswold v. Connecticut,* 381 U.S. 479 (1965).

The identification and protection of fundamental rights is an enduring part of the judicial duty to interpret the Constitution. That responsibility, however, "has not been reduced to any formula." *Poe v. Ullman,* 367 U.S. 497, 542 (1961) (Harlan, J., dissenting). Rather, it requires courts to exercise reasoned judgment in identifying interests of the person so fundamental that the State must accord them its respect. See *ibid.* That process is guided by many of the same considerations relevant to analysis of other constitutional provisions that set forth broad principles rather than specific requirements. History and tradition guide and discipline this inquiry but do not set its outer boundaries. See *Lawrence.* That method respects our history and learns from it without allowing the past alone to rule the present.

The nature of injustice is that we may not always see it in our own times. The generations that wrote and ratified the Bill of Rights and the Fourteenth Amendment did not presume to know the extent of freedom in all of its dimensions, and so they entrusted to future generations a charter protecting the right of all persons to enjoy liberty as we learn its meaning. When new insight reveals discord between the Constitution's central protections and a received legal stricture, a claim to liberty must be addressed.

Applying these established tenets, the Court has long held the right to marry is protected by the Constitution. In *Loving v. Virginia,* 388 U.S. 1 (1967), which invalidated bans on interracial unions, a unanimous Court held marriage is "one of the vital personal rights essential to the orderly pursuit of happiness by free men." The Court reaffirmed that holding in *Zablocki v. Redhail,* 434 U.S. 374 (1978), which held the right to marry was burdened by a law prohibiting fathers who were behind on child support from marrying. The Court again applied this principle in *Turner v. Safley,* 482 U.S. 78 (1987), which held the right to marry was abridged by regulations limiting the privilege of prison inmates to marry. Over time and in other contexts, the Court has reiterated that the right to marry is fundamental under the Due Process Clause. See, *e.g., M.L.B. v. S.L. J.,* 519 U.S. 102 (1996); *Cleveland Bd. of Ed. v. LaFleur,* 414 U.S. 632 (1974); *Griswold; Skinner v. Oklahoma ex rel. Williamson,* 316 U.S. 535 (1942); *Meyer v. Nebraska,* 262 U.S. 390 (1923).

It cannot be denied that this Court's cases describing the right to marry presumed a relationship involving opposite-sex partners. The Court, like many institutions, has made assumptions defined by the world and time of which it is a part. This was evident in *Baker v. Nelson,* 409 U.S. 810 [(1972)], a one-line summary decision issued in 1972, holding the exclusion of same-sex couples from marriage did not present a substantial federal question.

Still, there are other, more instructive precedents. This Court's cases have expressed constitutional principles of broader reach. In defining the right to marry these cases have identified essential attributes of that right based in history, tradition, and other constitutional liberties inherent in this intimate bond. See, *e.g., Lawrence; Turner; Zablocki; Loving; Griswold.* And in assessing whether the force and rationale of its cases apply to same-sex couples, the Court must respect the basic reasons why the right to marry has been long protected. See, *e.g., Eisenstadt; Poe* (Harlan, J., dissenting).

This analysis compels the conclusion that same-sex couples may exercise the right to marry. The four principles and traditions to be discussed demonstrate that the reasons marriage is fundamental under the Constitution apply with equal force to same-sex couples.

A first premise of the Court's relevant precedents is that the right to personal choice regarding marriage is inherent in the concept of individual autonomy. This abiding connection between marriage and liberty is why *Loving* invalidated interracial marriage bans under the Due Process Clause. Like choices concerning contraception, family relationships, procreation, and childrearing, all of which are protected by the Constitution, decisions concerning marriage are among the most intimate that an individual can make. See *Lawrence.* Indeed, the Court has noted it would be contradictory "to recognize a right of privacy with respect to other matters of family life and not with respect to the decision to enter the relationship that is the foundation of the family in our society." *Zablocki.*

Choices about marriage shape an individual's destiny. As the Supreme Judicial Court of Massachusetts has explained, because "it fulfils yearnings for security, safe haven, and connection that express our common humanity, civil marriage is an esteemed institution, and the decision whether and whom to marry is among life's momentous acts of self-definition." *Goodridge.*

The nature of marriage is that, through its enduring bond, two persons together can find other freedoms, such as expression, intimacy, and spirituality. This is true for all persons, whatever their sexual orientation. See *Windsor.* There is dignity in the bond between two men or two women who seek to marry and in their autonomy to make such profound choices. Cf. *Loving* ("[T]he freedom to marry, or not marry, a person of another race resides with the individual and cannot be infringed by the State").

A second principle in this Court's jurisprudence is that the right to marry is fundamental because it supports a two-person union unlike any other in its importance to the committed individuals. This point was central to *Griswold v. Connecticut,* which held the Constitution protects the right of married couples to use contraception. Suggesting that marriage is a right "older than the Bill of Rights," *Griswold* described marriage this way:

"Marriage is a coming together for better or for worse, hopefully enduring, and intimate to the degree of being sacred. It is an association that promotes a way of life, not causes; a harmony in living, not political faiths; a bilateral loyalty, not commercial or social projects. Yet it is an association for as noble a purpose as any involved in our prior decisions."

And in *Turner,* the Court again acknowledged the intimate association protected by this right, holding prisoners could not be denied the right to marry because their committed relationships satisfied the basic reasons why marriage is a fundamental right. The right to marry thus dignifies couples who "wish to define themselves by their commitment to each other." *Windsor.* Marriage responds to the universal fear that a lonely person might call out only to find no one there. It offers the hope of companionship and understanding and assurance that while both still live there will be someone to care for the other.

As this Court held in *Lawrence,* same-sex couples have the same right as opposite-sex couples to enjoy intimate association. *Lawrence* invalidated laws that made same-sex intimacy a criminal act. And it acknowledged that "[w]hen sexuality finds overt expression in intimate conduct with another person, the conduct can be but one element in a personal bond that is more enduring." But while *Lawrence* confirmed a dimension of freedom that allows individuals to engage in intimate association without criminal liability, it does not follow that freedom stops there. Outlaw to outcast may be a step forward, but it does not achieve the full promise of liberty.

A third basis for protecting the right to marry is that it safeguards children and families and thus draws meaning from related rights of childrearing, procreation, and education. See *Pierce v. Society of Sisters,* 268 U.S. 510 (1925); *Meyer.* The Court has recognized these connections by describing the varied rights as a unified whole: "[T]he right to 'marry, establish a home and bring up children' is a central part of the liberty protected by the Due Process Clause." *Zablocki* (quoting *Meyer*). Under the laws of the several States, some of marriage's protections for children and families are material. But marriage also confers more profound benefits. By giving recognition and legal structure to their parents' relationship, marriage allows children "to understand the integrity and closeness of their own family and its concord with other families in their community and in their daily lives." *Windsor.* Marriage also affords the permanency and stability important to children's best interests.

As all parties agree, many same-sex couples provide loving and nurturing homes to their children, whether biological or adopted. And hundreds of thousands of children are presently being raised by such couples. Most States have allowed gays and lesbians to adopt, either as individuals or as couples, and many adopted and foster children have same-sex parents. This provides powerful confirmation from the law itself that gays and lesbians can create loving, supportive families.

Excluding same-sex couples from marriage thus conflicts with a central premise of the right to marry. Without the recognition, stability, and predictability marriage offers, their children suffer the stigma of knowing their families are somehow lesser. They also suffer the significant material costs of being raised by unmarried parents, relegated through no fault of their own to a more difficult and uncertain family life. The marriage laws at issue here thus harm and humiliate the children of same-sex couples. See *Windsor*.

That is not to say the right to marry is less meaningful for those who do not or cannot have children. An ability, desire, or promise to procreate is not and has not been a prerequisite for a valid marriage in any State. In light of precedent protecting the right of a married couple not to procreate, it cannot be said the Court or the States have conditioned the right to marry on the capacity or commitment to procreate. The constitutional marriage right has many aspects, of which childbearing is only one.

Fourth and finally, this Court's cases and the Nation's traditions make clear that marriage is a keystone of our social order. Alexis de Tocqueville recognized this truth on his travels through the United States almost two centuries ago:

> "There is certainly no country in the world where the tie of marriage is so much respected as in America . . . [W]hen the American retires from the turmoil of public life to the bosom of his family, he finds in it the image of order and of peace . . . . [H]e afterwards carries [that image] with him into public affairs." 1 Democracy in America 309.

In *Maynard v. Hill*, 125 U.S. 190 (1888), the Court echoed de Tocqueville, explaining that marriage is "the foundation of the family and of society, without which there would be neither civilization nor progress." Marriage, the *Maynard* Court said, has long been "'a great public institution, giving character to our whole civil polity.'" This idea has been reiterated even as the institution has evolved in substantial ways over time, superseding rules related to parental consent, gender, and race once thought by many to be essential.

For that reason, just as a couple vows to support each other, so does society pledge to support the couple, offering symbolic recognition and material benefits to protect and nourish the union. Indeed, while the States are in general free to vary the benefits they confer on all married couples, they have throughout our history made marriage the basis for an expanding list of governmental rights, benefits, and responsibilities. These aspects of marital status include: taxation; inheritance and property rights; rules of intestate succession; spousal privilege in the law of evidence; hospital access; medical decisionmaking authority; adoption rights; the rights and benefits of survivors; birth and death certificates; professional ethics rules; campaign finance restrictions; workers' compensation benefits; health insurance; and child custody, support, and visitation rules. Valid marriage under state law is also a significant status for over a thousand provisions of federal law. See *Windsor*. The States have contributed to the fundamental character of the marriage right by placing that institution at the center of so many facets of the legal and social order.

There is no difference between same- and opposite-sex couples with respect to this principle. Yet by virtue of their exclusion from that institution, same-sex couples are denied the constellation of benefits that the States have linked to marriage. This harm results in more than just material burdens. Same-sex couples are consigned to an instability many opposite-sex couples would deem intolerable in their own lives. As the State itself makes marriage all the more precious by the significance it attaches to it, exclusion from that status has the effect of teaching that gays and lesbians are unequal in important respects. It demeans gays and lesbians for the State to lock them out of a central institution of the Nation's society. Same-sex couples, too, may aspire to the transcendent purposes of marriage and seek fulfillment in its highest meaning.

The limitation of marriage to opposite-sex couples may long have seemed natural and just, but its inconsistency with the central meaning of the fundamental right to marry is now manifest. With that knowledge must come the recognition that laws excluding same-sex couples from the marriage right impose stigma and injury of the kind prohibited by our basic charter.

Objecting that this does not reflect an appropriate framing of the issue, the respondents refer to *Washington v. Glucksberg,* 521 U.S. 702 (1997), which called for a "'careful description'" of fundamental rights. They assert the petitioners do not seek to exercise the right to marry but rather a new and nonexistent "right to same-sex marriage." *Glucksberg* did insist that liberty under the Due Process Clause must be defined in a most circumscribed manner, with central reference to specific historical practices. Yet while that approach may have been appropriate for the asserted right there involved (physician-assisted suicide), it is inconsistent with the approach this Court has used in discussing other fundamental rights, including marriage and intimacy. *Loving* did not ask about a "right to interracial marriage"; *Turner* did not ask about a "right of inmates to marry"; and *Zablocki* did not ask about a "right of fathers with unpaid child support duties to marry." Rather, each case inquired about the right to marry in its comprehensive sense, asking if there was a sufficient justification for excluding the relevant class from the right.

That principle applies here. If rights were defined by who exercised them in the past, then received practices could serve as their own continued justification and new groups could not invoke rights once denied. This Court has rejected that approach, both with respect to the right to marry and the rights of gays and lesbians. See *Loving*; *Lawrence*.

The right to marry is fundamental as a matter of history and tradition, but rights come not from ancient sources alone. They rise, too, from a better informed understanding of how constitutional imperatives define a liberty that remains urgent in our own era. Many who deem same-sex marriage to be wrong reach that conclusion based on decent and honorable religious or philosophical premises, and neither they nor their beliefs are disparaged here. But when that sincere, personal opposition becomes enacted law and public policy, the necessary consequence is to put the imprimatur of the State itself on an exclusion that soon demeans or stigmatizes those whose own liberty is then denied. Under the Constitution, same-sex couples seek in marriage the same legal treatment as opposite-sex couples, and it would disparage their choices and diminish their personhood to deny them this right.

The right of same-sex couples to marry that is part of the liberty promised by the Fourteenth Amendment is derived, too, from that Amendment's guarantee of the equal protection of the laws. The Due Process Clause and the Equal Protection Clause are connected in a profound way, though they set forth independent principles. Rights implicit in liberty and rights secured by equal protection may rest on different precepts and are not always co-extensive, yet in some instances each may be instructive as to the meaning and reach of the other. In any particular case one Clause may be thought to capture the essence of the right in a more accurate and comprehensive way, even as the two Clauses may converge in the identification and definition of the right. See *M.L. B.*; *Bearden v. Georgia,* 461 U.S. 660 (1983). This interrelation of the two principles furthers our understanding of what freedom is and must become.

The Court's cases touching upon the right to marry reflect this dynamic. In *Loving* the Court invalidated a prohibition on interracial marriage under both the Equal Protection Clause and the Due Process Clause. The Court first declared the prohibition invalid because of its unequal treatment of interracial couples. It stated: "There can be no doubt that restricting the freedom to marry solely because of racial classifications violates the central meaning of the Equal Protection Clause." With this link to equal protection the Court proceeded to hold the prohibition offended central precepts of liberty: "To deny this fundamental freedom on so unsupportable a basis as the racial classifications embodied in these statutes, classifications so directly subversive of the principle of equality at the heart of the Fourteenth Amendment, is surely to deprive all the State's citizens of liberty without due process of law." The reasons why marriage is a fundamental right became more clear and compelling from a full awareness and understanding of the hurt that resulted from laws barring interracial unions.

The synergy between the two protections is illustrated further in *Zablocki*. There the Court invoked the Equal Protection Clause as its basis for invalidating the challenged law, which, as already noted, barred fathers who were behind on child-support payments from marrying without judicial approval. The equal protection analysis depended in central part on the Court's holding that the law burdened a right "of fundamental importance." It was the essential nature of the marriage right, discussed at length in *Zablocki,* that made apparent the law's incompatibility with requirements of equality. Each concept—liberty and equal protection—leads to a stronger understanding of the other.

Indeed, in interpreting the Equal Protection Clause, the Court has recognized that new insights and societal understandings can reveal unjustified inequality within our most fundamental institutions that once passed unnoticed and unchallenged. To take but one period, this occurred with respect to marriage in the 1970's and 1980's. Notwithstanding the gradual erosion of the doctrine of coverture, invidious sex-based classifications in marriage remained common through the mid–20th century. These classifications denied the equal dignity of men and women. One State's law, for example, provided in 1971 that "the husband is the head of the family and the wife is subject to him; her legal civil existence is merged in the husband, except so far as the law recognizes her separately, either for her own protection, or for her benefit." Ga.Code Ann. §53–501 (1935). Responding to a new awareness, the Court invoked equal protection principles to invalidate laws imposing sex-based inequality on marriage. See, *e.g.*, *Kirchberg v. Feenstra*, 450 U.S. 455 (1981); *Wengler v. Druggists Mut. Ins. Co.*, 446 U.S. 142 (1980); *Califano v. Westcott*, 443 U.S. 76 (1979); *Orr v. Orr*, 440 U.S. 268 (1979); *Califano v. Goldfarb*, 430 U.S. 199 (1977) (plurality opinion); *Weinberger v. Wiesenfeld*, 420 U.S. 636 (1975); *Frontiero v. Richardson*, 411 U.S. 677 (1973). Like *Loving* and *Zablocki*, these precedents show the Equal Protection Clause can help to identify and correct inequalities in the institution of marriage, vindicating precepts of liberty and equality under the Constitution.

Other cases confirm this relation between liberty and equality. In *M.L.B. v. S.L. J.*, the Court invalidated under due process and equal protection principles a statute requiring indigent mothers to pay a fee in order to appeal the termination of their parental rights.In *Eisenstadt v. Baird*, the Court invoked both principles to invalidate a prohibition on the distribution of contraceptives to unmarried persons but not married persons. And in *Skinner v. Oklahoma ex rel. Williamson*, the Court invalidated under both principles a law that allowed sterilization of habitual criminals.

In *Lawrence* the Court acknowledged the interlocking nature of these constitutional safeguards in the context of the legal treatment of gays and lesbians. Although *Lawrence* elaborated its holding under the Due Process Clause, it acknowledged, and sought to remedy, the continuing inequality that resulted from laws making intimacy in the lives of gays and lesbians a crime against the State. *Lawrence* therefore drew upon principles of liberty and equality to define and protect the rights of gays and lesbians, holding the State "cannot demean their existence or control their destiny by making their private sexual conduct a crime."

This dynamic also applies to same-sex marriage. It is now clear that the challenged laws burden the liberty of same-sex couples, and it must be further acknowledged that they abridge central precepts of equality. Here the marriage laws enforced by the respondents are in essence unequal: same-sex couples are denied all the benefits afforded to opposite-sex couples and are barred from exercising a fundamental right. Especially against a long history of disapproval of their relationships, this denial to same-sex couples of the right to marry works a grave and continuing harm. The imposition of this disability on gays and lesbians serves to disrespect and subordinate them. And the Equal Protection Clause, like the Due Process Clause, prohibits this unjustified infringement of the fundamental right to marry. See, *e.g., Zablocki,*; *Skinner*.

These considerations lead to the conclusion that the right to marry is a fundamental right inherent in the liberty of the person, and under the Due Process and Equal Protection Clauses of the Fourteenth Amendment couples of the same-sex may not be deprived of that right and that liberty. The Court now holds that same-sex couples may exercise the fundamental right to marry. No longer may this liberty be denied to them. *Baker v. Nelson* must be and now is overruled, and the State laws challenged by Petitioners in these cases are now held invalid to the extent they exclude same-sex couples from civil marriage on the same terms and conditions as opposite-sex couples.

IV

There may be an initial inclination in these cases to proceed with caution — to await further legislation, litigation, and debate. The respondents warn there has been insufficient democratic discourse before deciding an issue so basic as the definition of marriage. In its ruling on the cases now before this Court, the majority opinion for the Court of Appeals made a cogent argument that it would be appropriate for the respondents' States to await further public discussion and political measures before licensing same-sex marriages.

Yet there has been far more deliberation than this argument acknowledges. There have been referenda, legislative debates, and grassroots campaigns, as well as countless studies, papers, books, and other popular and scholarly writings. There has been extensive litigation in state and federal courts. Judicial opinions addressing the issue have been informed by the contentions of parties and counsel, which, in turn, reflect the more general, societal discussion of same-sex marriage and its meaning that has occurred over the past decades. As more than 100 *amici* make clear in their filings, many of the central institutions in American life — state and local governments, the military, large and small businesses, labor unions, religious organizations, law enforcement, civic groups, professional organizations, and universities — have devoted substantial attention to the question. This has led to an enhanced understanding of the issue — an understanding reflected in the arguments now presented for resolution as a matter of constitutional law.

Of course, the Constitution contemplates that democracy is the appropriate process for change, so long as that process does not abridge fundamental rights. Last Term, a plurality of this Court reaffirmed the importance of the democratic principle in *Schuette v. BAMN,* 572 U.S. _____ (2014), noting the "right of citizens to debate so they can learn and decide and then, through the political process, act in concert to try to shape the course of their own times." Indeed, it is most often through democracy that liberty is preserved and protected in our lives. But as *Schuette* also said, "[t]he freedom secured by the Constitution consists, in one of its essential dimensions, of the right of the individual not to be injured by the unlawful exercise of governmental power." Thus, when the rights of persons are violated, "the Constitution requires redress by the courts," notwithstanding the more general value of democratic decisionmaking. This holds true even when protecting individual rights affects issues of the utmost importance and sensitivity.

The dynamic of our constitutional system is that individuals need not await legislative action before asserting a fundamental right. The Nation's courts are open to injured individuals who come to them to vindicate their own direct, personal stake in our basic charter. An individual can invoke a right to constitutional protection when he or she is harmed, even if the broader public disagrees and even if the legislature refuses to act. The idea of the Constitution "was to withdraw certain subjects from the vicissitudes of political controversy, to place them beyond the reach of majorities and officials and to establish them as legal principles to be applied by the courts." *West Virginia Bd. of Ed. v. Barnette,* 319 U.S. 624 (1943). This is why "fundamental rights may not be submitted to a vote; they depend on the outcome of no elections." *Ibid.* It is of no moment whether advocates of same-sex marriage now enjoy or lack momentum in the democratic process. The issue before the Court here is the legal question whether the Constitution protects the right of same-sex couples to marry.

This is not the first time the Court has been asked to adopt a cautious approach to recognizing and protecting fundamental rights. In *Bowers,* a bare majority upheld a law criminalizing same-sex intimacy. That approach might have been viewed as a cautious endorsement of the democratic process, which had only just begun to consider the rights of gays and lesbians. Yet, in effect, *Bowers* upheld state action that denied gays and lesbians a fundamental right and caused them pain and humiliation. As evidenced by the dissents in that case, the facts and principles necessary to a correct holding were known to the *Bowers* Court. That is why *Lawrence* held *Bowers* was "not correct when it was decided." Although *Bowers* was eventually repudiated in *Lawrence,* men and women were harmed in the interim, and the substantial effects of these injuries no doubt lingered long after *Bowers* was overruled. Dignitary wounds cannot always be healed with the stroke of a pen.

A ruling against same-sex couples would have the same effect—and, like *Bowers,* would be unjustified under the Fourteenth Amendment. The petitioners' stories make clear the urgency of the issue they present to the Court. James Obergefell now asks whether Ohio can erase his marriage to John Arthur for all time. April DeBoer and Jayne Rowse now ask whether Michigan may continue to deny them the certainty and stability all mothers desire to protect their children, and for them and their children the childhood years will pass all too soon. Ijpe DeKoe and Thomas Kostura now ask whether Tennessee can deny to one who has served this Nation the basic dignity of recognizing his New York marriage. Properly presented with the petitioners' cases, the Court has a duty to address these claims and answer these questions.

Indeed, faced with a disagreement among the Courts of Appeals—a disagreement that caused impermissible geographic variation in the meaning of federal law—the Court granted review to determine whether same-sex couples may exercise the right to marry. Were the Court to uphold the challenged laws as constitutional, it would teach the Nation that these laws are in accord with our society's most basic compact. Were the Court to stay its hand to allow slower, case-by-case determination of the required availability of specific public benefits to same-sex couples, it still would deny gays and lesbians many rights and responsibilities intertwined with marriage.

The respondents also argue allowing same-sex couples to wed will harm marriage as an institution by leading to fewer opposite-sex marriages. This may occur, the respondents contend, because licensing same-sex marriage severs the connection between natural procreation and marriage. That argument, however, rests on a counterintuitive view of opposite-sex couple's decisionmaking processes regarding marriage and parenthood. Decisions about whether to marry and raise children are based on many personal, romantic, and practical considerations; and it is unrealistic to conclude that an opposite-sex couple would choose not to marry simply because same-sex couples may do so. See *Kitchen v. Herbert*, 755 F.3d 1193, 1223 (C.A.10 2014) ("[I]t is wholly illogical to believe that state recognition of the love and commitment between same-sex couples will alter the most intimate and personal decisions of opposite-sex couples"). The respondents have not shown a foundation for the conclusion that allowing same-sex marriage will cause the harmful outcomes they describe. Indeed, with respect to this asserted basis for excluding same-sex couples from the right to marry, it is appropriate to observe these cases involve only the rights of two consenting adults whose marriages would pose no risk of harm to themselves or third parties.

Finally, it must be emphasized that religions, and those who adhere to religious doctrines, may continue to advocate with utmost, sincere conviction that, by divine precepts, same-sex marriage should not be condoned. The First Amendment ensures that religious organizations and persons are given proper protection as they seek to teach the principles that are so fulfilling and so central to their lives and faiths, and to their own deep aspirations to continue the family structure they have long revered. The same is true of those who oppose same-sex marriage for other reasons. In turn, those who believe allowing same-sex marriage is proper or indeed essential, whether as a matter of religious conviction or secular belief, may engage those who disagree with their view in an open and searching debate. The Constitution, however, does not permit the State to bar same-sex couples from marriage on the same terms as accorded to couples of the opposite sex.

V

These cases also present the question whether the Constitution requires States to recognize same-sex marriages validly performed out of State. As made clear by the case of Obergefell and Arthur, and by that of DeKoe and Kostura, the recognition bans inflict substantial and continuing harm on same-sex couples.

Being married in one State but having that valid marriage denied in another is one of "the most perplexing and distressing complication[s]" in the law of domestic relations. *Williams v. North Carolina*, 317 U.S. 287 (1942) (internal quotation marks omitted). Leaving the current state of affairs in place would maintain and promote instability and uncertainty. For some couples, even an ordinary drive into a neighboring State to visit family or friends risks causing severe hardship in the event of a spouse's hospitalization while across state lines.

In light of the fact that many States already allow same-sex marriage—and hundreds of thousands of these marriages already have occurred—the disruption caused by the recognition bans is significant and ever-growing.

As counsel for the respondents acknowledged at argument, if States are required by the Constitution to issue marriage licenses to same-sex couples, the justifications for refusing to recognize those marriages performed elsewhere are undermined. The Court, in this decision, holds same-sex couples may exercise the fundamental right to marry in all States. It follows that the Court also must hold—and it now does hold—that there is no lawful basis for a State to refuse to recognize a lawful same-sex marriage performed in another State on the ground of its same-sex character.

* * *

No union is more profound than marriage, for it embodies the highest ideals of love, fidelity, devotion, sacrifice, and family. In forming a marital union, two people become something greater than once they were. As some of the petitioners in these cases demonstrate, marriage embodies a love that may endure even past death. It would misunderstand these men and women to say they disrespect the idea of marriage. Their plea is that they do respect it, respect it so deeply that they seek to find its fulfillment for themselves. Their hope is not to be condemned to live in loneliness, excluded from one of civilization's oldest institutions. They ask for equal dignity in the eyes of the law. The Constitution grants them that right.

The judgment of the Court of Appeals for the Sixth Circuit is reversed.

It is so ordered.

Chief Justice ROBERTS, with whom Justice SCALIA and Justice THOMAS join, dissenting.

Petitioners make strong arguments rooted in social policy and considerations of fairness. They contend that same-sex couples should be allowed to affirm their love and commitment through marriage, just like opposite-sex couples. That position has undeniable appeal; over the past six years, voters and legislators in eleven States and the District of Columbia have revised their laws to allow marriage between two people of the same sex.

But this Court is not a legislature. Whether same-sex marriage is a good idea should be of no concern to us. Under the Constitution, judges have power to say what the law is, not what it should be. The people who ratified the Constitution authorized courts to exercise "neither force nor will but merely judgment." The Federalist No. 78 (A.Hamilton)(capitalization altered).

Although the policy arguments for extending marriage to same-sex couples may be compelling, the legal arguments for requiring such an extension are not. The fundamental right to marry does not include a right to make a State change its definition of marriage. And a State's decision to maintain the meaning of marriage that has persisted in every culture throughout human history can hardly be called irrational. In short, our Constitution does not enact any one theory of marriage. The people of a State are free to expand marriage to include same-sex couples, or to retain the historic definition.

Today, however, the Court takes the extraordinary step of ordering every State to license and recognize same-sex marriage. Many people will rejoice at this decision, and I begrudge none their celebration. But for those who believe in a government of laws, not of men, the majority's approach is deeply disheartening. Supporters of same-sex marriage have achieved considerable success persuading their fellow citizens—through the democratic process—to adopt their view. That ends today. Five lawyers have closed the debate and enacted their own vision of marriage as a matter of constitutional law. Stealing this issue from the people will for many cast a cloud over same-sex marriage, making a dramatic social change that much more difficult to accept.

The majority's decision is an act of will, not legal judgment. The right it announces has no basis in the Constitution or this Court's precedent. The majority expressly disclaims judicial "caution" and omits even a pretense of humility, openly relying on its desire to remake society according to its own "new insight" into the "nature of injustice." As a result, the Court invalidates the marriage laws of more than half the States and orders the transformation of a social institution that has formed the basis of human society for millennia, for the Kalahari Bushmen and the Han Chinese, the Carthaginians and the Aztecs. Just who do we think we are?

It can be tempting for judges to confuse our own preferences with the requirements of the law. But as this Court has been reminded throughout our history, the Constitution "is made for people of fundamentally differing views." *Lochner v. New York,* 198 U.S. 45 (1905) (Holmes, J., dissenting). Accordingly, "courts are not concerned with the wisdom or policy of legislation." *Id.,* at 69 (Harlan, J., dissenting). The majority today neglects that restrained conception of the judicial role. It seizes for itself a question the Constitution leaves to the people, at a time when the people are engaged in a vibrant debate on that question. And it answers that question based not on neutral principles of constitutional law, but on its own "understanding of what freedom is and must become." I have no choice but to dissent.

Understand well what this dissent is about: It is not about whether, in my judgment, the institution of marriage should be changed to include same-sex couples. It is instead about whether, in our democratic republic, that decision should rest with the people acting through their elected representatives, or with five lawyers who happen to hold commissions authorizing them to resolve legal disputes according to law. The Constitution leaves no doubt about the answer.

I

Petitioners and their *amici* base their arguments on the "right to marry" and the imperative of "marriage equality." There is no serious dispute that, under our precedents, the Constitution protects a right to marry and requires States to apply their marriage laws equally. The real question in these cases is what constitutes "marriage," or—more precisely—*who decides* what constitutes "marriage"?

The majority largely ignores these questions, relegating ages of human experience with marriage to a paragraph or two. Even if history and precedent are not "the end" of these cases, *ante,* at 4, I would not "sweep away what has so long been settled" without showing greater respect for all that preceded us. *Town of Greece v. Galloway,* 572 U.S. _____ (2014).

A

As the majority acknowledges, marriage "has existed for millennia and across civilizations." For all those millennia, across all those civilizations, "marriage" referred to only one relationship: the union of a man and a woman. As the Court explained two Terms ago, "until recent years, . . . marriage between a man and a woman no doubt had been thought of by most people as essential to the very definition of that term and to its role and function throughout the history of civilization." *United States v. Windsor.*

This universal definition of marriage as the union of a man and a woman is no historical coincidence. Marriage did not come about as a result of a political movement, discovery, disease, war, religious doctrine, or any other moving force of world history — and certainly not as a result of a prehistoric decision to exclude gays and lesbians. It arose in the nature of things to meet a vital need: ensuring that children are conceived by a mother and father committed to raising them in the stable conditions of a lifelong relationship. . . .

The premises supporting this concept of marriage are so fundamental that they rarely require articulation. The human race must procreate to survive. Procreation occurs through sexual relations between a man and a woman. When sexual relations result in the conception of a child, that child's prospects are generally better if the mother and father stay together rather than going their separate ways. Therefore, for the good of children and society, sexual relations that can lead to procreation should occur only between a man and a woman committed to a lasting bond.

Society has recognized that bond as marriage. And by bestowing a respected status and material benefits on married couples, society encourages men and women to conduct sexual relations within marriage rather than without. As one prominent scholar put it, "Marriage is a socially arranged solution for the problem of getting people to stay together and care for children that the mere desire for children, and the sex that makes children possible, does not solve." J.Q. Wilson, The Marriage Problem 41 (2002).

This singular understanding of marriage has prevailed in the United States throughout our history. The majority accepts that at "the time of the Nation's founding [marriage] was understood to be a voluntary contract between a man and a woman." Early Americans drew heavily on legal scholars like William Blackstone, who regarded marriage between "husband and wife" as one of the "great relations in private life," and philosophers like John Locke, who described marriage as "a voluntary compact between man and woman" centered on "its chief end, procreation" and the "nourishment and support" of children. To those who drafted and ratified the Constitution, this conception of marriage and family "was a given: its structure, its stability, roles, and values accepted by all."

The Constitution itself says nothing about marriage, and the Framers thereby entrusted the States with "[t]he whole subject of the domestic relations of husband and wife." *Windsor*. There is no dispute that every State at the founding — and every State throughout our history until a dozen years ago — defined marriage in the traditional, biologically rooted way. The four States in these cases are typical. Their laws, before and after statehood, have treated marriage as the union of a man and a woman. Even when state laws did not specify this definition expressly, no one doubted what they meant. The meaning of "marriage" went without saying.

Of course, many did say it. In his first American dictionary, Noah Webster defined marriage as "the legal union of a man and woman for life," which served the purposes of "preventing the promiscuous intercourse of the sexes, . . . promoting domestic felicity, and . . . securing the maintenance and education of children." 1 An American Dictionary of the English Language (1828). An influential 19th-century treatise defined marriage as "a civil status, existing in one man and one woman legally united for life for those civil and social purposes which are based in the distinction of sex." J. Bishop, Commentaries on the Law of Marriage and Divorce 25 (1852). The first edition of Black's Law Dictionary defined marriage as "the civil status of one man and one woman united in law for life." Black's Law Dictionary 756 (1891) (emphasis deleted). The dictionary maintained essentially that same definition for the next century.

This Court's precedents have repeatedly described marriage in ways that are consistent only with its traditional meaning. Early cases on the subject referred to marriage as "the union for life of one man and one woman," *Murphy v. Ramsey,* 114 U.S. 15 (1885), which forms "the foundation of the family and of society, without which there would be neither civilization nor progress," *Maynard v. Hill,* 125 U.S. 190, (1888). We later described marriage as "fundamental to our very existence and survival," an understanding that necessarily implies a procreative component. *Loving v. Virginia*; see *Skinner v. Oklahoma ex rel. Williamson*. More recent cases have directly connected the right to marry with the "right to procreate." *Zablocki*.

As the majority notes, some aspects of marriage have changed over time. Arranged marriages have largely given way to pairings based on romantic love. States have replaced coverture, the doctrine by which a married man and woman became a single legal entity, with laws that respect each participant's separate status. Racial restrictions on marriage, which "arose as an incident to slavery" to promote "White Supremacy," were repealed by many States and ultimately struck down by this Court. *Loving*.

The majority observes that these developments "were not mere superficial changes" in marriage, but rather "worked deep transformations in its structure." They did not, however, work any transformation in the core structure of marriage as the union between a man and a woman. If you had asked a person on the street how marriage was defined, no one would ever have said, "Marriage is the union of a man and a woman, where the woman is subject to coverture." The majority may be right that the "history of marriage is one of both continuity and change," but the core meaning of marriage has endured. . . . .

II

Petitioners first contend that the marriage laws of their States violate the Due Process Clause. The Solicitor General of the United States, appearing in support of petitioners, expressly disowned that position before this Court. The majority nevertheless resolves these cases for petitioners based almost entirely on the Due Process Clause.

The majority purports to identify four "principles and traditions" in this Court's due process precedents that support a fundamental right for same-sex couples to marry. In reality, however, the majority's approach has no basis in principle or tradition, except for the unprincipled tradition of judicial policy-making that characterized discredited decisions such as *Lochner v. New York.* Stripped of its shiny rhetorical gloss, the majority's argument is that the Due Process Clause gives same-sex couples a fundamental right to marry because it will be good for them and for society. If I were a legislator, I would certainly consider that view as a matter of social policy. But as a judge, I find the majority's position indefensible as a matter of constitutional law.

A

Petitioners' "fundamental right" claim falls into the most sensitive category of constitutional adjudication. Petitioners do not contend that their States' marriage laws violate an *enumerated* constitutional right, such as the freedom of speech protected by the First Amendment. There is, after all, no "Companionship and Understanding" or "Nobility and Dignity" Clause in the Constitution. They argue instead that the laws violate a right *implied* by the Fourteenth Amendment's requirement that "liberty" may not be deprived without "due process of law."

This Court has interpreted the Due Process Clause to include a "substantive" component that protects certain liberty interests against state deprivation "no matter what process is provided." *Reno v. Flores,* 507 U.S. 292 (1993). The theory is that some liberties are "so rooted in the traditions and conscience of our people as to be ranked as fundamental," and therefore cannot be deprived without compelling justification. *Snyder v. Massachusetts,* 291 U.S. 97 (1934).

Allowing unelected federal judges to select which unenumerated rights rank as "fundamental"—and to strike down state laws on the basis of that determination—raises obvious concerns about the judicial role. Our precedents have accordingly insisted that judges "exercise the utmost care" in identifying implied fundamental rights, "lest the liberty protected by the Due Process Clause be subtly transformed into the policy preferences of the Members of this Court." *Washington v. Glucksberg*; see Kennedy, Unenumerated Rights and the Dictates of Judicial Restraint 13 (1986) (Address at Stanford) ("One can conclude that certain essential, or fundamental, rights should exist in any just society. It does not follow that each of those essential rights is one that we as judges can enforce under the written Constitution. The Due Process Clause is not a guarantee of every right that should inhere in an ideal system.").

The need for restraint in administering the strong medicine of substantive due process is a lesson this Court has learned the hard way. The Court first applied substantive due process to strike down a statute in *Dred Scott v. Sandford*. There the Court invalidated the Missouri Compromise on the ground that legislation restricting the institution of slavery violated the implied rights of slaveholders. The Court relied on its own conception of liberty and property in doing so. It asserted that "an act of Congress which deprives a citizen of the United States of his liberty or property, merely because he came himself or brought his property into a particular Territory of the United States . . . could hardly be dignified with the name of due process of law." In a dissent that has outlasted the majority opinion, Justice Curtis explained that when the "fixed rules which govern the interpretation of laws [are] abandoned, and the theoretical opinions of individuals are allowed to control" the Constitution's meaning, "we have no longer a Constitution; we are under the government of individual men, who for the time being have power to declare what the Constitution is, according to their own views of what it ought to mean."

Dred Scott's holding was overruled on the battlefields of the Civil War and by constitutional amendment after Appomattox, but its approach to the Due Process Clause reappeared. In a series of early 20th-century cases, most prominently *Lochner v. New York,* this Court invalidated state statutes that presented "meddlesome interferences with the rights of the individual," and "undue interference with liberty of person and freedom of contract." In *Lochner* itself, the Court struck down a New York law setting maximum hours for bakery employees, because there was "in our judgment, no reasonable foundation for holding this to be necessary or appropriate as a health law."

The dissenting Justices in *Lochner* explained that the New York law could be viewed as a reasonable response to legislative concern about the health of bakery employees, an issue on which there was at least "room for debate and for an honest difference of opinion." *Id.,* at 72 (opinion of Harlan, J.). The majority's contrary conclusion required adopting as constitutional law "an economic theory which a large part of the country does not entertain." *Id.,* at 75 (opinion of Holmes, J.). As Justice Holmes memorably put it, "The Fourteenth Amendment does not enact Mr. Herbert Spencer's Social Statics," a leading work on the philosophy of Social Darwinism. The Constitution "is not intended to embody a particular economic theory. . . . It is made for people of fundamentally differing views, and the accident of our finding certain opinions natural and familiar or novel and even shocking ought not to conclude our judgment upon the question whether statutes embodying them conflict with the Constitution."

In the decades after *Lochner,* the Court struck down nearly 200 laws as violations of individual liberty, often over strong dissents contending that "[t]he criterion of constitutionality is not whether we believe the law to be for the public good." *Adkins v. Children's Hospital of D. C.,* 261 U.S. 525, 570 (1923) (opinion of Holmes, J.). By empowering judges to elevate their own policy judgments to the status of constitutionally protected "liberty," the *Lochner* line of cases left "no alternative to regarding the court as a . . . legislative chamber." L. Hand, The Bill of Rights 42 (1958).

Eventually, the Court recognized its error and vowed not to repeat it. "The doctrine that . . . due process authorizes courts to hold laws unconstitutional when they believe the legislature has acted unwisely," we later explained, "has long since been discarded. We have returned to the original constitutional proposition that courts do not substitute their social and economic beliefs for the judgment of legislative bodies, who are elected to pass laws." *Ferguson v. Skrupa,* 372 U.S. 726 (1963); see *Day–Brite Lighting, Inc. v. Missouri,* 342 U.S. 421 (1952) ("we do not sit as a super-legislature to weigh the wisdom of legislation"). Thus, it has become an accepted rule that the Court will not hold laws unconstitutional simply because we find them "unwise, improvident, or out of harmony with a particular school of thought." *Williamson v. Lee Optical of Okla., Inc.,* 348 U.S. 483 (1955).

Rejecting *Lochner* does not require disavowing the doctrine of implied fundamental rights, and this Court has not done so. But to avoid repeating *Lochner*'s error of converting personal preferences into constitutional mandates, our modern substantive due process cases have stressed the need for "judicial self-restraint." Our precedents have required that implied fundamental rights be "objectively, deeply rooted in this Nation's history and tradition," and "implicit in the concept of ordered liberty, such that neither liberty nor justice would exist if they were sacrificed." *Glucksberg.*

Although the Court articulated the importance of history and tradition to the fundamental rights inquiry most precisely in *Glucksberg,* many other cases both before and after have adopted the same approach. See, *e.g., District Attorney's Office for Third Judicial Dist. v. Osborne,* 557 U.S. 52 (2009); *Flores*; *United States v. Salerno,* 481 U.S. 739 (1987); *Moore v. East Cleveland,* 431 U.S. 494 (1977) (plurality opinion); see also *id.,* at 544 (White, J., dissenting) ("The Judiciary, including this Court, is the most vulnerable and comes nearest to illegitimacy when it deals with judge-made constitutional law having little or no cognizable roots in the language or even the design of the Constitution."); *Troxel v. Granville,* 530 U.S. 57 (2000) (KENNEDY, J., dissenting) (consulting " '[o]ur Nation's history, legal traditions, and practices' " and concluding that "[w]e owe it to the Nation's domestic relations legal structure . . . to proceed with caution" (quoting *Glucksberg*)).

Proper reliance on history and tradition of course requires looking beyond the individual law being challenged, so that every restriction on liberty does not supply its own constitutional justification. The Court is right about that. But given the few "guideposts for responsible decisionmaking in this unchartered area," "an approach grounded in history imposes limits on the judiciary that are more meaningful than any based on [an] abstract formula." *Moore* (plurality opinion). Expanding a right suddenly and dramatically is likely to require tearing it up from its roots. Even a sincere profession of "discipline" in identifying fundamental rights, does not provide a meaningful constraint on a judge, for "what he is really likely to be 'discovering,' whether or not he is fully aware of it, are his own values," J. Ely, Democracy and Distrust 44 (1980). The only way to ensure restraint in this delicate enterprise is "continual insistence upon respect for the teachings of history, solid recognition of the basic values that underlie our society, and wise appreciation of the great roles [of] the doctrines of federalism and separation of powers." *Griswold v. Connecticut* (Harlan, J., concurring in judgment).

B

The majority acknowledges none of this doctrinal background, and it is easy to see why: Its aggressive application of substantive due process breaks sharply with decades of precedent and returns the Court to the unprincipled approach of *Lochner.*

1

The majority's driving themes are that marriage is desirable and petitioners desire it. The opinion describes the "transcendent importance" of marriage and repeatedly insists that petitioners do not seek to "demean," "devalue," "denigrate," or "disrespect" the institution. Nobody disputes those points. Indeed, the compelling personal accounts of petitioners and others like them are likely a primary reason why many Americans have changed their minds about whether same-sex couples should be allowed to marry. As a matter of constitutional law, however, the sincerity of petitioners' wishes is not relevant.

When the majority turns to the law, it relies primarily on precedents discussing the fundamental "right to marry." *Turner v. Safley*; *Zablocki*; see *Loving*. These cases do not hold, of course, that anyone who wants to get married has a constitutional right to do so. They instead require a State to justify barriers to marriage as that institution has always been understood. In *Loving,* the Court held that racial restrictions on the right to marry lacked a compelling justification. In *Zablocki,* restrictions based on child support debts did not suffice. In *Turner,* restrictions based on status as a prisoner were deemed impermissible.

None of the laws at issue in those cases purported to change the core definition of marriage as the union of a man and a woman. The laws challenged in *Zablocki* and *Turner* did not define marriage as "the union of a man and a woman, *where neither party owes child support or is in prison*." Nor did the interracial marriage ban at issue in *Loving* define marriage as "the union of a man and a woman *of the same race*." Removing racial barriers to marriage therefore did not change what a marriage was any more than integrating schools changed what a school was. As the majority admits, the institution of "marriage" discussed in every one of these cases "presumed a relationship involving opposite-sex partners."

In short, the "right to marry" cases stand for the important but limited proposition that particular restrictions on access to marriage *as traditionally defined* violate due process. These precedents say nothing at all about a right to make a State change its definition of marriage, which is the right petitioners actually seek here. Neither petitioners nor the majority cites a single case or other legal source providing any basis for such a constitutional right. None exists, and that is enough to foreclose their claim.

2

The majority suggests that "there are other, more instructive precedents" informing the right to marry. Although not entirely clear, this reference seems to correspond to a line of cases discussing an implied fundamental "right of privacy." *Griswold*. In the first of those cases, the Court invalidated a criminal law that banned the use of contraceptives. *Id.*, at 485–486. The Court stressed the invasive nature of the ban, which threatened the intrusion of "the police to search the sacred precincts of marital bedrooms." In the Court's view, such laws infringed the right to privacy in its most basic sense: the "right to be let alone." *Eisenstadt v. Baird*; see *Olmstead v. United States,* 277 U.S. 438, 478 (1928) (Brandeis, J., dissenting).

The Court also invoked the right to privacy in *Lawrence v. Texas,* 539 U.S. 558 (2003), which struck down a Texas statute criminalizing homosexual sodomy. *Lawrence* relied on the position that criminal sodomy laws, like bans on contraceptives, invaded privacy by inviting "unwarranted government intrusions" that "touc[h] upon the most private human conduct, sexual behavior . . . in the most private of places, the home."

Neither *Lawrence* nor any other precedent in the privacy line of cases supports the right that petitioners assert here. Unlike criminal laws banning contraceptives and sodomy, the marriage laws at issue here involve no government intrusion. They create no crime and impose no punishment. Same-sex couples remain free to live together, to engage in intimate conduct, and to raise their families as they see fit. No one is "condemned to live in loneliness" by the laws challenged in these cases — no one. At the same time, the laws in no way interfere with the "right to be let alone."

The majority also relies on Justice Harlan's influential dissenting opinion in *Poe v. Ullman,* 367 U.S. 497, (1961). As the majority recounts, that opinion states that "[d]ue process has not been reduced to any formula." But far from conferring the broad interpretive discretion that the majority discerns, Justice Harlan's opinion makes clear that courts implying fundamental rights are not "free to roam where unguided speculation might take them." They must instead have "regard to what history teaches" and exercise not only "judgment" but "restraint." Of particular relevance, Justice Harlan explained that "laws regarding marriage which provide both when the sexual powers may be used and the legal and societal context in which children are born and brought up . . . form a pattern so deeply pressed into the substance of our social life that any Constitutional doctrine in this area must build upon that basis."

In sum, the privacy cases provide no support for the majority's position, because petitioners do not seek privacy. Quite the opposite, they seek public recognition of their relationships, along with corresponding government benefits. Our cases have consistently refused to allow litigants to convert the shield provided by constitutional liberties into a sword to demand positive entitlements from the State. See *DeShaney v. Winnebago County Dept. of Social Servs.,* 489 U.S. 189 (1989); *San Antonio Independent School Dist. v. Rodriguez,* 411 U.S. 1 (1973). Thus, although the right to privacy recognized by our precedents certainly plays a role in protecting the intimate conduct of same-sex couples, it provides no affirmative right to redefine marriage and no basis for striking down the laws at issue here.

3

Perhaps recognizing how little support it can derive from precedent, the majority goes out of its way to jettison the "careful" approach to implied fundamental rights taken by this Court in *Glucksberg*. It is revealing that the majority's position requires it to effectively overrule *Glucksberg,* the leading modern case setting the bounds of substantive due process. At least this part of the majority opinion has the virtue of candor. Nobody could rightly accuse the majority of taking a careful approach.

Ultimately, only one precedent offers any support for the majority's methodology: *Lochner v. New York*. The majority opens its opinion by announcing petitioners' right to "define and express their identity." The majority later explains that "the right to personal choice regarding marriage is inherent in the concept of individual autonomy." This freewheeling notion of individual autonomy echoes nothing so much as "the general right of an individual to be *free in his person and in his power to contract in relation to his own labor.*" *Lochner* (emphasis added).

To be fair, the majority does not suggest that its individual autonomy right is entirely unconstrained. The constraints it sets are precisely those that accord with its own "reasoned judgment," informed by its "new insight" into the "nature of injustice," which was invisible to all who came before but has become clear "as we learn [the] meaning" of liberty. The truth is that today's decision rests on nothing more than the majority's own conviction that same-sex couples should be allowed to marry because they want to, and that "it would disparage their choices and diminish their personhood to deny them this right." Whatever force that belief may have as a matter of moral philosophy, it has no more basis in the Constitution than did the naked policy preferences adopted in *Lochner*. See 198 U.S., at 61 ("We do not believe in the soundness of the views which uphold this law," which "is an illegal interference with the rights of individuals . . . to make contracts regarding labor upon such terms as they may think best").

The majority recognizes that today's cases do not mark "the first time the Court has been asked to adopt a cautious approach to recognizing and protecting fundamental rights." On that much, we agree. The Court was "asked"—and it agreed—to "adopt a cautious approach" to implying fundamental rights after the debacle of the *Lochner* era. Today, the majority casts caution aside and revives the grave errors of that period.

One immediate question invited by the majority's position is whether States may retain the definition of marriage as a union of two people. Although the majority randomly inserts the adjective "two" in various places, it offers no reason at all why the two-person element of the core definition of marriage may be preserved while the man-woman element may not. Indeed, from the standpoint of history and tradition, a leap from opposite-sex marriage to same-sex marriage is much greater than one from a two-person union to plural unions, which have deep roots in some cultures around the world. If the majority is willing to take the big leap, it is hard to see how it can say no to the shorter one.

It is striking how much of the majority's reasoning would apply with equal force to the claim of a fundamental right to plural marriage. If "[t]here is dignity in the bond between two men or two women who seek to marry and in their autonomy to make such profound choices," why would there be any less dignity in the bond between three people who, in exercising their autonomy, seek to make the profound choice to marry? If a same-sex couple has the constitutional right to marry because their children would otherwise "suffer the stigma of knowing their families are somehow lesser," why wouldn't the same reasoning apply to a family of three or more persons raising children? If not having the opportunity to marry "serves to disrespect and subordinate" gay and lesbian couples, why wouldn't the same "imposition of this disability," serve to disrespect and subordinate people who find fulfillment in polyamorous relationships? See Bennett, Polyamory: The Next Sexual Revolution? Newsweek, July 28, 2009 (estimating 500,000 polyamorous families in the United States); Li, Married Lesbian "Throuple" Expecting First Child, N.Y. Post, Apr. 23, 2014; Otter, Three May Not Be a Crowd: The Case for a Constitutional Right to Plural Marriage, 64 Emory L.J.1977 (2015).

[handwritten margin note: But Immutable]

I do not mean to equate marriage between same-sex couples with plural marriages in all respects. There may well be relevant differences that compel different legal analysis. But if there are, petitioners have not pointed to any. When asked about a plural marital union at oral argument, petitioners asserted that a State "doesn't have such an institution." But that is exactly the point: the States at issue here do not have an institution of same-sex marriage, either.

4

Near the end of its opinion, the majority offers perhaps the clearest insight into its decision. Expanding marriage to include same-sex couples, the majority insists, would "pose no risk of harm to themselves or third parties." This argument again echoes *Lochner,* which relied on its assessment that "we think that a law like the one before us involves neither the safety, the morals nor the welfare of the public, and that the interest of the public is not in the slightest degree affected by such an act."

Then and now, this assertion of the "harm principle" sounds more in philosophy than law. The elevation of the fullest individual self-realization over the constraints that society has expressed in law may or may not be attractive moral philosophy. But a Justice's commission does not confer any special moral, philosophical, or social insight sufficient to justify imposing those perceptions on fellow citizens under the pretense of "due process." There is indeed a process due the people on issues of this sort—the democratic process. Respecting that understanding requires the Court to be guided by law, not any particular school of social thought. As Judge Henry Friendly once put it, echoing Justice Holmes's dissent in *Lochner,* the Fourteenth Amendment does not enact John Stuart Mill's On Liberty any more than it enacts Herbert Spencer's Social Statics. And it certainly does not enact any one concept of marriage.

The majority's understanding of due process lays out a tantalizing vision of the future for Members of this Court: If an unvarying social institution enduring over all of recorded history cannot inhibit judicial policymaking, what can? But this approach is dangerous for the rule of law. The purpose of insisting that implied fundamental rights have roots in the history and tradition of our people is to ensure that when unelected judges strike down democratically enacted laws, they do so based on something more than their own beliefs. The Court today not only overlooks our country's entire history and tradition but actively repudiates it, preferring to live only in the heady days of the here and now. I agree with the majority that the "nature of injustice is that we may not always see it in our own times." As petitioners put it, "times can blind." But to blind yourself to history is both prideful and unwise. "The past is never dead. It's not even past." W. Faulkner, Requiem for a Nun 92 (1951).

III

In addition to their due process argument, petitioners contend that the Equal Protection Clause requires their States to license and recognize same-sex marriages. The majority does not seriously engage with this claim. Its discussion is, quite frankly, difficult to follow. The central point seems to be that there is a "synergy between" the Equal Protection Clause and the Due Process Clause, and that some precedents relying on one Clause have also relied on the other. Absent from this portion of the opinion, however, is anything resembling our usual framework for deciding equal protection cases. It is casebook doctrine that the "modern Supreme Court's treatment of equal protection claims has used a means-ends methodology in which judges ask whether the classification the government is using is sufficiently related to the goals it is pursuing." The majority's approach today is different:

"Rights implicit in liberty and rights secured by equal protection may rest on different precepts and are not always co-extensive, yet in some instances each may be instructive as to the meaning and reach of the other. In any particular case one Clause may be thought to capture the essence of the right in a more accurate and comprehensive way, even as the two Clauses may converge in the identification and definition of the right."

The majority goes on to assert in conclusory fashion that the Equal Protection Clause provides an alternative basis for its holding. Yet the majority fails to provide even a single sentence explaining how the Equal Protection Clause supplies independent weight for its position, nor does it attempt to justify its gratuitous violation of the canon against unnecessarily resolving constitutional questions. In any event, the marriage laws at issue here do not violate the Equal Protection Clause, because distinguishing between opposite-sex and same-sex couples is rationally related to the States' "legitimate state interest" in "preserving the traditional institution of marriage."

It is important to note with precision which laws petitioners have challenged. Although they discuss some of the ancillary legal benefits that accompany marriage, such as hospital visitation rights and recognition of spousal status on official documents, petitioners' lawsuits target the laws defining marriage generally rather than those allocating benefits specifically. The equal protection analysis might be different, in my view, if we were confronted with a more focused challenge to the denial of certain tangible benefits. Of course, those more selective claims will not arise now that the Court has taken the drastic step of requiring every State to license and recognize marriages between same-sex couples.

IV

The legitimacy of this Court ultimately rests "upon the respect accorded to its judgments." That respect flows from the perception—and reality—that we exercise humility and restraint in deciding cases according to the Constitution and law. The role of the Court envisioned by the majority today, however, is anything but humble or restrained. Over and over, the majority exalts the role of the judiciary in delivering social change. In the majority's telling, it is the courts, not the people, who are responsible for making "new dimensions of freedom . . . apparent to new generations," for providing "formal discourse" on social issues, and for ensuring "neutral discussions, without scornful or disparaging commentary."

Nowhere is the majority's extravagant conception of judicial supremacy more evident than in its description—and dismissal—of the public debate regarding same-sex marriage. Yes, the majority concedes, on one side are thousands of years of human history in every society known to have populated the planet. But on the other side, there has been "extensive litigation," "many thoughtful District Court decisions," "countless studies, papers, books, and other popular and scholarly writings," and "more than 100" *amicus* briefs in these cases alone. What would be the point of allowing the democratic process to go on? It is high time for the Court to decide the meaning of marriage, based on five lawyers' "better informed understanding" of "a liberty that remains urgent in our own era." The answer is surely there in one of those *amicus* briefs or studies.

Those who founded our country would not recognize the majority's conception of the judicial role. They after all risked their lives and fortunes for the precious right to govern themselves. They would never have imagined yielding that right on a question of social policy to unaccountable and unelected judges. And they certainly would not have been satisfied by a system empowering judges to override policy judgments so long as they do so after "a quite extensive discussion." In our democracy, debate about the content of the law is not an exhaustion requirement to be checked off before courts can impose their will. "Surely the Constitution does not put either the legislative branch or the executive branch in the position of a television quiz show contestant so that when a given period of time has elapsed and a problem remains unresolved by them, the federal judiciary may press a buzzer and take its turn at fashioning a solution." Rehnquist, The Notion of a Living Constitution, 54 Texas L.Rev. 693, 700 (1976). As a plurality of this Court explained just last year, "It is demeaning to the democratic process to presume that voters are not capable of deciding an issue of this sensitivity on decent and rational grounds." *Schuette v. BAMN.*

The Court's accumulation of power does not occur in a vacuum. It comes at the expense of the people. And they know it. Here and abroad, people are in the midst of a serious and thoughtful public debate on the issue of same-sex marriage. They see voters carefully considering same-sex marriage, casting ballots in favor or opposed, and sometimes changing their minds. They see political leaders similarly reexamining their positions, and either reversing course or explaining adherence to old convictions confirmed anew. They see governments and businesses modifying policies and practices with respect to same-sex couples, and participating actively in the civic discourse. They see countries overseas democratically accepting profound social change, or declining to do so. This deliberative process is making people take seriously questions that they may not have even regarded as questions before.

When decisions are reached through democratic means, some people will inevitably be disappointed with the results. But those whose views do not prevail at least know that they have had their say, and accordingly are — in the tradition of our political culture — reconciled to the result of a fair and honest debate. In addition, they can gear up to raise the issue later, hoping to persuade enough on the winning side to think again. "That is exactly how our system of government is supposed to work."

But today the Court puts a stop to all that. By deciding this question under the Constitution, the Court removes it from the realm of democratic decision. There will be consequences to shutting down the political process on an issue of such profound public significance. Closing debate tends to close minds. People denied a voice are less likely to accept the ruling of a court on an issue that does not seem to be the sort of thing courts usually decide. As a thoughtful commentator observed about another issue, "The political process was moving . . . , not swiftly enough for advocates of quick, complete change, but majoritarian institutions were listening and acting. Heavy-handed judicial intervention was difficult to justify and appears to have provoked, not resolved, conflict." Ginsburg, Some Thoughts on Autonomy and Equality in Relation to *Roe* v. *Wade,* 63 N.C.L.Rev. 375, 385–386 (1985) (footnote omitted). Indeed, however heartened the proponents of same-sex marriage might be on this day, it is worth acknowledging what they have lost, and lost forever: the opportunity to win the true acceptance that comes from persuading their fellow citizens of the justice of their cause. And they lose this just when the winds of change were freshening at their backs.

Federal courts are blunt instruments when it comes to creating rights. They have constitutional power only to resolve concrete cases or controversies; they do not have the flexibility of legislatures to address concerns of parties not before the court or to anticipate problems that may arise from the exercise of a new right. Today's decision, for example, creates serious questions about religious liberty. Many good and decent people oppose same-sex marriage as a tenet of faith, and their freedom to exercise religion is — unlike the right imagined by the majority — actually spelled out in the Constitution.

Respect for sincere religious conviction has led voters and legislators in every State that has adopted same-sex marriage democratically to include accommodations for religious practice. The majority's decision imposing same-sex marriage cannot, of course, create any such accommodations. The majority graciously suggests that religious believers may continue to "advocate" and "teach" their views of marriage. The First Amendment guarantees, however, the freedom to "*exercise* " religion. Ominously, that is not a word the majority uses.

Hard questions arise when people of faith exercise religion in ways that may be seen to conflict with the new right to same-sex marriage — when, for example, a religious college provides married student housing only to opposite-sex married couples, or a religious adoption agency declines to place children with same-sex married couples. Indeed, the Solicitor General candidly acknowledged that the tax exemptions of some religious institutions would be in question if they opposed same-sex marriage. There is little doubt that these and similar questions will soon be before this Court. Unfortunately, people of faith can take no comfort in the treatment they receive from the majority today.

Perhaps the most discouraging aspect of today's decision is the extent to which the majority feels compelled to sully those on the other side of the debate. The majority offers a cursory assurance that it does not intend to disparage people who, as a matter of conscience, cannot accept same-sex marriage. That disclaimer is hard to square with the very next sentence, in which the majority explains that "the necessary consequence" of laws codifying the traditional definition of marriage is to "demea[n] or stigmatiz[e]" same-sex couples. The majority reiterates such characterizations over and over. By the majority's account, Americans who did nothing more than follow the understanding of marriage that has existed for our entire history — in particular, the tens of millions of people who voted to reaffirm their States' enduring definition of marriage — have acted to "lock . . . out," "disparage," "disrespect and subordinate," and inflict "[d]ignitary wounds" upon their gay and lesbian neighbors. These apparent assaults on the character of fairminded people will have an effect, in society and in court. Moreover, they are entirely gratuitous. It is one thing for the majority to conclude that the Constitution protects a right to same-sex marriage; it is something else to portray everyone who does not share the majority's "better informed understanding" as bigoted.

In the face of all this, a much different view of the Court's role is possible. That view is more modest and restrained. It is more skeptical that the legal abilities of judges also reflect insight into moral and philosophical issues. It is more sensitive to the fact that judges are unelected and unaccountable, and that the legitimacy of their power depends on confining it to the exercise of legal judgment. It is more attuned to the lessons of history, and what it has meant for the country and Court when Justices have exceeded their proper bounds. And it is less pretentious than to suppose that while people around the world have viewed an institution in a particular way for thousands of years, the present generation and the present Court are the ones chosen to burst the bonds of that history and tradition.

* * *

If you are among the many Americans—of whatever sexual orientation—who favor expanding same-sex marriage, by all means celebrate today's decision. Celebrate the achievement of a desired goal. Celebrate the opportunity for a new expression of commitment to a partner. Celebrate the availability of new benefits. But do not celebrate the Constitution. It had nothing to do with it.

I respectfully dissent.

Justice SCALIA, with whom Justice THOMAS joins, dissenting.

I join THE CHIEF JUSTICE's opinion in full. I write separately to call attention to this Court's threat to American democracy.

The substance of today's decree is not of immense personal importance to me. The law can recognize as marriage whatever sexual attachments and living arrangements it wishes, and can accord them favorable civil consequences, from tax treatment to rights of inheritance. Those civil consequences—and the public approval that conferring the name of marriage evidences—can perhaps have adverse social effects, but no more adverse than the effects of many other controversial laws. So it is not of special importance to me what the law says about marriage. It is of overwhelming importance, however, who it is that rules me. Today's decree says that my Ruler, and the Ruler of 320 million Americans coast-to-coast, is a majority of the nine lawyers on the Supreme Court. The opinion in these cases is the furthest extension in fact—and the furthest extension one can even imagine—of the Court's claimed power to create "liberties" that the Constitution and its Amendments neglect to mention. This practice of constitutional revision by an unelected committee of nine, always accompanied (as it is today) by extravagant praise of liberty, robs the People of the most important liberty they asserted in the Declaration of Independence and won in the Revolution of 1776: the freedom to govern themselves.

I

Until the courts put a stop to it, public debate over same-sex marriage displayed American democracy at its best. Individuals on both sides of the issue passionately, but respectfully, attempted to persuade their fellow citizens to accept their views. Americans considered the arguments and put the question to a vote. The electorates of 11 States, either directly or through their representatives, chose to expand the traditional definition of marriage. Many more decided not to. Win or lose, advocates for both sides continued pressing their cases, secure in the knowledge that an electoral loss can be negated by a later electoral win. That is exactly how our system of government is supposed to work.

The Constitution places some constraints on self-rule — constraints adopted *by the People themselves* when they ratified the Constitution and its Amendments. Forbidden are laws "impairing the Obligation of Contracts," denying "Full Faith and Credit" to the "public Acts" of other States, prohibiting the free exercise of religion, abridging the freedom of speech, infringing the right to keep and bear arms, authorizing unreasonable searches and seizures, and so forth. Aside from these limitations, those powers "reserved to the States respectively, or to the people" can be exercised as the States or the People desire. These cases ask us to decide whether the Fourteenth Amendment contains a limitation that requires the States to license and recognize marriages between two people of the same sex. Does it remove *that* issue from the political process?

Of course not. It would be surprising to find a prescription regarding marriage in the Federal Constitution since, as the author of today's opinion reminded us only two years ago (in an opinion joined by the same Justices who join him today): "[R]egulation of domestic relations is an area that has long been regarded as a virtually exclusive province of the States." [and] "[T]he Federal Government, through our history, has deferred to state-law policy decisions with respect to domestic relations." [*Windsor*]

But we need not speculate. When the Fourteenth Amendment was ratified in 1868, every State limited marriage to one man and one woman, and no one doubted the constitutionality of doing so. That resolves these cases. When it comes to determining the meaning of a vague constitutional provision — such as "due process of law" or "equal protection of the laws" — it is unquestionable that the People who ratified that provision did not understand it to prohibit a practice that remained both universal and uncontroversial in the years after ratification. We have no basis for striking down a practice that is not expressly prohibited by the Fourteenth Amendment's text, and that bears the endorsement of a long tradition of open, widespread, and unchallenged use dating back to the Amendment's ratification. Since there is no doubt whatever that the People never decided to prohibit the limitation of marriage to opposite-sex couples, the public debate over same-sex marriage must be allowed to continue.

But the Court ends this debate, in an opinion lacking even a thin veneer of law. Buried beneath the mummeries and straining-to-be-memorable passages of the opinion is a candid and startling assertion: No matter *what* it was the People ratified, the Fourteenth Amendment protects those rights that the Judiciary, in its "reasoned judgment," thinks the Fourteenth Amendment ought to protect. That is so because "[t]he generations that wrote and ratified the Bill of Rights and the Fourteenth Amendment did not presume to know the extent of freedom in all of its dimensions. . . ." One would think that sentence would continue: ". . . and therefore they provided for a means by which the People could amend the Constitution," or perhaps ". . . and therefore they left the creation of additional liberties, such as the freedom to marry someone of the same sex, to the People, through the never-ending process of legislation." But no. What logically follows, in the majority's judge-empowering estimation, is: "and so they entrusted to future generations a charter protecting the right of all persons to enjoy liberty as we learn its meaning." The "we," needless to say, is the nine of us. "History and tradition guide and discipline [our] inquiry but do not set its outer boundaries." Thus, rather than focusing on *the People's* understanding of "liberty" — at the time of ratification or even today — the majority focuses on four "principles and traditions" that, *in the majority's view,* prohibit States from defining marriage as an institution consisting of one man and one woman.

This is a naked judicial claim to legislative — indeed, *super*-legislative — power; a claim fundamentally at odds with our system of government. Except as limited by a constitutional prohibition agreed to by the People, the States are free to adopt whatever laws they like, even those that offend the esteemed Justices' "reasoned judgment." A system of government that makes the People subordinate to a committee of nine unelected lawyers does not deserve to be called a democracy.

Judges are selected precisely for their skill as lawyers; whether they reflect the policy views of a particular constituency is not (or should not be) relevant. Not surprisingly then, the Federal Judiciary is hardly a cross-section of America. Take, for example, this Court, which consists of only nine men and women, all of them successful lawyers who studied at Harvard or Yale Law School. Four of the nine are natives of New York City. Eight of them grew up in east- and west-coast States. Only one hails from the vast expanse in-between. Not a single Southwesterner or even, to tell the truth, a genuine Westerner (California does not count). Not a single evangelical Christian (a group that comprises about one quarter of Americans), or even a Protestant of any denomination. The strikingly unrepresentative character of the body voting on today's social upheaval would be irrelevant if they were functioning as *judges,* answering the legal question whether the American people had ever ratified a constitutional provision that was understood to proscribe the traditional definition of marriage. But of course the Justices in today's majority are not voting on that basis; *they say they are not.* And to allow the policy question of same-sex marriage to be considered and resolved by a select, patrician, highly unrepresentative panel of nine is to violate a principle even more fundamental than no taxation without representation: no social transformation without representation.

II

But what really astounds is the hubris reflected in today's judicial Putsch. The five Justices who compose today's majority are entirely comfortable concluding that every State violated the Constitution for all of the 135 years between the

Fourteenth Amendment's ratification and Massachusetts' permitting of same-sex marriages in 2003. They have discovered in the Fourteenth Amendment a "fundamental right" overlooked by every person alive at the time of ratification, and almost everyone else in the time since. They see what lesser legal minds — minds like Thomas Cooley, John Marshall Harlan, Oliver Wendell Holmes, Jr., Learned Hand, Louis Brandeis, William Howard Taft, Benjamin Cardozo, Hugo Black, Felix Frankfurter, Robert Jackson, and Henry Friendly — could not. They are certain that the People ratified the Fourteenth Amendment to bestow on them the power to remove questions from the democratic process when that is called for by their "reasoned judgment." These Justices *know* that limiting marriage to one man and one woman is contrary to reason; they *know* that an institution as old as government itself, and accepted by every nation in history until 15 years ago, cannot possibly be supported by anything other than ignorance or bigotry. And they are willing to say that any citizen who does not agree with that, who adheres to what was, until 15 years ago, the unanimous judgment of all generations and all societies, stands against the Constitution.

The opinion is couched in a style that is as pretentious as its content is egotistic. It is one thing for separate concurring or dissenting opinions to contain extravagances, even silly extravagances, of thought and expression; it is something else for the official opinion of the Court to do so.

If, even as the price to be paid for a fifth vote, I ever joined an opinion for the Court that began: "The Constitution promises liberty to all within its reach, a liberty that includes certain specific rights that allow persons, within a lawful realm, to define and express their identity," I would hide my head in a bag. The Supreme Court of the United States has descended from the disciplined legal reasoning of John Marshall and Joseph Story to the mystical aphorisms of the fortune cookie. [relocated footnote — eds.]

Of course the opinion's showy profundities are often profoundly incoherent. "The nature of marriage is that, through its enduring bond, two persons together can find other freedoms, such as expression, intimacy, and spirituality." (Really? Who ever thought that intimacy and spirituality [whatever that means] were freedoms? And if intimacy is, one would think Freedom of Intimacy is abridged rather than expanded by marriage. Ask the nearest hippie. Expression, sure enough, *is* a freedom, but anyone in a long-lasting marriage will attest that that happy state constricts, rather than expands, what one can prudently say.) Rights, we are told, can "rise . . . from a better informed understanding of how constitutional imperatives define a liberty that remains urgent in our own era." (Huh? How can a better informed understanding of how constitutional imperatives [whatever that means] define [whatever that means] an urgent liberty [never mind], give birth to a right?) And we are told that, "[i]n any particular case," either the Equal Protection or Due Process Clause "may be thought to capture the essence of [a] right in a more accurate and comprehensive way," than the other, "even as the two Clauses may converge in the identification and definition of the right." (What say? What possible "essence" does substantive due process "capture" in an "accurate and comprehensive way"? It stands for nothing whatever, except those freedoms and entitlements that this Court *really* likes. And the Equal Protection Clause, as employed today, identifies nothing except a difference in treatment that this Court *really* dislikes. Hardly a distillation of essence. If the opinion is correct that the two clauses "converge in the identification and definition of [a] right," that is only because the majority's likes and dislikes are predictably compatible.) I could go on. The world does not expect logic and precision in poetry or inspirational pop-philosophy; it demands them in the law. The stuff contained in today's opinion has to diminish this Court's reputation for clear thinking and sober analysis.

* * *

Hubris is sometimes defined as o'erweening pride; and pride, we know, goeth before a fall. The Judiciary is the "least dangerous" of the federal branches because it has "neither Force nor Will, but merely judgment; and must ultimately depend upon the aid of the executive arm" and the States, "even for the efficacy of its judgments." [The Federalist No. 78 (A.Hamilton).] With each decision of ours that takes from the People a question properly left to them—with each decision that is unabashedly based not on law, but on the "reasoned judgment" of a bare majority of this Court—we move one step closer to being reminded of our impotence.

Justice THOMAS, with whom Justice SCALIA joins, dissenting.

The Court's decision today is at odds not only with the Constitution, but with the principles upon which our Nation was built. Since well before 1787, liberty has been understood as freedom from government action, not entitlement to government benefits. The Framers created our Constitution to preserve that understanding of liberty. Yet the majority invokes our Constitution in the name of a "liberty" that the Framers would not have recognized, to the detriment of the liberty they sought to protect. Along the way, it rejects the idea—captured in our Declaration of Independence—that human dignity is innate and suggests instead that it comes from the Government. This distortion of our Constitution not only ignores the text, it inverts the relationship between the individual and the state in our Republic. I cannot agree with it.

I

. . . I have elsewhere explained the dangerous fiction of treating the Due Process Clause as a font of substantive rights. *McDonald v. Chicago* (THOMAS, J., concurring in part and concurring in judgment). It distorts the constitutional text, which guarantees only whatever "process" is "due" before a person is deprived of life, liberty, and property. Worse, it invites judges to do exactly what the majority has done here—"'roa[m] at large in the constitutional field' guided only by their personal views" as to the "'fundamental rights'" protected by that document. *Planned Parenthood of Southeastern Pa. v. Casey,* 505 U.S. 833 (1992) (Rehnquist, C. J., concurring in judgment in part and dissenting in part).

By straying from the text of the Constitution, substantive due process exalts judges at the expense of the People from whom they derive their authority. Petitioners argue that by enshrining the traditional definition of marriage in their State Constitutions through voter-approved amendments, the States have put the issue "beyond the reach of the normal democratic process." But the result petitioners seek is far less democratic. They ask nine judges on this Court to enshrine their definition of marriage in the Federal Constitution and thus put it beyond the reach of the normal democratic process for the entire Nation. . . .

II

Even if the doctrine of substantive due process were somehow defensible — it is not — petitioners still would not have a claim. To invoke the protection of the Due Process Clause at all — whether under a theory of "substantive" or "procedural" due process — a party must first identify a deprivation of "life, liberty, or property." The majority claims these state laws deprive petitioners of "liberty," but the concept of "liberty" it conjures up bears no resemblance to any plausible meaning of that word as it is used in the Due Process Clauses.

A

1

As used in the Due Process Clauses, "liberty" most likely refers to "the power of locomotion, of changing situation, or removing one's person to whatsoever place one's own inclination may direct; without imprisonment or restraint, unless by due course of law." 1 W. Blackstone, Commentaries on the Laws of England 130 (1769) (Blackstone). That definition is drawn from the historical roots of the Clauses and is consistent with our Constitution's text and structure.

. . . The Framers drew heavily upon Blackstone's formulation, adopting provisions in early State Constitutions that replicated Magna Carta's language, but were modified to refer specifically to "life, liberty, or property." State decisions interpreting these provisions between the founding and the ratification of the Fourteenth Amendment almost uniformly construed the word "liberty" to refer only to freedom from physical restraint. . . . [Given this history], it is hard to see how the "liberty" protected by the [Fifth Amendment's Due Process] Clause could be interpreted to include anything broader than freedom from physical restraint.

If the Fifth Amendment uses "liberty" in this narrow sense, then the Fourteenth Amendment likely does as well. Indeed, this Court has previously commented, "The conclusion is . . . irresistible, that when the same phrase was employed in the Fourteenth Amendment [as was used in the Fifth Amendment], it was used in the same sense and with no greater extent." [*Hurtado v. California*, 110 U.S. 516 (1884).] . . . That the Court appears to have lost its way in more recent years does not justify deviating from the original meaning of the Clauses.

2

Even assuming that the "liberty" in those Clauses encompasses something more than freedom from physical restraint, it would not include the types of rights claimed by the majority. In the American legal tradition, liberty has long been understood as individual freedom *from* governmental action, not as a right *to* a particular governmental entitlement.

[T]he founding-era idea of civil liberty as natural liberty constrained by human law necessarily involved only those freedoms that existed *outside of* government. As one later commentator observed, "[L]iberty in the eighteenth century was thought of much more in relation to 'negative liberty'; that is, freedom *from,* not freedom *to,* freedom from a number of social and political evils, including arbitrary government power." J. Reid, The Concept of Liberty in the Age of the American Revolution 56 (1988). Or as one scholar put it in 1776, "[T]he common idea of liberty is merely negative, and is only the *absence of restraint.*" R. Hey, Observations on the Nature of Civil Liberty and the Principles of Government §13, p. 8 (1776). When the colonists described laws that would infringe their liberties, they discussed laws that would prohibit individuals "from walking in the streets and highways on certain saints days, or from being abroad after a certain time in the evening, or . . . restrain [them] from working up and manufacturing materials of [their] own growth." Each of those examples involved freedoms that existed outside of government.

B

Whether we define "liberty" as locomotion or freedom from governmental action more broadly, petitioners have in no way been deprived of it.

Petitioners cannot claim, under the most plausible definition of "liberty," that they have been imprisoned or physically restrained by the States for participating in same-sex relationships. To the contrary, they have been able to cohabitate and raise their children in peace. They have been able to hold civil marriage ceremonies in States that recognize same-sex marriages and private religious ceremonies in all States. They have been able to travel freely around the country, making their homes where they please. Far from being incarcerated or physically restrained, petitioners have been left alone to order their lives as they see fit.

Nor, under the broader definition, can they claim that the States have restricted their ability to go about their daily lives as they would be able to absent governmental restrictions. Petitioners do not ask this Court to order the States to stop restricting their ability to enter same-sex relationships, to engage in intimate behavior, to make vows to their partners in public ceremonies, to engage in religious wedding ceremonies, to hold themselves out as married, or to raise children. The States have imposed no such restrictions. Nor have the States prevented petitioners from approximating a number of incidents of marriage through private legal means, such as wills, trusts, and powers of attorney.

Instead, the States have refused to grant them governmental entitlements. Petitioners claim that as a matter of "liberty," they are entitled to access privileges and benefits that exist solely *because of* the government. They want, for example, to receive the State's *imprimatur* on their marriages — on state issued marriage licenses, death certificates, or other official forms. And they want to receive various monetary benefits, including reduced inheritance taxes upon the death of a spouse, compensation if a spouse dies as a result of a work-related injury, or loss of consortium damages in tort suits. But receiving governmental recognition and benefits has nothing to do with any understanding of "liberty" that the Framers would have recognized.

To the extent that the Framers would have recognized a natural right to marriage that fell within the broader definition of liberty, it would not have included a right to governmental recognition and benefits. Instead, it would have included a right to engage in the very same activities that petitioners have been left free to engage in — making vows, holding religious ceremonies celebrating those vows, raising children, and otherwise enjoying the society of one's spouse — without governmental interference. At the founding, such conduct was understood to predate government, not to flow from it. . . . Petitioners misunderstand the institution of marriage when they say that it would "mean little" absent governmental recognition.

Petitioners' misconception of liberty carries over into their discussion of our precedents identifying a right to marry, not one of which has expanded the concept of "liberty" beyond the concept of negative liberty. Those precedents all involved absolute prohibitions on private actions associated with marriage. *Loving v. Virginia*, for example, involved a couple who was criminally prosecuted for marrying in the District of Columbia and cohabiting in Virginia. They were each sentenced to a year of imprisonment, suspended for a term of 25 years on the condition that they not reenter the Commonwealth together during that time. In a similar vein, *Zablocki v. Redhail* involved a man who was prohibited, on pain of criminal penalty, from "marry[ing] in Wisconsin or elsewhere" because of his outstanding child-support obligations. And *Turner v. Safley*, involved state inmates who were prohibited from entering marriages without the permission of the superintendent of the prison, permission that could not be granted absent compelling reasons. In *none* of those cases were individuals denied solely governmental recognition and benefits associated with marriage.

The suggestion of petitioners and their *amici* that antimiscegenation laws are akin to laws defining marriage as between one man and one woman is both offensive and inaccurate. "America's earliest laws against interracial sex and marriage were spawned by slavery." P. Pascoe, What Comes Naturally: Miscegenation Law and the Making of Race in America 19 (2009). For instance, Maryland's 1664 law prohibiting marriages between " 'freeborne English women' " and " 'Negro Sla[v]es' " was passed as part of the very act that authorized lifelong slavery in the colony. Virginia's antimiscegenation laws likewise were passed in a 1691 resolution entitled "An act for suppressing outlying Slaves." "It was not until the Civil War threw the future of slavery into doubt that lawyers, legislators, and judges began to develop the elaborate justifications that signified the emergence of miscegenation law and made restrictions on interracial marriage the foundation of post-Civil War white supremacy." Laws defining marriage as between one man and one woman do not share this sordid history. The traditional definition of marriage has prevailed in every society that has recognized marriage throughout history. It arose not out of a desire to shore up an invidious institution like slavery, but out of a desire "to increase the likelihood that children will be born and raised in stable and enduring family units by both the mothers and the fathers who brought them into this world." And it has existed in civilizations containing all manner of views on homosexuality. [relocated footnote—eds.]

In a concession to petitioners' misconception of liberty, the majority characterizes petitioners' suit as a quest to "find . . . liberty by marrying someone of the same sex and having their marriages deemed lawful on the same terms and conditions as marriages between persons of the opposite sex." But "liberty" is not lost, nor can it be found in the way petitioners seek. As a philosophical matter, liberty is only freedom from governmental action, not an entitlement to governmental benefits. And as a constitutional matter, it is likely even narrower than that, encompassing only freedom from physical restraint and imprisonment. The majority's "better informed understanding of how constitutional imperatives define . . . liberty,"—better informed, we must assume, than that of the people who ratified the Fourteenth Amendment—runs headlong into the reality that our Constitution is a "collection of 'Thou shalt nots,'" *Reid v. Covert,* 354 U.S. 1 (1957) (plurality opinion), not "Thou shalt provides."

III

The majority's inversion of the original meaning of liberty will likely cause collateral damage to other aspects of our constitutional order that protect liberty.

A

The majority apparently disregards the political process as a protection for liberty. . . . Although men, in forming a civil society, "give up all the power necessary to the ends for which they unite into society, to the majority of the community," John Locke, [Second Treatise of Civil Government], they reserve the authority to exercise natural liberty within the bounds of laws established by that society. To protect that liberty from arbitrary interference, they establish a process by which that society can adopt and enforce its laws. In our country, that process is primarily representative government at the state level, with the Federal Constitution serving as a backstop for that process. As a general matter, when the States act through their representative governments or by popular vote, the liberty of their residents is fully vindicated. This is no less true when some residents disagree with the result; indeed, it seems difficult to imagine *any* law on which all residents of a State would agree. What matters is that the process established by those who created the society has been honored.

That process has been honored here. The definition of marriage has been the subject of heated debate in the States. Legislatures have repeatedly taken up the matter on behalf of the People, and 35 States have put the question to the

People themselves. In 32 of those 35 States, the People have opted to retain the traditional definition of marriage. That petitioners disagree with the result of that process does not make it any less legitimate. Their civil liberty has been vindicated.

B

Aside from undermining the political processes that protect our liberty, the majority's decision threatens the religious liberty our Nation has long sought to protect. . . . Numerous *amici* — even some not supporting the States — have cautioned the Court that its decision here will "have unavoidable and wide-ranging implications for religious liberty." In our society, marriage is not simply a governmental institution; it is a religious institution as well. Today's decision might change the former, but it cannot change the latter. It appears all but inevitable that the two will come into conflict, particularly as individuals and churches are confronted with demands to participate in and endorse civil marriages between same-sex couples.

The majority appears unmoved by that inevitability. It makes only a weak gesture toward religious liberty in a single paragraph. And even that gesture indicates a misunderstanding of religious liberty in our Nation's tradition. Religious liberty is about more than just the protection for "religious organizations and persons . . . as they seek to teach the principles that are so fulfilling and so central to their lives and faiths." Religious liberty is about freedom of action in matters of religion generally, and the scope of that liberty is directly correlated to the civil restraints placed upon religious practice.

Although our Constitution provides some protection against such governmental restrictions on religious practices, the People have long elected to afford broader protections than this Court's constitutional precedents mandate. Had the majority allowed the definition of marriage to be left to the political process — as the Constitution requires — the People could have considered the religious liberty implications of deviating from the traditional definition as part of their deliberative process. Instead, the majority's decision short-circuits that process, with potentially ruinous consequences for religious liberty.

IV

Perhaps recognizing that these cases do not actually involve liberty as it has been understood, the majority goes to great lengths to assert that its decision will advance the "dignity" of same-sex couples. The flaw in that reasoning, of course, is that the Constitution contains no "dignity" Clause, and even if it did, the government would be incapable of bestowing dignity.

Human dignity has long been understood in this country to be innate. . . . The corollary of that principle is that human dignity cannot be taken away by the government. Slaves did not lose their dignity (any more than they lost their humanity) because the government allowed them to be enslaved. Those held in internment camps did not lose their dignity because the government confined them. And those denied governmental benefits certainly do not lose their dignity because the government denies them those benefits. The government cannot bestow dignity, and it cannot take it away. . . .

* * *

Our Constitution—like the Declaration of Independence before it—was predicated on a simple truth: One's liberty, not to mention one's dignity, was something to be shielded from—not provided by—the State. Today's decision casts that truth aside. In its haste to reach a desired result, the majority misapplies a clause focused on "due process" to afford substantive rights, disregards the most plausible understanding of the "liberty" protected by that clause, and distorts the principles on which this Nation was founded. Its decision will have inestimable consequences for our Constitution and our society. I respectfully dissent.

Justice ALITO, with whom Justice SCALIA and Justice THOMAS join, dissenting.

Until the federal courts intervened, the American people were engaged in a debate about whether their States should recognize same-sex marriage. The question in these cases, however, is not what States *should* do about same-sex marriage but whether the Constitution answers that question for them. It does not. The Constitution leaves that question to be decided by the people of each State.

I

The Constitution says nothing about a right to same-sex marriage, but the Court holds that the term "liberty" in the Due Process Clause of the Fourteenth Amendment encompasses this right. Our Nation was founded upon the principle that every person has the unalienable right to liberty, but liberty is a term of many meanings. For classical liberals, it may include economic rights now limited by government regulation. For social democrats, it may include the right to a variety of government benefits. For today's majority, it has a distinctively postmodern meaning.

To prevent five unelected Justices from imposing their personal vision of liberty upon the American people, the Court has held that "liberty" under the Due Process Clause should be understood to protect only those rights that are " 'deeply rooted in this Nation's history and tradition.' " *Washington* v. *Glucksberg*. And it is beyond dispute that the right to same-sex marriage is not among those rights. Indeed: "In this country, no State permitted same-sex marriage until the Massachusetts Supreme Judicial Court held in 2003 that limiting marriage to opposite-sex couples violated the State Constitution. Nor is the right to same-sex marriage deeply rooted in the traditions of other nations. No country allowed same-sex couples to marry until the Netherlands did so in 2000. What [those arguing in favor of a constitutional right to same sex marriage] seek, therefore, is not the protection of a deeply rooted right but the recognition of a very new right, and they seek this innovation not from a legislative body elected by the people, but from unelected judges. Faced with such a request, judges have cause for both caution and humility." *United States v. Windsor* (ALITO, J., dissenting)

For today's majority, it does not matter that the right to same-sex marriage lacks deep roots or even that it is contrary to long-established tradition. The Justices in the majority claim the authority to confer constitutional protection upon that right simply because they believe that it is fundamental.

II

Attempting to circumvent the problem presented by the newness of the right found in these cases, the majority claims that the issue is the right to equal treatment. Noting that marriage is a fundamental right, the majority argues that a State has no valid reason for denying that right to same-sex couples. This reasoning is dependent upon a particular understanding of the purpose of civil marriage. Although the Court expresses the point in loftier terms, its argument is that the fundamental purpose of marriage is to promote the well-being of those who choose to marry. Marriage provides emotional fulfillment and the promise of support in times of need. And by benefiting persons who choose to wed, marriage indirectly benefits society because persons who live in stable, fulfilling, and supportive relationships make better citizens. It is for these reasons, the argument goes, that States encourage and formalize marriage, confer special benefits on married persons, and also impose some special obligations. This understanding of the States' reasons for recognizing marriage enables the majority to argue that same-sex marriage serves the States' objectives in the same way as opposite-sex marriage.

This understanding of marriage, which focuses almost entirely on the happiness of persons who choose to marry, is shared by many people today, but it is not the traditional one. For millennia, marriage was inextricably linked to the one thing that only an opposite-sex couple can do: procreate.

Adherents to different schools of philosophy use different terms to explain why society should formalize marriage and attach special benefits and obligations to persons who marry. Here, the States defending their adherence to the traditional understanding of marriage have explained their position using the pragmatic vocabulary that characterizes most American political discourse. Their basic argument is that States formalize and promote marriage, unlike other fulfilling human relationships, in order to encourage potentially procreative conduct to take place within a lasting unit that has long been thought to provide the best atmosphere for raising children. They thus argue that there are reasonable secular grounds for restricting marriage to opposite-sex couples.

If this traditional understanding of the purpose of marriage does not ring true to all ears today, that is probably because the tie between marriage and procreation has frayed. Today, for instance, more than 40% of all children in this country are born to unmarried women. This development undoubtedly is both a cause and a result of changes in our society's understanding of marriage.

While, for many, the attributes of marriage in 21st-century America have changed, those States that do not want to recognize same-sex marriage have not yet given up on the traditional understanding. They worry that by officially abandoning the older understanding, they may contribute to marriage's further decay. It is far beyond the outer reaches of this Court's authority to say that a State may not adhere to the understanding of marriage that has long prevailed, not just in this country and others with similar cultural roots, but also in a great variety of countries and cultures all around the globe.

As I wrote in *Windsor* :

> "The family is an ancient and universal human institution. Family structure reflects the characteristics of a civilization, and changes in family structure and in the popular understanding of marriage and the family can have profound effects. Past changes in the understanding of marriage—for example, the gradual ascendance of the idea that romantic love is a prerequisite to marriage—have had far-reaching consequences. But the process by which such consequences come about is complex, involving the interaction of numerous factors, and tends to occur over an extended period of time.
>
> "We can expect something similar to take place if same-sex marriage becomes widely accepted. The long-term consequences of this change are not now known and are unlikely to be ascertainable for some time to come. There are those who think that allowing same-sex marriage will seriously undermine the institution of marriage. Others think that recognition of same-sex marriage will fortify a now-shaky institution.
>
> "At present, no one—including social scientists, philosophers, and historians—can predict with any certainty what the long-term ramifications of widespread acceptance of same-sex marriage will be. And judges are certainly not equipped to make such an assessment. The Members of this Court have the authority and the responsibility to interpret and apply the Constitution. Thus, if the Constitution contained a provision guaranteeing the right to marry a person of the same sex, it would be our duty to enforce that right. But the Constitution simply does not speak to the issue of same-sex marriage. In our system of government, ultimate sovereignty rests with the people, and the people have the right to control their own destiny. Any change on a question so fundamental should be made by the people through their elected officials."

III

Today's decision usurps the constitutional right of the people to decide whether to keep or alter the traditional understanding of marriage. The decision will also have other important consequences.

It will be used to vilify Americans who are unwilling to assent to the new orthodoxy. In the course of its opinion, the majority compares traditional marriage laws to laws that denied equal treatment for African–Americans and women. The implications of this analogy will be exploited by those who are determined to stamp out every vestige of dissent.

Perhaps recognizing how its reasoning may be used, the majority attempts, toward the end of its opinion, to reassure those who oppose same-sex marriage that their rights of conscience will be protected. We will soon see whether this proves to be true. I assume that those who cling to old beliefs will be able to whisper their thoughts in the recesses of their homes, but if they repeat those views in public, they will risk being labeled as bigots and treated as such by governments, employers, and schools.

The system of federalism established by our Constitution provides a way for people with different beliefs to live together in a single nation. If the issue of same-sex marriage had been left to the people of the States, it is likely that some States would recognize same-sex marriage and others would not. It is also possible that some States would tie recognition to protection for conscience rights. The majority today makes that impossible. By imposing its own views on the entire country, the majority facilitates the marginalization of the many Americans who have traditional ideas. Recalling the harsh treatment of gays and lesbians in the past, some may think that turnabout is fair play. But if that sentiment prevails, the Nation will experience bitter and lasting wounds.

Today's decision will also have a fundamental effect on this Court and its ability to uphold the rule of law. If a bare majority of Justices can invent a new right and impose that right on the rest of the country, the only real limit on what future majorities will be able to do is their own sense of what those with political power and cultural influence are willing to tolerate. Even enthusiastic supporters of same-sex marriage should worry about the scope of the power that today's majority claims.

Today's decision shows that decades of attempts to restrain this Court's abuse of its authority have failed. A lesson that some will take from today's decision is that preaching about the proper method of interpreting the Constitution or the virtues of judicial self-restraint and humility cannot compete with the temptation to achieve what is viewed as a noble end by any practicable means. I do not doubt that my colleagues in the majority sincerely see in the Constitution a vision of liberty that happens to coincide with their own. But this sincerity is cause for concern, not comfort. What it evidences is the deep and perhaps irremediable corruption of our legal culture's conception of constitutional interpretation.

Most Americans—understandably—will cheer or lament today's decision because of their views on the issue of same-sex marriage. But all Americans, whatever their thinking on that issue, should worry about what the majority's claim of power portends.

Discussion

1. *Obergefell and fundamental rights. Obergefell v. Hodges* holds that the fundamental right to marriage protected by the Due Process Clause extends to same-sex couples. *Lawrence v. Texas* was ambiguous on whether the liberty interest in same-sex relations was fundamental. By contrast, *Obergefell* clearly states that gays and lesbians enjoy a fundamental right to marry. Does this now

clarify that *Lawrence* is also a case about fundamental rights? If gays and lesbians enjoy a fundamental right to marry, do they also enjoy a fundamental right to sexual relations, or is right this limited only to married couples?

2. *Tradition! Obergefell* is an extended essay on tradition, but the majority and the dissent have very different ways of articulating what constitutionally protected tradition is and how we determine its contours.

Justice Kennedy argues that constitutionally protected traditions are those which are consistent with the underlying reasons why a social tradition is valuable to us today. "[I]n assessing whether the force and rationale of its cases apply to same-sex couples, the Court must respect the basic reasons why the right to marry has been long protected." Accordingly, he recites four features of marriage that make it valuable to us today and then argues that same-sex marriage applies to all of them. His opinion assumes that tradition—or at the very least, constitutionally protected tradition—is something that present generations can reason about and rationally extend or alter. Kennedy's recitation of how the couples in the case met, fell in love, married, lived, and raised children in *Obergefell* is more than an attempt to tug at our heartstrings. He also wants to show that the reason we sympathize with these couples and their plight is the same reason we sympathize with the hardships and sacrifices of married couples generally.

Roberts, Scalia, and especially Alito, identify constitutionally protected traditions with long-standing social practices. They view tradition as the accumulated wisdom of previous generations. Therefore we should not disturb the judgments of previous generations because we are very likely to make a mistake. Present generations are likely to view the world from a very narrow perspective—our own lifetimes—and therefore if we try to make significant changes based on contemporary judgments and reasons we are likely to produce unintended and undesirable consequences, as well as destroying institutions of long-standing.

These different conceptions of tradition presume contrasting views about human knowledge and moral growth. Kennedy regards the evolution of tradition as beneficially shaped by increases in knowledge and understanding. Repeatedly he speaks of "new awareness," "new insight," or "enhanced understanding" of new facts and moral truths that result from deliberation and political interaction. These new insights and understandings should properly be incorporated into the constitutional tradition, altering what the tradition means for us today.

The dissenters, by contrast, do not think that present generations are necessarily getting any wiser, even if their values may have changed. At one point in his dissent, Chief Justice Roberts, almost in exasperation, exclaims, "Just who do we think we are?"

Kennedy emphasizes that traditional practices change over time and are always changing. Hence he offers a history of changing conceptions of marriage—from arranged marriages to marriage for love to the gradual decline of coverture rules to the emergence of companionate marriage between equals. Roberts and Alito, by contrast, emphasize that core features of the institution of marriage have not changed for centuries, and can be found in almost all civilizations, ancient and modern. (Note Chief Justice Roberts' reference to "the Kalahari Bushmen and the Han Chinese, the Carthaginians and the Aztecs.") The changes that Kennedy describes are not central to the core of the tradition, while the union of one man and one woman is central.

It is tempting to identify the dissenters with Edmund Burke, who famously criticized the French Revolution, and to view Kennedy as opposed to Burkeanism. Certainly the dissenters would like to brand Kennedy as a revolutionary or Jacobin, heedlessly destroying a valued institution at the center of society. But Kennedy's use of tradition is also Burkean in its own way. In particular Kennedy emphasizes change through respect for tradition that results from discussion and lived experience — as opposed to change that occurs through violence and revolutionary upheaval. Kennedy emphasizes the natural evolution and growth of previous commitments through debate, contestation and social practice. Our commitments evolve as they we apply them to changed factual circumstances and our wisdom grows through encountering those changed circumstances in practical terms. We can have greater confidence in our judgments achieved in this way because, unlike previous generations, we have the benefit of their experience, while they do not have the benefit of ours.

3. *Bye, Bye, Glucksberg.* Justice Kennedy's opinion in *Obergefell* unceremoniously overrules the reasoning if not the specific results in *Washington v. Glucksburg*, without saying so directly. In order to reject a constitutional right to assisted suicide, *Glucksberg* offered a very narrow test of when courts could recognize new implied fundamental rights. (See the discussion in the Note on Tradition as a Source of Fundamental Rights, Casebook, pp. 1533-1541). The Chief Justice well understands this: "It is revealing that the majority's position requires it to effectively overrule *Glucksberg,* the leading modern case setting the bounds of substantive due process."

Obergefell makes clear, however, that *Glucksberg* has never really been "the leading modern case on substantive due process" and implied fundamental rights. Rather, *Glucksberg* has been especially attractive to *critics* of implied fundamental rights because it seems to limit implied fundamental rights to practices, when described very concretely, that have a very long history of protection. Taken seriously, almost none of the Court's key substantive due process decisions would meet *Glucksberg's* test. That is why critics of implied fundamental rights tend to like it.

Indeed, Chief Justice Rehnquist — no fan of implied fundamental rights himself — wrote *Glucksberg* in 1997 precisely to lay down a marker so that federal judges would stop trying to imply fundamental rights. Unfortunately for Rhenquist, he didn't succeed. The Court hasn't taken *Glucksberg* very seriously since it was decided. Not in *Lawrence,* not in *Windsor*, and certainly not in *Obergefell.*

In *Obergefell,* Justice Kennedy essentially limits *Glucksberg* to its facts:

> "*Glucksberg* did insist that liberty under the Due Process Clause must be defined in a most circumscribed manner, with central reference to specific historical

practices. Yet while that approach may have been appropriate for the asserted right there involved (physician-assisted suicide), it is inconsistent with the approach this Court has used in discussing other fundamental rights, including marriage and intimacy. *Loving* did not ask about a "right to interracial marriage"; *Turner* did not ask about a "right of inmates to marry"; and *Zablocki* did not ask about a "right of fathers with unpaid child support duties to marry." Rather, each case inquired about the right to marry in its comprehensive sense, asking if there was a sufficient justification for excluding the relevant class from the right.

That principle applies here. If rights were defined by who exercised them in the past, then received practices could serve as their own continued justification and new groups could not invoke rights once denied. This Court has rejected that approach, both with respect to the right to marry and the rights of gays and lesbians. See *Loving*; *Lawrence*."

Another way of putting this is that the debate between Justice Brennan and Justice Scalia in *Michael H. v. Gerald D.* is over, and Justice Brennan won. In *Michael H.*, Justice Scalia (joined by Chief Justice Rehnquist) argued that traditions of liberty should be construed as narrowly as possible — "the most specific level at which a relevant tradition protecting, or denying protection to, the asserted right can be identified." Justice Brennan argued that constitutional traditions of liberty should be construed abstractly and broadly, so that some existing practices might actually be inconsistent with our traditions properly understood in their best light. At the time, Scalia's account had real difficulties accounting for the Court's jurisprudence up to that point; it wasn't really consistent with *Eisenstadt*, much less *Roe*. But that was fine with Scalia — he didn't want to extend these decisions any further.

Compare Justice Brennan's and Justice Kennedy's view of tradition with that of the second Justice Harlan, who famously wrote of "the balance struck by this country, having regard to what history teaches are the traditions from which it developed as well as the traditions from which it broke. That tradition is a living thing." Justice Harlan emphasized that sometimes following tradition means rejecting some traditional practices or assumptions that we now believe are no longer consistent with our traditions considered in their best light. Our traditions are living because they change over time, for example, by becoming more inclusive.

The Chief Justice quotes part of this famous passage from *Poe v. Ullman* in his dissent. But he leaves out the words "as well as the traditions from which it broke. That tradition is a living thing." In contrast to the Chief Justice in *Obergefell*, Justice Harlan was arguing that sometimes the best way to read our traditions is as evolving, and therefore as rejecting some previous practices that we previously regarded as part of our traditions. In like fashion, Justice Kennedy argued that the best way to understand our traditions of marriage is as evolving — we have gradually been moving toward a view of marriage as a bond of commitment between two equals, which is as compatible with same-sex marriage as it is with opposite-sex marriage. Kennedy argues that when our traditions of liberty are considered in their best light, same-sex marriage is fully consistent with those traditions, rather than opposed to them.

4. *Polygamy.* The Chief Justice points out that Justice Kennedy's Due Process arguments don't adequately distinguish same-sex marriage from polygamy: "[The majority] offers no reason at all why the two-person element of the core definition of marriage may be preserved while the man-woman element may not. Indeed, from the standpoint of history and tradition, a leap from opposite-sex marriage to same-sex marriage is much greater than one from a two-person union to plural unions, which have deep roots in some cultures around the world. If the majority is willing to take the big leap, it is hard to see how it can say no to the shorter one." Chief Justice Roberts also argues that each of the four reasons for protecting the right to marry "would apply with equal force to the claim of a fundamental right to plural marriage."

If *Obergefell* had been decided on traditional equal protection grounds, the issue would not arise in the same way. The Court might point out that limiting marriage to two persons of either sex does not discriminate either on the basis of sex or sexual orientation.

Does Kennedy have a good response to Chief Justice Roberts? Does polygamy present a realistic possibility of social problems that same-sex marriage does not? Judge Richard Posner argues that in traditional polygamous societies, wealthy and powerful men tend to collect multiple wives, and this makes it more difficult for other men to find partners. See Richard A. Posner, The Chief Justice's Gay Marriage Dissent is Heartless, Slate, June 27, 2015, at http://www.slate.com/articles/news_and_politics/the_breakfast_table/features/2015/scotus_roundup/supreme_court_gay_marriage_john_roberts_dissent_in_obergefell_is_heartless.single.html Of course, analogies to how polygamy operates in traditional societies may or may not tell us much; we don't yet know how polygamy will work in modern society — whether, for example, powerful women would also collect many husbands, whether adults would form families of roughly equal men and women, and whether members of polygamous families would be more equal than in traditional societies.

At this point in history, do you expect the Supreme Court to extend constitutional protection to plural marriage? Given the current state of American politics and culture, why might the Court extend marriage to same-sex couples but not recognize plural marriage? Are any of these reasons discussed in the opinion?

5. *Equality in* Obergefell. In *Obergefell v. Hodges*, Justice Kennedy holds that bans on same-sex marriage also violate the Equal Protection Clause. However, his equal protection analysis does not discuss the standard doctrinal tiers of scrutiny. He does not hold that restricting marriage to opposite-sex couples violates sex equality, as some *amici* proposed. He does not hold that sexual orientation is a suspect classification, as the Obama Administration urged the Court to do. He does not suggest that limiting marriage to opposite-sex couples involves unconstitutional animus, as he did in *Windsor*; nor does he say that the ban fails "rational basis with a bite," because it is premised on irrational prejudice.

At the very end of the opinion Kennedy includes language that suggests that the exclusion of gay couples would violate even the ordinary rational basis standard, because the states' justification — that keeping gays from marrying will encourage straights to marry — makes no sense: "it is unrealistic to conclude that an opposite-sex couple would choose not to marry simply because same-sex couples may do so." Yet Kennedy does not argue that the exclusion violates rational basis.

Even so, Kennedy's argument for treating same-sex marriage as part of the fundamental right to marry has many significant equality ideas. He states that "[t]here is no difference between same- and opposite sex couples with respect to" marriage's usefulness in grounding the social order. He argues that excluding same-sex couples "teaches that gays and lesbians are unequal in important respects." and that "[i]t demeans gays and lesbians for the State to lock them out of a central institution of the Nation's society." He adds that "laws excluding same-sex couples from the marriage right impose stigma and injury of the kind prohibited by our basic charter."

As in *Lawrence v. Texas*, the language of stigma and demeaning sounds in civil equality and the anti-subordination principle. Indeed, later in the opinion, Kennedy says: "the challenged laws abridge central precepts of equality. . . . [they are] essentially unequal: same-sex couples are denied all the benefits afforded to opposite-sex couples and are barred from exercising a fundamental right. Especially against a long history of disapproval of their relationships, this denial . . . works a grave and continuing harm. The imposition of this disability on gays and lesbians serves to disrespect and subordinate them. And the Equal Protection Clause, like the Due Process Clause, prohibits this unjustified infringement of the fundamental right to marry."

This sounds very much like an anti-subordination rationale. Moreover, together with other parts of the opinion, Kennedy seems to be carefully laying the groundwork for arguing that gays and lesbians have suffered a long history of discrimination, and that they are excluded from important opportunities for reasons that have nothing to do with their contribution to society. (In fact, at one point, Kennedy even suggests that sexual orientation is akin to an immutable characteristic, arguing that the "immutable nature [of same-sex couples] dictates that same-sex marriage is their only real path to this profound commitment [of marriage].") If one added that gays and lesbians are a minority without significant representation in "the Nation's decision-making councils," one would have a pretty good argument for treating sexual orientation as a suspect classification. (This was the Obama Administration's argument as amicus curiae.) Nevertheless, having set up virtually all of the elements for this conclusion, Kennedy does not reach it.

Instead, Kennedy's equal protection argument emphasizes that equality and liberty are two sides of a coin — that they are two different perspectives on a problem that shine light on each other: "Each concept — liberty and equality — leads to a stronger understanding of the other." Hence selective denials of fundamental rights deny equal dignity. Accordingly, Justice Kennedy, in a very interesting passage, reinterprets the sex equality cases of the 1970s as protecting the equal dignity of men and women in the right to marry.

Kennedy's account of equality is perhaps closest to two ideas in previous jurisprudence. The first is in *Casey* and in Justice Ginsburg's dissent in *Carhart II*. Both opinions are officially about the liberty protected by the Due Process Clause, but both argue that women's interest in reproductive liberty is tied to their equal status as citizens. One could read *Obergefell*—together with *Lawrence*—as drawing on and expanding these ideas of liberty as equal citizenship status (although, interestingly the abortion cases are never mentioned in the majority opinion).

The second idea comes from *Skinner v. Oklahoma* and from some of the Warren Court's decisions on the rights of the poor, especially *Harper v. Virginia Board of Elections* (discussed in the Casebook at pp. 1779-1802). This is the "fundamental rights" strand of equal protection doctrine. The government violates equal protection when it discriminates against or selectively burdens the exercise of a fundamental right or interest. One could also read *Obergefell* as part of this line of cases. Because marriage is a fundamental right (or more correctly, a *fundamental interest*, as discussed below), the state cannot deny the right to marry arbitrarily to a group of citizens without a compelling interest. Here the state does not even have a reasonable justification, so, *a fortiori*, the discrimination is unconstitutional.

6. *The doctrine and the dissents.* If Justice Kennedy generally avoids analyzing the case in terms of black-letter levels-of-scrutiny doctrine, so do the dissents. None of the dissents directly explain why the state governments' asserted justification for denying same-sex couples the right to marry passes the rational basis test. As noted above, the states' justification is fairly weak. The reason is that, after *Lawrence* and *Windsor*, the states could not argue that the laws were designed to enforce religious or moral objections to homosexual behavior, or that they reflected anxiety and fears about homosexuality. What arguments can you find in the dissents for why the state laws would nevertheless pass rational basis?

7. *Lochner, I say, Lochner!* Note the Chief Justice's repeated use of *Lochner*. What does *Lochner* stand for in his opinion? The Chief Justice believes that courts should not make up new constitutional rights out of whole cloth; he denounces the idea of five unelected lawyers undermining democracy and imposing their own ideological convictions on the rest of the country. Are these sentiments consistent with the Chief Justice's majority opinion in *Shelby County v. Holder*, which announces a new doctrine of "equal sovereignty of the states," and which strikes down key parts of an important civil rights statute passed by overwhelming majorities in Congress? At oral argument in *Shelby County* Justice Scalia suggested that the very fact that the Voting Rights Act was passed by such overwhelming margins was a reason that the courts needed to strike it down.

Is *Obergefell* different than *Shelby County* because the latter involved structure rather than rights? What then, of the fact that all four dissenters joined Justice Kennedy's opinion in *Citizens United v. FEC*? How do we tell when judges have committed the sin of *Lochner*?

8. *They'll never take our dignity.* In dissent, Justice Thomas objects to the majority's argument that limiting marriage to opposite-sex couples denies same-sex couples their dignity. He notes that the term "dignity" does not appear in the Constitution. He argues that dignity is innate and that no man-made institution can take away this dignity. Even the inherent dignity of slaves, he argues, could not be taken away by the vicious institution of slavery. Thomas's argument is that natural rights and human dignity preexist the state and therefore it is wrong to assume that the state could or should bestow dignity on anyone.

Does this argument adequately engage with the majority? Of course, Kennedy might respond, Thomas is correct that human dignity is innate and cannot be taken away by the state. That is precisely why the Constitution values it. Rather, the issue is government actions that deny *appropriate respect* for human dignity. When the state fails to accord people the equal concern and respect that they deserve, this violates the Equal Protection Clause of the Constitution. Properly *recognizing* and *respecting* dignity is not the same thing as *creating* dignity or being the *source* of dignity.

9. *Fundamental rights and fundamental interests.* Another way of stating Kennedy's argument is that the state has an obligation to respect and recognize the inherent dignity of the people who live within its borders. The state fails to do this when it arbitrarily denies the rights and benefits of marriage to a class of its citizens without adequate public justification. Although the state may not have to provide those rights and benefits in the first place, once it has given them out, it may not make arbitrary distinctions in who receives them.

This restatement, however, suggests an important point. It may be better to call marriage a *fundamental interest* than a *fundamental right*. The difference is that the state does not have to provide a fundamental interest at all, but once it does, it must bestow and protect it equally among the members of the political community. Instead of having a bundle of rights called "marriage," for example, the state could simply allow private marriage ceremonies and enforce civil contracts between couples. Nevertheless, once the state creates a bundle of legal rights and calls it "marriage," it cannot arbitrarily limit who enjoys that bundle of rights.

10. *Why did Justice Kennedy not use standard equal protection law?* As noted above, Justice Kennedy avoided the standard language of equal protection scrutiny. There are many possible reasons for this. First, as a libertarian, Kennedy may simply be more comfortable talking about liberty. Second, Kennedy might not want to take on all of the legal consequences of creating a new suspect classification—the first since the 1970s—without more consideration about the consequences for legal doctrine in a host of different areas. Third, Kennedy may not be particularly enamored of the formalism of existing equal protection categories, which in many cases tend to obscure the real issues at stake.

Fourth, employing heightened scrutiny under the equal protection clause has its own problems. A threshold question is whether the statutes involved in the marriage cases classify on the basis of *sex* or *sexual orientation*. If the latter, does limiting marriage to one man and one woman constitute *facial discrimination* on the basis of sexual orientation, or does it merely have a *disparate impact* on sexual orientation minorities? If the latter, could the plaintiffs prove discriminatory purpose within the meaning of *Feeney*—that is, could they show that all of the states' laws were enacted *because of*, not *in spite of*, the effect on gays and lesbians? Potentially, all of these problems could be surmounted—for example, Kennedy could have just employed a sex equality argument. But each of the alternatives would raise difficulties that he might have wanted to avoid.

Fifth, Kennedy might have decided against using the "rational basis with a bite" or "animus" lines of cases because he did not think that he could easily show that *all* of the state laws defining marriage in terms of opposite-sex couples were passed because of malice or irrational prejudice against gays and lesbians. Some of these laws were quite old. If he declared that all of them were based in animus, he would be declaring all of the people who voted for them had bad intentions or were prejudiced, or both. Instead, he simply states that whatever their motivations, the laws they produced had the effect of demeaning and subordinating gays and lesbians. Is this an important difference?

Although Kennedy's opinion has a lot of equality ideas in it, it does not offer a very clear account of how doctrine should develop. That may be deliberate. But it will mean that the lower courts will have to spend a lot of time puzzling out how best to apply Kennedy's arguments to a host of other issues, including, for example, state discrimination in adoption, family formation, employment, housing, and education.

11. *Religious liberty as the next battleground in the culture wars.* Just as *Obergefell* leaves open questions of discrimination based on sexual orientation, it does not resolve how courts will balance the dignitary interests and rights to equal treatment of gays and lesbians against claims of religious freedom by opponents of gay rights. Culture war issues have changed in recent years in anticipation of increasing protection for gay rights and same-sex marriage. Disputes about homosexuality and reproductive rights are increasingly being reframed as questions of religious liberty. Opponents of same-sex marriage, abortion, and contraception argue that they have a right not to cooperate or be complicit with what they regard as sinful conduct. See Douglas NeJaime and Reva B. Siegel, Conscience Wars: Complicity-Based Conscience Claims in Religion and Politics, 124 Yale L. J. 2516 (2015). Chief Justice Roberts' dissent notes some of the potential conflicts between same-sex marriage and religious belief and practice that may arise in the future.

As noted in the Casebook (pp. 780-81), in 1990, the Supreme Court, in an opinion by Justice Scalia, severely limited the ability of religious minorities to object to laws of general application that burden the exercise of their religion. Employment Division v. Smith, 494 U.S. 872 (1990). In response, Congress passed the Religious Freedom Restoration Act (RFRA), which, after the decision in *City of Boerne v. Flores*, (Casebook pp. 780-790), binds only the federal government. Nevertheless, many states have passed their own versions of RFRA. Interpretation and application of federal and state versions of RFRA will likely be a key site of disputes about whether religious objectors may refuse to do business with same-sex couples or with gays and lesbians more generally.

12. *Obergefell, Democratic Constitutionalism, and Judicial Review.* All of the dissenters in *Obergefell* criticize the majority for preempting the decisions of state legislatures across the country and prematurely ending the debate on same-sex marriage. Justice Kennedy offers two different kinds of responses, which, at first glance, seem in some tension with each other. On the one hand, quoting Justice Jackson in West Virginia Bd. of Ed. v. Barnette, 319 U.S. 624 (1943), he argues that "fundamental rights may not be submitted to a vote; they depend on the outcome of no elections." The relevant question is not how much public support there is for same-sex marriage, but whether the right is fundamental. For this reason, Kennedy explains, the Court was wrong in *Bowers v. Hardwick* and should have begun to protect gay rights in 1986, if not earlier.

Elsewhere in the opinion, however, Kennedy reasons quite differently. He argues that "changed understandings of marriage are characteristic of a Nation where new dimensions of freedom become apparent to new generations, often through perspectives that begin in pleas or protests and then are considered in the political sphere and the judicial process." He then spends several paragraphs summarizing the long fight for gay equality, describing numerous interactions between judicial decisions, the political process, and civil society. In an appendix to the decision he lists all of the state courts and lower federal courts that have passed on the question of same-sex marriage. And immediately before he quotes Justice Jackson in *Barnette*, he spends several paragraphs emphasizing the amount of public deliberation over same-sex marriage: "There have been referenda, legislative debates, and grassroots campaigns, as well as countless studies, papers, books, and other popular and scholarly writings, [as well as] extensive litigation in state and federal courts." All of this, he explains, "has led to an enhanced understanding of the issue—an understanding refined in the arguments now presented for resolution as a matter of constitutional law."

In these parts of the opinion, Justice Kennedy is describing what Robert Post and Reva Siegel have called "democratic constitutionalism"—the process by which continual interactions between civil society actors, political actors, and judges shape the constitutional ideas and judgements of the time. Robert C. Post & Reva Siegel, Roe Rage: Democratic. Constitutionalism and Backlash, 42 Harv. C.R.-C.L. L. Rev. 373 (2007).

Justice Kennedy bases his constitutional arguments on "changed understandings," and "new awareness" of the rights of women, gays and lesbians—but those changed understandings and that new awareness did not occur only in the mind of Tony Kennedy. Rather, mechanisms of social influence, which operate in politics, law and culture, changed many Americans' minds about liberty and equality. These mechanisms of social influence moved arguments about same-sex marriage, from "off-the-wall" to "on-the-wall." Interactions between culture, law, and politics continually reshape constitutional commonsense, thus enabling judges like Kennedy to reach the conclusions that they reach. Judges, as part of the culture, absorb the results of this process of cultural debate by osmosis. For that reason, judges need not and should not consult public opinion polls or statistical measures of public will in order to recognize that the practical meanings of liberty and equality, judgements about what is just and unjust, and the felt sense of what is reasonable and unreasonable have changed.

The process of social influence is "democratic" in the sense that it is interactive and participatory on multiple levels, but it is not "democratic" in the sense that judges are responding directly to elections and the wishes of either politicians or public opinion. Indeed, when Justices make decisions like *Obergefell*, there is often significant public support for what they do, but there is also usually some substantial segment of public opinion that strongly disagrees — and there are usually politicians who view the Court's decisions as an opportunity to mobilize against the Court.

13. Obergefell *and democratic legitimacy*. Post and Siegel offer their model of democratic constitutionalism only as a descriptive account of constitutional change. Jack Balkin argues that this model explains how the processes of living constitutionalism enjoy long-term democratic legitimacy. See Jack M. Balkin, Living Originalism (2011). One can only speak of legitimacy from a long-term perspective because at any point in time there is unlikely to be a one-to-one correspondence between the public's views about the Constitution on any particular subject and the views of the federal judiciary. For every *Obergefell*, there is a *Citizens United*, or vice-versa, depending on one's substantive views. The point, rather, is that by processes of social influence, the decisions of the federal judiciary stay connected to long-term shifts in public views about constitutional values.

According to Balkin's account, the contemporary democratic legitimacy of the Constitution comes from two sources. First, legitimacy comes from the basic framework—the original meaning of the constitutional text and its choice of rules, standards, and principles. Second, the Constitution's contemporary legitimacy comes from constitutional constructions that are built on the basic framework–which include judicial precedents.

The democratic legitimacy of the basic framework derives from acts of adoption and subsequent amendment by We the People. The democratic legitimacy of constitutional constructions built on the framework comes from the processes of democratic constitutionalism (or living constitutionalism). These help ensure that constitutional constructions are connected to long-term shifts in the public's constitutional values. Both sources produce the Constitution's contemporary democratic legitimacy, and both are important to maintaining that legitimacy.

The four dissenters in *Obergefell* strongly object to the majority's confirmation of a sea change in American attitudes about same-sex marriage. The irony is that the dissenters' presence on the Supreme Court, and their conservative jurisprudence, are also the result of the same processes of democratic constitutionalism, albeit working in a different direction. The conservative mobilizations of the 1980s and afterwards led to judicial appointments, political protests, and litigation campaigns. These features of democratic constitutionalism on the right brought conservative constitutional values into ascendance and are reflected in many of the judicial precedents appearing in this casebook.

PAVAN v. SMITH
2017 WL 2722472

PER CURIAM:

As this Court explained in *Obergefell v. Hodges,* 576 U.S. ____, 135 S.Ct. 2584 (2015), the Constitution entitles same-sex couples to civil marriage "on the same terms and conditions as opposite-sex couples." In the decision below, the Arkansas Supreme Court considered the effect of that holding on the State's rules governing the issuance of birth certificates. When a married woman gives birth in Arkansas, state law generally requires the name of the mother's male spouse to appear on the child's birth certificate—regardless of his biological relationship to the child. According to the court below, however, Arkansas need not extend that rule to similarly situated same-sex couples: The State need not, in other words, issue birth certificates including the female spouses of women who give birth in the State. Because that differential treatment infringes *Obergefell* 's commitment to provide same-sex couples "the constellation of benefits that the States have linked to marriage," we reverse the state court's judgment.

The petitioners here are two married same-sex couples who conceived children through anonymous sperm donation. Leigh and Jana Jacobs were married in Iowa in 2010, and Terrah and Marisa Pavan were married in New Hampshire in 2011. Leigh and Terrah each gave birth to a child in Arkansas in 2015. When it came time to secure birth certificates for the newborns, each couple filled out paperwork listing both spouses as parents—Leigh and Jana in one case, Terrah and Marisa in the other. Both times, however, the Arkansas Department of Health issued certificates bearing only the birth mother's name.

The department's decision rested on a provision of Arkansas law, Ark.Code §20–18–401 (2014), that specifies which individuals will appear as parents on a child's state-issued birth certificate. "For the purposes of birth registration," that statute says, "the mother is deemed to be the woman who gives birth to the child." §20–18–401(e). And "[i]f the mother was married at the time of either conception or birth," the statute instructs that "the name of [her] husband shall be entered on the certificate as the father of the child." §20–18–401(f)(1). There are some limited exceptions to the latter rule—for example, another man may appear on the birth certificate if the "mother" and "husband" and "putative father" all file affidavits vouching for the putative father's paternity. *Ibid.* But as all parties agree, the requirement that a married woman's husband appear on her child's birth certificate applies in cases where the couple conceived by means of artificial insemination with the help of an anonymous sperm donor. See also Ark.

Code §9–10–201(a) (2015) ("Any child born to a married woman by means of artificial insemination shall be deemed the legitimate natural child of the woman and the woman's husband if the husband consents in writing to the artificial insemination").

The Jacobses and Pavans brought this suit in Arkansas state court against the director of the Arkansas Department of Health—seeking, among other things, a declaration that the State's birth-certificate law violates the Constitution. The trial court agreed, holding that the relevant portions of §20–18–401 are inconsistent with *Obergefell* because they "categorically prohibi[t] every same-sex married couple . . . from enjoying the same spousal benefits which are available to every opposite-sex married couple." But a divided Arkansas Supreme Court reversed that judgment, concluding that the statute "pass[es] constitutional muster." In that court's view, "the statute centers on the relationship of the biological mother and the biological father to the child, not on the marital relationship of husband and wife," and so it "does not run afoul of *Obergefell*." Two justices dissented from that view, maintaining that under *Obergefell* "a same-sex married couple is entitled to a birth certificate on the same basis as an opposite-sex married couple.".

The Arkansas Supreme Court's decision, we conclude, denied married same-sex couples access to the "constellation of benefits that the Stat[e] ha[s] linked to marriage." *Obergefell*. As already explained, when a married woman in Arkansas conceives a child by means of artificial insemination, the State will—indeed, *must*—list the name of her male spouse on the child's birth certificate. And yet state law, as interpreted by the court below, allows Arkansas officials in those very same circumstances to omit a married woman's female spouse from her child's birth certificate. As a result, same-sex parents in Arkansas lack the same right as opposite-sex parents to be listed on a child's birth certificate, a document often used for important transactions like making medical decisions for a child or enrolling a child in school.

Obergefell proscribes such disparate treatment. As we explained there, a State may not "exclude same-sex couples from civil marriage on the same terms and conditions as opposite-sex couples." Indeed, in listing those terms and conditions—the "rights, benefits, and responsibilities" to which same-sex couples, no less than opposite-sex couples, must have access—we expressly identified "birth and death certificates." That was no accident: Several of the plaintiffs in *Obergefell* challenged a State's refusal to recognize their same-sex spouses on their children's birth certificates. In considering those challenges, we held the relevant state laws unconstitutional to the extent they treated same-sex couples differently from opposite-sex couples. That holding applies with equal force to §20–18–401.

Echoing the court below, the State defends its birth-certificate law on the ground that being named on a child's birth certificate is not a benefit that attends marriage. Instead, the State insists, a birth certificate is simply a device for recording biological parentage—regardless of whether the child's parents are married. But Arkansas law makes birth certificates about more than just genetics.

As already discussed, when an opposite-sex couple conceives a child by way of anonymous sperm donation—just as the petitioners did here—state law requires the placement of the birth mother's husband on the child's birth certificate. And that is so even though (as the State concedes) the husband "is definitively not the biological father" in those circumstances. Arkansas has thus chosen to make its birth certificates more than a mere marker of biological relationships: The State uses those certificates to give married parents a form of legal recognition that is not available to unmarried parents. Having made that choice, Arkansas may not, consistent with *Obergefell*, deny married same-sex couples that recognition. . . . As the petitioners point out, other factual scenarios (beyond those present in this case) similarly show that the State's birth certificates are about more than genetic parentage. For example, when an Arkansas child is adopted, the State places the child's original birth certificate under seal and issues a new birth certificate—unidentifiable as an amended version—listing the child's (non-biological) adoptive parents. [relocated footnote—eds.]

The petition for a writ of certiorari and the pending motions for leave to file briefs as *amici curiae* are granted. The judgment of the Arkansas Supreme Court is reversed, and the case is remanded for further proceedings not inconsistent with this opinion.

It is so ordered.

Justice GORSUCH, with whom Justice THOMAS and Justice ALITO join, dissenting.

Summary reversal is usually reserved for cases where "the law is settled and stable, the facts are not in dispute, and the decision below is clearly in error." Respectfully, I don't believe this case meets that standard.

To be sure, *Obergefell* addressed the question whether a State must recognize same-sex marriages. But nothing in *Obergefell* spoke (let alone clearly) to the question whether §20–18–401 of the Arkansas Code, or a state supreme court decision upholding it, must go. The statute in question establishes a set of rules designed to ensure that the biological parents of a child are listed on the child's birth certificate. Before the state supreme court, the State argued that rational reasons exist for a biology based birth registration regime, reasons that in no way offend *Obergefell*—like ensuring government officials can identify public health trends and helping individuals determine their biological lineage, citizenship, or susceptibility to genetic disorders. In an opinion that did not in any way seek to defy but rather earnestly engage *Obergefell*, the state supreme court agreed. And it is very hard to see what is wrong with this conclusion for, just as the state court recognized, nothing in *Obergefell* indicates that a birth registration regime based on biology, one no doubt with many analogues across the country and throughout history, offends the Constitution. To the contrary, to the extent they speak to the question at all, this Court's precedents suggest just the opposite conclusion. See, *e.g., Michael H. v. Gerald D.,* 491 U.S. 110 (1989); *Tuan Anh Nguyen v. INS,* 533 U.S. 53 (2001). Neither does anything in today's opinion purport to identify any constitutional problem with a biology based birth registration regime. So whatever else we might do with this case, summary reversal would not exactly seem the obvious course.

What, then, is at work here? If there isn't a problem with a biology based birth registration regime, perhaps the concern lies in this particular regime's exceptions. For it turns out that Arkansas's general rule of registration based on biology does admit of certain more specific exceptions. Most importantly for our purposes, the State acknowledges that §9–10–201 of the Arkansas Code controls how birth certificates are completed in cases of artificial insemination like the one before us. The State acknowledges, too, that this provision, written some time ago, indicates that the mother's husband generally shall be treated as the father — and in this way seemingly anticipates only opposite-sex marital unions.

But if the artificial insemination statute is the concern, it's still hard to see how summary reversal should follow for at least a few reasons. First, petitioners didn't actually challenge §9–10–201 in their lawsuit. Instead, petitioners sought and the trial court granted relief eliminating the State's authority under §20–18–401 to enforce a birth registration regime generally based on biology. On appeal, the state supreme court simply held that this overbroad remedy wasn't commanded by *Obergefell* or the Constitution. And, again, nothing in today's opinion for the Court identifies anything wrong, let alone clearly wrong, in that conclusion. Second, though petitioners' lawsuit didn't challenge §9–10–201, the State has repeatedly conceded that the benefits afforded nonbiological parents under §9–10–201 must be afforded equally to both same-sex and opposite-sex couples. So that in this particular case and all others of its kind, the State agrees, the female spouse of the birth mother must be listed on birth certificates too. Third, further proof still of the state of the law in Arkansas today is the fact that, when it comes to adoption (a situation not present in this case but another one in which Arkansas departs from biology based registration), the State tells us that adopting parents are eligible for placement on birth certificates without respect to sexual orientation.

Given all this, it seems far from clear what here warrants the strong medicine of summary reversal. Indeed, it is not even clear what the Court expects to happen on remand that hasn't happened already. The Court does not offer any remedial suggestion, and none leaps to mind. Perhaps the state supreme court could memorialize the State's concession on §9–10–201, even though that law wasn't fairly challenged and such a chore is hardly the usual reward for seeking faithfully to apply, not evade, this Court's mandates.

I respectfully dissent.

Discussion

1. *Legislative snafu or cultural resistance?* Arkansas's birth certificate law was written before same-sex marriage became commonplace. It reflects traditional common-law assumptions, which privileged marriage over biology in determining parenthood in two ways. The first is the marital presumption, codified in §20–18–401(f)(1), that the father of a child is the husband of the birth mother. The marital presumption privileges the interest in legitimating descent,

smoothing property transmission, preserving marital stability (and protecting manly honor) over biological accuracy. The second feature of traditional family law that privileged the state's interest in marriage over biology was that children born outside of marriage lacked many rights, unless paternity was established by lawsuit or the father willingly acknowledged paternity.

When same-sex couples began to employ assisted reproductive technology (ART) using anonymous sperm donors, a problem arose: should children born in this way be treated as legitimate? Arkansas responded by analogizing this situation to the common-law marital presumption, as codified in Ark. Code §9–10–201(a) (2015). If the husband consented to the use of ART, the child is treated as "the legitimate natural child of the woman and the woman's husband." Here once again, Arkansas has privileged its interests in marriage over biological accuracy.[3]

These legal rules meant, of course, that the public health benefits of easily being able to determine the genetic parentage of a child would sometimes be undermined. Nevertheless, the state was quite willing to trade off information about biological descent for the more important purposes of supporting marriage, promoting family stability, and making it easier to legally assign parental responsibility.

Flash forward to the present. The U.S. Supreme Court has held that same-sex married couples are entitled to all of the rights and benefits of opposite-sex married couples. What is the best way of translating the state's balance of concerns in family law into a changed factual context? Put another way, will same-sex couples be entitled to the marital presumption and the analogous rules that apply for opposite-sex couples using ART?

Presented with this question, the Arkansas Supreme Court argued that the state's interest in recording biological parentage was more central to the state's purposes than its interest in reducing illegitimacy and ensuring family stability. But if that has not been the case where opposite-sex couples are concerned, why should it now be so in the context of same-sex married couples?

What work is the renewed focus on biology doing here? When same-sex married couples emerge on the scene, it now seems important to assert that one member of the couple is not the "real" (i.e., biological) parent of the child. But, in a same-sex marriage, that fact should be obvious if the mother and her spouse are listed on the birth certificate. Moreover, in opposite-sex marriage, the state has made clear that it does *not* want to signal that the husband is not the "real" father, even if this would defeat the asserted public health benefits of tracing genetic parentage. By reinterpreting the statutory scheme to be primarily concerned with biology and genetic descent (and not the traditional goals of family law), that Arkansas Supreme Court justifies marking same-sex couples as different from opposite-sex couples.

3. On the history of how states dealt with artificial reproductive technology, and its consequences for same-sex marriage, see Doug NeJaime, The Nature of Parenthood, 126 Yale L. J. 2260 (2017).

This may suggest one reason why the majority of the Court thought it important to reverse summarily. As we have seen in the sex equality cases, an emphasis on "biology" is often doing cultural work as well. The U.S. Supreme Court, recognizing this, insists that states adapt to changed circumstances in ways that treat, as much as possible, opposite and same-sex couples with equal concern and respect. The dissenting Justices, by contrast, want to read *Obergefell* more narrowly. Therefore, they also emphasize that the state's purpose is to emphasize biological connection, and not (perhaps ironically) the promotion of "family values."